The Red Cross and the Holocaust

Was the International Committee of the Red Cross aware of the appalling sufferings of the victims of the concentration camps? How much did it know about the deportation and extermination of the Jews in Europe? Did it try to protect the persecuted Jews? In what ways could it have helped them, given the neutrality which was the basis of its foundation? These questions have remained unanswered for more than fifty years and have sparked off bitter debates. Jean-Claude Favez here presents a startling new assessment, thanks to his unrivalled access to the archives of the Red Cross. This magisterial work, the fruit of many years of research, includes much hitherto unpublished archive material, as well as a chronology, biographical notes, and a statement by the current leaders of the Red Cross. Anyone interested in the complexity and tragedy of the Holocaust will find this compelling reading.

JEAN-CLAUDE FAVEZ was formerly Rector of the University of Geneva.

The Red Cross and the Holocaust

Jean-Claude Favez

Edited and translated by
John and Beryl Fletcher

CAMBRIDGE
UNIVERSITY PRESS

PUBLISHED BY THE PRESS SYNDICATE OF THE UNIVERSITY OF CAMBRIDGE
The Pitt Building, Trumpington Street, Cambridge CB2 1RP, United Kingdom

CAMBRIDGE UNIVERSITY PRESS
The Edinburgh Building, Cambridge CB2 2RU, United Kingdom
http://www.cup.cam.ac.uk
40 West 20th Street, New York, NY 10011–4211, USA   http://www.cup.org
10 Stamford Road, Oakleigh, Melbourne 3166, Australia
and Editions de la Maison des Sciences de l'Homme,
54 Boulevard Raspail, 75270 Paris Cedex 06, France

Originally published in French as *Une mission impossible?*
by Editions Payot Lausanne 1988
and © Editions Payot Lausanne

First published in English by Cambridge University Press 1999 as
The Red Cross and the Holocaust
English translation © Maison des Sciences de l'Homme and
Cambridge University Press 1999

Printed in the United Kingdom at the University Press, Cambridge

Typeset in Plantin 10/12pt [CE]

A catalogue record for this book is available from the British Library

Library of Congress cataloguing in publication data

Favez, Jean-Claude.
[Une mission impossible? French]
The Red Cross and the Holocaust / by Jean-Claude Favez; edited and translated
by John and Beryl Fletcher.
    p.   cm.
Includes bibliographical references and index.
ISBN 0 521 41587 X (hb)
1. Holocaust, Jewish (1939–1945).
2. World War, 1939–1945 – Jews – Rescue.
3. International Committee of the Red Cross.
I. Title.
D804.6.F38   1999
362.87'81'08992404–dc21   99–11233   CIP

ISBN 0 521 41587 X hardback
ISBN 2 7351 08384 hardback (France only)

'La question israélite sur le continent européen appartient strictement, selon l'avis des gouvernements intéressés, au domaine de la politique intérieure. . .'
(Note from the ICRC to the British Foreign Office, 5 April 1943)

Contents

viii   Contents

Author's preface to the English-language edition: A past that returns to haunt us

New thinking about the Shoah

If all history is contemporary history, the reader needs to know before even opening this book that the English-language version presented here is being published some ten years after it appeared in French, so that with the exception of a few titles added to the bibliography and the abridgement or dropping of some chapters, the text remains essentially that of 1988.

During the last few years, historical research on the Shoah has dug ever deeper and spread ever further. New documents, new questions and new debates have led to the publication of thousands of books and articles, and have resulted in fresh light being shed on such notorious disputes as the rather pointless one in my view between functionalists and intentionalists. Studied above all in its Jewish context, the Shoah now occupies a central position in the history of World War II, to such an extent that people have come to speak, as Renée Poznanski does, of a veritable revenge of historiography over history. According to Omar Bartov, an authority on the involvement of the state police and the Wehrmacht in the massacres in the East, today's specialists concentrate *inter alia* upon eyewitness accounts, memoirs and different forms of literary representation.

Swiss neutrality under the spotlight

It is important to bear this in mind even if the subject of this book is the International Committee of the Red Cross (ICRC) and its work during World War II on behalf of deportees and concentration camp detainees, since historiography has evolved in relation to this topic as well, particularly in the last three years with the problems over escheated deposits, Nazi gold and refugees denied entry that the collective memory of the Swiss nation has suddenly had to confront. These issues are not in themselves new, and the recent discoveries relate to facts already familiar to specialists, so why has it taken fifty years for the comforting certainties of the received interpretation of Swiss neutrality to be brought into doubt? The question transcends traditional considerations about generational conflict or the role of the media; the truth is that we are still none too clear about what has happened in the last three years, except that it will offer historians in the future a worthy topic for investigation. What is certain is that the controversy surrounding attacks by foreigners has for the first time since 1945 involved all shades of opinion and called into question not only individual memory of the official line, but the way very many Swiss people have tended to view themselves and their past: it has taken the form of a crisis of national identity which will, I believe, leave deep scars.

In spite of difficulties of access to public archives until the 1970s and the almost total closure until a few months ago of company files, including those of the ICRC (itself a private institution), it would be inaccurate to claim that Swiss historians had not done their work properly, but it is true to say that most of them did it without casting doubt on the received interpretation consistent with patriotism in time of war. From that viewpoint the questions that could have been asked, about such matters as the stamping of passports of German Jews in 1938 with a distinctive mark to keep track of those seeking asylum in Switzerland, or the limits of neutrality in the case of Franco-Swiss military collaboration revealed in the documents uncovered at La Charité-sur-Loire, lost some of their explosive potential, and the administrative investigations undertaken at the request of the Swiss authorities by historians and legal experts to provide answers and furnish rebuttals, like the Ludwig report on refugee policy or Professor Bonjour's history of Swiss neutrality in World War II, represented at once an advance in understanding and a balanced justification of the past, so that the first real break occurred in 1983 with the publication of the *New History of Switzerland and the Swiss* by a team of young historians concerned less with flouting taboos and undermining myths from William Tell to General Guisan (the army commander from 1939 to 1945) than with making available to a wider public the most recent advances in historical scholarship; even so, the controversy they aroused remained limited in scope and hardly on the scale that might have been expected from the work's bestseller status.

Since the 1930s the emergence of totalitarian regimes and the increasing threat of war gave rise among many Swiss people to the knee-jerk reaction of clinging to the most traditional values of the past: not only armed neutrality but the particular characteristics of Switzerland in general were going to safeguard the country's independence. This image of a homogeneous, exclusive national community shifted unbrokenly from World War II to the Cold War, justifying a foreign policy rooted in the principle of participating but not belonging that enabled Switzerland to enjoy the fruits of economic growth without compromising her sovereignty. Neutrality was thus the lodestar of government action and the ICRC, the Don Suisse and humanitarian action the price of her abstention from world affairs. The deaf ear turned by the authorities and by Swiss banks in the 1960s to the pleas of Holocaust victims which we now find so shocking was not merely the expression of selfishness – an attitude that was far from being the exclusive preserve of the twenty-three cantons, after all – it was the incarnation of the *Sonderfall Schweiz*, of the isolationist statute justifying the missions of good offices and humanitarian aid accepted by authorities and citizens alike.

I must, however, correct the perfunctory and unfair impression which may have been given by what I have just said with regard to all those who went to the assistance of people in need by reminding the reader that throughout the twentieth century intellectuals, artists, churchmen and churchwomen have denounced such exploitation of solidarity and challenged the prevailing order and the historiography which legitimised it. In the 1960s the rise of the consumer society led to a growing malaise that inspired many essays, pamphlets and articles, and more recently two events have helped give a collective dimension to such criticism and doubts: the fall of the Berlin Wall in 1989 and the narrowness of the vote by which in 1992 the Swiss people rejected the treaty on the European Economic Area. The dismantling of the Wall was the final nail in the coffin of wartime patriotism, and their unwillingness to accept even a limited form of union with Europe has left the Swiss helplessly isolated and turned in upon themselves: the subtle blend of conservatism and modernism that since the eighteenthth century had constituted the bedrock of the identity of the Swiss Confederation failed to withstand the shock of this retreat into the past; the manner in which the nation perceived itself was shaken to its foundations and history, no longer able to offer any firm bearings or clear certainties, lost all meaning. Conditions were therefore ripe in 1995 for the question of Swiss attitudes during World War II to become the subject of doubt and controversy.

The ICRC confronts its past

Much of what I have been saying applies equally to the ICRC, as I hope the reader will agree, since one of the leading themes in this book is precisely that the ICRC was operating during World War II in a context marked by the humanitarian work of the Confederation and by the defence of Swiss neutrality. The state's presence manifested itself in several ways. In the political domain, that is in the deployment of ways and means, the obvious though relatively infrequent case was direct intervention. I set out in a later chapter the circumstances surrounding the ICRC's decision in October 1942 not to launch a public appeal denouncing human rights violations; other less obtrusive instances could be cited, so habitual was the Confederation's historic and pragmatic inclination to ask the international Red Cross to serve the nation's neutrality, the ICRC contributing thereby to the achievement of its own aims and to the reinforcement of its authority and effectiveness, including with regard to the federal government.

The Swiss presence was a fact of life at both the individual and the institutional level. The patriotism of national defence, for example, formed part of the ideological environment from which the Red Cross could not entirely escape, despite the universal character of its religious and political neutrality and of the criteria it invoked in the fulfilment of its mission.

But what was taken for granted by the World War II generation could and did later become the subject of questions, doubts and objections. The ICRC and the Swiss Confederation were sharply criticised for what they failed to do on behalf of the victims of that conflict. Then attention turned to other matters. In opening its World War II archives to historians the ICRC decided, as did the Confederation, to go back over that past in order to explain itself, this time to new generations and in a different context. The publication of this book in French in the late 1980s marked a first step in this revisitation of history. The recent opening of the archives represents a further progression in the continuing search for truth. Now people can assess for themselves the extent to which the efforts currently being made by Switzerland to dispel the shadows of the past will foster a truer understanding of the work of the international Red Cross during World War II.

Jean-Claude Favez
September 1998

Acknowledgements

A number of people have helped us in the work of editing and translating this book. The author, Professor Jean-Claude Favez, has been unstinting in his encouragement and has answered our questions with unfailing courtesy and promptness. Richard Fisher of Cambridge University Press has been patient and supportive in ways that few translators are privileged to enjoy. We are deeply grateful to both of them, as we are to Frances Nugent for the care and attention she brought to the task of copy-editing the typescript. Our daughter Harriet generously gave of her time to assist us with the translation of the chapter on Slovakia and the first part of the chapter on Romania, and large sections of the manuscript were typed with speedy efficiency by our son Hilary. We wish to acknowledge too a grant from the School of Modern Languages and European Studies at the University of East Anglia which helped us materially to expedite the completion of this book, the expert work of Dr Jean Boase-Beier in translating the German documents in the Appendix, the ready willingness of other colleagues in the University to give us the benefit of their specialised knowledge of the field, and the eagerness of final year French honours students in the Advanced Translation seminar to offer suggestions, several of which are incorporated in the chapter on France.

The documents in the Appendix (apart from document II which is reproduced here in the original English) were translated from German by Jean Boase-Beier.

John Fletcher
Beryl S. Fletcher

Chronology

This chronology is restricted in the main to events discussed in the book, with issues concerning the Red Cross in the left-hand column and other important dates on the right

1933–1938

30 January 1933 Hitler becomes Chancellor in Germany

28 February 1933 The decree on the protection of the German state and people lifts the constitutional guarantee on fundamental liberties

20 March 1933 Dachau opened

1 April 1933 Boycott of Jewish shops, doctors, lawyers, etc.

18 May 1933 First discussion in the ICRC about growing political violence in Germany

November 1933 ICRC–DRK accord on the routing of individual enquiries about concentration camp detainees

1933–35 In a series of laws and decrees Jews are excluded from German public service and society

1 May 1935 Boissier memorandum on political detainees

15 September 1935 Nuremberg laws for the protection of German blood and honour and on Reich citzenship

19–27 October 1935 Carl J.
Burckhardt visits Lichtenburg,
Esterwegen and Dachau

9–15 May 1936 Burckhardt's
official visit to Germany

13 March 1938 Austria annexed
by the Reich

July 1938 Evian conference on
German Jewish refugees.
Intergovernmental Committee for
Refugees set up

19 August 1938 Guillaume Favre
visits Dachau

9–10 November 1938
Kristallnacht. Jews excluded from
economic life

19 November 1938 French
démarche to the ICRC

24 November 1938 Red Cross
League enquiry on Jewish refugees

28 December 1938 ICRC approach
to the DRK on behalf of political
and racial detainees

30 December 1938 ICRC enquiry
to national Red Cross societies on
the needs of countries accepting
Jewish refugees

1939

9 January 1939 The DRK
rejects the ICRC's démarche of
28 December 1938

24 January 1939 Heydrich heads
the Jewish Emigration Office

17 May 1939 the British White
Paper limits the number of Jewish

emigrants to the Palestine
Mandate to 75,000 up to the end
of March 1944

4 July 1939 RVJD set up

1 September 1939 Launch of
euthanasia programme for mental
patients (suspended on 24 August
1941)
Outbreak of war in Europe

2 September 1939 The ICRC
presents its action programme and
offers its services to the countries
at war

9 September 1939 Memorandum
to the belligerents reminding them
of the need to respect human
rights, protect civilians and outlaw
certain forms of warfare

27 September 1939 RSHA set up
under SS control

2 October 1939 The ICRC refines
its proposals of 9 September
concerning civilians: to apply the
Tokyo project or grant civilians
de facto POW status

7 October 1939 Himmler put in
charge of racial reorganisation in
the East as *Reichskommissar* for the
strengthening of the German race

October–November 1939 Marcel
Junod's second mission to
Germany and occupied Poland

October 1939 Beginning of
deportations to Poland. Jewish
reserve set up in the Lublin
district, a policy abandoned in
March 1940

22 December 1939 The DRK
confirms that the ICRC can send
parcels to the concentration camps

1940

12 March, 12 May 1940 Appeals
for the protection of civilian
populations

March 1940 Burckhardt mission
to Berlin

17 August 1940 Eric Descoeudres
and Roland Marti visit Buchenwald

13 September 1940 Deportations
from Vienna, Mährisch-Ostrau,
Teschen and Stettin

3 October 1940 'Statut des Juifs'
promulgated by the Vichy regime
in France

November 1940 Setting up of the   November 1940 Construction of
CMS by the ICRC and Red Cross   Warsaw ghetto
League
Alec Cramer visits refugee camps in
southern France

1941

2 January 1941 Concentration
camps and internees divided into
three categories according to the
seriousness of the sentence

29 March 1941 Vichy sets up the
'Commissariat aux questions
juives'

22 June 1941 Germany attacks the
Soviet Union. The
'Einsatzkommandos' go into
action

23 June 1941 The ICRC offers its
services to the belligerents in the
East; the USSR does not respond

Summer 1941 Greek population aid activities launched

31 July 1941 Goering's written order entrusting Heydrich with overall responsibility for the solution of the Jewish problem

20 August 1941 The DRK informs the ICRC of the suspension of all concentration camp enquiries

August 1941 Burckhardt in Berlin

August 1941 Massacre of the Galician Jews settled in Hungary

27 August 1941 Members of the resistance in the Eastern territories and communists ordered to be deported to the concentration camps

16 September 1941 Coordinating Commission examines the plight of Franco-Spanish POWs deported to Mauthausen; the issue is raised with Hartmann

September 1941 First gassing by Zyklon B of invalids and Soviet POWs at Auschwitz I

October–November 1941 The ICRC cannot decide whether or not to intervene over the execution of hostages in France

Mid-October 1941 German Jews deported to Lodz

22–24 October 1941 Execution of nintety-eight hostages in France. RSHA bans Jewish emigration from Europe

Autumn 1941 Deportation and massacre of Romanian Jews in Transnistria

December 1941 The ICRC fails to persuade the British to lift the blockade to allow supplies into the Polish camps and ghettos
The war spreads to the Pacific; the ICRC offers its services and organises its delegations in Asia

December 1941 Chelmno extermination camp opened (gassing with lorries)

7 December 1941 *Nacht und Nebel* decree

1942

20 January 1942 Wannsee conference and the 'Final Solution of the Jewish problem'

January 1942 Massacre of Jews and Serbs at Novi-Sad

March–April 1942 Rohmer mission for the CMS in Hungary, Romania and Slovakia

16 March 1942 Suzanne Ferrière reminds Hartmann of the ICRC's questions following the DRK's 20 August 1941 letter

16 March 1942 Concentration camps placed under SS economic control

17 March 1942 Beginning of the Reinhardt operation. Belzec, Sobibor, Maidanek and Treblinka brought into service in turn to wipe out the Eastern ghettos

27 March 1942 First trainload of deportees from Compiègne to Auschwitz

30 March 1942 Barbey letter to Marti (démarche requesting permission to send help to the Compiègne internees)

March–June 1942 Slovak Jews deported to Auschwitz

15 April 1942 Setting up under ICRC auspices of the Fondation pour l'organisation des transports de la CR

16 April 1942 Gallopin note to Marti (démarche seeking to ascertain the final destination of deportees to the East)

29 April, 1 May 1942 In response
to the démarche of 16 March 1942,
the DRK announces it can no
longer furnish information about
non-Aryan detainees

15 May 1942 ICRC leaders meet
in top-level session

20 May 1942 Roland Marti told to
relaunch the 16 April 1942 démarche

1 June 1942 Burckhardt writes to
Grawitz about the Dutch hostages

9 June 1942 The Slovak Red Cross
asks the ICRC to intervene

2 July 1942 Dannecker–Bousquet
agreement on the deportation of
French Jews

16–17 July 1942 The big 'Vél
d'hiv' round-up in Paris

22 July 1942 Deportations from
the Warsaw ghetto begin.
Auschwitz becomes the main
extermination camp

10 August 1942 Memorandum to
the USSR to try and get
negotiations restarted

Early August 1942 Schulte's
information reaches Riegner

13–18 August 1942 Marti mission
in the General-Government

20 August 1942 The DRK
announces the suspension of all
concentration camp enquiries

24 August 1942 The German
consulate in Geneva is handed the
four Engelbrechten notes dealing
inter alia with the Dutch hostages
and the Franco-Spanish inmates
in Mauthausen.

26 August 1942 Max von Wyss
arrives in Cracow for the CMS

26 August 1942 Big round-up of
Jews in the French unoccupied
zone

3 September 1942 The ICRC
replies to the Slovak Red Cross that
there is nothing it can do and
Jacques Chenevière writes to the
French Foreign Ministry about
their deportees

September 1942 Hartmann visits
Geneva

September 1942 The German
Justice Ministry hands over to the
SS for extermination as and when
it sees fit all 'Eastern' detainees
sentenced to more than three
years and even German nationals
condemned to serve more than
eight years in a concentration
camp

21 September 1942 Burckhardt
asks to see Himmler on behalf of
a deportee, Countess Lanskoranska

23 September 1942 Roland Marti
asked to intervene on behalf of the
Belgian hostages and deportees

24 September 1942 Démarche
(via a note to Marti) on
behalf of deported and interned
aliens

9 October 1942 During the Dieppe
Raid 'handcuffs crisis' the ICRC
reiterates the need for all concerned
to respect the Conventions

14 October 1942 An ICRC plenary
session drops the idea of a public
appeal against human rights abuses

22 October 1942 The ICRC again
reminds people of the need to respect
the Conventions

29 October 1942 Himmler gives
the go-ahead again to parcels to
certain categories of deportees

7 November 1942 Conversation
between Burckhardt and Paul C.
Squire

11 November 1942 The
Wehrmacht occupies the whole of
France

17 December 1942 Allied appeal
against the massacre of Jews

30 December 1942 The
Coordinating Commission drops
the 24 September 1942 démarche
and resolves instead to try sending
aid direct to the deportees

1943

18 January, 30 January 1943 Note
to Marti and letter from Huber in
this vein

27 January 1943 Without
questioning agreed action priorities
the Coordinating Commission
resolves to take on board the
question of Jews held in their
own country

2 February 1943 German defeat
at Stalingrad

15 February 1943 In its reply the
German Foreign Ministry expresses
strong reservations about the direct
aid démarche

March 1943 Julius Schmidlin in
Zagreb

22 March–4 April 1943 Max von
Wyss's visit to the General-
Government

March–May 1943 Salonika's Jews
deported

5 April 1943 ICRC note to the
British Foreign Office about boat
emigration

19 April–16 May 1943 Warsaw
ghetto uprising

May–June 1943 Fifty parcels sent
to concentration camps
Edouard Chapuisat and David de
Traz visit Central and Eastern
Europe

June 1943 Hartmann visits
Theresienstadt

24 July 1943 ICRC appeal to the
belligerents about methods of war

12 August–15 September 1943
Roland Marti's visit to Norway

23 August 1943 Appeal on behalf
of POWs' and civilian internees'
human rights

August 1943 Treblinka uprising

October 1943 Jean de Bavier
appointed delegate in Budapest

October 1943 Sobibor uprising

19 October 1943 Reinhardt
operation ends and Sobibor,
Belzec and Treblinka put out of
service

November 1943 Karl Kolb
appointed delegate in Budapest
where he joined de Steiger

November 1943 Burckhardt in
Berlin

11–21 December 1943 Karl Kolb
visits Transnistria

Late December 1943 René Henry
is sent to Sofia

30 December 1943 ICRC public
appeal to the belligerents about
reprisals and the increasing savagery
of methods of war

1944

22 January 1944 WRB set up

9 February 1944 Letter from Max
Huber to Mihaï Antonescu

15 February 1944 Memorandum
about the repatriation or
hospitalisation in a neutral country
of sick and wounded POWs

February 1944 Burckhardt's
intervention with Hartmann on
behalf of the Vittel internees
holding South American passports

15 March 1944 Special Aid   15–19 March 1944 The
Division set up   Wehrmacht intervenes in
                                   Hungary

2 May 1944 The WRB's démarche
to the ICRC to ask Berlin to
recognise the Jews as civilian
internees

Mid-May 1944 Frédéric Born
arrives in Budapest

                                   6 June 1944 D-Day: the Allies
                                   land in Normandy

23 June 1944 Maurice Rossel visits
Theresienstadt

5 July 1944 Bureau decision to
intervene in Hungary

                                   7 July 1944 Horthy suspends the
                                   deportation of Jews from Hungary

12 July 1944 New instructions
from the Federal Police Division
about the admission of refugees to
Switzerland

Mid-July 1944 Julius Schmidlin
visits three Croatian concentration
camps

20–21 July 1944 Robert Schirmer
gives Horthy Huber's message

26 July 1944 Burckhardt plan
for Hungary

3 August 1944 The ICRC
authorises the Romanian Red Cross
to use its flag for boat emigration

15 August 1944 Last trainload of
deportees leaves France

17 August 1944 Appeal for
humanitarian law to apply to
partisans

22 August 1944 318 Belsen
prisoners arrive in Switzerland

25 August 1944 Paris liberated

20 September 1944 Bureau decision
to make a démarche on behalf of
deportees

25 September 1944 General
instructions to delegates modified

2 October 1944 Huber's letter to
Ribbentrop about deportees
Huber's note on the notion of
civilian internees

15 October 1944 The Arrow-
Crosses seize power in Hungary

Late October 1944 Georges
Dunand arrives in Bratislava

25 November 1944 Himmler suspends exterminations at Auschwitz

10 December 1944 The ICRC awarded the Nobel Peace Prize for the second time

Early December 1944 1,352 Jews from Belsen arrive in Switzerland

15 December 1944 Huber's appeal to Mgr. Tiso

December 1944 Hans Bon in Italy Sub-delegation set up in Vienna

1945

January 1945 The Berlin delegation in negotiations with the SS leadership

1 February 1945 The German Foreign Ministry replies to the note of 2 October 1944

2 February 1945 Himmler's letter to Burckhardt

8 February 1945 J.-M. Musy arrives in Switzerland with 1,200 Jews from Theresienstadt

15 February 1945 The ICRC announces that it is undertaking a revision of the Conventions and drawing up new texts on humanitarian law
The ICRC replies to the Reich's note of 1 February 1945

2 March 1945 The Germans agree to the exchange of French, Belgian and Dutch civilians, women, children and old men

12 March 1945 Burckhardt–Kaltenbrunner meeting on the Arlberg road

5–11 April 1945 Three hundred
Ravensbrück women exchanged
by Switzerland

6 April 1945 Otto Lehner and Paul
Dunant at Theresienstadt

15 April 1945 Belsen liberated

20–21 April 1945 Willy Pfister and
Albert de Cocatrix witness the
evacuation of Oranienburg and
Ravensbrück

22 April 1945 Innsbruck meeting
between Hans Bachmann, Hans
Mayer and Ernst Kaltenbrunner

24–26 April 1945 Second
trainload of repatriated prisoners
from Mauthausen

26 April 1945 Robert Hort and
Raymond Moynier at Türckheim

27 April 1945 Louis Haefliger
enters Mauthausen
Démarche by Riegner and Red
Cross societies to the ICRC about
Jewish POWs

28 April 1945 Victor Maurer at
Dachau

2 May 1945 Paul Dunant takes up
residence at Theresienstadt

5 May 1945 Mauthausen liberated

8 May 1945 Germany surrenders
unconditionally

Abbreviations

The following abbreviations are used in the text and in the notes:

AA	Auswärtiges Amt (German Foreign Ministry)
ACPG	Agence centrale de renseignements des prisonniers de guerre (Central Agency for Prisoners of War)
AG	ICRC Archives, Geneva
AWJC	Archives of the World Jewish Congress, Geneva Office
BA	Bundsarchiv, Koblenz (German federal archive)
CCC	Colis aux camps de concentration (Concentration Camp Parcels Scheme)
CI or CICR	Comité international de la Croix-Rouge (ICRC)
CID	Civils internés divers (MCI, Miscellaneous Civilian Internees, ICRC service)
CIMADE	Comité inter-mouvements auprès des évacués (inter-movement evacuees committee)
CMS	Commission mixte de secours du CICR et de la LSCR (Joint Aid Commission of the ICRC and the Red Cross League)
CPI	Civilian Prisoners and Internees (PIC)
CR	Croix-Rouge (Red Cross)
CRF	Croix-Rouge française (French Red Cross)
DAS	Division d'assistance spéciale (Special Aid Division, ICRC service)
Delasem	Italian Jewish communities aid committee
DIE	Division des intérêts étrangers (Foreign Interests Division of the DPF)
DPF	Département politique fédéral (Swiss Federal Political Department)
DRK	Deutsches Rotes Kreuz (German Red Cross)
DZAP	Deutsches Zentralarchiv, Potsdam (German central archive)
FA	Swiss Federal Archives, Berne

HIJEFS	Schweizerischer Hilfsverein für jüdische Flüchtlinge im Ausland (Swiss Aid Committee for Jewish Refugees Abroad)
ICRC	International Committee of the Red Cross
IfZ	Institut für Zeitgeschichte (Munich Contemporary History Institute)
IMPA	Immigration en Palestine (Palestine Immigration Service, ICRC)
IMS	International Migration Service
Joint	American Jewish Joint Distribution Committee
JUS	Jüdische Unterstützungsstelle (Jewish Assistance Office)
KL or KZ	Konzentrationslager (concentration camp)
LSCR	Ligue des Sociétés de la Croix-Rouge (Red Cross League)
MCI	Miscellaneous Civilian Internees (CID)
NA	National Archives, Washington
NGO	Non-governmental organisation
NN	*Nacht und Nebel* (Night and Fog)
NS	Nationalsozialistisch (Nazi)
NSDAP	Nationalsozialistische Deutsche Arbeiterpartei (Nazi party)
OKH	Oberkommando des Heeres (German army High Command)
OKW	Oberkommando der Wehrmacht (German armed forces High Command)
OSE	Œuvre de secours aux enfants (children's aid charity)
PIC	Prisonniers et internés civils (CPI, commission of the ICRC)
PMS	Personal Message Scheme (Service)
POW	Prisoner of war
PRO	Public Record Office, Kew
PVB	Procès-verbaux du Bureau du CICR (ICRC Bureau minutes)
PVCC	Procès-verbaux de la Commission centrale, puis de co-ordination, du CICR (ICRC Central Committee, later Coordinating Committee, minutes)
PVCICR	Procès-verbaux du CICR (ICRC minutes)
PVDAS	Procès-verbaux de la DAS (Special Aid Division minutes)
PVPIC	Procès-verbaux de la PIC (CPI minutes)
PVSvCi	Procès-verbaux des Services civils de l'Agence centrale des prisonniers de guerre (ACPG civilian services minutes)
RC	Red Cross

Relico	Comité d'assistance à la population juive frappée par la guerre (Aid Committee to Jewish People Caught Up in the War)
RGO	Rada Glowna Opiekuncza (Polish central mutual aid committee)
RICR	*Revue internationale de la Croix-Rouge (International Journal of the Red Cross)*
RSHA	Reichssicherheitshauptamt (Reich Central Security Bureau)
RVJD	Reichsvereinigung der Juden in Deutschland (Reich Association of Jews in Germany)
SA	Sturmabteilungen (stormtroops)
SCIU	Save the Children International Union
SD	Sicherheitsdienst (security service)
SdN	Société des Nations (League of Nations)
Sipo	Sicherheitspolizei (security police)
SS	Schutzstaffeln (protection squad)
UB	Universitätsbibliothek Basel (Basel University Library)
UGIF	Union générale des Israélites de France (Union of French Jews)
UISE	Union internationale de secours aux enfants (Save the Children International Union)
WJC	World Jewish Congress
WRB	War Refugee Board
YMCA	Young Men's Christian Association

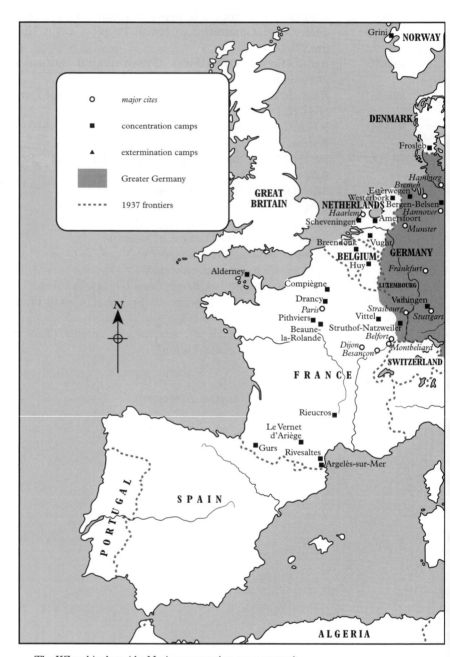

The KZ archipelago (the Nazi concentration camp system).

ESTONIA

LATVIA

SWEDEN

LITHUANIA

GERMANY
Danzig ⬜Stutthof

Neuengamme⬛
Ravensbrück⬤
GERMANY⬛ Oranienburg-
⬜Sachsenhausen Cheimno   ▲Treblinka
⬤Berlin   ▲Cheimno
Gardelegen⬛   Warsaw   ▲Sobibor
Dore-Mittelbau⬛ POLAND   ⬛Maidanek
⬛⬤Halle Dresden⬛ Gross-Rosen ▲Belzec
Buchenwald⬛   Auschwitz-
⬛Theresienstadt   Birkenau
Prague⬤   ▲⬛○Cracow
⬤Flossenburg
Nurnberg⬤ CZECHOSLOVAKIA
           ⬛Novaki
         Gusen⬛ Vyhne
Dachau⬛ ⬜Mauthausen ⬛Szered
  ⬤Munich Vienna ⬛Vamosmikola
Kaufering⬛ Linz   ⬛Kistarcsa
AUSTRIA   ⬛Szarvas
        ⬛Merano   HUNGARY
      ⬛Bolzano / Gries

0   100   200 miles
0   160   320 kilometres

RUSSIA

ROMANIA

YUGOSLAVIA
  ⬛Stara Gradiska
    ⬛Jasenovac

BULGARIA

ITALY

Civitella⬛
del Tronto

ALBANIA

TURKEY

Fossolo⬛
di Carpi   Larissa⬛
        ⬛Ferramonti- GREECE
         Tarsia   Thebes⬛
                    Athens

TUNISIA

anity and a semblance of civilised conduct where military opera-
s were concerned.

he problem that the Conventions had not foreseen and therefore did
cover was deliberate and systematic brutality towards civilians
ninating in mass extermination. When first in the 1930s the Third
h, and then in the 1940s Axis allies like Italy, German satellites like
atia and defeated countries with puppet regimes like France, began
ecuting their Jewish citizens, the ICRC considered that its statutes
the international agreements (the 'Conventions') under which it
rated did not allow it to intervene. More than that, as this book
es abundantly clear, it was terrified that any action on behalf of
ims of racist legislation would be seriously counter-productive, the
st-case scenario being denial of access to POW camps in German-
trolled territory. In other words, fruitless attempts to save the Jews
ht be punished by the banning of all humanitarian activity however
timately grounded in Conventions which Germany had signed. The
RC was acutely conscious of what that would mean: after all, it was
verless to prevent the deaths of the vast numbers of Soviet POWs
) died in conditions of scarcely imaginable cruelty, of hunger, cold
disease (where they were not shot out of hand on surrender), simply
ause the USSR was not a signatory to the Conventions.

he Jews, unfortunately, were not combatants covered by these
nventions, but civilians subject to the laws of their respective coun-
s, so much as the ICRC might deplore the severity (and later on the
tal savagery) of such legislation, it felt it was powerless to act.
haps the most chilling document in the entire book is Mgr. Tiso's
tification of his country's antisemitic policies (document VII in the
pendix) which flabbergasted even a hardened diplomat like Jean-
enne Schwarzenberg, the same ICRC official who set out for the
pteenth time the Committee's position on the issue. 'The Jewish
blem presents the IRCR with particular difficulties', he wrote with
iracteristic understatement, and went on to say:

he ICRC for its part makes no distinctions where race is concerned, it cannot
all that totally ignore the internal legislation of certain sovereign states which
practise such distinctions. Care must be taken that the ICRC's interventions
behalf of the Jews, although entirely of a humanitarian nature, are not
isidered – wrongly, of course – as taking up a position vis-à-vis such internal
islation, and thus assuming a political character incompatible with the
nciple of neutrality which lies at the heart of everything the ICRC does.[1]

iat, in a nutshell, is what this book is all about. It is quite true that the
RC made no distinction between Jews and those whom the Nazis
led Aryans. The trouble was, others did. One of the most sinister

Introduction

John Fletcher

The wisdom of hindsight

Of all forms of wisdom, hindsight is by general
merciful, the most unforgiving. Had the Allies kno
know now, they would surely have chosen to bomb *F*
and other Nazi extermination camps, even at the cos
among the inmates, rather than allow the industrialis
and other racial minorities to continue. But as v
painfully aware, those in charge of the strategic
thought otherwise: better to get the war over as qui<
save the victims of persecution that way. What few
grasp then – and that, if not an excuse, is at least an e
exclusively the Nazis' attention was focused on th
their conquests *Judenfrei*. No rational person could
to penetrate the minds of those for whom the achiev
called 'the Final Solution to the Jewish problem' wa
tance than winning the war itself. It is in that context
on behalf of the Jews by the Red Cross in general, a
Committee (the ICRC) in particular, has to be eval
an attempt to do that, with fairness, objectivity and a
as the horrific nature of the subject-matter allows.

To adapt the title of the original French edition, d
World War II find itself embroiled in a 'mission
after all a charitable organisation whose historic role
was the protection of sick and wounded soldiers on
of prisoners of war in enemy hands; as such, it I
strictest neutrality. If it was seen to favour one side
if that side now seems clearly to have been the 'ri<
jeopardising its primary function and provoking t
into repudiating the famous Conventions whicl
legitimacy and, in a situation of total war, at leas
theatre's western and southern fronts, preserve

aspects of Nazi propaganda was the way it induced people who otherwise were free of all taint of racism to speak in terms of a Jewish 'problem'. Where there is a problem, the evil suggestion followed, there must be a solution. In the late 1930s, for well-meaning men and women of a tolerant outlook and liberal instincts such as those who served on the ICRC or worked for it, often in a voluntary capacity, that solution was to be sought in emigration (Madagascar was even mooted by some authorities as a possible homeland for the European Jews). Few people seem to have seen through the Nazi sleight-of-hand and asked pointedly 'what problem?' Once it was accepted, even tacitly and reluctantly, that the Jews constituted a problem, the first step had been taken on the road that led ultimately to Auschwitz and the other factories of death, all in pursuance of what was referred to in that truly breath-taking German euphemism, '*Endlösung*', 'Final Solution'.

The argument in brief

In outline the account given in this book is as follows.

On 20 January 1942 the notorious Wannsee Conference took place. At this meeting in Berlin representatives of all the German ministries and agencies involved in the deportation and extermination of the Jews launched what they termed the 'Final Solution of the Jewish problem' in Europe. We know what was decided at the conference because the minutes taken by Adolf Eichmann, head of the Jewish section in the RSHA, the Reich's Central Security Bureau, were found after the war and produced in evidence at Nuremberg. From the point of view of the present study, two things are of particular importance in this document. Firstly, that even amongst themselves those high-ranking civil servants and officers, almost all members of the Nazi party or the SS, disguised the reality. They did not speak of mass slaughter or of extermination, but only of death by labour and of Jewish resettlement in Eastern Europe. The 'terrible secret' of which Walter Laqueur speaks in his influential book[2] was a well-kept secret even in the higher echelons of the administration in the Third Reich. Secondly, all the plans laid at Wannsee and afterwards required the active participation of thousands of people in the police and the railways in the occupied territories and in the satellites and the countries allied to the Reich. Certainly the policy of the 'Final Solution' was the inevitable outcome of Hitler's rabid antisemitism, but it would never have succeeded to the extent that it did without the ready cooperation of many individuals who were neither German nor Nazis. It is nevertheless the case that for the most part these people saw only one aspect of the operations against the Jews and were able to claim afterwards that they had been unaware of the full horror of what was going on.

As for the role of the ICRC in all this, it is worth recalling that it was founded in 1863 by five prominent people in Geneva as a non-governmental humanitarian organisation. Despite the adjective 'International' its members have always been Swiss citizens, that is residents of a neutral country. They seek chiefly to maintain and develop the ties between the national Red Cross societies, to act as fair-minded intermediaries between the belligerents in time of war, to care for soldiers wounded in battle or taken prisoner, and to promote the observance and improvement of humanitarian law, of which the best-known elements are the Geneva Conventions of 1864 and 1929 and the Hague Convention of 1907 relating to POWs. At the outbreak of World War II, however, civilians were for the most part not protected by these international accords, since the Tokyo agreement adopted at the 1934 Red Cross conference in Japan[3] had by 1939 not been ratified by national governments. In any case, the Tokyo project concerned only civilian aliens detained by a belligerent at the outbreak of hostilities or held hostage by an enemy army occupying the country of which they were citizens. On behalf of the first category the ICRC obtained in autumn 1939 first from the German authorities and then through reciprocity from the French and British governments the same treatment as that accorded to POWs under the 1929 Geneva Convention, so that during the war the Committee's delegates visited civilian internees in their camps and sent them parcels from their families and relief organisations where such supplies were allowed through the Allied and German blockades.

But besides these prisoners there were other civilian victims of the war, such as the inmates of the concentration camps opened by the Nazis before the war for the incarceration (and so-called re-education) of their political opponents and of people whom they considered socially undesirable like homosexuals or racially tainted like Gypsies and Jews. From December 1941 onwards, too, people suspected or convicted of resistance activity against the Wehrmacht in the occupied territories were deported to concentration camps in the Reich, and by December 1944, despite the very high death-rate from cold, hunger, disease and ill treatment, their numbers had grown to 800,000.

Since international humanitarian law did not protect or provide relief for political prisoners held by their own government, the ICRC could only act on their behalf on its own initiative and with great caution. Thus it was only with the Nazis' full consent that members of the Committee were able to visit German concentration camps in 1935 and 1938.

Furthermore in pursuance of their aim of domination in Europe the Nazis did not wage war only against their neighbours; they wanted to wipe out the Jewish race and to enslave the peoples of Eastern Europe as well. From 1933 to 1940 the Third Reich deprived the German Jews of their nationality, civil rights, freedom of movement, and so on, then step by step tried to expel to other countries the Jews made foreigners in their own state. But the results of this policy were disappointing. The annexation of Austria, Bohemia-Moravia and Poland made the Reich master of more Jews than ever. Moreover emigration from Europe became more difficult. In 1917 the British foreign secretary Arthur Balfour had promised the Zionists a national home in Palestine, but after the peace treaties the British actually restricted entry to the Mandate so as to placate the Arabs and maintain order in the country, and in the 1930s no government was willing to grant entry to Jews from Germany, except those in transit, because of high unemployment caused by the economic crisis.

So in 1940 the Germans began to assemble the Jews in ghettos, first of all in Poland. Then, after the attack against the Soviet Union on 22 June 1941, the SS sent in the *Einsatzgruppen* to carry out mass killings in the rear of the Wehrmacht's advance, and in autumn 1941 specialists in execution by gas, who had murdered between 10,000 and 20,000 mentally ill Germans on secret orders from Hitler since 1939, looked for suitable sites to build extermination camps on Poland's eastern border. In September 1941 the first gas chamber experiments were conducted on invalid Russian troops at Auschwitz which up till then had been a camp for POWs and Polish detainees, and in December of the same year operations began at the Chelmno installations, with the extermination camps of Belzec, Sobibor and Treblinka opening a few months later. The Holocaust, Jewry's greatest tragedy, was well under way.

Thereafter Red Cross delegates were able to visit the POW and civilian internee camps in Germany as they could in Great Britain and the United States, but they were denied access to the concentration camps, let alone the extermination camps (which were not real camps at all but merely the last stop on the line for the deportation trains), with two minor exceptions. In Buchenwald two delegates visited a group of Dutch civilian hostages twice (in 1940 and 1941), and an ICRC delegate and a small Danish Red Cross contingent were allowed a one-day visit to the camp-ghetto at Theresienstadt. Old and well-known Jews were sent to this camp, and the Red Cross visit had been prepared by the SS with flowers, an orchestra, guides and brief informal periods of communication between the visitors and the inmates. But actually

Theresienstadt, in common with similar installations, was a transit camp on the way to Auschwitz.

In autumn 1944 many delegates turned up at the gates of such concentration camps as Buchenwald, Dachau and Mauthausen on the pretext of verifying the arrival of parcels for the foreign detainees which after 1943 the ICRC, other relief organisations and inmates' relatives were allowed to send. The delegates spoke to the camps' SS commandants or to their deputies, but by this time the truth about the camps and the extermination programme was well enough known in the world. From 1940–41 onwards representatives of national Red Cross societies had transmitted to Geneva information both about the detainees' terrible plight and about the expulsions, incarceration and ill treatment of Jews, especially mass executions by SS squads in the East. What seemed at first just rumour was soon corroborated by accurate reports from eyewitnesses about deportations and mass murder. Even this did not amount to confirmation of a meticulously planned total extermination, since that was the most closely guarded secret of the Third Reich, but it was so alarming and so firmly based on the convergence of information from such a wide variety of sources that as early as the end of December 1941 the ICRC sought to respond to the distress calls from and the questions asked by relatives and national Red Cross societies.

The papers in the ICRC archives do not make it possible even today to be certain precisely when the Committee and its leaders realised the truth about the Final Solution. Carl J. Burckhardt, who was vice-president at the time, was apparently told in August 1942 by the Geneva representative of the WJC, Gerhart Riegner, who had been his student in the 1930s, but he also seems to have been tipped off by people in the German Foreign Ministry with whom he had been friends since before the war. What is clear is that in November 1942 Burckhardt confirmed to the American consul in Geneva, Paul C. Squire, that the Nazis had embarked on a programme to exterminate all the Jews in Germany. But the ICRC did not wait for confirmation of the plan to start thinking about its responsibilities and of ways in which it might help the Jews.

It still continued to rely, however, on the national Red Cross societies, even when in August 1941 the DRK (German Red Cross), whose nominal president was the Duke of Saxe-Coburg-Gotha but whose real head was none other than the SS's chief medical officer, Dr Ernst Grawitz, announced that it could no longer provide information about any Jew in the hands of the German police authorities. Further than that the ICRC felt it could not go, since, from the strict point of view of the law of nations, its competence did not extend to the victims of civil wars or political repression such as Jews who had been stripped of their previous citizenship or had been abandoned by their governments to the tender mercies of the Nazi authorities.

From December 1941 to the spring of 1942, in response to calls for help from France, the ICRC and its delegation in Berlin tried unsuccessfully to get permission to send parcels to the camp at Compiègne near Paris, which from the end of March 1941 onwards served as the departure point for trains going to Auschwitz. The DRK, the army and the German Foreign Ministry all turned a deaf ear even when the ICRC knew the name and address of the deportee. On 7 December 1941 the OKW issued the notorious order *NN*, *Nacht und Nebel* ('Night and Fog', later used as a title by Alain Resnais for his landmark documentary on the Nazi concentration camp system *Nuit et brouillard*) that authorised the deportation of French civilians accused of resistance activities to Mauthausen, perhaps the harshest camp of all. In summer 1942 some ICRC members thought that they could intervene on behalf of such deportees under the terms of the Tokyo project and accordingly on 24 September 1942 their chief delegate in Berlin, Roland Marti, delivered a verbal note to the German Foreign Ministry requesting the right for these detainees to receive visits from the Red Cross and letters and parcels from their relatives, but this plea too fell on deaf ears.

By the end of 1942, therefore, the ICRC had to admit that prudent, discreet démarches of this sort had got it nowhere. Up until then the organisation had seldom issued public calls; it did however have recourse to such means to denounce, for example, the use of gas in World War I (February 1918) or bombing raids on civilian targets (Whitsun 1940). Nevertheless, in midsummer 1942 it did prepare such a scheme that while not mentioning the Jews explicitly appealed against the worsening of conditions for civilians caught up in the war. A majority of the ICRC's twenty-three members voted in favour of such a public call but remained divided over the form it should take. The Swiss authorities became alarmed; when the Wehrmacht was sweeping all before it was not the moment, they felt, to antagonise the Nazi regime and put Switzerland's neutrality at risk. So the warning from Berne on the one hand, and the fear on the other that arising out of the Dieppe Raid 'handcuffs crisis'[4] the Reich would repudiate the Geneva Conventions, led the ICRC to give up the idea of a public call. Worse, German violations of the Conventions were allowed to pass without protest, as for example when the Wehrmacht separated French Jewish POWs from their fellow countrymen and sent them to military hospitals on the Eastern Front, or when Polish POWs were forced to work in German munitions factories.

Since the rescue of the Jews seemed impossible, the ICRC decided at the turn of 1942–43 to act on two fronts: sending relief supplies to the deportees (the Concentration Camp Parcels Scheme) and appealing directly to governments in the Reich's allies and satellites. Valuable as the parcels were, they could only be sent to detainees whose name and camp address were known to the sender, thereby of course excluding people sent to extermination camps, the very existence of which was a Nazi secret. Of the Axis allies and satellites, only Bulgaria resisted German pressure to adopt antisemitic measures, and with the exception of Hungary the ICRC's delegates were free to act on behalf of the Jews only when the Germans were in full retreat, that is from autumn 1944 onwards. By then, tragically, nearly all the Jews from these countries had been killed.

The Nazis refused to the very last to let the ICRC into the concentration camps, even after agreement had been reached – very belatedly, on 1 February 1945 – between de Gaulle's provisional French government, the Belgians and the Dutch on the one hand and the Reich on the other for the application on a basis of reciprocity of the Tokyo project to civilian detainees, especially the very large number of French people stranded in Germany. By this time indeed there was widespread anxiety that in a bloody *Götterdämmerung* the retreating Nazis would blow up the camps and slaughter all the inmates, so secret high-level contacts took place between the ICRC and the SS to forestall such an apocalypse. Hans Bon, the delegate in northern Italy, got in touch with SS General Karl Wolff, who was negotiating with the Allied powers over his own surrender, to have the deportations suspended, and on 12 March 1945 in a summit encounter near Feldkirch on the Swiss-Austrian border Burckhardt met Ernst Kaltenbrunner, the personal representative of Heinrich Himmler, who was desperately trying to save his own skin. The two negotiators agreed that the ICRC should take under its wing all concentration camp internees, including such Jews as had survived, but except at Mauthausen and Theresienstadt local camp commandants refused to cooperate with the Red Cross. Allied military commanders for their part accorded a higher priority to liberating and repatriating their own POWs than to rescuing civilian internees other than those who were very ill. In the end the remnants of the KZ archipelago collapsed in disorder, with ICRC delegates often arriving too late and with too few resources to be of much use, but at least the whole ghastly tragedy was over.

The response of the ICRC

In a letter to the author of 19 March 1988 Cornelio Sommaruga responded on behalf of the ICRC to Professor Favez's findings; at the latter's request the Committee's comments were published in full on pages 376–9 of the original edition and are summarised below.[5]

After conveying to the author the Committee's congratulations and thanks for his painstaking and detailed examination of the ICRC's archives to which he had been granted unrestricted access, for his objective analysis of the relevant papers, and for his skilful synthesis of the material provided in a scholarly work of reference, M. Sommaruga confirmed that the ICRC's desire for light to be shed on a particularly painful chapter in the history of Europe and of the ICRC itself had been satisfied, particularly with regard to the question of how much the ICRC knew of the 'Final Solution' and what it tried and was able to do on behalf of victims of Nazi persecution. The ICRC did, however, have some reservations: too much stress had been placed, it felt, on work done at headquarters in Geneva to the detriment of the activities of delegates on the ground, and it would have preferred a more balanced approach in this respect; likewise, not enough allowance had been made for the fact that the ICRC had many other tasks to perform, particularly with regard to POWs and civilian internees, and could not simply put all its efforts into helping victims of racially motivated persecution. The ICRC was not satisfied either that Professor Favez's account had established with sufficient rigour what precisely it knew about the 'Final Solution' or what, when it did know, it had tried doing about it. Moreover, although this would have involved considerably more research in the archives than Professor Favez was able to undertake, the ICRC would have preferred him to proceed systematically through the files to see how reports, eyewitness accounts and other information reached the Committee, and in particular it would have liked him to indicate the dates when documents actually arrived in Geneva as well as the dates when they were dispatched, since there was often a timelag, due to the conditions of war, between the sending of information and the decisions taken at headquarters in response to it. The ICRC deeply regretted the complete absence in its archives of documents and eyewitness accounts of the informal contacts between its leaders (especially Max Huber and Carl Burckhardt) and the information they exchanged verbally, but thought that more weight could have been given to oral evidence on the subject from surviving members of the wartime organisation.

While M. Sommaruga conceded that Professor Favez's book showed that the ICRC was slow to realise the totally exceptional nature of what was going on in the camps in Eastern Europe and to undertake a re-examination of its priorities in consequence, he doubted whether, in the face of the greatest disaster in human history and civilisation's most egregious failure, a public appeal, such as the one envisaged in October

1942 and discussed at length in this book, would have done much good. On the contrary it might well have made matters worse, given the Nazis' determination to deal with what they called the 'Jewish problem', and jeopardised the ICRC's work on behalf of POWs. Only discreet actions (on behalf particularly of civilian aliens – Jewish as well as non-Jewish – in German hands) met with some success, albeit out of all proportion to the effort required and the sheer scale of the Nazi extermination programme. With the benefit of hindsight, however, the ICRC ought perhaps to have pressed the Allies and the neutral countries to accord a higher priority to saving the Jews and tried harder to persuade the less enthusiastic Axis partners and satellites to suspend or at least delay the deportations. Where Germany itself and occupied Poland were concerned, however, the ICRC was still of the opinion that the situation of the Jews was utterly hopeless, and although this emerged from Professor Favez's account it was not stressed sufficiently. Likewise, adequate prominence had not been given to the ICRC's efforts in 1939 and 1940 to secure provisional adoption of the Tokyo project concerning civilian aliens in enemy hands; had this been achieved in time the ICRC would have possessed the legal authority, which in the event it cruelly lacked, to intervene on behalf of Jews holding other than German passports.

The present edition

In editing this book, which in the original runs to over 400 closely printed pages, we have with the author's agreement made a number of changes. Nothing of substance has been omitted, although some sections have been reordered and several documents (especially internal ICRC memoranda) have been summarised rather than translated in full; where this has been done page references to the texts in the French edition are indicated in a note. On the other hand, greater prominence has been given to a number of important Nazi documents (which in the first edition are given in French in the main text) by having them translated directly from the original German and placed in an appendix. The French version makes extensive use of boxes set apart from the text and of digressions placed between chapters; in some cases the author asked us to delete these, but in other cases the information they contain has been incorporated in the main text or included in a note. Finally, the author has deleted chapters 1 to 3 inclusive of the original and has provided us with an abridged version instead; this has been translated and forms our chapter 1.

Part I

The Background

1   The Red Cross, political prisoners and racial persecution before 1939

Introduction

On 30 January 1939 Hitler made a speech in the Reichstag in which he declared: 'if international Jewish finance within Europe or beyond its shores was to be successful in embroiling its populations in a new world war, the outcome would not be the bolshevisation of the world and the resultant triumph of Jewry, but the wholesale destruction of the Jewish race in Europe'.[1] If his contemporary listeners were disturbed by his threat, today we are struck rather by the uncanny accuracy of the Führer's bloodcurdling prophecy concerning the fate of the European Jews. This shift in emphasis shows how far history has moved on and highlights the watershed of Auschwitz. Auschwitz has since 1945 come to encapsulate everything to do with antisemitism. Far from the Holocaust tending to fade, the shadow it casts over historical discussion of World War II has steadily increased. We are much better placed now to grasp that whereas the Allies' strategy tended to play down freeing those suffering racial persecution, the Nazis had for their part made their struggle to the death with the Jews the fundamental and secret aim of their dream of world conquest.

Religious leaders, moral authorities and charitable organisations like the Red Cross have suffered more than national governments from this shift in the collective unconscious. Even before the guns had fallen silent in Europe the International Committee of the Red Cross (ICRC) was considering how to deal with the question of what it had known about the fate of those persecuted for their race and what had been done to come to their assistance.[2] It is significant – and surprising – that after vacillating for years between owning up to its failures on the one hand and emphasising on the other how hard it had tried, it decided in the end, by examining its own archives, to arrive at conclusions about this terrible past, as if history could give definitive answers to satisfy each successive generation's curiosity.

So while this book goes over familiar ground to some extent, it also seeks to understand why the issues were not viewed then in the same light as we view them now. For this reason it does not deal solely with racial persecution, but also with concentration camps and with civilian internees, because that was the way the Red Cross envisaged things at the time. And since this study of humanitarian endeavour focuses on the ICRC and not on the victims, it is necessary first to introduce the institution briefly, to indicate the resources it had at its disposal, and to outline its chief concerns; but also, and more importantly, to set out the principles at stake, since it is in the light of those principles that one must interpret – and indeed understand – the policy of the international Red Cross. The words of one of its finest servants should always be borne in mind: 'So long as the eye is denied imagination's magnifying glass, charity can see nothing clearly.'[3]

The Red Cross as an institution and an idea

The ICRC, a non-governmental body staffed entirely by Swiss citizens, has been the driving force of the organisation since its foundation in 1863. Since 1919 the national Red Cross societies have been grouped in the League, and in 1928 the statutes of the international Red Cross were adopted, but neither of these events affected the ICRC's role as moral arbiter, as guardian of the Geneva Conventions, or as neutral and impartial intercessor, especially in time of war, in the domain of help to the sick and wounded of armies in the field, and of protection of prisoners of war.

On the eve of the outbreak of World War II the ICRC was still far from being the institution we are familiar with today, one which is solidly entrenched as a result of the proliferation of various forms of upheaval and armed conflict. The Committee in the narrow sense of the word was then its chief incarnation, consisting in 1939 of twenty-three members, all unpaid, of whom four were women playing an active part. Election to the committee was by cooption from within the circumscribed milieu of the liberal-conservative Protestant middle class in Geneva, and its social and cultural cohesiveness was striking, being largely unaffected either by the presidency from 1928 onwards of Max Huber, a Swiss government legal expert and leading member of Zurich's industrial bourgeoisie, or by the cooption, in the 1930s, of two serving Swiss federal councillors, Philippe Etter and Guiseppe Motta, both of whom were Catholics.[4] Opening up the committee in this way did, however, strengthen the national roots of the institution whose neutrality was based not only on the citizenship of its members but also on its non-governmental character.

There is no doubt that the ICRC sought to be independent of the Helvetic Confederation, and the Swiss authorities likewise stressed their wish to respect its complete freedom of action. They were nevertheless happy to provide it with financial, material and diplomatic support which turned out to be vital during World War II. And whilst they stoutly defended the prerogatives of the Confederation as protecting power, they did not in the least mind including the work of the international Red Cross in the list of services rendered by Swiss neutrality. This means that when all was said and done they took a very close interest in the Committee's activities, one of whose members, Edouard de Haller, was put in charge, from 1942 onwards, of the coordination of humanitarian aid in his capacity as delegate of the Federal Council for International Assistance and Cooperation. During the Second World War, the red cross on white ground and the white cross on red ground seemed to have been unfurled in the same cause, an impression held by most foreigners and shared by many Swiss citizens between 1940 and 1945.

The ICRC frequently drew attention to its right under its statutes to take the initiative in humanitarian matters.[5] Historically and doctrinally this right affected both practical action and international law. In 1929 an international conference met at its suggestion to consider the lessons of World War I; it revised the first Geneva Convention on the protection of sick and wounded combatants and added a second aimed at providing cover for prisoners of war and at defining the role in that regard of the Protecting Powers, without prejudice to the services which the ICRC could furnish by opening an information agency and by visiting those who had been captured.[6] The very real progress in law represented by these two 1929 Conventions should not disguise the fact that on the other hand enemy alien war victims, together with hostages and inter-nees, were still without protection when hostilities broke out in 1939. For some of these, though, the International Committee of the Red Cross managed, towards the end of autumn 1939, to persuade the belligerents to apply part of the draft convention which the Committee had had adopted by the 1934 Tokyo conference of the Red Cross and which a diplomatic conference, scheduled to take place in 1940, was due to examine and adopt.[7]

In this way enemy aliens interned on a belligerent's territory were able to benefit from treatment similar to that which the second Geneva convention of 1929 stipulated for prisoners of war: they were to be allowed to send and receive letters, to get parcels, to be visited by the Red Cross and by the Protecting Powers, and even to take up employ-ment and to be joined by their families.

No international convention covered political prisoners, and this at a time when social unrest, revolution and civil war were greatly swelling their numbers.[8] In the shadow of World War I and the Bolshevik Revolution, the ICRC intervened on the ground by trying to visit political prisoners in several countries, particularly in Central and Eastern Europe. Its thinking on the subject evolved in parallel, and its Commission for Political Prisoners – created in 1935, it bore witness to the importance the Red Cross would henceforth attach to the problem – unhesitatingly concluded that the Red Cross had both the right and the duty to intervene. As the exercise of this right obviously constituted intervention in the internal affairs of a sovereign state, the interests of the victims required it to be undertaken solely through the national Red Cross society of the state concerned. But if it happened that the national society ducked the issue, or was unable to act, then it fell to the ICRC to do so, even off its own bat and on the basis of queries and rumours. And if it came up against a veto from the national Red Cross or governmental authorities, it ought then to threaten to make public both the reasons for its request to intervene and the refusal it had come up against. In spring 1935, according to a memorandum adopted by the Commission, 'the Committee's prestige is not compromised when, having done all it can to defend a humanitarian cause, it suffers a setback. What damages its authority is doing nothing or acting with excessive prudence.'[9]

It is obviously regrettable that this viewpoint – developed, admittedly, in a context different from that of all-out war – did not inspire better thinking in the 1940s. But as early as June 1938 the sixteenth conference of the Red Cross, held in London at the height of the Spanish crisis, marked a step backwards, since the resolution it adopted on political detainees stopped short of real action, merely requesting the Committee and national societies to press ahead with the study of the most appropriate means of ensuring the application of the guiding principles of the Red Cross in conditions of civil war.[10]

The situation in the Third Reich

The Commission's viewpoint on political prisoners in 1935, and the subsequent attitude of the Committee on the issue of political detainees in general, are inseparable from the experiences of concentration camps in the Third Reich between 1933 and 1938. This is particularly interesting for what it reveals of the intentions and *arrière-pensées* of the ICRC's leaders at a time when the Red Cross's energies were not absorbed by Convention activities and the fear of Germany had not reached the extremes of terror which were to paralyse so many courageous initiatives in Switzerland between 1940 and 1943.

From spring 1933 onwards, the International Committee, like other humanitarian organisations, received appeals on behalf of German detainees in the concentration camps.[11] It is interesting to note, in the light of what follows, that President Huber considered, as did his colleagues, that as a matter of principle this problem fell within the ICRC's remit, in the name of general humanitarian obligations and in pursuance of the duty to take the initiative which the Committee claimed for all victims of conflict or repression. In fact, however, the requests reaching Geneva went unanswered until the Swedish Red Cross intervened in its turn to prod the German Red Cross Society (DRK) into action to improve the lot of the detainees.[12]

This move embarrassed both the DRK, caught up in the eddies of the *Gleichschaltung*,[13] and the ICRC, whose moral authority was being called into question, albeit in a fraternal spirit, by this Scandinavian initiative. Max Huber, with the full backing of the vice-president of the DRK, Paul Draudt, who could be trusted as an old friend, finally got the DRK not only discreetly to reassure the Swedes, but also to undertake to pass on to the police authorities in the new regime the names of imprisoned persons whose fate the ICRC, at the request of relatives or of third parties, was seeking information about.

So the president of the ICRC cut the ground from under the feet of the Swedes in the hope of strengthening the position of friends of the Red Cross in Germany, and enabled the ICRC not to appear indifferent or powerless in the face of police repression in the Reich,[14] even if requests for information addressed to Geneva remained few in number right up to the moment when the DRK stopped supplying details about non-Aryans in the summer of 1941.

A year later, in 1934, a fresh request for visits reached Geneva. This time it was the German authorities – at the highest level, it appears – who called upon the ICRC to visit the camps where Austrian Nazis (and even some German sympathisers) arrested after the failure of the coup in Vienna, and the death of the Austrian chancellor Engelbert Dollfuss, had been interned.[15] Caught between the fear of antagonising the Nazi regime, with the risk of jeopardising further the situation of the DRK, and the fear of laying himself open to exploitation by Goebbels' propaganda machine by undertaking an inspection, Huber prevaricated. He tried, unsuccessfully this time, to get either the Austrian Red Cross or the Yugoslav Red Cross to intervene (some of the coup members had fled to Yugoslavia). In the end, during Huber's absence on sick leave, the ICRC decided to send to Vienna Dr Louis Ferrière, brother of

committee member Suzanne Ferrière; he carried out a visit in which the
Nazis in the meantime had lost all interest, so that his report could be
published without causing any embarrassment.

ICRC members who backed the Vienna visit were looking for a
reciprocal gesture on the part of the Reich, that is permission for the
ICRC to be allowed to enter German camps.[16] Max Huber was uneasy
about this démarche, in spite of the firm tone of the Commission for
Political Prisoners' memorandum mentioned earlier.

Finally, through the good offices of Paul Draudt, he got permission in
the summer to carry out a visit, which at the time was nothing out of the
ordinary. In any case it was unclear right up to the last whether the
ICRC would be allowed to undertake the kind of thorough inspection it
was used to. In the end four camps were chosen: Lichtenburg, Esterwegen, Dachau and Oranienburg. The camp at Oranienburg had not
yet opened, so it had to be left out. The visit took place in the last week
of October 1935 and was carried out by Carl J. Burckhardt, a member
of an old Basel family and professor at the Institute of Advanced
International Studies at Geneva. It was backed up by discussions
between him and prominent members of the regime such as Reinhard
Heydrich, head of the *Sicherheitsdienst* (SD), whom Burckhardt wrote
about in vivid terms (even if they cannot be corroborated) in his book
My Danzig Mission, written in the 1960s.

Burckhardt's criticisms focused chiefly on the moral conditions of
detention, particularly the fact that political prisoners were not segre-
gated from common criminals and that the length of their sentence was
left at the discretion of the Gestapo. The very concise written report he
presented to his ICRC colleagues was not however published, in
accordance with the undertaking he had given the Germans,[17] and it is
impossible to ascertain if his extremely circumspect remarks on the
moral state of the detainees were brought to the Führer's attention by
the German Red Cross. In any case, as far as fundamentals were
concerned, they met with a pretty negative response from Heydrich.[18]
All in all, the regime, using every possible opportunity to show its
respectable face as it prepared to host the Olympic Games, had no
reason to complain of the way it was treated by the ICRC. Burckhardt
was therefore invited by the DRK on Hitler's orders to make an official
visit in May 1936.[19] From his conversations in Berlin he concluded that
the fate of concentration camp detainees had improved – probably true
by reason of the *détente* surrounding the Olympic Games, but this had
nothing to do with his visit of October 1935 – and he expressed
admiration, which may have been sincere or merely diplomatic, for the
achievements of the regime in implementing various infrastructure

projects (such as roads and social housing) which he described as 'positively Faustian'.[20]

A second ICRC visit to Dachau was carried out on 19 August 1938 by a member of the Committee, Colonel Guillaume Favre, a former army instructor, accompanied by a doctor. This visit added nothing new either as far as fundamentals were concerned, since this report too was not published and the two Swiss inspectors were on the whole favourably impressed by the material conditions and the organisation in the barracks: 'Generally speaking – once allowance has been made for the fact that the very idea of a concentration camp, and particularly the lack of segregation of very different categories of prisoner, is an affront to a free citizen's way of thinking – we have in all objectivity to recognise that the camp at D[achau] is a model of its kind in so far as the way it is built and run is concerned.'[21]

But just to get Max Huber to agree to arrange this visit with his German opposite number in behind-the-scenes discussions at the London Red Cross conference in June 1938, members of the Committee who were keeping a close eye on detention in the Third Reich, such as Suzanne Ferrière, had to exert considerable pressure[22] and to accept that Colonel Favre's mandate reflected as much President Huber's attitude of weary prudence as the concern to achieve a positive diplomatic breakthrough. The ICRC envoy's mission was in fact to 'be in a position to reassure public opinion about the living conditions of people held in the concentration camps. Public opinion is misled by all sorts of alarming rumours, very probably groundless, about the treatment of people held in these camps. To reassure public opinion, it is necessary to find out what living conditions are like, and it would also be desirable to facilitate as far as possible the emigration abroad of anyone freed seeking to leave Germany whom Germany wishes to expel.'[23]

The year 1938 saw a worsening in the situation of the Jews, with the Nazis employing all possible means to force them to emigrate. Hastily convened by President Roosevelt, the Evian Conference could do no more than refer the insoluble problem of the reception of the persecuted to an intergovernmental committee set up in London. Although Suzanne Ferrière was closely involved through her work in the International Migration Service, the ICRC kept a low profile on the question of Jewish emigration, in line with Swiss public opinion, faced with the ever more restrictive measures taken by Switzerland from 1933 onwards to stem the influx of asylum seekers from the Reich.[24]

Although the introduction of the distinctive sign 'J' in the passports of German Jews, announced by a communiqué of the Federal Council on 4 October 1938, gave rise to little angry reaction, the acts of violence on

Kristallnacht on 9 November following provoked a deep sense of shock. The ICRC was called upon to get involved – and this was a new phenomenon – by a certain number of national Red Cross societies.

This posed a challenge all the greater for the fact that the powerful American Red Cross Society got the League involved as well. The League had in any case moved its secretariat to Geneva after the crisis which led the Western powers to capitulate at Munich.[25] Once again Max Huber vacillated between abstention, an attitude which posed a threat to the ICRC's authority, and intervention, which risked alienating the Germans to the possible detriment of those elements in the DRK that had remained sound. It was becoming increasingly doubtful whether it sufficed any longer to forward to the DRK requests for information about people who had disappeared, as had been done regularly since November 1933, since such a letterbox function constituted a pretty derisory response to the violence meted out to the Jews, and it could no longer serve as a figleaf when in November 1938 the Quai d'Orsay, perhaps at the suggestion of the Roosevelt administration, asked the ICRC to study ways in which it might assist in organising in various interested countries the reception of Jewish refugees.[26]

Whatever the political cost to itself, the ICRC replied in the end to the French in fairly negative terms, referring the question of the organisation of assistance to national Red Cross societies, the coordination of aid to the international Red Cross (that is the League rather than itself), and the question of emigration to the intergovernmental committee and other competent authorities.[27] The same line was taken in spring 1939 when the Swedish Red Cross launched a proposal for international action in favour of refugee camps, an idea which in the end came to nothing,[28] but here again the ICRC considered that it was up to national societies to act, since the issue principally concerned political victims and detainees. This did not prevent the ICRC intervening off its own bat, as for instance at the end of 1938 when it unsuccessfully took up with the DRK its concern over the material circumstances of the detainees in the camps at the approach of winter and over the alleged ill treatment of prisoners in Buchenwald concentration camp.[29]

In 1935 the Commission for Political Prisoners had suggested that the ICRC publish the relevant documents in support of démarches which had met with a refusal to cooperate. On this occasion the Bureau in January 1939 merely noted that the acting president of the German Red Cross had declined to collaborate, the minutes of the meeting concluding tersely that 'the Red Cross idea is changing'.[30]

So, despite the efforts of a few of its members, the ICRC remained extremely cautious, both as far as German political detainees and as far as imprisoned or exiled Jews were concerned. Personal sympathy for conservative aspects of fascist regimes, and antisemitic elements – insofar as they existed – do not suffice to explain such an attitude. They were widespread in Switzerland – as they were in France and Great Britain – but in Red Cross circles they were, if anything, less marked. And the carefully calculated acts of caution of someone like Burckhardt, for example, were not restricted to the issue of concentration camps: they were fairly generally characteristic of private humanitarian diplomacy in Geneva. Nevertheless, Max Huber's reservations call for particular comment, since the fears of which they were the expression led the president increasingly to highlight the ICRC's political and philosophical neutrality in the name of an overriding concern for the interests of the victims. As he wrote in 1934: 'the Red Cross is action, action based on the self-denial not only of the person who brings succour, but on the part of the institution as well; which is why the Red Cross seeks to work hand in glove with all who are ready to help others, without enquiring into their motives'.[31]

Such noble sentiments did not, however, take account of the tight grip in which national Red Cross societies were held by totalitarian regimes. The ICRC was faced with this in Soviet Russia from 1919 onwards, in Italy from 1922, and in Germany from 1933 onwards. Such totalitarian takeovers not only undermined the very basis of the movement, they threatened to dislocate it on the international level. The risk of this so distressed Max Huber that he could envisage no other response than the strict application of the law and the constant reaffirmation of Red Cross principles, based in his own case on strongly held Christian beliefs. Even before the war, his public statements had become less and less geared to practical action, and in the end served no other purpose than to conceal his impotence by dodging the real issues, as is shown rather pathetically, for instance, by his little book of 1943 entitled *The Good Samaritan*.

So, even before war broke out, we can discern some of the elements which were to prevent the Red Cross dealing adequately with the Holocaust, and to make it very difficult for those involved to think and act in the decisive manner which the extreme gravity of the problem confronting them required.

2   Secrecy, rumour, information

When the victorious Allied armies opened the camps in 1945 and reports of racial extermination by the Nazis were confirmed, the question arose, never to be satisfactorily answered, of how much was known and understood about what had been going on in the Reich and its occupied territories.

To recapitulate the basic features of the information sources we are concerned with here: before the war, when the concentration camps were filled chiefly with Germans, both Aryan and non-Aryan, the Nazis made no attempt at systematic concealment of what was going on, not only because the prison population was constantly changing, but also because the camps had a kind of educational role to play in the mobilisation of German society around the person of the Führer. During the war, deportation from occupied territories to camps set up by the Reich extended and systematised the deployment of this weapon of terror. As the decree 'Night and Fog' of 7 December 1941 made brutally clear, the aim was to ensure the disappearance of those who threatened the security of the occupying power, to paralyse, by silence and mystification, the relatives and friends of the disappeared and, through them, the rest of the population in the occupied territories. Ignorance, by pushing forward the horizon of dread, proved more effective than death, which created martyrs and provoked acts of revenge. It was, nevertheless, possible to obtain some information about the concentration camps during the war, especially as correspondence with prisoners not subject to the 'Night and Fog' regime continued, albeit fitfully, and because the Nazis did sometimes free deportees. But such information was patchy, fragmentary and shrouded in mystery.

Extermination began in 1941 cloaked in secrecy and cunningly disguised, as the choice of the eastern territories for the installation of camps, ghettos and the bulk of the gas chambers shows. Those who were intent upon seeing the Final Solution carried out were certainly not fearful of the reactions of foreign governments and of international public opinion, even less of the judgement of history, being convinced for the most part that they were acting in conformity with the eternal laws of the universe. But they did have reason to fear wavering and doubts on the part of civil servants and military officers. And in spite of controlling a formidable police machine, they were not certain what German opinion would feel; the suppression of all freedom of expression meant that the regime lacked reliable information on public attitudes. But the feeling aroused by the euthanasia programme, which led eventually to its partial suspension, was an opportune reminder of the uncertain nature, indeed the limits, of the Führer's seemingly iron grip on German society.

Nevertheless the Nazi leadership never intended the massacre really to be a secret, whether from a feeling of triumphalism in their cause, or from a wish to frighten people. More than once, after 1939, Hitler publicly proclaimed the eradication of international Jewry as punishment for the war which they had allegedly provoked. This was well known. But the discourse conveyed nothing. It was seen in the context of prewar antisemitic policies, of war propaganda and of passions brought to fever pitch by war. It described nothing: it revealed nothing that showed it meant business.

Well disguised as it was, the Final Solution could not wholly escape the notice of a number of people: in the East, of Wehrmacht soldiers in contact with SS troops involved in mass executions, or of local governors and populations living in the eastern territories; in the West, of police in occupied countries ordered to carry out mass round-ups, of German railway officials and train drivers who kept the deportation trains moving, and so on.

The question here arises of what such unintended witnesses made of the actions they were involved in or of the scenes they observed; next, of what they tried, or were able, to pass on to the outside world; and finally, at the other end of the communication chain, with what imagination or courage those whom they managed to contact sought to understand and confront the reality of what they were told, to escape the twilight state between knowledge and ignorance that according to Visser't Hooft characterised, far more than antisemitism did, the indifference and disbelief with which public opinion in Allied and neutral countries greeted news of the Final Solution.[1]

Many books have been devoted to these questions, such as Christopher Browning's on the German Foreign Ministry,[2] and more especially *The Terrible Secret* by Walter Laqueur.[3] In spite of mistakes of detail, this book remains an indispensable source of information about the circulation and reception of information on the Holocaust, and Laqueur's general remarks, especially his caveat against the wisdom of

hindsight in such a sensitive matter, are particularly relevant in the case
of the ICRC.

I shall therefore look first at the sources of the Red Cross's information, then at the forms it took, and finally at what that information
amounted to, giving examples of each, and will conclude with some
observations about the ICRC's members and organisation; these will
serve to link this chapter, which is about what the ICRC knew, with
chapter 3, which deals with what it did or what it tried to do.

Channels of communication

During World War II Switzerland was one of the few points of contact
between the belligerents for all sorts of exchanges, of people, goods and
information. More than Sweden or Portugal, on the periphery as far as
the continental theatre of operations was concerned, Switzerland was at
the hub of all kinds of such international traffic as continued during
hostilities. Foreign legations in Berne, including those of governments in
exile in London, saw their importance considerably enhanced. It was the
same in Geneva, despite the sluggishness of the international organisations. The German Consulate-General, in the rue Charles Bonnet,
remained active despite the Nazis' withdrawal from the League of
Nations and the League's subsequent paralysis; until 1945 it was an
important outpost of the Reich, one not simply subordinated to the
German legation in Berne. Wolfgang Krauel, consul-general until March
1943, his successor Herbert Siegfried, and several of their colleagues
such as Maximilian von Engelbrechten, were unsympathetic to Nazism,
and moved in the same circles as the secretary of state for foreign affairs,
Ernst von Weizsäcker, who happened to be a friend of Carl J. Burckhardt. At the trial of Third Reich diplomats in 1946, a witness described
the secret agreement made in 1940 between the German consulate and
the Churches' Ecumenical Council in Geneva to facilitate contact and
coordinate activity between all those who strove to promote humane
treatment of internees and prisoners of war and oppose Nazi barbarism.

The ICRC naturally benefited considerably from this situation. For,
in addition to the international institutions which continued ticking over
in Geneva, numerous international relief organisations, often quite large
if non-governmental bodies, set up their headquarters, or their
European office, in the city. These included the Save the Children
International Union (UISE), the International Migration Service
(whose executive vice-chair was Suzanne Ferrière, an ICRC member),
the YMCA, the Quakers (whose local official, Rosswell MacLelland,
when the War Refugee Board was set up later, became President

Roosevelt's personal representative in Berne), and the Churches' Ecumenical Council then in the process of being set up, headed by Pastor Visser't Hooft and Pastor Freudenberg. The offices of several Jewish organisations were also located in Geneva, such as the World Jewish Congress (whose representative Gerhart M. Riegner – the first person to bring hard information about racial extermination to the world's attention in 1942 – had left the Reich in 1933 at the age of twenty-two, and had attended Burckhardt's lectures at the Institute of Advanced International Studies in Geneva), the Permanent Bureau of the Jewish Agency for Palestine at the League of Nations (Richard Lichteim and Mieczeslaw Kahany), the Palestine Bureau in Switzerland (Samuel Scheps), together with other organisations which the ICRC was to work closely with throughout the war, such as the Joint (American Jewish Joint Distribution Committee) whose representative, Saly Mayer of St Gall, chairman of the Federation of Swiss Jewish Communities from 1936 to 1942, was to be someone whom the ICRC turned to particularly frequently, or the HIJEFS (Schweizerischer Hilfsverein für jüdische Flüchtlinge im Ausland, the Swiss Aid Committee for Jewish Refugees Abroad, headed by Isaac Sternbuch in Montreux), or Relico (Aid Committee for Jewish War Victims, chairman Adolf Silberschein), which acted for the World Jewish Congress, and so on.

With all these representatives and organisations ICRC members maintained close links ranging from the occasional exchange of correspondence to regular face-to-face meetings. For example, until 1939 and after 1942 the ICRC and the German Bureau of the World Jewish Congress sent each other written information coming mostly out of Western Europe, and on several occasions from 1942 onwards Riegner met Burckhardt, whose colleague at the Institute of Advanced International Studies was Paul Guggenheim, the World Jewish Congress's legal expert. Such valuable personal contacts did not however mean that there existed between all these institutions any system of regular collaboration, even over the exchange of information, because such contacts did not eliminate rivalry and indeed friction, not even between Jewish organisations, such as the persistent hostility between the Joint and the World Jewish Congress. They did, however, provide an ideal breeding ground for pressure groups. Riegner, who was only grudgingly tolerated by the police authorities and whose residence permit was not renewed from 1940 to 1943, was adept at leaning on people, managing on more than one occasion to mobilise around him representatives of Red Cross societies in occupied countries, of governments in exile like the Czechoslovak Republic's ambassador Jaromir Kopecki, of the Churches' Ecumenical Council, and so on, to put pressure on the ICRC to act.

To this international network should be added the Swiss dimension. The full story of what precisely was known in Switzerland about racial and political persecution has not yet been told, but the outlines can be sketched in. Swiss diplomats serving abroad were one source of information, through their contacts with the authorities when dealing with problems posed by Jews of Swiss nationality and Jews from Allied countries whose interests Switzerland represented. Swiss army medical missions worked on the Eastern Front. In October 1942 the head of the Police Division of the Swiss Department of Justice and Police, Heinrich Rothmund, visited Oranienburg and had talks about the Jewish question with the head of the Gestapo Heinrich Müller in particular, but learned little of note.[4] In Switzerland itself German deserters seeking asylum were debriefed at length. Some, particularly an NCO in February 1942, gave precise details about mass executions they witnessed on the Eastern Front.[5] Finally the Swiss press, despite strict government controls, published items of information and comment. Too many Swiss people had personal or business dealings with the Reich, and too many Germans lived in Switzerland, for rumours and scraps of information not to circulate.

None of this of course means that the authorities, still less public opinion, had a clear, all-round picture before 1944 of what was going on. Certain incidents since come to light prove moreover that the authorities were unwilling for the sort of information whose retrieval I have pursued to be subject to scrutiny, still less cause them to review existing policy.

Beyond press coverage, was the ICRC kept informed of what the Swiss federal authorities knew? This question prompts another: who could have told the others anything about the Jews and the concentration camps? One wonders, given the sympathy felt for the Nazi regime by the Swiss ambassador to Berlin, and given the skill and flair of the head of the ICRC delegation Roland Marti. In Switzerland itself, at the highest level, were things any different? Supposing the Swiss Council for International Mutual Assistance's delegate Edouard de Haller had learnt from his brother-in-law Pierre Bonna, head of the Swiss diplomatic corps, something known to the general staff, the intelligence service, the Political Department, or some other government body, would he have belied his habitual caution by alerting the ICRC? And even if he had, were his opposite numbers in the ICRC so different from him that their reaction would have been other than his? The concise minutes of their weekly discussions prove that the fate of the Jews is raised on and off as early as 1942 between Edouard de Haller and representatives of the ICRC and that more than one possible course of action was discussed, but none of this makes it possible to decide what the parties to the discussions actually knew, or what picture they formed of the persecution.

Broadly speaking the ICRC's information was of two kinds: that which reached it through its own channels – this was the only information it felt free to follow up in due course – and that which was sent in by external informants.

The ICRC's channels were, firstly, its missions, secondly the permanent delegations which during the conflict undertook, jointly with the Protecting Power, visits to camps of POWs and civilian internees and carried out other humanitarian tasks, and thirdly ICRC members' and senior officers' personal contacts. Missions usually consisted of visits to political internees, such as the journeys by Burckhardt and Favre to the Reich in 1935 and 1938. As will be seen in the next chapter, there were no other missions until June 1944 to concentration camps, let alone extermination camps. Certain delegates, however, were able to approach and even visit camps and other centres where political or racial prisoners were held, in several countries, especially Italy and France, but also Buchenwald in Germany, on the occasion of an inspection in favour of a group of civilian internees held as hostages. Lastly, delegates on visits to POW and civilian internee camps occasionally met detainees in labour battalions (Auschwitz) or gathered from POWs information about deportees (Rawa-Ruska).

At the beginning of the war the ICRC launched several missions, mainly to establish the necessary liaison with the Central Agency for Prisoners of War and to carry out visits. Other missions made possible direct contacts with the heads of national Red Cross societies and government representatives, such as the tour undertaken by Edouard Chapuisat and a member of the Secretariat, David de Traz, to Budapest, Bratislava, Bucharest, Sofia and Zagreb.

Apart from such one-off activities, the ICRC gradually put in place a whole network of delegations, with at its centre the Berlin delegation, the largest and best resourced, dealing with the greatest number of camps and extending over the whole of occupied Europe including France and Belgium. It was in constant touch with the German Red Cross and government (for civilian affairs and general matters, with the Legal Division of the Foreign Ministry and its RI Department headed by Conrad Roediger, and for prisoners of war, with the German High Command (OKW) through the office of information on POWs and war casualties). In the eastern territories, especially in the General-Government and in the Protectorate of Bohemia-Moravia, the ICRC was unable to set up a delegation and had to settle for a few hasty visits by Marti or by representatives of the Joint Aid Commission; nor was it able to establish permanent representation in the Netherlands.

The Joint Commission of the International Red Cross also sent delegates, some to the Balkans to buy foodstuffs (such as the Rohner and Steiger missions to Romania in 1942), and others to the occupied territories, to pave the way for humanitarian aid and to check that donations got to their recipients. It was in constant touch with the DRK, and it was through the Joint Commission, for instance, that the ICRC's Commission for Civilian Prisoners and Internees learned in 1942 that it was possible to send medicines to Theresienstadt, which both confirmed the existence of this Jewish camp and immediately raised hopes of being able to do the same in other camps like Auschwitz.[6]

To this web of relationships must be added personal contacts. Carl J. Burckhardt and Max Huber were men of international standing, well known and highly regarded in Germany. On the Joint Aid Commission, the director (industrialist Robert Boehringer) and some delegates (such as the Baltic baron André de Pilar) kept numerous links with their former German homeland. Even if these contacts did not yield much in the way of specific items of information, they certainly made it possible for people to appraise with greater certainty and imaginative grasp than would otherwise have been the case the sometimes fantastic rumours being spread abroad and the various scraps of information going the rounds.

The national Red Cross societies were the ICRC's most immediate and credible external intelligence network since they were themselves in direct contact both with the camps and detention or transit centres and with aid organisations like the Community Aid Service for Emigrants in France or the Quakers. Moreover, they were often asked – even the DRK was – to dispatch gifts and aid direct to victims in the Eastern ghettos. To correspond with the national societies the ICRC had a variety of means at its disposal: firstly direct correspondence; secondly its delegates on the ground, as well as visits to Geneva by those in charge of national societies; and thirdly their designated permanent representatives who, although they did not make up a diplomatic corps properly speaking – the only truly accredited representative to the ICRC of a Ministry for Foreign Affairs was the Italian Count Guido Vinci, first political secretary of the *fascio* in Geneva – they did facilitate the exchange of information. The DRK did not have a permanent representative, but the head of its external relations section, Walter G Hartmann, went to Geneva eighteen times between 1939 and 1945, and as a devoted, albeit wary upholder of the Red Cross ethos, he was probably one of the most dependable sources of information about what was going on in the Reich that the ICRC was able to rely upon.

Forms the information took

The foregoing description of the channels of communication does not by itself account for the problem of information; we must also look at the forms it took. What the delegates, representatives and Committee members saw and heard, and the manner in which they reported it, was conditioned by three factors which transcended the individual, by three points of reference: firstly the Geneva Conventions and the Red Cross doctrine, which defined powers and jurisdiction; secondly, the political situation, which set out parameters of feasibility; and thirdly the mission statements themselves which were given, often in fairly general terms, to delegates before they set off from Geneva. For example when Carl J. Burckhardt and Guillaume Favre went to Germany in 1935 and 1938 they knew that they were operating outside the Red Cross's normal scope and were primarily making a political gesture. The ICRC was concerned to prove to those urging it to act that it could and did do something, while avoiding at the same time being exploited by the Nazi propaganda machine, which is why the two envoys concentrated their remarks on the comfort, health and psychological condition of the detainees, following the pattern of inspections in POW camps. From 1939 to September 1944 delegates' instructions reflected ICRC policy in prioritising POWs and civilian internees in its relief efforts.

This legal and political curb on the way things were perceived and expressed operated strongly during the war against the Jews, who were a taboo subject as far as the Germans were concerned, and an awkward one for Red Cross doctrine, since Jews did not constitute a nation either in international law or with regard to humanitarian law or to the ICRC, which could not without flagrant contradiction allow itself to be influenced in its actions by racial criteria.

The Red Cross's delegates and staff approached the suffering caused by war in a manner which was both professionally neutral and diplomatically evasive. Used as they were to dealing with outside contacts through negotiation – that is, in a neutral, self-controlled fashion – they never quite shook off, even in their relations with each other, the habit of caution, so that reports of camp visits and of discussions are noticeably reticent. Internal correspondence and face-to-face conversations in Geneva struck a more personal note, but in both cases the terms used to describe the unimaginable were at best diplomatic and at worst woefully inadequate. For instance, what are we to make of Mlle Ferrière's statement to Miss Warner of the British Red Cross about the deportation of Jews: 'it is a very tragic situation and we cannot do anything about it'?[7] Shortly after the wholesale deportation of Jews from Rome in

October 1943 the ICRC's delegate in the Italian capital, Wolf de Salis, reported in the following terms the events which shook public opinion (even the Vatican) and which he could not help being *au fait* with, if only at one remove:

The Situation of the Jews in Italy. The situation of the Jews in northern Italy seems exactly the same as here in Rome, where many people are being arrested and detained. The army chiefs have absolutely no say in the matter; the whole operation is in the exclusive hands of the SS, who are answerable to no-one, not even to the military High Command, so I'm afraid that for the present we cannot possibly hope to intervene either. Our task is more and more wearing on the nerves, and there is the extra fatigue caused by having to work long hours of overtime virtually every day. People we were looking after, as well as unofficial helpers, even neighbours, are continually being arrested on charges which carry the most serious consequences. Political detainees in prison are being partially transferred from Italian to German hands and a huge number of Italians are trying to go into hiding. Illegality stalks the land and people are turning to us on all sides in the hope of getting some advice.[8]

While we are continually aware of the uniqueness of the very notion of the Final Solution, for many contemporaries each step seemed just one further turn of the screw. Our sensibilities today are offended at seeing people using everyday words to describe what seems to us undescribable. But that was the reality: there is no getting away from it. The ICRC's way of seeing things was therefore no different in this regard from that of the much better informed Allied governments who, even after taking on board the possibility that the Jews would be completely wiped out, concluded that military victory alone would save this people too and so modified neither their strategy nor their tactics to help this particular group of victims. With all due allowance the ICRC's reaction was not dissimilar, except that the Red Cross was an institution devoted to the relief of suffering for all war victims: putting the Jews and even political prisoners on the same footing as victims covered by the various Geneva Conventions would not suffice, since they needed special attention. But prioritising intervention on their behalf would undoubtedly have had disastrous consequences for POWs, civilian detainees and even the ICRC itself.

Such questions show that until the end of the war victims of racial and political persecution did not get the attention they deserved; they were known in ICRC parlance as 'administrative internees' from 1943 onwards, and the passing, via the ICRC, of requests for information from families, national Red Cross societies and aid organisations to the German Red Cross, and back again, did not provoke special comment; whether it concerned Mlle de Posnansky's agency which gathered information on individual cases, or the ICRC's Agency for Miscellaneous Civilian Internees (CID, Civils internés divers), or the national branches of the Central Prisoners of War Bureau (ACPG, Agence centrale de renseignements des prisonniers de guerre), the ICRC stuck to the 1933 Huber–Draudt agreement and remained a mere channel of information, one-way for the most part, subject to conditions laid down by the Germans. For the ACPG was not equipped – through lack of instructions, organisation and perhaps resources – to coordinate systematically the analysis of individual index cards. When the food parcels service to the concentration camps was launched, it provided a hitherto unhoped-for opportunity for transforming piecemeal activities into a large-scale collective operation. But here again no attempt was made to use the information gained to establish the full extent of persecution and repression by supplementing the information provided by the delegates. What the ICRC seems to have been seriously deficient in throughout the war was any overall picture of what was going on, not through lack of information, but because its organisation was ill fitted for the task of collating intelligence and putting it into context, so as to enable that intelligence to be properly interpreted and correctly understood.

What the information amounted to

When war broke out, the ICRC was not unaware of the concentration camps, of antisemitic persecution in Germany, or of the emigration issue, so the question arises to what extent that knowledge may have made it less receptive to the worsening of persecution. Walter Laqueur has reminded us how much the peddling of alleged atrocities by both German and Allied propaganda in the First World War helped to reinforce scepticism over news of the Final Solution, a phenomenon in any case which the majority of rational people found beyond their comprehension. It is arguable that the camp visits of 1935 and 1938, together with others, had a similar effect by confining the ICRC's attention to conditions which were certainly harsh but perfectly adequate from a material point of view and, after all, commonplace enough at the time.

From the mass of documents in the ICRC archives, many of which are indirectly quite informative, I have selected only a few items. To avoid hindsight judgements I have given preference to texts whose significance arises both from the detail and precision of their contents and from the trust the ICRC put in their source. This means that the bulk came from delegates and representatives (the only fully acknowledged source) but that some derived from national Red Cross societies and from organisations with which the ICRC traditionally enjoyed relations of trust. I have aimed to quote wherever possible and to paraphrase where considerations of length make this appropriate. For before any inquiry into what, if anything, the ICRC was able to imagine or intuit about the Nazis' racial strategy, scholarly integrity demands that what it learned piecemeal about the persecutions, deportations and massacres be set out clearly and in strict chronological sequence.

In spite of the numerous things it had to attend to on behalf of POWs and civilian internees when war was declared, the ICRC did not lose sight of the Jews and their fate. In September 1939 the Jewish World Congress, the Jewish Palestine Agency and the American Jewish Joint Distribution Committee all urged the ICRC in Geneva to intervene to get news of Polish Jews and to send them aid, since all communication between Poland and the outside world was cut off. But at the same time the ICRC was aware that Viennese Jews were being expelled to Poland, and the ICRC's delegate-at-large Marcel Junod was sent to find out more during his visit to Berlin in November 1939.[9] At the end of December President Huber drew to the Central Commission's attention (it functioned at the time as the ICRC executive) that the situation of the Jews in the Lublin region appeared critical and that he thought it dangerous to herd such a large number of people into such limited space;[10] shortly afterwards he spoke to Walter Hartmann about it.

The requests for humanitarian assistance and information were confirmed by Junod's eyewitness account of his visit to Warsaw as an offshoot of his Reich mission in November 1939. There he not only saw in the distance barbed wire surrounding the ghetto (as he records in his memoirs[11]), but he had discussions with the chairman of the Council of Elders in the Jewish community and brought back an anonymous undated document (given to him by the Swiss legation in Berlin) which describes in precise detail the evacuation (*Aussiedlung*) of the Jews and reveals inside knowledge of decisions taken and plans drawn up as early as September 1939 (see Appendix, document I).

The document begins by recalling that the evacuation of the Jews from Greater Germany began on 17 October 1939 on the orders of the head of the SS, Heinrich Himmler, and was being conducted in four phases: firstly about 150,000 people from Bohemia-Moravia, next about 65,000 from Vienna, then about 30,000 from the new *Reichsgaue* of Posen and West Prussia, and finally about 240,000 from the old Reich. The Jewish communities in these regions were obliged to organise and finance the evacuation themselves under the supervision of Gestapo chief Adolf Eichmann, from whose HQ in Mährisch-Ostrau the deportations were being coordinated. Deportees were authorised to take with them no more than 300 Reichmarks, the rest of their possessions (property, furniture and personal effects) being compulsorily sold off. They were to be told officially that they were being taken to a re-education and resettlement camp, and indeed the first transports were sent to Nisko-on-the-San, south-east of Lublin, where the deportees were interned partly in war-torn villages and partly in barbed-wire camps. In both cases the deportees were responsible for repairing their own houses or building their own barrack huts. Since the river San marked the new German–Soviet border, barbed-wire entanglements were positioned along the banks to prevent anyone escaping into Russian-held territory. (The Stettin Jews, some 1,100 in all, were deported to the Lublin region; 300 died of hunger and disease en route.)

All the towns and villages in this border region were progressively to be emptied of their German, Polish and Ukrainian populations so as to make a huge reservation of about 800 square kilometres inhabited exclusively by Jews, surrounded by barbed wire and guarded by an SS unit. They were to be joined by a million and a half Polish Jews, and the entire forced operation was to be completed by 1 April 1940. The timetable was difficult to keep to, however, the document concedes, since many Jews managed to escape or commit suicide: between 20 October and 2 November 1939, for instance, eighty-two Jews (of whom thirty-six were women) committed suicide in Vienna alone.[12]

In December 1939 Hartmann assured Max Huber that the deportations had ceased for the time being, but that camp visits were out of the question for the moment.[13] On 19 February 1940 the *Neue Zürcher Zeitung* published an article by its Berlin correspondent which gave an eyewitness account of the deportation of the Stettin Jews during the night of 12 to 13 February, and announced forthcoming operations at Danzig, Königsberg, etc. This article can be seen in the ICRC archives[14] but that did not prevent a cabled question from Tel-Aviv, 'answer whether Jewish congregation Stettin deported', getting the extraordinary reply 'Sorry unable answer such questions being outside scope our activity';[15] the Committee clearly felt that it was not at liberty to transmit uncorroborated information to a third party.

Nevertheless first-hand intelligence sent by the ICRC delegation in Berlin did continue to arrive in Geneva. In summer 1940 Pierre Descoeudres was able to learn from a Jewish intellectual who had fled from Stettin what everyday life was like for the many tens of thousands of social outcasts who were still living in the capital of the Reich. Out of the half-million German Jews in 1933 an estimated 250,000 remained in 1940, Descoeudres was told, of whom 96,000 lived in overcrowded conditions in Berlin under the constant threat of deportation to Lublin and suffered a whole range of restrictions (fewer food coupons, severely limited shopping hours, 9 p.m. curfew), and were confined (the intelligentsia as much as the others) to heavy labouring jobs such as road building and coal loading. All the synagogues in the city had been set on fire, and the only organisation which was doing anything for the German Jews was the American Joint.[16]

Pierre Descoeudres was also able to visit Buchenwald with Roland Marti in the summer of 1940 (see p. 159), where they remarked upon the presence of German Jewish internees,[17] and in November 1941 the Berlin delegation witnessed the daily deportation of Jews to the General-Government (formerly Poland). That Geneva was kept informed of the details of the operation is made clear in a note by Dr Exchaquet (an ICRC delegate in Germany) arising from a long conversation he had with a Jewish doctor on 20 November 1940 on the situation of Berlin Jews. 'Although the matter is outside the remit of your delegates in Germany', Exchaquet wrote, 'I'm passing on the news to the Committee for whom it will perhaps be of some interest.' After this telling understatement Exchaquet went on:

There were still about 60,000 Jews in Berlin at the beginning of November. As far as I can tell from those whom I run across in the street, they are people of modest means, and many of them look poverty-stricken. A large number of the men are employed as road sweepers, and all Jews are made to wear an identifying yellow star sewn on to their clothes at chest level bearing the word 'JUDE'.

From the start of November the authorities seem to have begun the systematic evacuation of all Berlin Jews in successive trainloads of about 3,000 each. Several such transports have already left and the next is scheduled for 27 November. According to the plan currently being carried out, all the Jews in Berlin will have been evacuated by April.

This is how things are done: on the day fixed for the transport, they are taken from their homes in the evening and herded into a synagogue where they are minutely searched. All their money and jewellery are confiscated and they are made to sign a document renouncing their civil rights. They are allowed to take only what they can carry with them, about 50 kg of luggage. During the following night they are put on a train to the East and taken to the ghetto of a large town, such as Poznan or Lodz.[18]

The ICRC delegation in Germany and, to a lesser degree, ICRC missions and delegations in other countries, were not the only source of information reaching Geneva. National Red Cross societies in Allied and neutral countries sent in their questions and search lists, and those in occupied or Axis countries who were in even more direct contact with the populations subjected to persecution, with the obvious exception of the DRK, made their voices heard frequently in Geneva.

Information was also gathered and passed on by the charitable organisations. A good example is the memorandum addressed to Max

Huber and Carl J. Burckhardt on the situation in Poland by Pastor Visser't Hooft, secretary-general of the Churches' Ecumenical Council, on 29 October 1941. This document – at once a piece of information, a testimony and an appeal – began by quoting an objective and reliable observer who had brought back news from a recent visit to that country; according to him, in the grossly overcrowded and badly bombed cities, especially Warsaw, famine and typhus raged, and infant mortality was running at 26 per cent. American and Polish charities were distributing some food ('a mere drop in the ocean'), and a large consignment of US medical supplies was expected to arrive from Lisbon any day.

Hooft went on to describe the deportation of Jews from Berlin to Lodz in terms similar to those in Exchaquet's note quoted above, except that Hooft estimated each trainload as consisting of 7,000 deportees, and added that 20,000 Jews from the Rhineland, 2,000 from Prague, and an unspecified number from Vienna were being sent to Poland, where able-bodied men were made to build roads behind the Eastern Front and women were drafted into the munitions factories. Deportees were limited to one suitcase each and 10 RM and manifestly lacked adequate clothing against the cold and rain. Hooft had little doubt that measures such as these, inflicted upon people who had suffered so much already that they lacked the strength to cope, heralded the total expulsion of Jews from Germany and former Czechoslovakia.

Hooft concluded by insisting that it was the responsibility of the Christian churches to raise their voices to protect the Jews and deliver a stern warning to their persecutors, and suggested that the Red Cross send a delegate, ideally a doctor, to the Warthegau (especially Lodz) and the General-Government (especially the Lublin region) to assess the most urgent needs in terms of medicine, sanitation and clothing of the Jewish and Polish populations. The Churches' Ecumenical Council was for its part prepared to call upon all affiliated churches, especially in the United States, to lend their full support to the ICRC's aid programme.[19]

Contacts like these enabled the ICRC to be informed promptly of the suspension in autumn 1941 of Jewish emigration from Nazi Europe; Mlle Ferrière, in her capacity as vice-chair of the International Emigrants' Aid Agency, informed the British Red Cross on 19 November.[20] A month later Burckhardt got confirmation of the policy change when he met officials of the High Commission for Refugees,[21] and Roland Marti sent further particulars from Berlin.

So it was in full knowledge of the facts that Jean Pictet, one of the ICRC's secretaries, wrote on 15 December 1941 to tell the British Red Cross that old people and children were not allowed to leave Germany and Poland, even if they held immigration visas for other countries.[22] This did not prevent Frédéric Barbey responding in these terms to the Hungarian Red Cross's appeal for help:

We understand only too well the seriousness of deportation of Hungarian Jews under such terrible conditions to occupied Poland and Galicia. Unfortunately, despite the immense sympathy we feel for this mass of suffering humanity, we find ourselves quite unable at the moment to intervene in the way you ask . . . The enquiry you envisage involves a whole series of démarches and raises such grave issues of principle that merely spelling them out could seriously jeopardise what little we have, with infinite difficulty, been able to achieve.[23]

On 20 January 1942 in Wannsee, a suburb of Berlin, representatives of the ministries and agencies concerned drew up measures for coordinating their efforts to group and deport Jews to the East, with a view to making them disappear. By the same date the ICRC for its part was well aware that Jews in Nazi Europe were being maltreated and constituted an even more piteous and threatened category of victim than all the others, for as we have seen the ICRC was placed in possession of direct, detailed and reliable evidence on the point, not least by its own delegates.

But, at the same time, this same category, which appeared to be the focus of special treatment, remained a taboo subject in the eyes of the ICRC, something not even to be alluded to at the risk of jeopardising either the whole of its operations or (as the reply to the Hungarian Red Cross quoted above shows) in the slender hope of maintaining contact with the camps through the DRK.

From spring 1942 onwards the same sources enabled the ICRC to follow the sequence of deportations, if not in every detail at least with a sufficient degree of precision to allow it to conclude that an overall plan was in operation and to seek to gauge its aims and scope. In February Roland Marti in Berlin reported the deportation of 3,000 Jews from the capital to the General-Government,[24] and in September the Germans' intention to transfer to the East the Jews in the General-Government.[25] Relatives and friends of the deportees alerted the ICRC too. National Red Cross societies, such as the Slovak and the French ones, also enquired what was going on in the camps in the East, especially at Auschwitz, the name of which had cropped up earlier – in April 1942 – in connection with the deportation of Slovak Jews.[26] And in summer 1942 Marti notified the ICRC that while Berlin Jews were indeed being deported to the East, those aged seventy and over were being sent to Theresienstadt, a town of 10,000 inhabitants which, once emptied of its population, was planned to become an exclusively Jewish town. Neither they nor any other Jews were allowed to get in touch with their families.[27]

The round-ups organised in France in summer 1942, first in the occupied and then in the unoccupied zone, made an impression in Switzerland all the stronger for occurring in a neighbouring country. Apart from news and descriptions in the French-speaking Swiss press, detailed intelligence poured into ICRC headquarters, if not on the fate of the deportees, at least on what took place in front of numerous eyewitnesses. Dr Cramer made available to the ACPG as early as 1 September a copy of Pastor Boegner's 20 August protest forwarded on behalf of the Council of the Protestant Federation of France to Marshal Pétain, as well as carbon copies of two detailed memoranda on the application of measures taken against foreign Jews in non-occupied France sent to Tracy Strong, secretary-general of the World Alliance of YMCAs in Geneva, by the Alliance's delegate in France.[28]

The answer to the question of when the ICRC reached the conclusion that organised, systematic massacre was taking place must be the second half of 1942 when, as Walter Laqueur has shown, hard intelligence began to coalesce, firstly in Polish émigré circles in London, then in the American Jewish organisations, and finally in Allied chancelleries, culminating in the UN declaration of 17 December 1942. This did not settle all doubts and questions, especially amongst Jewish observers, not only because it was cautiously worded, but also because of the timelag between the receipt of intelligence and public opinion absorbing it.

As is well known, the Final Solution began in the East with the deployment of *Einsatzgruppen* who racially and politically 'cleansed' the territories occupied in the wake of conquest by the Wehrmacht. In mid-February 1942, i.e. seven or eight months after the operation began, Marti drew attention to the appalling treatment meted out to Soviet POWs in a camp. Basing his statement on information supplied by a German officer, he reported that, unlike the Wehrmacht, which preferred to put civilians to good use in support of the German war effort, SS troops systematically murdered POWs and civilians alike in the occupied territories.[29]

The harsh treatment of Soviet POWs was known at the time. The USSR did not sign the 1929 prisoner of war code. The ICRC showed acute concern about it and in December 1941 Junod went to Berlin to try and give some impetus to the negotiations on this topic which the ICRC had vainly been trying to press forward with. But Roland Marti's information now contained, albeit vaguely, a new element, one that touched upon the role of the SS, the fate of civilians, and the systematic nature of the massacre.

In March–April 1942, Werner Rohner was sent on a mission to Austria, Hungary, Romania and Slovakia on behalf of the Joint Aid

Commission, and brought back detailed information about the 1941 deportations together with a note, addressed to Carl J. Burckhardt, about antisemitism in those countries. Rohner drafted the note from his own observations, from conversations he had had, and from documents he had been passed, but here too the picture is blurred. The policy of segregation and persecution is mentioned in the same breath as civilian massacres and remarks about refugees and émigrés. The conclusion has to be read in the spirit of the time:

The fact of the matter is that Jews are being persecuted, deprived of their livelihood, and deported.

By depriving the Jews of work and any means of making a living, the authorities are condemning them to a slow death. Even if some individuals do deserve to be punished, it is unjust to hit out at all Jews, and quite inadmissible to inflict suffering on women and children.[30]

Between 13 and 18 August 1942 Marti visited the regions of Cracow and Lemberg where deportees were arriving in large numbers, and inevitably met groups of Jewish labourers. More interesting still, he learned from POWs at Rawa-Ruska, one of the three most feared POW punishment camps in Germany, of the beatings and killings perpetrated near the camp by the Ukrainian police against Jews awaiting deportation.[31]

Of course none of this means that by summer 1942 the ICRC had grasped the full extent of the tragedy, but it did know enough to agree that a general process was at work to separate non-Aryan internees from the rest and transfer them to the East, except apparently those whose country of origin was represented by a Protecting Power which could intervene, such as Switzerland for the British and North Americans. These deportees were moreover denied all communication with their families and any support from the ICRC, which was unable to obtain any information about their fate since the German authorities considered them criminals.

It was at the beginning of August 1942, as a result of a letter from the German industrialist Eduard Schulte, that Gerhart Riegner alerted the World Jewish Congress in New York that the Nazis were planning general extermination by poison gas.[32] If we are now keenly aware with what slowness this information overcame Allied disbelief, we are less well informed, because of the lack of documentary evidence, about what happened in Berne, where the head of the Police Aliens Department, Heinrich Rothmund, had been put in the picture by the president of the Federation of Jewish Communities in Switzerland, and we do not know either at what moment precisely or in what form the first indications of the Final Solution reached the ICRC, but Gerhart Riegner insists today that he and Paul Guggenheim made a full oral statement about the sinister conclusions they had arrived at to Burckhardt, Suzanne Ferrière and Lucie Odier in August or at the latest the beginning of September 1942. In mid-October Riegner passed to the ICRC Isak Lieber's report which confirmed previous eyewitness accounts from Latvia assembled by Gabriel Zivian.[33] Lieber had been arrested on 12 August in Brussels and deported first to Upper Silesia, then to the Eastern Front, where he learned from a German officer that Jews unfit for work were being exterminated. Lieber managed to escape, and reached Geneva via France at the end of an incredible two-month odyssey.[34]

The ICRC's information during the autumn of 1942 also derived from questions put to it, since these formed an early reaction to the various rumours which were circulating. The US State Department,[35] followed by the British Red Cross, amongst others, sought confirmation of the rumours, but Madame Frick, who dealt with civilians and deportees, told the Coordinating Commission on 21 October that she could not provide any, even though she accepted that Jews were being transported in 'unfavourable conditions'.[36] At the same time the Vatican reported to the Roosevelt administration in similar terms, and then, in November, agreed that Polish Jews were being exterminated.

The spotlight now falls on Burckhardt, who in early November confirmed to the US consul in Geneva Paul C. Squire that, according to two well-informed German sources, Hitler had in 1941, they believed, ordered Germany to be made *Judenfrei*, that is, cleared of Jews. Only American sources record this interview with Squire,[37] but it is confirmed by the fact that Burckhardt passed on the same information to his colleague Paul Guggenheim before the end of October, since on 29 October Guggenheim also confided in Squire. Moreover, when on 17 November he and Mlle Ferrière met Riegner, Burckhardt spoke of the deportations and mass executions as a certainty, about which he had also had a conversation with Ernst Kundt, who had worked in the External Relations Department of the DRK during the First World War.[38]

Two questions arise from this. Firstly, did the fact that he spoke of the massacre of entire populations mean that Burckhardt was already aware of the Final Solution? Secondly, if he was, did he pass this information on to colleagues and to fellow members of the ICRC? He made no mention of extermination or total liquidation of the Jews to either Squire or Riegner; otherwise they would certainly have noted the fact. He could, of course, have sought to play down the significance of what he knew given the ICRC's decision not to make any public declaration; equally he may have been simply repeating what he had learned from

German sources. For as Squire noted when sending his government the report of his conversation of 7 November with Burckhardt, if a territory must be *Judenfrei* by a given date, how could this be achieved other than through the deaths of those concerned?

The issue of the transmission of information within the ICRC is more sensitive. If, as he affirms, Riegner spoke to Burckhardt, Mlle Ferrière and Mlle Odier in August 1942, or at the latest in September, about the extermination plan, that only serves to reinforce the claim, made many times subsequently, that the note of 24 September was drafted with the sole purpose of attempting a démarche on behalf of the Jews under cover of intervention on behalf of alien civilian internees deported to the Reich. But it is true that in any case the ICRC was already in possession of plenty of information about deportation, most recently from nearby France. On the other hand, if the confirmation by two German sources conveyed by Burckhardt between the end of October and 17 November first to Guggenheim, then to Squire, and finally to Riegner, occurred before the ICRC meeting on 14 October devoted to the discussion of the public declaration, or even before the drafting of the ICRC's reply to the US government on French deportees, the only conclusion to be drawn is that Burckhardt kept his suppositions to himself, or else that he felt that what he knew was not likely to modify the agreed policy. The telegram in which the ICRC replied to the US State Department had actually been shown to Burckhardt, who had been unable to attend the meeting of the Coordinating Commission on 21 October. It is dated 2 November 1942, that is less than a week before Burckhardt's conversation with Paul C. Squire, and it confirms that despite widespread public concern and despite the fact that the Central Information Agency was finding that enquiries in the East had been brought to a complete halt, the ICRC refused categorically to get involved in the Jewish question. The telegram stated that while the ICRC was doing all it could for deportees, it had no hard information about the fate of Jews sent to Poland, and in any case it would have 'serious misgivings about passing on information to a government about the fate of people not nationals of the country making the enquiry': in other words, since the Jews concerned were not American citizens, the Committee was unwilling to give the US administration any information at all.[39]

From mid-November onwards, new reliable information did, however, arrive to confirm people's worst fears, even if I have been unable to find trace in the ICRC's files of any reaction to the United Nations appeal of 17 December 1942. Marti reported from Berlin that French-speaking Jews had been seen in the Riga area 'herded together', and the weakest eliminated, and he mentioned 60,000 Jews having been liquidated in Latvia.[40] Adolf Silberschein, a former member of the Polish Diet, brought Burckhardt early in December a whole sheaf of accounts, not it is true of the use of gas, but of the *Einsatzgruppen*'s massacres in Poland.[41] The Norwegian Red Cross in exile, prompted by rumours circulating in London, asked the ICRC to intervene to stop the deportation of Norwegians to the Reich so as to prevent their liquidation in Poland. Pastor Adolf Freudenberg, a German émigré and secretary of the Refugees Aid Agency of the Churches' Ecumenical Council, handed over a document dated 14 January 1943 which confirmed not only the disappearance of Berlin's Jews and those from the Warsaw ghetto, but also mentioned the use of gas. At the end of January Riegner sent detailed information, backed by eyewitness testimony from the Jewish community, about the Transnistrian deportations.

Later on further documents arrived to make people realise what was going on. The Swiss Human Rights League stepped in, probably on information from Riegner; and the Polish Red Cross in London sent a list of concentration and prison camps on which the names of the 'death' camps Treblinka, Belzec, Pelkinia and Sobibor appeared. This report, dated 8 March 1943, was quite specific:

These camps have, significantly, acquired the name 'camps of the deceased'. At Treblinka detainees are gassed, electrocuted or shot. Two special machines have been sent there to dig grave pits. The huge number of bodies and the shallowness of the graves produced such a stench in the neighbourhood of Treblinka that the country people had to leave their homes. Lithuanians, Latvians and Ukrainians are employed as executioners in the camps and are from the outset scheduled to be killed themselves once their sinister job, for which they are well paid by the Germans, is done.[42]

On 15 April 1943 Marti reported that only 1,400 Jews were left in Berlin and would soon be evacuated to Auschwitz, Pless, Lublin, Riga and Reval, and he added 'There is no news or trace of the 10,000 Jews who left Berlin between 28.2.43 and 3.3.43 and who are now presumed dead'.[43] The Geneva Secretariat replied thanking Marti for the information and added that it was anxious to discover the deportees' new addresses, for all the world as if they had merely moved house.[44]

From the second half of 1943 onwards, and particularly from the summer of 1944, the ICRC's information increased both in quality and quantity. National Red Cross societies, humanitarian organisations and above all Jewish communities and associations sent a growing amount of information, much of it direct and detailed, such as the account of the deportation of Rome's Jews[45] or, to take one example among many, the Hungarian Jews' *Zentralrat* report which Born, the ICRC delegate in Hungary, forwarded to Geneva on 28 October 1944.[46]

Naturally the ICRC gave particular credence to what its own members saw and heard, and here too intelligence snowballed. In June 1943 Edouard Chapuisat and David de Traz brought back from their mission to south-eastern Europe a rich harvest of information on the persecutions gathered often at the highest level of state, church or Red Cross organisation. The particular drive of 1944, first in Romania and then in Hungary, put the delegates on the ground in close and continuous touch with the day-to-day reality of the arrest, segregation and deportation of the Jews. Even the dispatch of parcels to the concentration camps yielded interesting statistical data in 1944–5, though it was not in fact made use of other than for addressing the packets. In December 1944, for example, Marti passed on the number of internees in Sachsenhausen, broken down by nationality, with the exception of Germans and Ukrainians;[47] three weeks earlier he had reported a reliable source on the arrival at Oranienburg of Dutch internees from s'Hertogenbosch, and followed it up with their numbers and the different concentration camps they had been sent on to. Sometimes the ICRC's delegates in the Reich were able to locate a whole population, such as the Danes in Germany who were the subject of a note from Marti dated 22 August 1944.[48]

These delegates did in fact get to certain camps in the Reich, such as Oranienburg-Sachsenhausen, Ravensbrück, Buchenwald and Dachau, and conversed on the doorstep with SS personnel in charge. They sought to ascertain that food parcels were being forwarded and distributed properly and sometimes managed to get a glimpse inside.[49] But even when they could not gain access or get all the information they wanted from the Germans, the ICRC had in 1944 gone beyond merely finding out where the principal concentration camps were. Through delegates' discreet contacts, escapees' statements and the collation of intelligence reaching it, the ICRC was in a position to get a clear idea of how some camps were organised and even to know with some degree of certainty by then what regime applied in them.

On 29 September 1944, Rossel went from Teschen (a POW camp) to Auschwitz, and on the road kept passing labour units – men and women in striped concentration-camp uniform – going with their SS guards to, or returning from, the mines or fields where they were employed. On the same trip Rossel went to Oranienburg and Ravensbrück too where, as at Auschwitz, though he never got beyond the offices of the *Kommandantur*, he did manage to bring back a number of details about the organisation, detainee population, daily routine and corporal punishment in the camps. He also brought back information about the Auschwitz gas chambers which shows how widely news spread within the concentration camp system: at Teschen a British officer asked if Rossel was aware of the rumours about an ultramodern 'shower room' in which detainees where gassed in batches,[50] and at Ravensbrück Jewish women who had been lucky enough to have been allowed to leave Auschwitz (which they described as a '90 per cent extermination camp') reported that prisoners there, nearly all of whom were Jews, had their number tattooed in blue on their arm, and that many – the sick, the old, and children in particular – were left in a special block to starve before being taken away in groups to be gassed.[51]

One of Rossel's Ravensbrück informants spoke of Jewish children being sterilised, but there was no clear proof of this; Marti on the other hand had as early as June drawn attention in confidence to operations carried out on Polish women,[52] and in November Mme Frick was so upset about medical experiments upon prisoners that she wrote 'if nothing can be done, the wretched victims should be sent the means of committing suicide; this would perhaps be more humane than giving them food'.[53]

If in common with other religious or humanitarian organisations and with Allied or neutral governments, the ICRC did manage to gather intelligence, it was unable to exercise visiting rights in the concentration camps, nor a fortiori in the extermination camps, and its delegates, as we have seen, had to be satisfied with talking to those in charge.[54] Nevertheless the stubbornness of some delegates did provide it with interesting if belated evidence, such as Rossel's report on his forced entry in December 1944 to the Reichsvereinigung der Juden in Berlin's Iranische Strasse, the Jewish director of which was terrified out his wits that the Gestapo would learn of the Red Cross representative's visit before he himself could inform them as he was compelled to do under the rules of secrecy governing his organisation.[55]

In ways like this the ICRC's leading members gradually became aware of the reality of the Final Solution. Early in February 1944, for example, Burckhardt did not deny it when the deputy high commissioner for refugees George Kullman asked him if it was true that only 140,000 out of three million Polish Jews remained; Burckhardt merely answered that he had received confidential reports on the subject, documents circulating at the League of Nations.[56]

This is the context in which to evaluate the information that delegate Rossel obtained at Theresienstadt on 23 June 1944. We shall see later the reasons which led the ICRC to insist the German authorities allow it to go into the ghetto-camp. In point of fact Theresienstadt was not entirely an unknown quantity in 1944, for the head of external relations in the DRK, Walter Hartmann, had, a year almost to the day before

Rossel, been able to go there himself during a tour of inspection stage-managed by the SS. On his return to Berlin, he conveyed his gloomy impressions to André de Pilar, the delegate of the Joint Aid Commission of the international Red Cross, who reported them to the ICRC, and to Riegner himself, in July 1943.

On the very day of his own visit, 23 June 1944, Rossel wrote down what he had seen and learned on a strictly confidential basis, as had been agreed with the SS.[57] The question is not so much whether he was taken in by his stroll through the model village à la Potemkin which characterised the ghetto, whether he suspected the existence of another camp, the small fortress, which his hosts took good care not to draw to his attention, and whether he realised that the photographs he was allowed to take and send to Geneva were no more truthful than movie stills. Ultimately the basic question is not whether his naïvety was sham or real; it is what conclusions the ICRC drew from his fifteen-page report.

The Nazis maintained that Theresienstadt was a model facility in which the Jews who had been brought there lived in peace and tranquillity, and Rossel's report seemed to confirm their version because it asserted that Theresienstadt was an *Endlager*, a terminus-camp. But doubt was immediately cast on this by Schwarzenberg, head of the Special Aid Division, who enquired of Rossel, obviously to no purpose, what had happened to the 30,000 people said to have been deported to Auschwitz and who accounted for the discrepancy he had noted between two figures for the population of Theresienstadt known to the Red Cross.[58]

So the ICRC decided against passing on Rossel's general observations to third parties, such as national Red Cross societies, governments, or Jewish organisations on the grounds that Theresienstadt was, at the very least, a camp of privileged inmates and that in any case no conclusions could be drawn about the fate of Jews in German hands on the basis of a visit to a single confinement facility.

Besides, other reports arrived in the same month of June 1944 containing terrible news about the fate of the Jews. Through the Czechoslovak minister Jaromir Kopecki the ICRC received a copy of the evidence which two young Slovak escapees from Auschwitz, Rudolf Vrba and Fred Wetzlar, gave Allied newspapers and governments[59] causing a real public outcry.[60] In July Willem Visser't Hooft and Paul Vogt passed the ICRC two documents on the deportation of the Hungarian Jews and the extermination at Auschwitz[61] which in essentials confirmed the testimony of the Slovak escapees. These first-hand statements were increasingly being complemented by contacts with eyewitnesses such as the Swiss citizen Mme Strauss-Meyer, who called in at the ICRC at the end of May 1944 to recount what she had seen at Drancy where she had worked for a time as a secretary.[62]

In the face of so much information convergence the ICRC's replies to questions put to it in 1944 seem remarkable for their caution. Since it was unable to conduct enquiries effectively on the spot, either in Germany or in the occupied countries, its official policy was to do no more than compile a register of names submitted to it and send help, while filtering carefully the information it gave out, especially in response to queries from Jewish organisations. It did, however, react vigorously when – for instance after Rossel's visit to Theresienstadt – the German government on the one hand, and the World Jewish Congress on the other, sought its endorsement of their arguments or their accusations.

Knowledge carries a heavy responsibility where humanitarian organisations are concerned. Faced with the build-up of proof in 1944 the ICRC came increasingly under pressure, not only from without but also from within. At the beginning of the year Burckhardt was still able to maintain that the Jewish question was outside the ICRC's remit and that the latter had no need of an intelligence unit, even if it was obliged to create machinery to deal with the many requests it received. By the summer this position was no longer tenable and the ICRC began to change course; then the information it held became relevant to its new attitude.

To know is not the same thing as to comprehend. The ICRC experienced the same difficulties where the Final Solution was concerned as the best-informed Allied governments, neutral countries or religious and humanitarian organisations did when it came to thinking the unthinkable. And to know is not enough to be able to will; even where there is a will, there is not necessarily a way. Having seen what the ICRC's information amounted to and before considering the decisions it took, we need to look more closely at the institution and at the way it functioned.

The ICRC: organisational aspects

I am not going to attempt a comprehensive description of the ICRC's decision-making processes (which were particularly complex, as we shall see), but will concentrate instead on the interplay between the organisation and the individuals who made it up.

In 1939 the International Committee of the Red Cross was a modest institution, despite the recent expansion of its activities during the Ethiopian and Spanish conflicts: it consisted of a Secretariat, archives section, accounts department, the *Revue Internationale de la Croix-Rouge*'s editorial staff and services concerned with the Spanish War, making fifty-seven people in all, under the supervision of the Bureau, as stipulated in the statutes, and of a number of committees, made up of members of the ICRC, responsible for dealing with current problems.[63] Its administrative growth through World War II was spectacular: on 31 December 1944 it employed 1,454 people in Geneva and 814 in the rest of Switzerland. To the number of delegates and deputy-delegates abroad – that came to 179 – must be added the delegations' staff, sometimes recruited locally.[64] Large buildings such as the Metropole Hotel, the Electoral Palace and the Carlton Hotel, its current headquarters, housed the activities of the Secretariat, of the Central Agency for Prisoners of War, of the Aid Division, not to mention the premises in the Cours des Bastions where the Joint Aid Commission of the International Red Cross had its head office.

The ICRC's finances and organisation, its management and administration, were of recurrent concern throughout the war and even after it. I do not intend to rehearse their history – it is obviously complex, given the growth in staff and increase in responsibilities – but rather to deal with those aspects which are relevant to my theme and especially to the discussion of what was known and of how what was known was interpreted.

The organisational problems revolved around the two central issues of management and administration. It is true, as the ICRC claimed in 1948, that its decisions in this area were guided above all by the desire to create an effective organisation able to respond to shifting circumstances, but the fact remains that changes made both in management and in administration were marked by improvisation, amateurism and even friction between individuals.[65]

Throughout the war the ICRC carried on as it had always done, defining principles and setting out the main thrust of its general policy in plenary session. But its twenty to twenty-five members, only some of whom devoted sufficient time to voluntary work on behalf of the Red Cross, could not hope to manage the institution in concert, or even oversee its day-to-day running. As early as 1938 a small committee called the War Activities Committee prepared actively for mobilisation; on 14 September 1939 it became the Central Committee and later took on the functions delegated under the statutes to the Bureau. In November 1940, using the powers granted him, chairman Max Huber drew up a plan for the division of labour which provided for a series of committees made up of ICRC members, each responsible for a particular branch of activity. To ensure overall control the Central Committee became the Coordinating Committee; because it was assigned to peacetime duties the Bureau was effectively marginalised. In March 1943 there was a fresh reorganisation: the Coordinating Committee was renamed the Bureau and so combined all peacetime and wartime responsibilities and powers. The ICRC's functions remained divided among a certain number of departments or agencies headed by boards or committees. It was from then on made explicit that paid officials would be responsible for running the areas with the heaviest work loads. How efficiently this functioned depended therefore on how well the ICRC members, usually part-time amateurs who held the real 'political' power, got on with the full-time professionals whose skills lay in running things.

The administration also had to be sorted out. Here too there were many changes which saw the small Secretariat of 1939 transformed first into the Central Secretariat of 1942, with its three secretaries responsible for general matters (Roger Gallopin for prisoners, the wounded, internees and civilians, Hans de Watteville for humanitarian aid and Claude Pilloud for the delegations), and then further transformed in 1944 into the General Secretariat with its four members of equal rank, Jean Duchosal (secretary-general), Hans Bachmann (humanitarian aid), Roger Gallopin (prisoners, internees and civilians), and Jean Pictet (legal and doctrinal matters). This restructuring and expansion of the Secretariat coincided with the regrouping of the various departments and agencies into Divisions.

During hostilities the ICRC's tasks were of two broad kinds: the first concerned the application of the Geneva Convention and the exchange of news and information; the second, the provision of material assistance to the different categories of war victim. Coordinating the two areas was not easy, however, either in management terms or in the daily reception and allocation of mail and reports. The head of the Central Agency, Jacques Chenevière, had to admit, whatever he felt about it, that activity coordination was more than one person could cope with, and that the problem could not be solved merely by strengthening the Central Secretariat, while the Coordinating Committee was too blunt an instrument to do the job, hence in May 1942 the creation, or more accurately the resurrection, of a body called the Prisoners of War and Civilian Internees Committee (Commission des prisonniers de guerre et internés civils, or PIC). It consisted of those ICRC members who dealt with such matters, that is Jacques Chenevière, Dr Cramer (Agency), Mlle Ferrière (non-internee civilians), Mme Frick (civilian internees) and Colonel Favre. It kept in constant touch with the administration through Roger Gallopin who at its meetings, normally held twice weekly, laid before the

Committee the most important letters received by the ICRC as well as general issues affecting prisoners of war, civilian internees and medical personnel.

As with the appointment in spring 1935 of a committee to deal with the question of political prisoners, the formation of such working groups inevitably raised issues of principle. In deciding to set up the PIC Committee, the ICRC's leading figures were not only responding to the need for administrative efficiency, they were also acknowledging in a way both the increasing scope and growing complexity of the issue of internees and the necessity of devising a strategy which would go further than the mere application of the Geneva Conventions and of ICRC doctrine. It is therefore in the papers of the PIC Committee that traces can be found of what essentially the ICRC knew about the internees' situation and of what it sought to achieve where they were concerned. At the end of 1942 and the beginning of 1943, the Coordinating Committee took once more, at Burckhardt's suggestion, a decision of some political importance: it entrusted Jean-Etienne Schwarzenberg, until then a 'specialist' on civilian internees under Mlle Ferrière's direction, with the handling of all matters concerning the Jews, issues which had up till then been dispersed, according to the nature of the problem, among several people and several agencies.[66]

In the summer of 1943, as we shall see, the ICRC began sending parcels to civilian prisoners, citizens of countries occupied by the Wehrmacht, who had been deported to Germany and held in concentration camps there. This work, conducted by the Humanitarian Aid Division directed by Hans Wasmer under the responsibility of Mlle Bordier and Mlle Odier, grew in scope and in particular made it possible to trace some of the *Schutzhäftlinge* (people in preventive detention). Hence the creation of a unit called 'colis aux camps de concentration', the CCC, or 'concentration camps parcels service', whose card index of addresses and information rose in twenty months from around fifty names to more than 90,000. Finally in March 1944 there was set up, not without some difficulty, a Special Aid Division ('Division d'assistance spéciale', or DAS) responsible for all humanitarian aid on behalf of civilians in enforced residence, including the Jews. The DAS worked on purchasing and dispatch with the Aid Division and the Pharmaceutical Service of the ICRC on the one hand and with the Joint Aid Commission of the international Red Cross on the other, but it was also in contact with the PIC, which now functioned under a PIC committee, and with the Central Agency, to which it passed information about people involved in the concentration camp parcels scheme. An *ad hoc* service provided the necessary liaison by sorting the incoming mail into

different categories and ensuring that information was exchanged
between the index files of the national services of the Central Agency
and those of the Special Aid Division.

In fact, this Central POW Agency was a veritable beehive, with its
enormous index files on prisoners and civilian internees compiled on the
basis of the thousands of letters which reached Geneva every day. In
1940, a special file index was created for Miscellaneous Civilian Internees ('civils internés divers', or CID), that is for all categories of civilians
not covered by the Geneva Conventions and deprived of Protecting
Powers: for the most part, stateless persons and Jewish émigrés. In
spring 1941 the civilian files, classified up till then by country, like those
of POWs, were combined into a general civilian file to which carbon
copies of the CID's documents were added. But managing the CID
(which had in fact absorbed the individual cases research service
formerly run by Mlle Posnansky) was no simple matter. As the 1948
report put it: 'In these circumstances the basis on which the CID
worked was very uncertain since there was no way of finding out the
destination of the trains deporting the people whom the service was
trying to trace.'[67] During 1942 the CID was in fact opened up to all
stateless people except holders of Nansen passports, and to all the Jews
from Germany and occupied countries deported to the East. In 1943
the files on deportees were transferred back to the national agencies, and
Mlle Arnold's CID then concerned itself mainly with German, Austrian
and stateless Jews. Requests to emigrate to Palestine, and other protection documents, were dealt with from December 1943 onwards by an
ad hoc service called IMPA. The chief significance attaching to these
administrative comings and goings is that they betray the ICRC's
uncertainty as to the position it ought to adopt towards certain categories of victim and as a result the way it groped towards a policy which
it did not yet dare to define.

Staying with the Central Agency for Prisoners of War one notes yet
another register, that of the camps and manpower service, which was
created in 1939 to hold all the information gathered on POW and
internment camps, whether they had been visited or not, and which
allowed the ICRC to draw up a list of the conditions under which
different categories of prisoners and detainees were held. In 1944 at the
ICRC's request this service started extending its intelligence-gathering
on Jews and deportees and making a monthly list of the camps where
they were held, rather than the quarterly list drawn up for POWs and
civilian internees, a sign of the times in itself and evidence, too, of
increasing attention being paid to the issue.

The hierarchy of functions which the flow-charts and descriptions of scope and function seem to establish is more apparent than real. The fact of entrusting a small group with the running of general affairs – the Central Committee, the Coordinating Committee, the Bureau – sat uneasily with the responsibilities which certain members enjoyed in their own committees, especially if that role was a long-established one, as was the case with Mme Frick where civilians were concerned, or Mlle Ferrière where emigration was the issue. So coordination was not easy even within the ruling group. Jacques Chenevière, as was his wont, complained to Max Huber about it:

There is in the ICRC's affairs a deplorable lack of discipline and liaison – of liaison both between certain members of staff and between some ICRC members too. For, too often, the coordinating committee is purely illusory: it is not consulted, or else it is informed only when people feel like it, and they frequently try to get its decisions changed afterwards, or they blithely alter them outside the committee. And yet this same committee is supposed to take responsibility for everything.[68]

This was in 1942. Two years later Chenevière made the same diagnosis but applied it this time to the Bureau:

I deeply regret, once again, that the Bureau, despite the illusion it very frequently suffers under that it possesses real authority, was, it seems to me, only informed very belatedly of something that was already far advanced . . . Such methods, I feel, create a regrettable sense of insecurity. One is driven to the conclusion that the Bureau often concentrates on trivial matters to the exclusion (almost) of essential problems. I appreciate that in the ICRC you often have to bear issues of personality in mind, which is hardly easy. Nevertheless I have already seen many cases where this 'internal' spirit of compromise causes or probably will cause much more serious external difficulties, which ultimately risk damaging the very institution itself. I may be wrong, but it is difficult for me to ignore what I sincerely believe to be the case.[69]

Chenevière was right that personality clashes played a not inconsiderable, albeit subterranean, role. For example, the setting up by Carl J. Burckhardt, its chairman, of the International Red Cross Joint Aid Commission led to a lengthy confrontation with Lucie Odier, in charge, since she joined the ICRC in 1930, of the development of aid agencies within national Red Cross societies and of the aid effort in Spain during the civil war, and the creator in 1939 of the ICRC's Aid Agency (later Aid Division).[70]

The ICRC's chairman Max Huber was thus confronted throughout the war with organisational and managerial problems, which led to his drawing up numerous flow-chart drafts, and sometimes with clashes between individuals where he had to pour oil on troubled waters. It can obviously be imagined that his poor state of health, which kept him on several occasions away from the ICRC and even from Geneva, particularly during the months, crucial from our perspective, of August, September, October, and November 1942, was a significant factor in the failure of leadership which Jacques Chenevière referred to more than once. But the chairman was perhaps also inclined to seek compromise before all else and, as his age and honours increased, to distance himself from day-to-day routine matters. His attitude towards the problem of the Jews and deportees therefore appears just another manifestation of the great caution and detachment which stands out so clearly today in the ICRC's wartime management. Moreover he so dominated the ICRC that it was to him, only a few weeks after his resignation at the end of 1944 for reasons of ill health and overwork, that his colleagues turned in order to replace – provisionally, it was thought – Burckhardt, whose departure to Paris as Switzerland's representative prevented his taking up in March 1945 the ICRC presidency to which he had just been appointed. So it is not easy to decide precisely how much influence Max Huber exerted on the ICRC's decision-making processes.

Its functional difficulties were inherent in its very nature: as Jacques Chenevière pointed out, it was 'an amalgam of good intentions' which fought shy of becoming 'an institution shouldering its responsibilities toward Switzerland and a deeply distressed world'.[71] Both the strength and the weakness of the ICRC lay in the fact that during World War II it remained, despite the development of its bureaucracy and the emergence of a new type of civil servant, a club of leading citizens and amateurs who differed little from each other. It constituted a strength in that such a membership profile made possible in theory rapid decision-making, a certain organisational flexibility, and the bold pursuit of individual initiative. It constituted a weakness in that individual rivalry was not constrained within institutional guidelines, and a number of decisions were taken on the spur of the moment only to be questioned later, or put off continually, or suspended because there was lacking any proper delegation of authority. For the same reasons papers containing important information were mislaid or failed to circulate properly, and sometimes time was wasted in fruitless discussions between inadequately briefed people.

So personalities played an all-important part at the highest level, that of the political leadership. To understand an institution it is insufficient just to study its flow-charts. For, to take but one example, the ICRC's members were not equal in responsibility, in knowledge, or in power. There were in fact at least three centres within the theoretically sovereign body: those in charge, who were in possession of information and who ran the organisation; the ordinary members, who ran little and knew less; and Carl J. Burckhardt, who often knew more than those in charge, who was less concerned than they with day-to-day management, but who intervened in the big political problems and often pursued a purely personal agenda.

The problem of the circulation of information, of internal communication and of participation in decision-making also arose between the ICRC's leading members and those who can be called its senior civil servants, the permanent officers of the institution, men such as Roger Gallopin, Jean Pictet, Hans Bachmann (Burckhardt's secular arm), and Jean-Etienne Schwarzenberg, who, as the person in charge of Jewish questions, is of particular importance in this study. Outwardly, they carried out the policy laid down by the ICRC and its committees. In reality, as in any similar set-up, they derived their power from their competence, their permanent presence, and their familiarity with the relevant papers and documents. But in considering the influence they exerted on political decision-making, given that they possessed the same information as the ICRC members in charge, we need to give due weight to individuals and to their responsibilities, intentions and relationships.

It was scarcely different for the delegates on the ground, even though headquarters viewed them simply as carrying out policy laid down in Geneva. In reality, given the slowness of ordinary correspondence (a letter subject to censorship took eight days from Geneva to Berlin), a tight control of telephones and telegrams, and a certain restraint in the use of the Swiss diplomatic bag, each outpost had largely to improvise on the basis of instructions given at the outset. Moreover initial training was of necessity cursory, and basic directives very general in nature, so that in fact delegates enjoyed considerable discretion, at the cost sometimes of the odd brush with Geneva, and their responsibilities, particularly in the case of top delegates such as Marcel Junod, Roland Marti, Pierre Descoeudres, Otto Lehner, Karl Kolb, Vladimir de Steiger and Frédéric Born, were considerable. So whatever the ICRC's unwieldiness, a feature it shared with most other institutions, it was people, here too, who played an essential role.

3   The door that stayed shut

This chapter goes to the heart of the matter: the ways the ICRC intervened with the German authorities on behalf of political prisoners and victims of racial persecution. There is, however, more to be said, and in the following chapters we will be looking at other concrete measures. Then the ICRC's activities will be scrutinised from a local perspective, since conditions varied according to whether occupied countries, allies or satellites of the Greater Germany were involved. Chapters 5 to 7 cover the period from the outbreak of war to the summer of 1944. Events in Hungary on the one hand, and the victorious advance of the Allies in the West on the other, made possible new initiatives which both permitted and required a special effort on behalf of prisoners and deportees; and that will be the subject of closing chapters 8 and 9.

As I have already emphasised, the fundamental criterion in the eyes of the belligerent states, and of necessity also in the eyes of the ICRC, was the existence of a protection regime based on Conventions. The Protecting Powers and the ICRC were justified in intervening to help and protect POWs who were nationals of states signatories to the 1929 Convention, and civilian internees from a belligerent state who found themselves at the outbreak of war on the territory of a hostile power, since that concession had been obtained by the ICRC from autumn 1939 onwards.

So from a strictly legal point of view, the people this book is concerned with, namely the concentration camp population, including the nationals of countries at war with the Reich who were arrested in occupied territories and deported as hostages, as suspects or as convicted prisoners, were not covered by the Conventions. The question then arises whether because of its lack of legal competence the ICRC was content with doing nothing, or whether, as André Durand writes in his history of the ICRC, 'since it was unable to enter the concentration camps, the ICRC sought to remove from them those categories of internees who were already protected by an international Convention or a multilateral agreement',[1] or indeed whether it explored every avenue by invoking the law (particularly Articles 42 to 56 of the Hague Convention), its own doctrine, or even its statutory right to take humanitarian initiatives. It was adequately apprised of inhuman treatment in the camps and of the tragic fate of racial deportees; so what needs to be asked is precisely what it imagined, attempted, or dared to do.

The DRK fails to cooperate

The immediate impact of the outbreak of war in Europe in early September 1939 was to concentrate the ICRC's attention and resources upon traditional, Convention-based tasks. The preparation of such activities had since the Munich alert been the responsibility of a body called the War Services Committee. This did not mean that other issues were neglected: any such assumption is belied by the success of efforts on behalf of enemy civilians interned at the outbreak of war on the belligerents' territory. Of note too is the fact that the setting up at the same time of national files on civilians and the exchange of information via civilian messages (the famous P61s of twenty-five words each) by the Central POW Agency involved the Jews too, even in the countries occupied by the Wehrmacht, and that the DRK, in the weeks following the occupation of Poland and the establishment of the General-Government, forwarded postal communications and requests for information about missing persons even where the Jews where concerned.

German victory in Poland and the appointment of Himmler (already supremo of the SS and of all German police forces) as *Reichskommissar* for the strengthening of the German race, gave fresh impetus to the struggle against the Jews; from this point onwards only rivalry between different power groupings in the Reich gave rise to the occasional hiccup in pushing forward the programme of racial reorganisation in Eastern Europe. The ICRC was quickly made aware of the worsening situation through the complaints and affidavits it received. The journey Junod made to the Government-General in November following the visit of the Joint's representatives to Geneva left no-one in any doubt about the reality of the deportations and of the regrouping in progress in the Lublin region, as Huber acknowledged on 27 December before the Central Committee and in direct discussions with Hartmann.[2] But other appeals for help, notably, as we shall see in the chapter on Poland, that on behalf of the Cracow professors, provided him with proof that it was not only the Jews but the entire civilian population of Poland that was threatened by measures of a totally unjustifiable brutality and scope. In the territories it controlled in the East, the Reich appeared indeed to believe that it was no longer bound by any legal constraint or humanitarian consideration.

The ICRC's reaction to this information was, as always, extremely cautious and restrained. In the early months of the war people at Geneva were distracted by other concerns, paralysed by what they already knew about Nazi political and antisemitic violence, and convinced that any direct Red Cross gesture over a matter which the Reich considered taboo would be futile, even counter-productive. So the ICRC members, with a few exceptions, did not pay a great deal of attention to what was going on in the East; worse still, like Burckhardt, who seems to have turned a deaf ear to Mme Frick-Cramer's repeated suggestion that the Germans be asked to allow a permanent delegation to be set up in Cracow, they did not really wish to be told what was going on. The documents relating to Burckhardt's mission to Berlin in March 1940 make no mention of any démarche on the subject. This does not prove conclusively that he did nothing about it, but it does show that anything he did do was not significant enough to be recorded in a written note.

The ICRC's silence at this time about events in Poland, Czechoslovakia and Austria is also explained by its hope of getting correspondence, and even some food and clothing, to the victims. In this respect its attitude on the question of Polish POWs is typical. Following the division of Poland the Reich considered these now stateless prisoners as mere civilian workers ready to do its bidding. Unlike the Protecting Power Sweden, which quickly gave in, the ICRC opposed the change in principle and maintained that so far as it was concerned the Polish POWs remained subject to the Geneva Convention. In actual fact, however, its reaction was more measured: it dropped the idea of pressing the point with the Germans, and accepted the *fait accompli* in the hope of being able to pursue its assistance in concrete ways: camp visits, aid parcels and the like. But in spring 1942 it had to admit that there was no possibility of this and that what it was maintaining was in reality a fiction. Besides, the question arose whether the Germans were also introducing racial discrimination in the application of the Geneva Convention. The ICRC became slowly and very reluctantly aware that, contrary to the assurances it had been given, POWs of Jewish faith, with the exception of English speakers, were sometimes the victims of discriminatory measures. It is true that here and there the policy of individual démarches produced the odd tangible result for the victims. When, as we shall see in the chapter devoted to Holland, some 200 civilian internees from the Dutch East Indies were taken to Buchenwald as hostages, the ICRC decided after much dithering not to make an issue of the violation of undertakings given by the Reich on the subject of civilian internees, and managed, at the end of months of negotiation, to get them transferred to a concentration camp in Holland where at least they no longer had to endure the rigours of the Thuringian winter.

From 1939 to 1941 the ICRC was everywhere in demand. What it knew of the fate of racial persecutees and concentration camp prisoners was still fragmentary, but the hope was still to be able to do something concrete on a case-by-case basis. Moreover, like Switzerland and indeed the whole of Europe, the ICRC was confronted by a victorious Germany, but a Germany which did not seem systematically hostile towards it. Quite the reverse: in the application of the Conventions, the Reich showed the ICRC more consideration than the United Kingdom, concerned above all to play the Protecting Power's card, did. In summer 1940 the German occupation authorities lent their support to the aid operation launched on Burckhardt's initiative in favour of the civilian populations of France and Belgium, and they showed similar understanding over the creation of the Joint Aid Committee. In the humanitarian sphere as well as in all the others, the Third Reich massively made its presence felt.

During the first two years of the war the ICRC made no attempt to enter the concentration camps or to challenge the refusal it had met with in January 1939 when it asked to be allowed to send food or clothing to the detainees. Its claim to deal with imprisoned persons therefore found expression solely through requests for information about missing people which the Search and Individual Cases Service, and later the civilian section of the Agency, forwarded to the German Red Cross.

But by the end of the Polish campaign the gap had begun to widen between the number of requests sent out and the number of replies received. The momentary interruption of mail deliveries to and from the occupied countries was not of course the sole reason, since the deportations put a big question mark over the information exchange set up in 1933 using the DRK's network.

In February 1940, during one of his visits to Geneva, Hartmann had to declare that the number of requests for information about Jews seemed too high, that letters about business matters were being smuggled in with family news (this was checked and shown to be false, of course, since all mail was censored by the Agency), and that in future the German Red Cross would only be able to furnish information in fairly important cases such as, for example, those where people given permission to emigrate were involved.[3] This warning provided only a short breathing space: on 20 August 1941 Hartmann asked the ICRC, because of the DRK's extra workload, to discontinue for the duration information requests about people held in concentration camps, and declared that henceforth any such messages would no longer be passed on.[4]

The bluntness of this announcement provoked the first in-depth discussion amongst the ICRC members about the fate of political prisoners. It took place at a particularly sensitive moment: on 22 June 1941 the Reich had attacked the Soviet Union. In a few weeks more than two million prisoners had fallen into the Wehrmacht's hands, but the USSR was not a signatory to the 1929 Convention on POWs and its national Red Cross society, like its government, had always kept the ICRC at arm's length. Besides, the war in the East was for the Nazis an ideological crusade. So Burckhardt, who was then concentrating his whole attention upon the negotiations over POWs in the East, had apparently no intention of making an issue of the interruption of enquiries about concentration camp internees, especially since such enquiries constituted at best an indirect form of interference. It was sufficient, in his opinion, to continue operating within the framework newly laid down by Berlin.[5]

However, another event occurred which encouraged Mme Frick-Cramer and Mlle Ferrière to press for more thought to be given to the matter: the situation of certain POWs in French uniform, mainly Spanish Republicans who had sought asylum in France and had enlisted in the French army and who, the Central Agency had found, were being deported to Mauthausen. On 16 September 1941 the Coordinating Committee, the highest operational authority, looked into these prisoners' cases and into the information received from the German Red Cross, and decided to take the matter up directly with the German Foreign Ministry.[6] Nothing came of this, partly because little cooperation could be expected from the Spanish authorities, and partly because the Germans would not budge from their position that the Spanish Republicans were political prisoners and not POWs. As a result, by the time Mauthausen was liberated, nearly 5,000 had perished out of a total of 8,000.

Behind the Spanish POWs lay other categories of prisoners: in spite of Huber's efforts not to mention them, they were present in spirit at the meeting on 16 September 1941, prompting the question whether in discussing repression the ICRC could ignore requests involving deportees of enemy nationality. On 19 September Mlle Ferrière tried again, and this time got the Committee to make a démarche covering both Mauthausen and concentration camp internees belonging to countries who were the Reich's enemies. But beforehand the problem was to be discreetly referred to the head of external relations of the DRK, Walter

Hartmann, on his next visit to Geneva, and two notes were drafted for the purpose, one concerning the POWs transferred to Mauthausen, the other being a reply to the DRK's letter of 20 August (in which, as already mentioned, Hartmann had announced that requests for information about concentration camp internees could no longer be entertained). In this reply the ICRC drew attention to the situation of concentration camp prisoners of enemy nationality and wondered whether they could not be granted the same status and treatment as civilians who had been interned on the territory of the Reich at the outbreak of war. The ICRC assured the DRK that there were not a lot of questions about such people; indeed since 20 August only six or seven cases were involved.

When he came to Geneva the attitude which Hartmann adopted was not wholly negative: in the case of missing persons considered civilian internees of enemy nationality, he made a concession to Mlle Ferrière that the DRK would go on receiving requests for information, and he promised to reply as soon as he got back to Berlin to the note handed to him on the subject.[7]

The winter of 1941–2, during which negotiations went on fruitlessly between the Reich and the Soviet Union about the fate of POWs, passed without written reply from Hartmann, in spite of reminders from Marti. During this time intelligence indicating a stepping-up of repression percolated through to Geneva: in particular, civilians were increasingly being taken hostage in occupied countries and deported to concentration camps in the Reich where they were classified as administrative internees in preventive detention who, unlike POWs or civilian internees, were not entitled to protection under the Geneva Convention. News was coming in, too, of the deterioration in the situation of the Jews: for example the High Commissioner for Refugees, Sir Herbert Emerson, personally informed Carl J. Burckhardt of the parlous situation in which the Jews found themselves, now that they had been forbidden to emigrate from Germany, Prince Charles of Sweden, president of the Swedish Red Cross, expressed his concern, too, about the fate of the Jews deported to the East, and Countess Dobrazensky of the Hungarian Red Cross (see pp. 233–4 below) requested aid for her Jewish compatriots deported in inhumane conditions to Galicia. So the ICRC was being challenged on all sides, and at the turn of the year 1941 to 1942, once charities like the Polish People's Aid Committee, chaired by the former American president Herbert Hoover, had managed, in spite of Allied blockade restrictions, to find supplies and distribute them to the civilian population in the General-Government, the question whether the Red Cross should assist deportees took on a particular urgency. So the Coordinating Committee turned all the more eagerly to the Joint Aid Commission once Max Huber had reiterated, at the general discussion on 9 December 1941, that the ICRC ought not to be deflected from its original objectives, since it was under extreme pressure already through its purely wartime activities.[8] But proxy action by the Joint Commission over aid to the Government-General ghettos, on the lines of what was being done for the camps in the south of France, would have required greatly increased means and effort on the one hand, and negotiating the partial lifting of the Allied blockade on the other. The failure of attempts to achieve this in London early in 1942[9] did not mean that the Joint Commission could do nothing for the civilian population in the East, but it did render impossible the kind of large-scale operation which those who looked to Geneva for help were crying out for.

In the middle of March 1942 the person in charge, Suzanne Ferrière, reminded Hartmann of his promise to take up with the competent authority whether there remained any possibility of pursuing enquiries about individual deportees, or whether the ICRC had to give up on an investigation service for which the DRK had up till then shown a certain sympathy. She harboured few illusions, however, and ended her message with the words 'we understand the enormous difficulties which this issue raises and are ready to fall in with your view and stop sending out information requests if you consider it necessary'.[10] The reply from Berlin consisted of two letters, signed by Hartmann and sent a month and a half later, which at one and the same time complement and partly contradict each other. In the first, dated 29 April 1942, the ICRC is notified that the German Red Cross will no longer be able to provide information about non-Aryan evacuees and so no further questions about them ought to be put to it; on the other hand, the DRK will continue to accept enquiries about enemy aliens interned in the Reich.[11] In the second letter, dated 1 May 1942 and addressed personally to Suzanne Ferrière, Hartmann adds that 'our negotiations at this end have reached the conclusion that the DRK cannot get hold of the information requested and that the ICRC has been so advised in the letter of 29 April'.[12]

Four months later, even the possibility of enquiring about enemy aliens vanished. In another 20 August letter (a year to the day after the first), the ICRC read this:

Further to the letter of 29 April 1942, the DRK announces that it is no longer in a position to obtain information about non-Aryans in territory occupied by the Wehrmacht and so asks that time-wasting requests for information about procedures and places of detention be avoided.[13]

Hartmann, who happened to be in Geneva when this reply was received, was able to do little more than confirm its terms, so there was practically nothing more that could be done for those deported to the East, whether they were of foreign nationality or not, and certainly not for Jews. All the ICRC could do in the circumstances was to take due note and from then onwards advise those who turned to it for help in tracing missing relatives that it 'had to limit itself to noting the requests sent to it, not being in a position to say if or when an answer could be given'.[14] This 'nothing doing' attitude needs to be qualified, however, since face to face Hartmann appears to have given the ICRC to understand that the DRK would try to make enquiries about enemy deportees as long as they were not Jewish, and he repeated this promise in the autumn of 1943 to Schwarzenberg without obviously being able to guarantee success in every case.[15]

Friedrich Forrer affirms for his part that the German Red Cross, or at least those of its leaders who tried to resist Nazism, would not have allowed the Reich Central Security Bureau's measures to be imposed directly onto it, although these measures increasingly forbade it to search for missing persons when the ICRC or the Red Cross societies of neutral countries requested it. Forrer mentions in particular a letter of 14 December 1941 from Hartmann's Amt Ausland to the RSHA and quotes a very tense conversation, which Hartmann is believed to have had about the matter with Adolf Eichmann on 1 June 1942. The discussion was of course fruitless except in gradually leading Hartmann, as head of foreign relations at the DRK, to give credence to the rumours about the extermination of the Jews.[16] The vagueness of the DRK's reports to the ICRC on its enquiries, and the noticeable contradictions between Hartmann's letters and what he seems to have said in Geneva during his visits from 1941 onwards, obviously strengthen the hypothesis that the policy of the SS encountered a degree of resistance within the DRK.

Searching for a solution, fearful of a reply

On 24 September 1942, the ICRC sent Roland Marti, its chief delegate in Germany, a note about deportees of foreign nationality imprisoned there. In order to set that note in context – it represented until October 1944 the ICRC's most direct démarche over the question that lies at the heart of this study – we need to go back several months in time and take on board the whole range of the ICRC's concerns.

During the winter of 1941–2 the ICRC's work expanded continually. With the American and Japanese entry into the war, new vast and distant theatres of operations opened up. The Russian campaign dragged on, while the number of prisoners kept rising without the negotiations between Geneva, Moscow and Berlin leading to anything tangible. Visits to prison and internment camps, the dispatch of aid, and the handling of correspondence of all kinds, meant that the number of delegates in Germany had to be increased, since there was no improvement in the lot of the victims the IRCR was concerned with; far from it. Last but not least, the civilian populations, whether interned or not, suffered more and more directly from the war and its consequences. The ICRC was called upon from all sides to give its protection, to search for the missing, to send aid and to offer succour, both moral and material. Jacques Chenevière, the ICRC's appointee at the head of the Central Bureau, was not alone in his concern. He was, as we have seen, particularly involved in questions of management and organisation. However, the problem here was not only one of efficiency: policy priorities needed to be established. At the beginning of 1942 he said to his colleagues: 'If the ICRC agrees to take on every activity which the world's suffering gives rise to, it will soon be overwhelmed and will lay itself open to the criticism that it did not first ensure that tasks laid down by tradition and convention were attended to first.'[17]

The discriminatory treatment meted out in certain camps to Jewish POWs, for instance, raised an issue both of principle and of tactics. Should they, as Max Huber believed, restate the doctrine even if that meant being unable to do anything else, or as Burckhardt argued, seek a more practical path which took account of the ICRC's whole range of activity?[18] So, at the start of 1942, everything pointed to the necessity for a general rethink. But, despite the urgency and importance of matters still left unresolved, it was only in mid-May, because of other commitments, that it was possible to convene the so-called 'hierarchy meeting' of the ICRC's leading members.

The reappraisal of objectives took place on 15 May and lasted two hours. It was not primarily nor even largely devoted to the Jews and to deportees. Nevertheless, the participants, all Committee members except Jean Pictet, the secretary, that is Max Huber (in the chair), Suzanne Ferrière and Marguerite Frick-Cramer, Jacques Chenevière, Carl J. Burckhardt, Alec Cramer and Frédéric Barbey, discussed first the problem of the German Jews on the basis of a note drafted by Mme Frick, Mlle Ferrière and Dr Alec Cramer. This document, dated late April 1942 and entitled 'How and to what extent the ICRC should become involved with the Jews', is worth looking at more closely.

In its essentials, the note affirms or reaffirms a by now familiar position:

a) In line with its traditions and statutes, with decisions of International Red Cross Conferences, and with the Conventions, the ICRC never discriminates on grounds of a religious, political or racial nature.

b) The only difference observable in law is that between Jews who belong to a nation at war with the interning power, and Jews of the same nationality as that power. The ICRC is entitled to intervene on behalf of the first category, since an international problem is involved.

And the note proposes a series of practical measures:

i) to request a visit to the Jewish camps in occupied France, whether their occupants are foreigners or French citizens, since the latter are in enemy hands;

ii) to try to organise aid, in particular by getting material assistance from Jewish organisations;

iii) to defend, in discussions with the Germans, the rights of Jewish POWs and equivalent civilian internees;

iv) finally (a more sensitive issue), to work to get news of deported Jews.[19]

The German Red Cross's reply to Mlle Ferrière's mid-March letter had not yet arrived, but it is significant that the note already casts doubt on the DRK's authority and suggests seeking other contacts in the Reich.

It would be an exaggeration to say that the decisions taken at this meeting amounted to a redefinition of aims: of the four measures adopted on the treatment of the Jews, two had been the subject of recent démarches by Marti, at the Foreign Ministry in Berlin, and a reply was still awaited. The first démarche, at the end of March, was signed by an ICRC member, Frédéric Barbey, indicating the importance attached to it. It referred to the Jewish detainees at Compiègne, most of whom were French; it was necessary to try and get much-needed supplies to them as a matter of urgency.[20] The second, sent in mid-April by the Secretariat, enquired into the whereabouts of the Jews from Compiègne and Drancy who had just been deported to the East.[21] The meeting held on 15 May therefore conferred a wider dimension on these two démarches. It laid great emphasis on the fact that people deported from France to Eastern Europe were classified by the ICRC are civilian internees in enemy hands, for whom the Committee felt justified in demanding the same treatment as POWs received. The DRK was not apprised of these two démarches; this confirmed that the privileged status it had enjoyed until then was now being abandoned.

Furthermore it was decided that the OKW, the German military High Command, would be asked about the treatment meted out to Jewish

POWs and medical personnel. For the moment no further action would be taken over Mme Frick-Cramer's proposal that deportees in the General-Government should be allowed to send news of themselves. Two other démarches would be undertaken, one on behalf of the Spaniards held, as we have seen, in Mauthausen, the other in support of POWs without a Protecting Power towards whom the ICRC felt a particular obligation.[22]

Applying these decisions proved far from easy. Four days after this meeting, on 19 May, Eduard Sethe, the deputy head of the legal department at the German Foreign Ministry and the person Roland Marti usually dealt with, told him that where Jews deported from France to the East were concerned, their whereabouts could not be revealed and no assistance could be channelled in their direction, because they were criminals who had threatened the security of the German armed forces and who therefore fell outside the Red Cross's remit.[23] This reply did not, however, take Marti aback. Instead he placed all his hopes in the démarche undertaken at the end of March to secure the possibility of sending aid to Compiègne. There was some hope that this could be achieved, given the many different categories of internees in the camp, some of whom had already been assisted by the ICRC.

Marti's hopes were to be dashed, however, since no formal reply was ever made to this proposal. During the summer of 1942, the ICRC's usual German informants, Consul Jacob-Ludwig Metternich and Walter Hartmann, both confirmed that since no action could be taken on behalf of the Jews the ICRC would do better not to raise the question in the first place.[24] The only possibility left open was that considered on 15 May, i.e. an intervention on behalf of alien deportees from occupied territories who could be said to be on the same footing, despite being held in concentration camps, as alien civilian internees.

Jean-Etienne Schwarzenberg was put in charge of this and prepared notes that had been agreed in principle at the 15 May meeting on priorities. But for both legal and political reasons he does not appear to have been convinced at the time that the ICRC should get involved in making a formal request to the Germans. In response to a démarche from the French Red Cross he discreetly suggested another approach, turning the issue that confronted the ICRC on its head: not to consider first the legality of what was possible and then decide upon a course of action, but to ask pragmatically whether or not one wished to do something and, if the answer was yes, to do it without feeling constrained to make a formal issue of it.[25]

The debate now moved to the CPI (Civilian Prisoners and Internees

Commission) set up in the spring of 1942; its members were Mme Frick-Cramer, Mlle Ferrière, M. Chenevière, M. Alec Cramer, M. Gallopin and M. Schwarzenberg. At the end of July 1942 four texts were ready; as things had moved on since then, they corresponded only partially to what had been decided at the 15 May meeting. Because Eduard Sethe, the representative of the German Foreign Ministry, could not come to Geneva, the four documents were handed to Maximilian von Engelbrechten, an official at the German consulate in Geneva responsible for POW issues, who passed them on during August to the Foreign Ministry in Berlin.

They bore upon the situation of the POWs and civilian internees deprived of a Protecting Power, the Mauthausen Spaniards, the visits the ICRC wished to make to POWs imprisoned for common law offences, and lastly the status of Dutch officers who upon demobilisation had been rearrested and deported as hostages to Stanislau, one of a number of punishment camps set up in Germany. As can be seen, the Jews and concentration camp deportees were nowhere mentioned. This highlights hesitation and perplexity on the part of the ICRC and even its feeling of impotence, which was reflected also in the negative reply sent at the same time to the Slovak Red Cross about racial persecution.

For Roland Marti things were simpler. On 20 August, the day that the German Red Cross sent notification from Berlin that it was suspending its services to deportees, he relaunched his démarche about the whereabouts of and how aid could be got to French deportees, since he had not yet received written confirmation of Sethe's verbal refusal of the preceding 19 May. But he did not think this new initiative would work. As far as he was concerned the only hope of achieving anything lay in a direct approach from the ICRC to Heinrich Himmler or the Ministry of Justice, even if it meant the risk of upsetting the Foreign Ministry. He felt the same about aid; this was (just to be seen to be trying to do something) a matter of increasing concern in Geneva. Marti was convinced that ICRC delegates would never be allowed into prisons or concentration camps, and that even if they were granted access, they would not be able to make a proper inspection. Whenever he raised these issues the German Red Cross, the Wehrmacht High Command and the Foreign Ministry all passed the buck to the Gestapo. Marti was after all the man on the ground and he knew the German officials and authorities concerned at first hand. He stressed that the ICRC should contact, direct from Geneva, the German Police and Justice Departments, who controlled the concentration camps, and not waste time with the Foreign Ministry or military High Command, as Burckhardt had recently once again attempted to do over aid supplies to Poland.[26]

At ICRC headquarters some progress was made, though not exactly in the direction Marti had proposed. The CPI Commission decided, on the advice of von Engelbrechten and probably on that of Walter Hartmann who was in Geneva at the time, to send a note to the German Foreign Ministry about the deportees. A similar approach was made to the French Foreign Ministry in Vichy; without speaking directly of political detainees, the letter confined itself to asking to be told the whereabouts and the names of the deportees, following numerous requests made to the Red Cross about them.[27] This message was sent with few illusions and apparently was never answered, or even acknowledged, in spite of the ICRC's close contacts in Geneva with Colonel André Garteiser, the French Red Cross's head of foreign affairs. But where political and racial prisoners were concerned the French Red Cross seems to have carried no more weight with its government than the DRK did in Germany.

The note to be sent to the Germans was drafted by Schwarzenberg, carefully checked by Burckhardt and signed by Roger Gallopin.[28] It was not to be sent direct to the Foreign Ministry but addressed to Marti, who was to undertake a verbal démarche and was free to decide, according to the way the discussion went, the best moment to submit it formally. The ICRC hoped to persuade German authorities to make concessions about the French deportees by taking up the case of German citizens held as enemy aliens in the United States, Great Britain and in Latin America, especially Brazil. But at no time did either the DRK or the Reich authorities enter into discussions of reciprocity on these lines.

Marti lost no time in making the démarche requested. He did so during a routine meeting with his usual interlocutor in the legal section of the German Foreign Ministry, *Geheimrat* Eduard Sethe. The reception Marti got was not unfriendly, but Sethe soon made it clear that he was sceptical about getting police permission to visit the camps. Marti then asked not for blanket authorisation but for a kind of sample visit, perhaps on the lines of those made in 1935 and 1938, and he mentioned Theresienstadt, where only old and sick people were held and where headquarters had told him it would be possible to send aid. Sethe was reasonably hopeful about the Theresienstadt detainees, or at least, he added vaguely, some categories among them. But his attitude had in truth been the same since the Compiègne démarche in late March to which, despite numerous reminders from Marti, he had only partially responded.

The fact is that the ICRC gave the distinct impression of dithering over the appeals made to it and the pressures it was subjected to, since its objectives were more contradictory than ever. If the 24 September note, under cover of dealing with alien civilian internees, was aimed at saving the Jews, it concerned only those of Western Europe, whose deportation at that time was causing great distress in Switzerland and the Anglo-Saxon countries, since the Jews of Poland, Czechoslovakia and so on, whose states had disappeared as far as the Nazis were concerned, could not be treated as enemy citizens any more than Germans or stateless people could. In that case, it might have made more sense to go in for a big gesture, perhaps in the form of a public appeal such as Jewish organisations were demanding of the Allies, the Vatican and the ICRC. But the so-called 'handcuffs' crisis, when Canadian commandos handcuffed German soldiers on the beach during the Dieppe raid in August 1942, and the tit-for-tat threat by the Reich authorities to repudiate the Geneva Convention on the treatment of POWs in their hands, greatly alarmed Burckhardt, who bore full responsibility during Max Huber's illness, convalescence and resulting absence from Geneva. This crisis, together with the need to wait for the German reply to the 24 September note, when added to the fears of the Swiss authorities and to a general conviction that any démarche was useless, all help explain why the decision of 14 October 1942 not to launch a protest about the violations of human rights was out of phase with the declaration of the Allies of 17 December 1942 concerning the Jewish massacres, a declaration which, it is true, was followed by no truly effective measure on the part of the Allies to come to the aid of peoples under threat.

The question then arises whether the ICRC's leaders considered a direct démarche to the Reich's rulers during the autumn of 1942. From a letter sent on 27 October 1942 to the ICRC by one of Himmler's aides, it would appear that Burckhardt had sought an audience with the SS chief on 21 September, i.e. three days before the dispatch of the note about the deportees. But the meeting, which in any case never took place, may have had another purpose: according to annotations on the document, confirmed forty-five years later by Hans Bachmann, it probably concerned, at least initially, an intervention on behalf of an individual who had been recommended to Burckhardt, Countess Karolina von Lanskoranska, whose release Burckhardt secured during his meeting with Ernest Kaltenbrunner, the head of the RSHA, the Reich Central Security Bureau, on the Arlberg road on 12 March 1945.[29]

In the absence of a reply from the German side, the conversations between Sethe and Marti about the 24 September note dragged on throughout the autumn. The ICRC faced a number of dilemmas, such as whether it should insist on a written reply, which could only be negative, or whether it should address itself directly to the police, as Marti kept recommending, or ask the Foreign Ministry for permission to visit the ghettos in Transnistria or in Theresienstadt, as Burckhardt suggested to Gerhart Riegner in mid-November, or whether it should simply give up, since all contacts with the Germans inclined it in that direction, and take up again the idea of sending the deportees aid that would indirectly benefit the Jews too. Marti and the CPI Commission thought it should.[30]

The ICRC did, after all, have lists of names drawn up from appeals for help and questions sent in by the families of those who had disappeared, and it might have been possible, on the basis of knowing the detainees' whereabouts and getting the necessary funds and parcels together, to make a concrete response to a critical situation without running up against an insurmountable issue of principle. On 30 December 1942 the ICRC's principal figures, during a meeting of the Coordinating Committee held in Burckhardt's absence on sick leave, resolved to give up trying to get a written reply to the 24 September note, and to examine instead the possibility of taking aid direct to the concentration camps.[31] A decisive step was thereby taken. Its implications are the subject of the next section, and the following chapter will look at the aid effort and evaluate what was achieved between late 1942 and the end of the war.

Same policy, different approach

The December 1942 decision was not supported unanimously. Mme Frick and Marcel Junod, the delegate at large dealing chiefly with the negotiations over POWs in the Russo-German conflict, thought that they should insist on getting information about Jewish deportees of foreign nationality or, at the very least, about the Aryans. Moreover it was felt that a démarche even over the sending of aid would have more chance of success if, as Marti recommended, it was addressed to Georg Thierack, the Reich's minister of justice. But one of Burckhardt's close aides brought up the familiar argument that the ICRC would thereby risk compromising its ability to act in other areas where its intervention was welcome.[32] This line of reasoning had as much influence as the failure of the 24 September démarche on the decision of the majority of the Coordinating Committee to stop banging on a door which remained firmly closed. This decision confirmed that the ICRC's growing interest in deportees and Jews did not mean a revaluation of its basic aims; instead it indicated that the ICRC was not going down that road, although this did not mean either that the ICRC was just going to do nothing when it was called upon to help.

The aid operation to deportees was not, however, launched under very good auspices. Attempts made during 1942 were hardly encouraging. In summer, the Coordinating Committee made clear its intention, starting with France and Greece, of bringing food aid to civilians interned on their own territory, abandoned for the most part and suffering great hardship. In the Italian-controlled part of Greece it was possible to help imprisoned civilians, including political prisoners and Jews, but Marti's démarches in Berlin on behalf of the French Jews of Compiègne and the Theresienstadt detainees met with no response, and Burckhardt's attempt to lean on the military High Command to bypass the political police succeeded only in increasing confusion between headquarters and the Berlin delegation. Besides, if the families of some categories of detainees in prisons and concentration camps were able to send small consignments of food for immediate consumption, the ICRC itself remained banned from getting aid into the camps, as the German Red Cross reminded it in 1939. Even if it had got the ban lifted, it would have had to find a way of convincing the Allies to allow through the blockade supplies that were subject to no check on distribution since the camps remained closed to all outside visitors, including the Red Cross. That is why, in the 24 September note, the ICRC, being fully aware of the situation, asked for parcels to be sent to deportees only by close relatives or by national Red Cross societies.

On the other hand the Joint Aid Committee, which was already supplying groups of Jews, for example in the camps in the south of France, and could get food, medicines and clothes donated to it through to civilian populations in German-controlled areas (Poland included) without much in the way of racial discrimination, received in autumn 1942 permission to proceed with the dispatch of medicines to Theresienstadt, that is to a Jewish camp in which it seemed German Jews were interned.[33] It looked like a precedent which could be used in support of aid not only to deportees or, as the ICRC was beginning to call them, administrative internees, but also to civilians interned in their own country, and it served as further encouragement to pursue the search for ways of assisting Jews and to revive the idea of an aid programme to concentration camps that might take the place of the protection refused by the Germans.[34]

Under Suzanne Ferrière's authority Jean-Etienne Schwarzenberg (in charge from now on of Jewish questions) prepared the necessary démarches. In accordance with the aim of making no distinction between Jews and other civilian alien internees, these démarches were aimed exclusively at the German Foreign Ministry and took the dual form of a note sent on 18 January 1943 to Marti and a personal letter from chairman Huber to the minister a few days later.

Marti's instructions pointed out that although the Reich did not grant the status of civilian internees to civilians arrested for various reasons, held in occupied countries, and sometimes transferred to prisons and concentration camps in Germany, the ICRC could not remain unconcerned about this category because they were, after all, citizens of an enemy country in the hands of a belligerent. Such 'administrative prisoners' were distinct from civilian internees. Since the ICRC's best endeavours to have them granted civilian internee status, at least as far as getting their addresses and news was concerned, had so far come to nothing, the ICRC was trying instead to get aid, especially food, to them. For this it was essential to have some means of checking how the aid was distributed, otherwise donors would not oblige; such checks could be carried out during occasional visits by delegates but could also involve the production of receipts, as already happened with Joint Committee aid to Poland. It was, however, indispensable for the ICRC to know at least where people were being held, their numbers, and the breakdown by nationality (Norwegians, Dutch, Poles, Belgians, French or Serbs). Although potential donors had not yet been approached to provide aid for their nationals held in German prisons or concentration camps, there was every hope (the ICRC's instructions to Marti concluded) that aid would be forthcoming if such donors could be assured that adequate safeguards were in place to ensure that any aid sent did not fall into the wrong hands.[35]

Contrary to Marti's fears, the first contacts with the Foreign Ministry were fairly positive, since Sethe even suggested the immediate dispatch of aid to those internees whose names and whereabouts in the Reich were known to the ICRC, including at the Dutch camp of Westerbork. Although only a score of deportees' names and addresses were listed, the go-ahead could be given for the dispatch of fifty parcels.

But these overtures were not really fresh concessions, since Himmler's order to allow food parcels to be sent by relatives to those detainees not subject to a severe punishment regime, Germans included, dated from 29 October 1942, and the Swedish Red Cross had already managed to send food and clothing to all Norwegians in German camps.[36] Furthermore, the need to know the whereabouts of the recipient that made any large-scale operation impossible, given the small number of prisoners located by the Central Agency at the time, not to mention the impossibility of entering the camps to ensure the parcels were correctly delivered, all conspired to make highly problematic the movement of aid from overseas through the Allied blockade.

The official Foreign Ministry reply to the January démarches confirmed these fears. It amounted to this. While Germany refused to allow aid to be sent to deportees in principle, it was prepared to allow exceptions to be made in respect of certain categories. People accused of serious crimes against the Reich – notably the *NN* or 'Night and Fog' – remained beyond the reach of help. Deportees convicted of less grave offences could receive books and clothes but not food, and on condition that the parcels came from their relatives, contained no message and were in conformity with fixed rules. Finally foreigners held in so-called preventive detention (*Schutzhäftlinge*) – among whom Marti hoped to be able to include genuine hostages as well – could receive general help. For this category the permission to send aid, already granted to relatives and to national Red Cross societies, was simply extended to the ICRC. No limit was placed on the number of parcels that could be sent, but amounts of food had to correspond to what the recipient needed, otherwise the surplus would be distributed to co-detainees. However – and this was an essential requirement – only parcels bearing a name would be delivered, so the sender had to know the name and address of the recipient.

Headquarters reacted with some disappointment, since only a limited number of addresses was on file and concerned above all a nationality, the Norwegians, who were being helped already. Moreover, proof that the recipient had got the parcel, generally insisted upon by donors, remained a problem because there was no-one in the concentration camps who in the absence of the addressee could be trusted to sign the acknowledgement slip. While asking Marti to press on with his démarche, Jacques Chenevière felt quite discouraged, noting bitterly that the ICRC had secured nothing more than others had and that Huber's letter had not had the slightest tangible effect.[37]

Marti did not see it that way. The preceding autumn he had shown himself very pessimistic about any approach to the Foreign Ministry over the principle of the deportees' status. Now he was urging action, calling for the famous fifty parcels to be sent. Their departure was put off for weeks by a series of delays demurely termed 'administrative', the most piquant of which was caused by stocks of marmalade running out. Marti was in no way surprised that the German Foreign Ministry ignored a new démarche that headquarters asked him to make in mid-May 1943, and redoubled his meetings with people in Berlin in direct contact with those privileged deportees, the Norwegians at Oranienburg.

In mid-June the dispatch of the parcels, accompanied like those of the Joint Committee by acknowledgement slips, met with unexpected success. This contrasted with the Foreign Ministry's silence over the principle of delivery checks. For of the fifty packets sent out, thirty receipts signed by the addressee were to come back. So the experiment planned at the end of 1942 and the beginning of 1943 seemed about to succeed, as was noted in the bulletin of triumph which Schwarzenberg sent to Huber on 11 August and which marked the beginning of the systematic dispatch of parcels to the concentration camps, as described in the next chapter.[38]

But before leaving this sequence of Committee decisions, marked by the note of 24 September 1942 and the adoption of proposals for concrete action on 30 December, we need to return to the Jewish issue to evaluate what effect these various decisions had. The business of the deportees was raised, some documents suggest, merely in order to get round the German refusal to enter into discussions about the Jewish problem. Here a question arose, and it was put by Huber himself on 27 January 1943, that is at the time when the aid effort to the camps was getting under way: did this mean that the ICRC – which from then on was going to concern itself with deported Jews not because they were Jewish but because they were deportees – was about to extend its solicitude to all Jews? The Coordinating Committee responded positively while refusing both to limit itself to the problem of the Jews and to compromise the whole of its activities for their sake.[39] This stand was not as contradictory as might at first appear, for it implied different theatres of operation. It was in any case followed by two concrete decisions, one relating to emigration possibilities, which could arise in Hungary and Romania, and the other to aid.

The emigration situation in these countries will be dealt with in later chapters; suffice it for the moment to stress the significance, tactical in a way, of the decision that had just been taken. Until then the question of racial and political persecution had been approached and dealt with by the ICRC in relation to the Third Reich. Certainly Germany made its weight felt throughout Europe; but seeing the problem from an exclusively German perspective could lead to the neglect of possibilities for action in at least some countries allied to the Reich and even in certain of its satellites. So the new European approach to persecution resulted in two concrete measures. De Steiger, an ICRC delegate in Bucharest working for the Joint Aid Commission, received instructions, worded with great care, to enquire into what help was necessary and possible in Transnistria and what possibilities of emigration existed. At the same time the idea of a mission to south-eastern Europe, which had been abandoned in the autumn of 1942, was revived, and led in May and June 1943 to David de Traz and ICRC member Edouard Chapuisat being sent to a series of capitals, mainly to strengthen links with national Red Cross societies and governments, to find out about local situations and needs, and to remind people of the existence and importance of the ICRC. In most of the countries visited – Hungary, Slovakia, Romania, Bulgaria and Croatia – the two men met the top political leaders, like prime minister Miklos Kallay in Budapest, the Romanian *Conducator* Marshal Ion Antonescu and his foreign affairs minister Mihaï Antonescu, as well as King Boris of Bulgaria and his prime minister Bodjan Filoff. In all these countries the Jewish question was raised and inspired the recommendations which Chapuisat and de Traz formulated on their return concerning the posting of ICRC delegates to Hungary, Slovakia and Bulgaria and the expansion of ICRC representation in Romania.[40] But everywhere they went the two emissaries also reminded the national Red Cross societies that it was their responsibility to aid political prisoners and victims of racial persecution in their own countries.

This emphasises, once again, that the 27 January 1943 decision did not represent a break with the ICRC's previous policy and attitude. True, the war situation had radically altered traditional conditions of internment. For this reason the instructions given to delegates could no longer take account of all existing categories of victim. By definition none could remain outside the Red Cross's remit, and no place of detention was excluded on principle from the ICRC's mission, but there had to be different levels of responsibility. That at least was what the leading members of the Committee kept repeating. What was true of the 15 May 1942 meeting, a meeting that went in for adjustments to, rather than any reappraisal of, basic ICRC aims, remained true in early 1943, in spite of the decision to do more for administrative detainees and Jews. On the issue of the deportation of the Salonika Jews (March–May 1943) which so violently upset the deputy-delegate there, Roger Burkhardt, that the Germans declared him *persona non grata*, Schwarzenberg stressed that the ICRC could do nothing to prevent it and so did not wish to embark on a démarche over it. It was up to the Greek Red Cross to see that food was distributed to those who risked starvation. The most the ICRC could do was to speak to the different Jewish organisations represented in Geneva to see if they could send a little money. To go beyond that was to overstep the limits the Bureau had set itself at its last meeting.[41]

Words and deeds

In the autumn of 1942, after much dithering, the ICRC had therefore turned its attention to the plight of detainees in concentration camps, amongst whom were Jews, by suggesting full assimilation – or if that were not possible, close comparison – with civilian alien internees. By giving up hope at the end of 1942 of getting a reply which was bound in any case to be negative, the ICRC in a way withdrew its own note. Until October 1944 it would not again raise the issue in a formal démarche, but was content from time to time to remind the Germans, in vain, of its concern, by mentioning the visits it carried out in several Allied countries to German civilian internees held as suspects or saboteurs and handed over for this reason to the police and not the Foreign Ministry.

Diplomatic démarches were then replaced by the sending of parcels to concentration camps: a concrete humanitarian gesture was substituted for unattainable legal protection. The effort to bring some relief from hunger, cold and isolation says something for the Red Cross in the conditions of silence – *Nacht und Nebel* – imposed by the sheer arbitrariness of totalitarianism. But proper recognition of such useful charity and of the succour it brought should not preclude its political evaluation, and that is the subject of this closing section.

The sending of food parcels to the concentration camps gave new impetus to the ICRC's efforts to enter them, since the Germans said no to any effective system of checking delivery and only tolerated the return of acknowledgement slips, sometimes signed by the addressees individually or collectively, and sometimes by the SS. In autumn 1942 Marti, in his discussions with Sethe about the 24 September note, had asked to be allowed to carry out a kind of test visit to Theresienstadt. His request was music to the ears of the SS, since the camp had become a kind of model institution, designed to mislead foreign visitors about racial extermination. The visit to Theresienstadt carried out by Walter Hartmann and his deputy Heinrich Niehaus in June 1943, about which the two representatives of the German Red Cross leaked information later, was part of a strategy of disinformation going up as far as Eichmann, if not beyond, and aimed among others at the DRK, the ICRC and the Vatican, which was also seeking authorisation for a visit by Mgr. Orsenigo, the apostolic nuncio in Berlin.[42] It is quite clear that Marti was unaware of this plan, but his wide German acquaintance and thorough knowledge of the situation enabled him to avoid the trap in 1943. Contrary to their hopes, the Nazis were not able to welcome Burckhardt himself to Theresienstadt; instead all they got was one of the members of the Berlin delegation, Dr Maurice Rossel, who, standing in for Marti who was in Switzerland at that moment, finally, on 23 June 1944, made the visit that had been put off several times.

The Germans did their job well: the camp was full of flowerbeds, and the staging was convincing. Rossel was not alone; two Danes, representing their government and the Danish Red Cross Society, were also present to find out about 400 Danish Jews who had recently been deported (a Swedish representative was also expected, but did not arrive). The three visitors were shown around by officials of the DRK, the Foreign Ministry and the RSHA, led by legation councillor Eberhardt von Thadden, the man who was responsible for liaison between the Foreign Ministry and Eichmann's RSHA Office in charge of Jewish questions, IVB4. They visited the old walled town, which had 35,000 inhabitants at the time, and spoke to members of the Council of Elders including its so-called chairman Paul Eppstein, and took photos. The inspection began about midday and ended with a dinner in their honour given in Hradkany Castle by the *Reichsprotektor* Karl-Hermann Frank, and a stroll through Prague the next day, Sunday.[43]

As already noted in chapter 2 (p. 44), Rossel promised the SS not to make public what he had seen.[44] His assertion that the ghetto was a permanent destination and not a mere transit camp – a claim in any case belied on the spot when the Danish envoys noticed the disappearance of a quarter of the people they were looking for – was immediately put in doubt by Schwarzenberg, who without knowing it showed the same scepticism as the Swiss consul in Prague after his meeting with Rossel. (There is evidence, however, that Rossel merely reported what he had seen, and was well aware of the carefully orchestrated nature of his visit.[45]) For all that Schwarzenberg let certain Jewish representatives in Geneva, like Gerhart Riegner, see the report. So the question arises as to how the two apparently contradictory attitudes should be interpreted. It may be that the ICRC's refusal to pass on officially the information it had gathered can be explained by the doubts surrounding certain passages in the report. It seems clear in fact that headquarters did not wish to make its mind up on the basis of a single visit, nor to allow the Germans a propaganda advantage (the deputy head of the press in the Reich had already exploited the visit in media terms). With regard to the chief purpose of his journey, checking on the parcel distribution in the concentration camps, Rossel gained no tangible information; his visit served merely to confirm the ICRC's doubts about the forwarding of surplus aid to camps in Upper Silesia like Auschwitz and Birkenau, a concession Hartmann claimed to have secured a year before.[46]

So getting into other camps remained a prime necessity. In the spring of 1944 a new opportunity offered itself when the Berlin delegation learned of the existence at Bergen-Belsen of a special Jewish camp consisting of people seeking emigration and holding *ad hoc* papers, genuine or forgeries, and of prominent Jews whom the Nazis hoped to exchange. From March to November 1944 Marti redoubled his démarches at the Foreign Ministry, the obvious interlocutor given the make-up of the camp's population. But the Ministry finally had to admit that it could not overcome the RSHA's intransigence. This did not discourage Schwarzenberg, who exhorted Marti to persevere in the task, even though the ICRC needed a more general authorisation to visit the camps before it could make up its own mind and in due course publish its views on the treatment of internees.[47]

It is true that from spring 1943 onwards, Marti, having failed to get Foreign Ministry permission to enter the camps, but encouraged by his contacts with the Oranienburg Norwegians, took it upon himself to get directly in touch with those in charge of some of the camps on the grounds that he needed to check parcel distribution there. In a year, until May 1944, he went in this way to Ravensbrück, Oranienburg, Dachau, Natzweiler and Buchenwald, and during 1944 the Berlin delegation continued and increased this activity. These discussions with camp commandants were not visits, and were aimed above all at gaining information about the nationality, number and names of detainees authorised to get parcels, but this did sometimes make it possible for the Red Cross to supplement the lists drawn up on the basis of the acknowledgement slips. Sometimes these came back signed by several detainees, and not just by the addressee, so that lists could also be added to in this way.

The exact number of those who received parcels, and even the number of detainees who made their names known to the ICRC, cannot now be ascertained. The International Enquiry Service at Arolsen today holds 96,184 receipts, to which should be added 20,070 supplementary signatures appearing on some of the slips. There is nothing to prove that this represents the grand total of receipts returned to Geneva; besides, some of the names occur twice or more, which one would expect, given that some detainees regularly received parcels. But ICRC sources give the number of parcels sent between November 1943 and May 1945 as anything from 750,000 to 1,112,000, the higher figure being given in the 1948 General Report. Because of German opposition, especially from summer 1944 onwards, a large number of both individual and collective parcel shipments were never acknowledged, a fact confirmed by complaints and comments from the Special Aid Division and the Berlin delegation. In November 1944 a breakdown by nationality drawn up by the Concentration Camp Parcels Service at M. Chenevière's request listed a total of only 9,525 names, of which 3,799 were Polish, 1,894 Norwegian, 1,641 French, 595 Dutch, 522 Jewish (with no other indication), 467 British, 202 Yugoslavian, 27 Czech, and so on. From this and other fragmentary information I have managed to glean and collate, it can be seen that the number of people located – not to be confused with the number of detainees who may have received one parcel or more – constitutes only a small percentage of the concentration camp population which, according to Nazi figures, amounted to some 715,000 people in January 1945. The system became more efficient, apparently, in the closing months of the war, in spite of the growing disruption of food supplies, especially, the documents show, in big camps like Buchenwald, Dachau and Ravensbrück. But the shipments relate in practice only to detainees under SS regimes I and II, and not to severe punishment prisoners in the 'Night and Fog' category, or those deported to Mauthausen.

As Hartmann promised, the DRK, or more precisely its Enquiry Bureau headed by Eduard Grüneisen, began from spring 1943 onwards to accept from the ICRC lists of deportees being sought, provided that the requests appeared to emanate from families. Of course not many replies were received. At the end of May 1943, the French Section of the Agency, the only one to have kept statistics in this area, noted that it was dealing with 1,441 cases in prisons and concentration camps, of which 61 per cent were Jewish, and that 713 enquiries had been made to the DRK up till then with a 37 per cent response rate.[48] At the beginning of 1944, the Agency estimated at 20 per cent the proportion of replies received in Geneva, taking the form, most of the time, of a notification of death or a statement that the person was still alive.

But as will be recalled, the 1942 interruptions concerned Jews above all. On this score the situation remained tragically blocked, since the quest for information, highly risky in Germany's allies or satellites, was more or less impossible in the Reich and the eastern territories, since the DRK got no information from the competent authorities. The ICRC's MCI (Miscellaneous Civilian Internees) service, which, since the return of index cards on administrative internees and Jews to the national agencies, handled only the cases of German, Austrian, Czech and stateless Jews, could not in practice ask anything of the ICRC's Berlin delegation, or find anything out except some details from Theresienstadt which came to it via the Reichsvereinigung der Juden. One of the paradoxes of the Final Solution is that the central organisation imposed by the Nazis on German Jews survived the almost total extermination of those it was put in charge of. So the MCI had to content itself with enriching its card index; by the spring of 1943 it contained nearly 40,000 names.

Finally, at the end of 1943, the German Red Cross asked the ICRC to indicate, on requests for information about missing people in occupied territories, if the person concerned was Aryan or not. The Central

Agency agreed to this because it meant cases could be dealt with more rapidly, but it also entailed the almost total abandonment of the Jews, who were treated henceforth according to blatantly racial criteria.[49] Moreover, in so doing it gave up until 1945 all hope of gleaning in spite of everything some information, by playing for instance on confusions of surname or location. At the end of 1944 the ICRC, noting the almost total blockage over the return of acknowledgement slips for concentration camp parcels, also decided to stop drawing up and sending to national Red Cross societies and the French POW Ministry lists of detainees enquired after or located, confining itself from then on to letting families know whether prisoners were alive or dead (on the basis either of acknowledgement slips, or of information sent via the DRK or obtained from any other source) without indicating their whereabouts.

All in all the sending of parcels to concentration camps, like its search activity in general, had contradictory effects on the ICRC's policy and attitudes towards victims of racial persecution and concentration camp detainees. In particular, the parcels scheme undeniably constituted a breakthrough in the domain of aid to victims, both materially and morally, and its significance for those who benefited from it should not be underestimated. However, in the eyes of leading figures it became an end in itself and its success overrode every other consideration. And finally it must be said that this aid work, which required much effort to get going and carried out, but which affected relatively few people considering the huge numbers of those imprisoned and persecuted, tended in the minds of some to get substituted for the rescue operation that the situation cried out for.

Even more generally, the pragmatic and practical approach adopted in spring 1943 allowed the ICRC to undertake several actions in favour of Jews and concentration camp detainees, especially in the Reich's allies and satellites, without calling into question either legally (which was not in its power) or politically the doctrinal framework and priority objectives of the Red Cross. This resulted, where the Reich was concerned, in the abandonment of, or failure until the summer of 1944 to take into consideration, any other angle than that of civilian alien internees held by a belligerent, and therefore any interlocutor other than the Foreign Ministry, to the detriment of another approach, that of political prisoners, which could have drawn inspiration from the reflections and principles of the 1930s and which would have pointed the ICRC in the direction of other power centres, like the police or the Justice Ministry. It was not until March 1945 that Burckhardt, by meeting Ernest Kaltenbrunner, the all-powerful head of the Reich Central Security Office (the RSHA), followed up in a way Marti's recommendations of summer

1942. It is of course a matter of supposition whether an approach to the problem through an initiative on behalf of political prisoners would have led to a different result. What is certain, on the other hand, is that this path was not followed, nor even really explored, and that the very success of the parcels scheme was probably not unconnected with this paralysis of imagination and initiative.

So until autumn 1944 delegates on the ground received difficult instructions. On the one hand, traditional missions under the Conventions had to remain at the centre of their activities. On the other hand, and according to circumstance, they acted, in the name of humanity, for all war victims, without endangering the overriding interests of POWs and civilian internees.[50] In these circumstances there were tensions, inevitably, between headquarters and certain particularly active delegates and those who reacted strongly to the sufferings of ill-treated civilians. A later chapter gives some examples of local difficulties, especially in Romania, Hungary and Italy, which were to last until the moment when Jean-Etienne Schwarzenberg himself, at the end of September 1944, suggested new instructions to take account of the political changes under way.[51]

The concentration camps parcels initiative, aid to the Jews in several countries, and the maintenance of traditional priorities allowed the ICRC to act in favour of new groups of victims while remaining true to its doctrine, respecting the Geneva Conventions, and maintaining neutrality, on which its credibility rested. But in embarking on an aid programme the ICRC took another risk, that of seeming unequal to the tragedy being played out; all the more so since it could not publicise widely the dispatch of parcels to concentration camps in case the Nazi central authorities put a stop to a practice tolerated but never clearly approved. Moreover, the public condemnation of the activities of a single belligerent, without reference to an international agreement, and without any possibility of making enquiries on the spot, seemed a gesture so risky as to be undertaken only if the situation became desperate. Gerhart Riegner, according to his own statement, agreed this with Burckhardt in November 1942. A public condemnation of the massacre of the Jews had therefore to be avoided, even though this meant that the time would inevitably come when no hope was left of being able to do anything about it. For different reasons the right moment for speaking out never came, either for Max Huber or Carl J. Burckhardt, whereas, for the Jewish organisations, the evidence of the Final Solution was soon to require that the Red Cross undertake not only material gestures but also speak out both as the world's conscience and in the name of its ideal of assistance to all victims of armed conflict.

During the war Burckhardt apparently remained on close terms with his colleague at the Advanced International Studies Institute, Paul Guggenheim, and above all with his former pupil, Gerhart Riegner, who said later how useful the information he had received had been. In spite of that, relations after 1942 between the ICRC and the Jewish organisations were not only to intensify but also – with some of them – to become increasingly strained.

On the one hand, indeed, the ICRC and the Joint Aid Committee collaborated with several charitable organisations which, by using the former as intermediaries, were able to get millions of Swiss francs' worth of currency, food, medicines and clothing to the victims of persecution. Relations became particularly close with Saly Mayer, who lived in St Gall and was president of the Federation of Swiss Jewish Communities from 1936 to December 1942, and through him with the Joint and more sporadically with the OSE, the Relico (Aid Committee to Jewish People Caught Up in the War, set up in 1939 by the World Jewish Congress), the Swiss Aid Committee for Jewish Refugees Abroad (HIJEFS), and, where the question of emigration or exchanges was concerned, with the Jewish Agency for Palestine, and so on. But this collaboration did not always betoken confidence. When in December 1942, for example, the ICRC considered sending food aid to Theresienstadt and the Polish ghettos in the hope that a delegate could go there, it secured the financial support of the World Jewish Congress. But the following February no Jewish organisation was invited to hear Mlle Ferrière outline confidentially the actions envisaged on behalf of the victims of racial persecution in the eastern territories, in Romania and in Hungary. The only organisations present were those close to the ICRC, such as the Churches' Ecumenical Council, the YMCA, the International Aid Service for Emigrants or the International Union for Aid to Children.[52] Thus the ICRC had no intention of going beyond the narrow domain of material aid, in which it felt it could act without raising any issue of principle, nor did it have any intention of letting it be supposed that its aims and the basic principles of its activity were in any way affected by the fact that it was concerned with – and indeed sought to concern itself with – a wider circle of war victims. That is why, for example, it refused to enter into discussions when the World Jewish Congress sought its help in urging the governments and national Red Cross societies of neutral countries to open their frontiers more widely to persecuted refugees,[53] to go along with the American Jewish Congress which asked it to conduct an enquiry into the massacres in Europe,[54] or to associate itself in summer 1943 with the appeal that the World Jewish Congress intended to make to Roosevelt, Churchill and Stalin, the three leaders of the Allied coalition, that the Allies immediately put at the disposal of welfare organisations under the aegis of the ICRC the sum of five million pounds sterling for aid to the populations of occupied Europe. For it felt that if it gave its blessing in advance to such an initiative, it would be announcing a change of policy and would risk annoying the Anglo-Americans because of the blockade and giving the impression of making overtures to the Soviet Union. Max Huber concluded that the refusal by one of the Allies of the proposal would be particularly damaging to the ICRC if it had already given it its blessing.[55] These hesitations also led the ICRC to vet carefully the information it passed on, and over events in Hungary in spring 1944 even to stop passing intelligence altogether to the World Jewish Congress.[56] It is true that national governments placed similar restrictions on information, as Riegner, for example, found out to his cost after passing on to Washington, through the US legation in Berne, his reports of late January 1943 about the situation in Transnistria.

Burckhardt's personal relations with Riegner, which were resumed in late 1942 after a few years' interruption, made no difference, therefore, any more than did the creation of the Special Aid Division in March 1944. While seeking to paper over the deep cracks in the Jewish world over the question of increasing the efficacy of aid (as in summer 1944 in the case of Hungary), the ICRC obviously felt more at ease with associations like the Joint, dedicated to concrete aid, and therefore ready to embrace its line of prudent and discreet activity, than with organisations like the World Jewish Congress, which demanded the setting up of rescue missions and recourse to political means. Until the end of spring 1944, the principled position of the ICRC did not vary, in spite of detailed substantiated reports then circulating about Hungary and Auschwitz. In face-to-face discussions with Gerhart Riegner and the Czechoslovak minister Jaromir Kopecki, Schwarzenberg reiterated on 27 June 1944 that the ICRC could not protest to the Germans about the Jews, because – as interested parties abroad clearly failed to understand – the ICRC lacked official channels of any kind to communicate with the German authorities about the Jews. If the United States wished to do something for the Jews, Schwarzenberg went on, they should go through the Protecting Power acting as intermediary, and offer a *quid pro quo*; but whatever they did they should do it quickly. All the ICRC could offer was to transmit these reports to certain German authorities and the German Red Cross. Kopecki agreed with Schwarzenberg and undertook to send to the ICRC an extract from the reports of Rudolf Vrba and Fred Wetzlar so that these could be forwarded to the German Red Cross.[57]

If the information about the concentration and extermination camps did not in itself cause a change of heart in the ICRC, the changing fortunes of war did justify in the summer of 1944 a gradual re-evaluation of its aims and objectives. The Allied victory was fraught with danger not only for the traditional position of Switzerland in Europe and especially for its neutrality, but also for the ICRC, as was seen in 1919. The attitude of the United States and therefore of the powerful American Red Cross almost spelt the end of the ICRC and a complete overhaul of the Red Cross's world.[58] The success of the parcels to the concentration camps initiative and the probability of speedy victory in the West increased the pressure on the ICRC to approach things anew, to make a protective gesture for once. France was particularly interested in this, since tens of thousands of its citizens were languishing for various reasons in concentration camps. The United States, which had taken upon itself, with the creation of the War Refugee Board, a particular responsibility for the Jewish question, was urging the ICRC to move in the same direction. The Reich was enfeebled and on the defensive; it would perhaps now show more understanding. The Swiss authorities, finally, pressed the ICRC to act, to widen its scope and to raise itself to the level of energetic action demanded by a continent once again at war.[59] In 1944, therefore, the ICRC's commitment in Hungary, which paralleled that of Switzerland's, heralded a new stage in activities undertaken on behalf of the victims of persecution and the inmates of the concentration camps.

4   Ways and means

What we have been looking at so far in the way of démarches planned or undertaken was, strictly speaking, a diplomacy of charity. But the ICRC still had other ways of getting things done. It is tempting to divide them into two broad categories, aid on the one hand, bringing help to victims, and rescue on the other, starting with the protection of individuals. In reality the two categories got mixed up. When it became clear that protection was impossible, and rescue even more so, the Red Cross turned to trying to give help in the form of consignments of food, clothing, drugs and medicines. While this assistance in kind was invaluable, especially towards the end of the war when the camps were suffering from malnutrition and overcrowding, it served also as a kind of substitute for the protection denied to many detainees. After all, deportees who were meant to disappear, those in the *Nacht und Nebel* category in particular, and Jews dumped in extermination camps precisely in order to be exterminated, were forbidden to receive parcels. But aid also served as a means of rescue which the ICRC hoped to carry out among certain allies of the Reich such as Romania and Hungary. That is why the present chapter concentrates on various forms of material assistance sent by the ICRC and the Joint Committee of the International Red Cross.

As far as rescue was concerned the ICRC remained virtually powerless, since in matters of emigration and prisoner exchanges states were solely competent. Protection of POWs did still, however, constitute one of the Red Cross's fundamental activities. In the application of the Geneva Conventions, it clashed with the World Jewish Congress not only over the degree of danger run by Jewish POWs and civilian internees, but – more surprisingly – over the connection to be made between the probability of discrimination against this category and the scope of the POW code, which forbade any difference of treatment not based on rank, physical fitness or gender. Indeed, the ICRC refused to the bitter end to consider extending the definition of civilian internees to any groups other than those designated in the Tokyo draft convention, whereas if it could not decide to do so unilaterally, it could at least have proposed the change. On the other hand, it defended its right to intervene when the Nazis attempted to categorise Jews and deportees as criminals. But it did not find, nor apparently did it seek, in earlier deliberations of international Red Cross conferences, in human rights legislation in general, or, in their absence, in universal humanitarian principles, the legal basis for action on their behalf.

Concern for its responsibilities towards POWs and civilian internees, and perhaps too towards Russian and German prisoners on the Eastern Front, had an influence not only on what preoccupied the ICRC, but also on its choice of ways and means, as is proved by the decision not to launch in October 1942 a public appeal against human rights violations. But this famous episode also shows how the ICRC sought effective action based above all upon its neutrality between warring states and upon its moral authority in the world of the Red Cross.

The non-appeal of 1942

One of the basic reproaches made to the ICRC about its activity in the Second World War was its silence in the face of public concern about racial persecution and mass deportation. During the war the ICRC was urged from several quarters to make a public protest against crimes committed in this area by the Reich. The ICRC failed to respond, for a whole complex of reasons that need to be more closely examined.

As a neutral intermediary in time of war, the ICRC intended to remain the moral guarantor of the Geneva Conventions and more generally of humanitarian law. This role derived from its statutes[1] and was inspired by tradition and the lessons of history. During the First World War, the ICRC received several complaints from national Red Cross societies which it always passed on to the other side. In the name of its general right to take humanitarian initiatives, it also spoke directly to governments, to remind them of the stipulations of the 1906 Convention, and to suggest measures in favour of POWs or victims of war. It sometimes used diplomatic channels and sometimes it appealed directly to public opinion, as in the case of the solemn condemnation, on 6 February 1918, of the use of poison gas, which, as can be imagined, provoked a lot of controversy. Indeed, the attacks on it from all sides provided bitter confirmation of the ICRC's impartiality; but they also tended to reinforce its already considerable distrust of public declarations. In 1936 the Ethiopian government appealed for the first time to Article 30 of the Geneva Convention. Italian bad faith obviously made it impossible for the desired enquiry to be carried out and, once again, the

ICRC found itself 'taken to task by the warring factions and used in the propaganda war'.[2] Max Huber was confirmed in his extreme reluctance to engage in public controversy and in his conviction that the Red Cross did not exist to make declarations, take up positions, or pronounce judgement, but to do something concrete on behalf of victims. In a world deeply divided ideologically and less and less faithful to the human values associated with the Christian liberal tradition from which the Red Cross sprang, Huber felt that the capital of trust that the organisation had built up and that was, in the last analysis, the only resource this private body possessed vis-à-vis national governments and Red Cross societies, had become an even more precious commodity than in the past and should not be squandered. At the outbreak of war in 1939 the ICRC therefore made it clear that it would exercise the greatest restraint in carrying out its functions in respect of violations of humanitarian law, and that this activity would be relegated to second place behind the tasks defined by the Conventions and by its reputation for impartiality and neutrality. It would normally conduct investigations only about breaches of the Conventions, and would merely pass on complaints from national Red Cross societies. And lastly, while it refused in advance to turn itself into a committee of enquiry or arbitration tribunal, it would lend its good offices to the setting up of such bodies.

Behind this extreme caution, and this great mistrust of public pronouncements, lay two basic concerns: effective action on behalf of the victims, and the upholding of the authority of the ICRC in the world of the international Red Cross. The idea of speaking out when governments were silent or evasive, especially in Convention grey areas, was not totally abandoned; it served as the background to many discussions, particularly over categories of victims not fully covered by the Conventions. This happened, as we have seen, in 1935 in the case of political prisoners, and occurred again early in 1940 when governments were called upon to agree a ban on the aerial bombardment of civilian targets.[3]

The origins of the draft appeal on violations of human rights

When in mid-May 1942 the ICRC's leaders reconsidered their priorities, they could not ignore the appeals they had received and even the attacks made upon them over the increasingly brutal methods by which the war was being fought. The American and Swedish criticisms were not entirely disinterested, but what was of greater significance were the doubts which their silence gave rise to in Switzerland and which the army command drew their attention to.[4] Some members of the Committee itself, such as Colonel Guillaume Favre, who died shortly afterwards, wondered whether the time had not come to raise the ICRC's voice again, for example about aerial bombardment.

The Coordinating Committee, on which the leading members of the ICRC sat, was not convinced. The potential gains from a solemn condemnation of hostage-taking or aerial bombardment were so problematical when weighed against the risks and the virtual certainty of failure that the Committee thought it preferable to maintain a wait-and-see non-committal attitude. Nevertheless, at the end of June 1942 it instructed one of its secretaries, Jean Pictet, to draft a circular restating the basic principles of humanitarian law concerning hostages, the bombing of civilian targets, and so on.[5]

But as doubts remained about the advisability of issuing any declaration at all, the Committee decided as a last resort to consult the whole ICRC in writing about the document.[6] At the end of August 1942, a draft (numbered 3) was sent to all members. The covering letter set out the arguments: firstly those against sending such an appeal, at least in the near future, on the grounds that it would have no practical effect and risked compromising certain relationships; and secondly those that justified it by reason of the role the ICRC intended playing in the defence of humanitarian principles. The letter stressed that the point at issue was not the terms in which the appeal was couched, but whether it was advisable to issue it at all. The decision to be taken was an important one, although most of those consulted were not informed in detail of the problems of the hour nor of the démarches currently being undertaken. Indeed, the Coordinating Committee does not appear to have been particularly anxious to give rise to a wider discussion about a gesture described nonetheless as one of real gravity, since consultation, as we have seen, was by letter only. In the last resort the small ruling group would decide by interpreting the general feeling, a fairly common method of reaching decisions. This time Max Huber was not directly involved. Detained first by illness and then by convalescence at La Lignière near Nyon, he took no part in the discussions of September and October, and he indicated in advance that he would fall in with the majority. On the other hand, an actor of considerable weight was to emerge from the wings in the shape of the Swiss government itself.

Edouard de Haller had been an honorary member of the ICRC since his appointment in January 1942 to the newly created post of Federal Council delegate to international aid charities. As soon as he received it, he sent the draft to his brother-in-law, Pierre Bonna, head of the Foreign Affairs Division of the Political Department, whose arguments directly inspired the reply he sent a few days later. What is more, he sought actively to bring other members round to his point of view – people like Jacques Chenevière, Paul Logoz, his cousin Rodolphe de Haller, and Albert Lombard. As far as he was concerned (the same applied to Pierre Bonna, and probably to federal councillor Marcel Pilet-Golaz, the head of the Swiss diplomatic service), however skilfully it was drafted, the appeal would achieve nothing and would put in jeopardy the traditional charitable activities of the ICRC. If the ICRC considered it necessary to express an opinion, perhaps just with regard to its role as moral guarantor of humanitarian principles, why – Edouard de Haller wondered – did it not do so by intervening discreetly and directly with the government concerned? Even if, in drawing attention to the matter, it got no reply or was rebuffed, it would have done its duty, Edouard de Haller told Max Huber.[7]

At the end of September 1942 the ICRC secretariat had to accept that the majority of replies – in all, twenty-one members out of twenty-three, and three honorary members had written in – were more or less favourable to a public statement. This was a big surprise to Edouard de Haller and to Philippe Etter, the Swiss president that year, who in 1940 had replaced Giuseppe Motta on the ICRC. It was therefore decided, at their request, to abandon the written consultation and call a plenary session at which Etter would exceptionally be present. The summary of the replies sent to all members in advance of the meeting was a straightforward précis of the arguments without attribution to individuals, so as not to draw attention to the fact that in the camp of those opposing a public appeal the two most clear-cut replies were from the two people most closely associated with the Federal authority.[8] Their position was indeed a delicate one. At the same time, it coincided with that of the ICRC's leaders. Jacques Chenevière, for example, did not give his opinion in writing, but in close consultation with de Haller watered down, even emasculated, Jean Pictet's draft, if its author is to be believed. Carl Burckhardt, for his part, advocated a direct and discreet démarche to Berlin rather than sending a text which would put everyone's backs up, the British because of the reference to aerial bombardment, the Germans by reason of the allusion to deportations.[9] But in spite of that, or perhaps precisely because of this basic agreement, before the meeting de Haller came to dread being the victim of what he called 'a manoeuvre to lay the blame for the scuppering of the appeal on the shoulders of the Federal Council or the Political Department'.[10]

The non-appeal

The fourth draft differed from the third in matters of detail only; attached to it was a summary of opinions, none of which was attributed to individual members. First of all, the draft stressed the ICRC's concern to seek ways of mitigating the evils of war generally, either on its own initiative or in pursuance of powers delegated to it. The draft then referred to the appeal concerning the protection of civilian populations against aerial bombardment dated 12 March and 12 May 1940, the protests of all kinds reaching Geneva, and messages in the same vein from national Red Cross societies. So the ICRC was being called upon from all sides to intervene, but it could only do so on the basis of two fundamental principles: (1) absolute neutrality, and (2) the constant search for the most effective way of helping war victims. But fulfilling its practical obligations did not absolve the ICRC from the duty of expressing its concerns about the ever-increasing ferocity of the conflict in the air and of economic warfare. The draft then turned to the question of civilian deportees:

Alongside civilian internees proper, certain categories of civilians belonging to various nationalities are being deprived of their liberty for reasons connected with the state of war, and are being deported. Or they are being taken hostage and risk being put to death for acts of which they are usually not the perpetrators.

When certain categories of war victim are accorded favourable treatment in the framework of the Conventions, the basic reason for this is the same as the principle underlying humanitarian law, that civilians enjoy general immunity and can never be afforded worse treatment than people for the protection of whom it is felt that special stipulations need to be drawn up. Because people who have participated more or less directly in armed conflict are afforded guarantees, civilians in general should be even better protected.

The International Committee of the Red Cross therefore calls upon the warring powers to grant civilians upon whom they feel it necessary to impose certain restrictions the benefit of arrangements at least as liberal as those enjoyed by POWs and civilian internees. Such arrangements can be summarised chiefly as follows: safeguarding their life and health, early notification of their place of detention or internment, freedom under certain conditions for them to correspond with their families, and to receive aid parcels and visits from representatives of a Protecting Power or the ICRC. Such guarantees were provided for in the Tokyo proposals, adopted by the XVth International Conference of the Red Cross, and relate to the condition and protection of civilians of enemy nationality who find themselves on the territory of a belligerent or on territory occupied by him.

After once more rehearsing various problems connected with the treatment of POWs, the draft concluded by drawing attention to instances where the belligerents had shown a positive attitude, such as in extending to civilian aliens the principles of the POW code, in facilitating sea transport under Red Cross colours of aid for war victims, and in desisting thus far from the use of chemical or bacteriological weapons. The draft stressed the need always to apply the principle of reciprocity by treating as a whole the measures taken by each state to improve the victims' lot.[11]

The plenary session, held at the Metropole Hotel on Wednesday 14 October 1942 from 3 p.m. to 5 p.m., was chaired in Max Huber's absence by Edouard Chapuisat who, though not a member of the Coordinating Committee, kept in close touch with the work of the ICRC. Two members normally kept away by age (Heinrich Zangger) and the pressure of other commitments (Philippe Etter) were present. One by one each member set out his or her position, sometimes suggesting a situation half-way between solemn, public protest and no declaration at all, such as a document which might be published in the *International Journal of the Red Cross* and which could take stock, three years into the war, of the human rights situation. If those supporting a half-way house position are added to those firmly in favour, a clear majority was for an appeal. This majority included in particular the four women on the ICRC, Mme Frick-Cramer and Mlle Ferrière, Mlle Odier and Mlle Bordier, former members like Edmond Boissier and Paul des Gouttes, practising doctors like Alec Cramer, and diplomats like the former Swiss envoy in Rome, Georges Wagnière. But Philippe Etter and Edouard de Haller had nothing to worry about. The leading members – the people who actually ran the ICRC – stuck to their guns in resisting the proposal, thereby making it possible for Edouard Chapuisat to pull off what Edouard de Haller himself described as a 'first-class fudge'.[12] The minutes make no attempt to conceal the deft way in which the proposal was shelved. Mme Frick-Cramer was reduced to hoping that, as a matter of urgency, the ICRC would intervene directly on the subject of deportations and economic warfare. She was told that, like any other member of the ICRC, she was free to submit proposals to the Coordinating Committee about any aspect of the ICRC's activities. Throughout the meeting, no mention appears to have been made of the information in the possession of members like Burckhardt.[13]

Furthermore, no document has been found indicating that the ICRC was approached by the Allies (as the Vatican was) over the Allied appeal of 17 December 1942. It is true that the British Foreign Office was well aware how powerless the ICRC was in gaining access to the concentration camps.[14] But with regard to the advisability of a public appeal, it is clear from references to it in his correspondence with Huber in October and November 1942, that the 'handcuffs' crisis (see p. 66 above) was especially influential in dictating the attitude of Carl J. Burckhardt in particular.

Not wishing to lag behind

The war was continuing, and growing in scope; the number of civilian victims was rising; humanitarian rules were increasingly being flouted. In such circumstances, with the gap ever widening between human rights and the reality of the fighting, saying nothing led to others being prompted to speak out. The support given in spring 1943 by the Geneva Association of Places of Sanctuary to a Spanish initiative on behalf of bombed civilian populations upset the ICRC considerably because of the confusion in the mind of the general public between itself and this modest organisation.[15] The Bureau, which had taken over the role of the Coordinating Committee, chose in the end to take a stand not in the form of an appeal but of a circular to national Red Cross societies. This dealt not only with the tasks shouldered by the ICRC in pursuance of the Conventions, but also with the unjust sufferings inflicted on civilian populations, including the threat of chemical weapons, against which the International Committee wished to mobilise the national societies.[16] But if the recipient seemed clearly defined this time, and if all thought of an appeal to the public seemed to have been abandoned as a result, it remained to be seen whether making a stand in this way on present issues and possible future developments was the right thing to do. Philippe Etter, consulted once again in person,[17] Max Huber, Jacques Chenevière and Carl J. Burckhardt at the Bureau, were not against the idea, but neither did they did wish to go back on the negative decision taken by the ICRC in plenary session the previous 14 October. In the end a succinct telegram, set out in fairly general terms, was sent to the belligerent governments and copied to Red Cross societies on 23 July 1943. The text was published in the August 1943 issue of the *International Journal of the Red Cross*:

Faced with the horrors, sufferings and injustices of war, the guiding principle of the International Committee of the Red Cross has always been to make clear its moral position and its wish to bring succour by deeds rather than by words. However in messages to governments at the outbreak of hostilities in 1939 then on 12 March and 12 May 1940 the International Committee expressed views on war methods fully in line with its traditions. The Committee earnestly reminds all belligerents of the contents of these documents. Faced with the violence of the fighting the International Committee of the Red Cross wishes yet again to entreat the belligerent powers whatever military considerations dictate to respect man's natural right to be treated according to the law, without arbitrariness and without being held to account for actions he bears no responsibility for. It also requests the powers not to resort to unwarranted acts of destruction and above all not to pernicious forms of warfare banned by international law.[18]

In the autumn of 1943 the ICRC had to accept that while this text had perhaps not had any unfortunate consequences, despite the publicity given to it, it had not caused much of a stir either. The intensification of the war and more especially the balance of power within the Red Cross world demanded that the ICRC get the credit more explicitly for its gesture. Burckhardt in particular worried about the ICRC's standing at the end of the war; he feared there was a risk that its position would be less favourable than it had been after 1918. This was due in part, he felt, to the fact that the ICRC had not been able to publicise its activities sufficiently in foreign countries, and in part to the Red Cross League's skill in getting the credit for the work of the Joint Aid Committee, ironically a body masterminded by the ICRC.[19]

So it was decided (without going back to the full Committee) not only to send the governments a reminder so as to publicise the stand taken in the *Journal*, but also, at Max Huber's suggestion, to convey to them a new message banning reprisals against POWs in any shape or form and expressing considerable anxiety about 'the continual worsening of methods of warfare involving in various ways, and increasingly, civilian populations, and property of no military importance but often of irreplaceable cultural value'.[20] In this text, dated 30 December 1943, no special mention was made of humanitarian law, even less of deportations and concentration camps; chairman Huber nevertheless felt that this message replaced, in a way, the more general appeal that had been dropped. But when it was published in the *Journal* and released to the press, it aroused little interest. So in March 1944 the ICRC made up its mind to publish without comment the list of twenty-two countries who answered the appeal of 23 July 1943, chiefly the USA, the Latin American Countries, Italy, the Free French and a few European states, but neither the Reich, nor Great Britain and the Commonwealth, nor the Soviet Union.[21]

Clearly, the public appeal on human rights violations was a failure. According to its records, the ICRC sent some thirty-nine notes, telegrams, letters, appeals and circulars to governments and national Red Cross societies between 2 September 1939 and 21 May 1945. Most of this correspondence concerned the application of the Conventions, such as the note of 30 July 1943 about the exchange and hospitalisation of the sick and seriously wounded, or the appeal of 23 August 1943 on the status of POWs and civilian internees; it touched too upon the life of the

Red Cross, such as circular no. 365 of 17 September 1941 on the constitution and particular circumstances of national societies in wartime; and some of it dealt with the situation of civilians, such as the appeals of 12 March 1940, 23 July and 30 December 1943, which have already been looked at. But all this effort put into information and all these position papers have not in the eyes of posterity been able to erase the memory of the decision, taken on 14 October 1942, not to go ahead with a public appeal. Quite the reverse: they make it even harder, with hindsight, to understand that decision. Before the end of the war the ICRC's leaders realised this. But that did not make up for their original failure of nerve. When the camps were opened and the horrors they had concealed were there for all to see, the ICRC's discomfiture was analysed with authority and frankness by Jacques Chenevière in an unpublished text of 1946 which, he said, 'was the description of a tragic problem and not an act of self-justification':

People have expressed surprise that the ICRC did not protest publicly while there was still time. But what could it have protested about? Its own power-lessness? But all the states that were signatories to the Conventions knew the reason and yet failed to make any protest themselves. Could it have protested against the brutal treatment the deportees claimed they were suffering from? But the ICRC had no way of confirming, even partially, such statements. Besides, experience proved that public protests by the ICRC not supported by observations of its own were fruitless, doing more harm than good. In the absence of hard proof they were taken by the accused country as evidence of *a priori* bias, and put at once in jeopardy the other activities which the Red Cross was duty bound under the Conventions to carry out.

Protests can be the last resort of the weak. Or they can be a quick way of salving our conscience and giving us the illusion of having done something. Even then, anyone indulging in them needs to be totally free of obligations that imply effective action. Some will always say 'the public must be told'. But that often amounts to a call for reprisals, and the Red Cross must never take the risk of stoking a fire that is ever ready to flare up. So it was in silence, though with all its strength, that the ICRC laboured on behalf of the deportees.[22]

Aid and assistance

It is not my aim to recount in detail the history of the Red Cross's aid efforts during World War II, or even to present more than a general overview of it: the third volume of the General Report[23] and the Report of the Joint Aid Committee[24] provide a great deal of information on the subject. I want more simply to supplement what was said above about the concentration camp aid parcels scheme with an assessment of the help given to detainees and victims of persecution. Even then it needs be understood that the aid often consisted of a whole series of individual gestures, sometimes covert in nature, which it is impossible to quantify exactly; that it is not always feasible to determine precisely the status of those who benefited; and that in the case of Jewish victims a probably quite sizeable proportion of what was sent went astray or was stolen before it ever reached its destination (how much can only be guessed at).

General overview

According to the General Report, the ICRC's aid effort between 1939 and 1946, leaving aside gifts sent from person to person, can be grouped under four main headings according to the category of beneficiary: POWs and civilian internees benefiting from the 1929 Convention; German and Italian POWs and civilian internees similarly helped between 1945 and 1946; civilians supplied first by the ICRC and then from 1941 by the Joint Aid Committee; and finally detainees, Jewish or 'Aryan', in prisons and concentration camps.

The figures in the General Report show that the latter category received 6,836 metric tons of merchandise representing 1.6 million parcels (1,112,000 by 8 May 1945, according to the Geneva Report, three-quarters of a million according to other ICRC estimates). Compared with this, 400,000 tons of merchandise were sent to POWs and civilian internees at a total cost of three billion Swiss francs, and 93,518 tons were sent by the Joint Committee (between 1941 and 1945, so leaving out of account the year 1946, the most significant as far as the Joint Committee's work was concerned), at a cost of about 196 million Swiss francs.

The totality of aid operations is impressive and represented a considerable proportion of the ICRC's overall effort, both in material and strategic terms.

On the day Germany surrendered, the ICRC had twenty-one depots in Switzerland with a total capacity of 105,000 tons. Three ships bearing the insignia of the ICRC, the Red Cross flag marked with the words 'C. International', had been acquired by the Red Cross Transportation Organisation; together with trains and lorries, they ploughed the high seas and plied the land routes. Through the ports of Lisbon and Marseilles and, at the end of the war, of Gothenburg and Lübeck, food, clothing and medicines reached the continent and were distributed in the camps, except of course in Russia and the territories under its control.

This vast enterprise posed innumerable organisational and operational problems, notably in getting through the Allied blockade and the

German counter-blockade. For while parcels were shipped either in
bulk or in the form of standard individual packets, from families,
national Red Cross societies, charitable organisations and governments,
free of charge and without hindrance, in accordance with the 1929
Convention and arrangements made for POWs and civilian internees,
forwarding supplies from overseas to civilian populations, with the
exception of medicines, came up against objections from the British and
the Americans, who were afraid that humanitarian aid would be diverted
to assist the Reich's war effort. The Reich, for its part, had encouraged
Burckhardt's aid scheme aimed in the summer of 1940 at the populations of France and Belgium, and later supported the creation of the
Joint Aid Committee. In a declaration dated 11 January 1941, it
guaranteed that gifts in cash and in kind for needy civilians in the
occupied territories would be collected from neutral countries and
distributed free of both duty and shipping charges by the German Red
Cross. Throughout the war, therefore, and even after 8 May 1945, the
Joint Committee and the ICRC conducted endless difficult negotiations
to secure the principle of their freedom of action, and the British
consistently turned it down, even though the discussions were closely
connected with those engaged in by Switzerland in order to protect its
own supplies and maintain, despite its encirclement by German-occupied Europe, minimal trade relations with the rest of the world. All this
quibbling hampered, at least until 1945, the Joint Committee's effectiveness, and sometimes disheartened both donors and recipients. But it did
occasionally get results. For instance, Burckhardt persuaded Vichy and
London to allow the ICRC to send help to the refugee camps in the
south of France where many stateless Jews were held. Unfortunately the
US entry into the war vitiated this effort to some extent. Later, too, the
Ministry of Economic Warfare relaxed its demands in respect of the aid
effort in Greece carried out jointly by the ICRC and Sweden. But
otherwise the Ministry continued to insist on making the issue of
navigation certificates subject to strict criteria, such as the nationality of
the recipients, the nature of the aid, and, most importantly of all, how
effective were the checks that supplies did not fall into the wrong hands.
The Joint Aid Commission therefore acquired its merchandise through
purchases in Switzerland, in neutral countries and in south-eastern
Europe. This was not the complete answer, since the Committee had no
funds of its own and donor monies too had to cross the Allied blockade
on financial transactions. In the main these were effected through the
Bank of International Settlements, the National Bank of Switzerland
and private banks, assisted by the ICRC's delegates in the various
capitals.

The first parcel distribution to POWs was carried out in 1939 by the same people who had been responsible during the Spanish civil war for the aid, paid for by donations, that the ICRC had sent to both sides. This aid service grew considerably as the war went on and was restructured several times. An Aid Committee, chaired by an ICRC member, Mlle Bordier, took charge from 1942 onwards of general policy and the coordination of the work of executive bodies like the Aid Division (run by Hans Wasmer), the Transportation and Communications Division (run by Walter Fülleman, answerable in its turn to a Transportation Committee), the agencies dealing with individual aid, pharmaceuticals, intellectual assistance, and so on.

In the summer of 1941 a second organisation was formally set up. The Joint Aid Committee of the international Red Cross was, as we have seen, Burckhardt's political brainchild. He chaired and motivated it. It was run by Robert Boehringer, an industrialist from the Basel region who had recently acquired Swiss nationality, and was registered as an association under Article 60 of the Swiss civil code. Its work and very existence made it closely dependent on the ICRC but did not put a strain upon its budget, since the Joint Committee deducted 2 per cent for administration from the purchasing funds it received and 1 per cent from the gifts in kind that it forwarded.

So much, then, for the general framework within which aid to concentration camp detainees and to the Jews was organised.

The Concentration Camp Parcels Scheme

On 11 August 1943 Schwarzenberg reported to chairman Huber on the success of the experiment conducted since mid-June. As we have seen, out of fifty food parcels sent to Norwegian detainees in concentration camps, more than thirty receipts came back signed, a percentage all the more remarkable for the fact that several addresses held by the ICRC were already old. Further shipments confirmed this early success; by mid-November a total of 882 parcels had been sent to the Reich, made up largely of 500 to Dutch prisoners, 269 to Norwegians, 52 to Poles and 31 to Jews (whom the statistics do not further differentiate). The camps affected included Oranienburg-Sachsenhausen, Buchenwald, Dachau, Ravensbrück, Neuengamme and Stutthof, as well as several prisons.[25]

Things were sufficiently advanced in the autumn of 1943, therefore, for the problem of organisation to need looking into. The first shipments were undertaken by the Individual Aid Agency with logistical support from the Joint Aid Committee, which made up the parcels and sent them off, and with financial backing in the form of a loan from the ICRC. It was undeniably necessary for the ICRC to hold on to responsibility for the operation, not just because of difficulties over financing (the ICRC had no funds to devote to it) but also because the matter was politically sensitive. So an agency attached to Burckhardt, called 'Colis aux camps de concentration' (Concentration Camps Parcels Scheme), or CCC, was set up. It was headed by Jean-Etienne Schwarzenberg, who wrote soon afterwards:

It was something of an adventure, since we were departing from the traditional basis of our work as defined by the Conventions. That was indeed the chief reason for not entrusting this new task to the Aid Division, which was concerned above all with individuals to whom the Convention applied, at least by extension. That is why we had to file the information we had managed to obtain and exploit it in a strictly confidential manner, especially deportees' names. We had to make sure for example that any information given to families was not at variance with German regulations.[26]

With the creation in the spring of 1944 of a Special Aid Division (Division d'assistance spéciale, or DAS) to take over the CCC's role, operations expanded considerably. The prospect of an Allied victory and the future shape of postwar Europe loomed ever larger in people's minds. Jewish organisations brought increasing pressure to bear on the ICRC, and the establishment by President Roosevelt on 22 January 1944 of the War Refugee Board created an important partner and interlocutor for the Red Cross, one the ICRC could not ignore since it was directly answerable to the White House.

The DAS was entrusted by the Bureau on 15 March 1944 with responsibility for 'all collective and individual aid operations on behalf of civilians in belligerent and occupied countries held in an enforced place of residence (deportees, political prisoners, administrative detainees and Jews) who do not qualify for protection under the Conventions'.[27] The Division was answerable to a committee chaired by Albert Lombard which, apart from Jacques Chenevière, was made up of members of the Secretariat, such as Roger Gallopin, Jean-Etienne Schwarzenberg, Hans Bachmann, and of Robert Boehringer, head of the Joint Aid Commission. Mme Frick and Mlle Ferrière, 'specialists' in refugee and civilian internee matters, and Mlle Bordier and Mlle Odier, the ICRC's experts on aid, did not sit on this committee. Jean-Etienne Schwarzenberg took over the running of it, and acted as liaison with the other ICRC services, the Joint Aid Commission and the Central Agency, and with outside bodies like the High Commission for Refugees, the War Refugee Board, the American Jewish Joint Distribution Committee, and so on. The DAS benefited from the organisational abilities of Marcel Leclerc, a retailer by profession and a Swiss of Romanian origin, whose wife was Jewish. It quickly became apparent, however, that its brief was too wide, as Schwarzenberg himself admitted, especially given the personnel and funds it had at its disposal. As so often in the ICRC, the Division suffered throughout its existence from chronically under-resourced administration, and this led to difficulties for which it would be criticised within the institution when its work came to be evaluated.

The November 1943 statistics bear this out. The German authorities would only allow food parcels to be sent to those not subject to a strict punishment regime, whose names and place of detention were known to the ICRC, which boiled down to people who had already received parcels occasionally from their relatives. So the Concentration Camps Parcels Scheme was in danger of going round in circles and benefiting those who least needed it. It had become clear that, assuming the Germans were willing to provide some sort of statistical breakdown by nationality, making shipments to categories of prisoner rather than to individuals was the only way of breathing new life into the enterprise. In mid-November 1943 Roland Marti and Luc Thudicum met the commandant of the camp at Oranienburg-Sachsenhausen and got him to agree to the dispatch of such collective parcels; and, thanks to the autonomy enjoyed by camp commandants in the Nazi concentration camp system, a similar concession was obtained for Ravensbrück. Encouraged by this and giving up, with the ICRC's agreement, on attempts to establish direct contact with the internees themselves, the delegates turned this time not to the Foreign Ministry but direct to Gestapo headquarters in Albrechtstrasse. In vain, as Marti reported at the end of January 1944: he met with a blanket refusal to allow parcels to be sent other than to named individuals.[28]

But, as we have seen, this did not prevent the gradual development of collective mailings, thanks to contacts with camp commandants built up systematically by Marti and his colleagues throughout the Reich. At the end of May 1944, the deputy commandant of Sachsenhausen sent in confidence the numbers of French, Czech, Polish, Belgian and Norwegian prisoners allowed to receive parcels, and he too promised receipts. A few days later a similar understanding was reached with the commandant of Stutthof. Not every such contact was as positive, of course, and by no means all the promises were kept. As to how many parcels actually reached the prisoners, this depended on the attitude of the commandant and varied from camp to camp, but at the end of spring 1944 Marti was able to announce that he was in touch with the main KZ sites on the territory of the Reich: Ravensbrück, Oranienburg-Sachsenhausen,

Dachau, Natzweiler, Buchenwald and Stutthof. More interesting still is
the fact that parcels not distributed at Dachau because of the death of
the recipient were no longer returned to Geneva, as occasionally happened, but were handed to another prisoner of the same nationality
who, by returning the acknowledgement slip signed with his name,
could be added to the list of recipients. In other cases, the acknowledgement slips came back signed by several people.

So a process was started which grew steadily in importance. To the
names given by families, national Red Cross societies, governments in
exile and charitable organisations, were added the individual signatures
on the acknowledgement slips of personal or collective mailings. And
the problem of maintaining a balance between the requests received and
the funds placed by donors at the disposal of particular groups of
prisoners became acute. It may seem surprising that such an operation
could develop like this in a world of camps and prisons in which (leaving
aside the extermination camps to which access was obviously quite out
of the question) thousands of men and women suffered ill treatment and
hunger, but such was the logic of the system that the Nazis aimed to
offer a quality service to those entitled to receive it, as demonstrated by
the story of the three parcels addressed to Buchenwald that were
forwarded to Natzweiler to which the recipients had been transferred.[29]

The concentration camps in the East were not completely closed
either. In the spring of 1944, some 450 acknowledgement slips arrived
from Auschwitz which, as we have seen, was not exclusively an extermination camp; indeed the officials of the DAS did not know whether they
were dealing with a concentration camp or a labour battalion. They did,
however, know that Jews were being held there, so they asked Marti to
proceed cautiously to investigate on the spot, something which had to
wait until Maurice Rossel was able to make a visit at the end of
September 1944 (see p. 42 above).

The growth of the parcels operation brought the issue of the blockade
back to the fore from the beginning of 1944 onwards. In August 1943
Schwarzenberg had recommended contacting London and Washington
to suggest that the Allies agree to accept acknowledgement slips as
sufficient to authorise a lifting of the blockade, since that was the only
means of checking that aid was not being diverted which the Germans
were prepared to accept. This proposal met with no more success than
the ICRC's many previous démarches on the subject, in spite of the
support it gained from national Red Cross societies and the High
Commission for Refugees, and despite efforts on the same lines by
governments in exile in London.

The situation was therefore becoming dangerously tense. The way the

military situation was developing meant that the internal markets on the
continent (apart from Switzerland and the Balkan countries) where the
Joint Commission bought its supplies were shrinking rapidly. The need
to get food and clothing, that is to hold navigation certificates rather
than credits, was increasing. During the transfer to Switzerland by the
War Refugee Board of $100,000 from the American Jewish Joint
Distribution Committee, the ICRC managed to divert part of the
money to other than Jewish war victims by buying concentration camp
parcels and, more generally, pharmaceutical products. But it had no
success in persuading Britain and the United States to relax the
blockade, less because of the ineffectiveness of its delegations in London
and Washington than because of the simple fact that Britons and
Americans were few in number in the concentration camps and that the
economic weapon was of overriding importance in the eyes of the
maritime powers.

In the summer of 1944 the situation changed yet again. With the end
of the war in sight, the Allies were now less afraid of seeing aid to
concentration camps and the Jews helping the Nazi war effort. The
ICRC had shown that the acknowledgement slips and contacts between
its delegates and camp commandants made possible a reasonable check
on distribution, since it could even suspend shipments where supplies
were systematically looted by the SS, as it did, for instance, in the case
of Mauthausen. But, more importantly, it was able to prove to Jewish
organisations and the American government that alongside some significant achievements (in Romania and Hungary essentially) its main
effort on behalf of the Jews was focused on the Concentration Camp
Parcels Scheme. In the autumn of 1944, without backing down on the
principle, the Roosevelt administration agreed to modifications in practice by allowing through the blockade 260,000 three-kilogram parcels
donated by the American Red Cross as well as the use of 50 tons of
merchandise from the shipwreck in the Mediterranean of the *Cristina* to
make up another 25,000 parcels. Moreover, the American Jewish Joint
Distribution Committee and the World Jewish Congress paid the International Red Cross and other organisations like the Quakers and the
YMCA several hundred thousand Swiss francs to buy on the continent
the wherewithal to make up several tens of thousands more parcels.

In this new phase of its work the ICRC was running a dual risk: on the
one hand vis-à-vis the American Jewish organisations, who were quick to
draw up a list of camps to be aided that was a good deal more
comprehensive than the institutions already involved, on the grounds
that the latter held very few Jews, with the exception of citizens of neutral
countries or of the Allied powers;[30] and on the other hand, vis-à-vis the

Americans, by lending the parcels scheme an importance it did not possess, since it all depended on a tacit agreement with the Germans and more especially with the camp commandants whom the ICRC's Berlin delegation lacked the means (with its eight delegates, later increased to twelve) to meet as often as necessary.[31] The difficulties that arose in the autumn of 1944 (when some commandants refused to accept collective parcels and others stopped sending back receipts, when reception was interrupted at Auschwitz and Stutthof, and when attempts at contact with Bergen-Belsen failed) showed how much the operation did indeed depend on Nazi goodwill, and compelled the ICRC to take permanent precautions, such as in December 1944, for example, no longer passing on to national Red Cross societies lists of deportees drawn up on the basis of acknowledgement slips and restricting shipments to a few reliable camps like Buchenwald, Dachau and Ravensbrück.

After most of France had been liberated the ICRC found itself faced with a paradoxical situation. The Allied governments, at the forefront of which was the new French administration, urged it to redouble its efforts and forward the same number of collective parcels as the regular individual ones, while the Germans were getting less and less cooperative.[32] The need among other problems to unblock the parcels system finally led both the Berlin delegation and the ICRC chairman to meet the top police authorities in the spring of 1945.

Aid to the Jews

The wartime effort on behalf of the Jews raised particular problems, of course. Jewish organisations had to accept that part of the aid placed at the Joint Commission's disposal was going to be allocated to other categories of victim. On the other hand Jews also benefited from gifts made available to the ICRC by national Red Cross societies and other charitable organisations. Accounting today for all the original gifts would involve the enormously time-consuming task of reconstituting the details from documents in Geneva and New York, and would in any case be misleading, as would approaching the problem from the distribution end, since delegates often had to improvise with the support of the authorities on the ground, and sometimes in spite of them, as the reports and assessments sent in by the delegates at the ICRC's request make clear. So no attempt will be made here to draw up a precise list of aid, since even at the time the ICRC was not able to see the full picture, but I will try rather to outline the main operations undertaken by the ICRC from the documents by which the organisation itself accounted for its efforts with the aim of defending and illustrating its policy.

In the autumn of 1942 Geneva was being inundated with requests
that food, clothing and medicines be sent to persecuted Jews, not only
from organisations like the World Jewish Congress which hoped among
other things to be able to include all Jews in the lifting of the blockade
agreed in favour of civilian internees, but also from governments, like
the United States, who were alarmed at the recent round-ups in France.

At first sight, the Red Cross's reply was being dictated by its experiences in the immediate past. The British had refused early in 1942 to
allow the Joint Commission to set up a vast aid operation to the ghettos
and the Polish civilian population. Aid to Jewish internees and deportees
was well nigh impossible, as the démarches of recent months over
Compiègne had just shown. The Germans would not agree, even for aid
purposes, to the ICRC treating concentration camp Jews, including
those who were citizens of enemy countries, as internees. There was,
however, the odd chink of light. As we have seen (p. 93 above), the Joint
Commission succeeded, with Vichy's agreement and London's acquiescence, in supplying the camps in the south of France, which held
numerous Jewish internees, thanks to the checks made by its delegates
on the spot; it was able, as we shall see in the chapter on Poland, to
extend its work to the General-Government, distributing the food and
especially the medicines it received according to a formula that did not
exclude Jews at large or in ghettos; it even kept an eye to some extent on
the DRK's distribution slips from the Jüdische Unterstützungsstelle
(JUS, Jewish Assistance Office) in Cracow; and, last but not least, it
managed to get a toe in the door at Theresienstadt, a camp still not
clearly pinpointed in the outside world, by obtaining permission to send
in medical supplies.

In a note to the Coordinating Committee at the end of 1942,
Schwarzenberg was therefore being candid in recognising that if the
ICRC had up till then said no to calls for help, this was especially
because such work, falling outside the scope of its traditional mission,
could only be justified on humanitarian grounds, and because, he said,
'there is a great danger that the good relations the ICRC maintains with
the competent authorities in Germany will be compromised, to the
detriment of its normal work, if it insists too much on this delicate
question, so closely bound up with a central dogma of the totalitarian
regime'. The experiences of the Joint Commission during the last few
months did indeed seem less negative than the ICRC implied whenever
it was approached.

So Schwarzenberg, who had just been put in charge of Jewish affairs,
proposed that the feeding of the civilian population be stepped up, not
only at Theresienstadt but also in the Polish ghettos, and to that end

charities and national Red Cross societies be approached and asked to press governments and Jewish organisations to secure funds and exemptions from the blockade.[33] But, as we saw earlier (p. 79), Suzanne Ferrière agreed in February 1943 to organise on behalf of the ICRC an information session on these issues to which Jewish organisations were not invited, even purely charitable ones, although they had already responded to an ICRC appeal for funds.[34]

In line with its decision to attempt to get aid to concentration camp prisoners rather than press for a reply to its note of 24 September 1942, the Coordinating Committee too came round to the idea of stepping up aid to Jews, since the two went hand in hand: getting aid into concentration camps was a way of succouring the Jews. The World Jewish Congress, kept in the picture through Burckhardt's contacts with its head Gerhart Riegner, was therefore asked to contribute, and at once complied by announcing its intention of making $12,000 a month available if it was able to get the necessary exemptions from the Allies.[35] On a visit to Germany delegate-at-large Marcel Junod was also asked to take up once more the question of aid to the Jews (Marti being responsible for negotiations with the Foreign Ministry about aid to civilian aliens interned in concentration camps) by going on if possible to Prague and Cracow to make direct contact with local branches of the German Red Cross. His instructions for this mission – which was also concerned with the issue of the news that Jewish alien deportees should give their families – stressed that the ICRC could not turn down all approaches made to it without jeopardising the atmosphere of friendly collaboration between all national Red Cross societies, and they drew attention to the fact that the Germans had already given their agreement in principle to the Joint Commission's work.[36]

But Junod's mission came to nothing and for several months talks on aid to concentration camps made no headway. There was still the decision of 27 January 1943 to try and do something for Jews being persecuted in their own countries, outside the Reich and the territories it occupied, but it needs to be remembered that this measure was carefully hedged about to comply with the familiar principles that inspired it. The instructions sent to Vladimir de Steiger, the delegate dealing with the Transnistrian deportees, stressed the need to proceed cautiously and discreetly because of the danger of jeopardising the ICRC's purpose, which was covertly to include the Jews in aid schemes aimed at civilians in occupied countries.[37]

In May 1943, even the Jüdische Unterstützungsstelle had to suspend its activities, and failure seemed complete. Riegner and Paul Guggenheim went to see Burckhardt and reminded him of his plans and purposes of the preceding November. There was not much he could say in reply. He did draw their attention to the ICRC's view that the Jews deported to the East were undeniably civilian internees to whom the Tokyo draft applied; he then touched upon the difficulties he was encountering in his negotiations with the blockade authorities, and asked for the World Jewish Congress's help in persuading the Allies to grant navigation certificates on behalf of the Jews; but what was the point, he wondered, if in the end the Germans refused to play ball? According to Riegner's record of the discussion, the meeting concluded with Burckhardt agreeing to undertake a new démarche with Walter Hartmann, who was then on a visit to Geneva.

As only one way of proceeding still seemed possible – sending medicines and food, even in collective form, to Theresienstadt – it was tempting to concentrate all effort on that and even try to extend its possibilities. But to do so required, as an absolute minimum, permission being given for Marti to visit the camp, but the Foreign Ministry refused, just as it turned down his suggestion to widen the circle of beneficiaries of aid to include other camps such as Auschwitz and Birkenau. As for the German Red Cross, it passed on the authorities' claim that there was no shortage of food and medicines in the Jews' camps (described as 'work camps') so it was quite unnecessary to send any.[38]

Nevertheless, during his visit in mid-May 1943, Hartmann did seem keen to respond to the questions which Burckhardt had undertaken to put to him, and on his return to Berlin got permission to go to Theresienstadt with his deputy Heinrich Niehaus. While this convinced the ICRC of the DRK's goodwill, it was merely an aspect of the SS's clever use of this camp to pull the wool over everybody's eyes (see p. 73 above).

The trick did not, however, quite come off, since Hartmann's inspection on 24 June 1943 tended rather to increase the DRK's suspicions and fears about the fate of the Jews, at least if André de Pilar, who met Hartmann in Berlin shortly after his return from the camp, is to be believed. All in all, the DRK's visit to Theresienstadt enabled the ICRC to check that aid was getting through, thereby confirming the acknowledgement slips signed by the leaders of this bogus community, and it led Hartmann to ask the SS for permission to send on to the camps in the East, especially the Auschwitz complex, any overflow of aid from Theresienstadt.[39] But this démarche, much as it was to the credit of the humanitarian motives of some members of the German Red Cross, obviously had no more practical impact than the announcement of the resumption of the services of the Jüdische Unterstützungsstelle in the

General-Government: just one more lie put out by the Nazi propaganda machine following the massacre of the Jewish population there.

Up to the summer of 1944, the Joint Commission's work on behalf of the Jews can be summed up, according to a list Carl J. Burckhardt published at the time,[40] briefly as follows:

1) In France, blankets, clothing and food were sent to the camps in the south, where many of the internees were Jewish, and medicines and tonics to Montpellier and Chambéry.
2) In Holland, medicines were delivered to the Joodsche Rad vor Amsterdam and to the camps at Westerbork and Vught.
3) In Italy, a consignment of medicines was sent to the Delasem.
4) In Latvia, a case of vaccine went to the Riga ghetto's main hospital.
5) In Poland, there were several shipments between 1941 and 1943, especially of food and medicines.
6) In Slovakia, several parcels of medicines and tonics were dispatched.
7) In Slovenia, medicines were sent to the children of Ljubliana.
8) At Theresienstadt, medicines, tonics and condensed foods (milk and flour) were supplied.

In addition there was the work on behalf of the Transnistrian deportees, which began in November 1943 (aid and repatriation), and the Hungarian operation in autumn and winter of 1944–5, together of course with the Concentration Camps Parcels Scheme. In Romania and Hungary, as will be seen in ensuing chapters, the ICRC played a useful role too in the transfer to local Jewish leaders of funds collected by the American Jewish Joint Distribution Committee, the World Jewish Congress, and so on.

This last point is a reminder that the ICRC and Joint Commission served above all as proxies, since the bulk of the aid in cash and in kind that they received was entrusted to them by national Red Cross societies, governments and organisations for distribution to specific groups. This meant that between an appeal for help and the dispatch of aid there could be a gap of several months during which the ICRC had to negotiate the collection of funds or gifts in kind and get permission for the blockade or counter-blockade to be lifted. It would have been simpler to stockpile clothing and pharmaceutical products on the continent, a suggestion never taken up by the Allies. On the other hand, if it could not always serve as the Red Cross's much-needed storehouse, Switzerland did offer a financial centre which maintained valuable relations with all the belligerents.

As the end of the war approached, funds placed at the ICRC's disposal on behalf of the Jews increased continually. The majority of aid operations to this group were carried out after the German capitulation, so fall outside the scope of this study, but the problems posed and solutions adopted were no different, since exchange controls and other impediments to international transfers remained in place long after the Liberation.

The American Jewish Joint Distribution Committee (the main provider of funds) for example put up 100,000 Swiss francs which were transferred to Romania in November 1943 to provide aid for the Transnistrian ghettos. Out of the donation of $100,000 that it managed with the help of the War Refugee Board to get into Switzerland in spring 1944, Sw Frs 100,000 was once more sent to Romania, but this time the ICRC was allowed to allocate some of the money to non-Jews, so about 100,000 francs was given to the ICRC's pharmaceutical service and the rest used to provide parcels for Jews at Cracow, Theresienstadt and Birkenau. Nevertheless the largest sums put at the ICRC's disposal by the American Jewish Joint Distribution Committee arrived after the summer of 1944; four million Swiss francs were sent to Romania in this way by the end of 1944.

The bulk of such funds was transferred through banks in various ways, but the ICRC always made sure it complied scrupulously with the legislation in force in Switzerland and the other countries concerned. In Romania and Hungary, for instance, the American Jewish Joint Distribution Committee's money was transferred from Switzerland by purchasing lei and pengös on the Swiss money markets, or with the agreement of the competent authorities in Berne by using through a clearing system Swiss deposits frozen abroad. But frequently, too, the lei and pengös were bought on the spot by the ICRC's delegate in exchange for credits drawn on funds deposited in Swiss francs by the Joint Distribution Committee in Switzerland in the ICRC's name, or against dollar credits repayable after the war and guaranteed by the Joint Distribution Committee and the War Refugee Board,[41] a solution which obviously appealed to rich Romanian and Hungarian Jews anxious to emigrate as soon as possible. And, lastly, delegates were entrusted with currency for their own expenses and for small individual acts of assistance which were all highly appreciated, but of which no trace remains.

Leaving Fortress Europe

Emigration

At the end of March 1944 the US administration sent chairman Max Huber a set of proposals to facilitate the emigration of Romanian Jews and in particular asked the ICRC to press the governments concerned to grant the *Tari*, which was ready to set sail, the necessary clearance. This transport could then lead to others, since the representative of the War Refugee Board in Ankara had offered the ICRC delegate in Turkey the use of another vessel.

But Schwarzenberg did not share the breezy optimism exuded by the American note. The ICRC had been trying for months to draw the attention of governments and other interested parties to the need to facilitate the emigration of Jews from the Balkan countries and to the possibilities opened up in this regard by the positive attitude of the Romanian and Hungarian authorities, but only after the setting up of the War Refugee Board by President Roosevelt two months earlier did the Red Cross's suggestions seem to find an echo on the American side, by which time it was too late: the Germans refused the necessary safe-conducts and tightened their grip on the two countries from which the Jews still had some chance of escaping. The head of the Special Aid Division concluded with some bitterness that nothing more could be done except to set out for the benefit of the Americans the full story of so much fruitless effort.[42]

But had the ICRC really tried everything, did it have any other plans up its sleeves, and how did it see emigration via the Black Sea being operated in practice? These questions will now be addressed.

Doors closing

Until the autumn of 1941 (when the Nazis put a stop to their relative tolerance and plugged the loopholes) it was still possible, if difficult, for Jews to emigrate from Western Europe. Many thousands of refugees from the Reich, from countries under its control, and from camps in the French unoccupied zone were able, with the help of the High Commission for Refugees, the Jewish Agency for Palestine, the American Jewish Joint Distribution Committee, the Quakers, and so on, to reach Palestine, Latin America and North America via North Africa, Spain and Portugal. But from then onwards this migratory flow, small enough in the view of the hundreds of thousands of Jews in Nazi hands, began to dry up. British controls on entry to Palestine were tightened up, and the United States strengthened their immigration requirements and slimmed down their consular network, at which point Pearl Harbor put a stop to all transatlantic emigration.

These developments did not greatly alter the ICRC's attitude, which was that problems of emigration were not covered by the Conventions and were the responsibility of national governments. Nevertheless, in line with its principle of complementarity, it remained interested in what some states were doing, especially in their capacity as Protecting

Powers. That was how as early as spring 1942 it got discreetly involved in a scheme (thought up by the Ankara representative of the Jewish Agency for Palestine, Chaïm Barlas) aimed at Jewish children in the Balkans, and agreed to pass on to the Romanian and Hungarian governments a request for exit visas for a total of 270 children. However, the scheme, which only managed with immense difficulty to get off the ground, was put a stop to by the intervention of the Gestapo in Bulgaria in March 1943 and their arrest of three young Polish Jews, and by Bulgaria's subsequent refusal to issue transit visas across its territory, since frontier crossings were now under German control. The ICRC, or more precisely its Bucharest delegate, was thus engaged in a delicate matter involving the Protecting Power and sovereign states. This pleased neither the British authorities (who always preferred official diplomatic contacts to the involvement of humanitarian organisations, even the international Red Cross), nor the Swiss federal government. The ICRC, which was trying at the same time to widen the scope of its activities to include Jews in the countries of Eastern Europe, but was afraid of getting overcommitted, was therefore very receptive to Edouard de Haller's warnings and more than willing to convey the necessary words of caution to the delegates concerned: Vladimir de Steiger in Bucharest and Gilbert Simond in Ankara.

But by this time the affair of the 270 children had become just one episode among many in the emigration field, because the deportation of the foreign Jews from France in the summer of 1942 had drawn attention once again to the plight of refugees in Western Europe and led the High Commission to redouble its efforts, the USA and the Dominican Republic having declared their willingness to accept a few thousand children, and the British government having agreed to the children, siblings or cousins of persons missing in France being invited over by their relations in the UK. In the heavily charged atmosphere of autumn 1942 – when the impact in Switzerland of events in France drove the Federal Council to undertake an unusual diplomatic démarche – the Coordinating Committee led by Jacques Chenevière breathed fresh life into an idea that seems to have been put to it several months earlier, that of transporting with the belligerents' agreement Jews wishing to emigrate from Europe to the New World aboard Swiss vessels which carried goods across the Atlantic in an easterly direction and returned empty to the USA.[43] At the request of the Coordinating Committee Jean Pictet prepared a preliminary draft, which, noting that the ICRC had not concerned itself much up till then with the Jewish question as a whole, sought to lay the foundations for a general study and sketched the outlines of a global response.

Truth to tell, Pictet had few illusions. Transporting from Europe the Jews from the territories controlled by the Reich was beyond the ability of the Red Cross, especially since neither the Axis powers nor the United States were likely to countenance such a large movement of population. So he reduced the proposal to deportees and individuals unfit for work or military service whom the Reich was keen to get rid of. Such people could be assembled in Switzerland, from where they would go on to the countries in the Americas that had agreed to have them. The operation would not be risk-free for Switzerland, because the Jewish question put everyone's backs up, or cost-free either, because the deportees would have to be fetched in part with Swiss rolling stock and shipped on Red Cross vessels paid for by, among others, the Swiss. But Switzerland would also stand to gain since the first Jews to be evacuated could be those that Switzerland was already harbouring and those who continued to cross more or less clandestinely into the country.[44]

In the immediate aftermath the draft of 1 October 1942 led to nothing concrete. On the contrary, the deputy high commissioner for refugees, George G. Kullmann, made a number of démarches to Mlle Ferrière during the month of October, none of which came to anything.[45] The ICRC lacked the means to intervene in a problem that concerned above all national policies – including Switzerland's – and that required it to act only when called upon by governments to do so. Besides, it was caught, like Swiss public opinion and the federal authorities themselves, on the horns of a dilemma: was the lifeboat only half-empty, or was it already half-full? Even in the discussions of March 1945 with the Nazis at the highest level we find, inextricably linked to the projects under consideration and a general desire to help, the concern, rarely mentioned overtly, to send to suffering populations where they were the necessary food aid, and humanitarian personnel, rather than see the refugees, prisoners and internees freed or on the run pouring into Switzerland and perhaps settling there.

The pros and cons of intervention

At the turn of the year 1942–43 the emigration issue took on a new dimension when the British government yielded to pressures from various quarters and agreed to issue immigration certificates for Palestine to the tune of 4,500 for children and 500 for accompanying adults, the White Paper of 1939 having, it will be recalled, laid down a maximum of 75,000 entry visas for Jews into the Mandate until 30 March 1944.[46] At the same time the Romanian authorities let it be known that they would allow a proportion of the Transnistrian deportees to emigrate, and confirmed this officially on several occasions in spring 1943, as did the Hungarian government.[47] So, early in the year, negotiations got under way in Bucharest between the Jewish Department, a governmental organisation led by Radu Lecca, the Romanian commissioner for Jewish affairs, and the Jewish Palestine Agency, which was considering entrusting a first trainload of 1,000 people to the Compagnie Internationale des Wagons-Lits. To ensure their protection, it was envisaged calling upon the ICRC.

Despite Pictet's note, or perhaps because of the issues it raised and the perspectives it opened up, the ICRC's reaction to the information and questions coming to it was not negative in principle. Part of Steiger's instructions, sent on 18 February, was to look into the possibilities of emigration; Mlle Ferrière, for some years the ICRC member in charge of the question, sought the advice and support of the international organisations concerned, such as the High Commission for Refugees, and made contacts on the ground in Palestine during her visit to South Africa.[48] Preparations for a planned tour of south-eastern European capitals, later to become the Chapuisat–de Traz mission, focused on this issue too, with Berne's agreement, so as to avoid the Protecting Power taking offence at what could be seen as interference in its sphere of competence.

Two major obstacles confronted emigrants on the outward journey: the attitude of the Germans, on whom could depend in the last resort the issue of exit or transit visas, and that of the British and Americans, who controlled the main host territories. Knowing that it could count on the agreement of the Romanian government – the most important player since Romania had direct access to the sea and therefore to neutral Turkey – the ICRC decided for the time being to confine itself to emigration to Palestine and to hold discussions with London with that end in view. Its note of 5 April 1943 to the Foreign Office reflected its response to the demands made upon it, its broad sympathy with those demands, and the conditions it laid down for any undertaking to assist emigration to Palestine. It said, in essence, that the ICRC had to tread carefully since governments in general, and the German government in particular, considered the Jewish question a purely domestic matter; nevertheless, the Committee had sent limited aid (chiefly medicines) to Jews in ghettos, and were looking into the possibility of assisting Jews deported to Transnistria from Romania who were suffering enormous privations. Moreover, the Committee had been asked to help Jews to emigrate to Palestine, and was prepared to consider allowing ships carrying Jews to sail under the Red Cross flag provided that neutral vessels, accompanied by an ICRC escort, were chartered and paid for by the organisations concerned, and used exclusively for emigrants and not for the shipment of goods. The ICRC was keen to have the views of the UK government on the subject and particularly on whether it was prepared to give its blessing in principle to the suggestion.[49]

This démarche coincided with the abortive Allied conference in Bermuda on refugees and failed to bring about any change in the British position. In early June 1943, H. M. Government sought the ICRC's help on the terms set out in the 5 April note. But the ICRC was in its eyes only an agent in a plan whose realisation depended at the time on a Swedish vessel anchored in the Baltic, the *Lynn Drottningholm*. This plan, like so many others, never got off the ground: over emigration, as over prisoner exchanges, the ICRC was looked upon merely as a subordinate partner in the policies decided by governments and Protecting Powers who, Schwarzenberg noted bitterly, had no more legal authority than the ICRC did to get involved in emigration.[50]

The German authorities did not even bother to reply to the ICRC's request, backed by the British, to recognise the mission of the *Lynn Drottningholm*, and the encouraging noises made to Edouard Chapuisat and David de Traz by their Romanian, Bulgarian and Hungarian contacts in May/June 1943 were so much hot air, since the Wehrmacht controlled the entire length of Bulgaria's southern frontier and had cut the land route to Turkey. Chapuisat tried in vain in July to make a personal, direct démarche to the official in charge of political affairs at the Foreign Ministry in Sofia. The Bulgarians seemed to have lost sovereignty over the question of transit through their own territory.

The ICRC was left with but one card up its sleeve: Romania, the only country keen to assist its Jewish nationals to emigrate rather than face deportation. Both the Swiss representative in Bucharest, René de Weck, and the ICRC's own delegate there, Vladimir de Steiger, encouraged it to continue its talks with the Romanian Red Cross, which seemed willing to organise transportation by the immensely preferable sea route to Istanbul, provided that safe-conducts could be secured for the vessels it chartered, safe-conducts which launches and other small craft obviously did not bother to obtain when, at the risk of their passengers' lives, they charged a small fortune to make the perilous crossing. The ICRC's dilemma was simple: should it refuse in principle to get involved in a risky enterprise, or should it embark on a venture which the Romanian Red Cross society, the Swiss ambassador, and the ICRC's delegate on the ground all believed fell within the scope of the Red Cross's humanitarian activities in general? It opted for the second solution, taking care to keep Berne on side, and laid down clearly in advance the narrow limits set for its intervention, while pressing its delegate, still supported by the Swiss ambassador, to get the deputy prime minister Mihaï Antonescu, to agree to the emigration plan. Diplomatic reticence and prudent calculation were probably both involved when the ICRC, concerned above all not to get embroiled in an enterprise that could have dangerous consequences for its basic traditional mission, sent a note to Bucharest handing over to the Romanian government and Red Cross the responsibility for the scheme. The note said, in essence, that the ICRC wished to have no direct part in it and intended to confine itself strictly to extending the protection of its flag to the vessels concerned.[51]

But Schwarzenberg was also aware that a policy of genuine support to Romanian organisations meant that the Bucharest delegation had to be strengthened, since Vladimir de Steiger had originally been sent only as a representative of the Joint Aid Committee, in charge of purchasing, to that part of Europe still spared the ravages of total war. So, naturally enough, Schwarzenberg asked for a specialist in maritime transportation to second de Steiger,[52] especially as the decision, made at the same time, to send a delegate to Budapest, Jean de Bavier, was also inspired by the emigration hopes raised by the Chapuisat–de Traz mission. Several months were to pass, however, before the person chosen as the maritime expert, Karl Kolb, could get the necessary visas to go and back up de Steiger and the Swiss representative in Bucharest and provide the link with Jean de Bavier in Budapest and Gilbert Simond in Ankara.

Two ships for an emigration that never was
Encouraged by the positive attitude of the Romanian government, itself backed by the ICRC's delegates in Bucharest, the local Red Cross society set about organising sea transportation for the 4,500 children and 500 adults for whom there were, in theory, entry visas to Palestine available. The plan was to charter a small ninety-ton Bulgarian wooden ship, the *Bellacita*, for twice-weekly sailings for three months from Constantza to Istanbul. On 19 December 1943, the Romanian Red Cross asked the ICRC to act as mediator to obtain for the vessel, which was flying the flag of a belligerent country, a safe-conduct from all the powers so that it could sail under the ICRC's protection. The ICRC approached the United States, the Reich and the United Kingdom direct; the USSR was contacted through the Turkish Red Cresent.

The British were not enthusiastic. Their own plans had stalled and they still did not look favourably upon the ICRC's intrusion into a domain that touched upon their vital interests and those of the Protecting Power. But, as Schwarzenberg pointed out, the failure of British plans showed just how powerless states were. Besides, he wondered, what else could you expect where populations who had no Protecting Power were concerned? Britain had referred the matter to Switzerland because certain Palestinian interests were involved, but it seemed to Schwarzenberg that 'the *personal* interest of the Jews concerned was more important than defending the interests of Palestine as a recipient country (*Zielland*)'.[53]

Everything would obviously depend on the Reich's response, but the German authorities did not even acknowledge receipt of the démarche, since they were determined not to give the Jews the opportunity to regroup outside their control. They had resolved not to compromise their pro-Arab policy by authorising emigration to Palestine, and to use instead other means for making the European Jews disappear. Faced with Nazi intransigence, the arguments of the ICRC cut no ice at all; it was reduced to lamenting that the Germans seemed to have no conception of how much self-restraint the ICRC had shown in not denouncing them publicly: 'it is hard sometimes for us to remain absolutely neutral', it confessed, 'but we are determined not to compromise the confidence which all the belligerents, especially the German government, has placed in us'.[54]

In spite of the Reich's silence on the issue, the ICRC found itself involved in emigration projects of even greater complexity. There were two reasons for this. The first was that soon after it was set up the War Refugee Board sent a representative to Istanbul, Ira A. Hirschmann. He had considerable funds at his disposal, and enjoyed a status and backing which enabled him to make contact direct with diplomats in post in Turkey, with the Turkish authorities, and with the Jewish Agency for Palestine. For the ICRC delegates, Gilbert Simond in Ankara and Karl Kolb in Bucharest, who for months had been energetically following up numerous contacts, Hirschmann was at one and the same time a precious help and a thorn in their side since he sought rapid solutions and tried to speed up contacts with London and Berlin, contacts in which the ICRC was involved.[55]

The second reason why the ICRC found itself involved in emigration projects was that Kolb in Bucharest was increasingly being appealed to by various Jewish organisations who devised schemes, often in competition with each other, to draw benefit from the relative openness of the Romanian authorities. Kolb's situation was being made all the more uncomfortable by the fact that he was under pressure from all sides to come out for one scheme or another, especially where several were inspired more by the lure of money than by humanitarian considerations. In the end he had to distance himself from, and even to disclaim, the dispatch of craft like the *Milka* or the *Maritza*, operated by groups in contact with him but who had lost patience and launched themselves on the Black Sea without visas, safe-conduct, or protective flag.

At headquarters in Geneva, where the anarchic development of the situation was being followed anxiously and with an inevitable delay because of the timelag, the ICRC tried on the one hand to restrain its delegate (not without a public row, as we shall see later in the chapter devoted to Romania), and on the other to stick to its guns on the issue of principle: that without German agreement, any use by the Romanian Red Cross of the organisation's flag would constitute a departure from the Tenth Hague Convention and could not in consequence be condoned by the ICRC. Only hospital ships were covered by this Convention; any other use of the flag had to be endorsed by all the belligerents involved; as the Germans had failed to oblige in the case of the *Bellacita*, the Red Cross flag could not be used for this or any subsequent journey. The ICRC concluded, with infinite regret, that its obligation to remain strictly neutral meant that it had to leave to Jewish organisations the task of organising the exodus of Jews from occupied Europe.[56]

In April 1944, the *Bellacita* affair seemed well and truly bogged down. When the boat did leave the Romanian coast, it was at its own risk, since the ICRC had got nothing from Berlin. But in Istanbul Hirschmann had managed to secure the services of a modern 4,000-ton vessel, the *Tari*, capable of carrying 1,500 passengers a time, under ICRC protection, from Constantza to Haïfa, and the question arose whether what they had refused to a Bulgarian ship, flying the flag of a belligerent, the Germans would perhaps allow to a neutral vessel. Once again, therefore, the ICRC was asked to seek a safe-conduct from the Reich authorities, and it agreed to do so in the light of the failure of its démarche over the *Bellacita* and its humanitarian obligations in an affair in which its delegate network appeared well and truly to have taken the place of national governments. But the latter were not absent from this new initiative. The Roosevelt administration proposed that neutrals intervene with the authorities in Berlin, and the Ankara cabinet, very clumsily according to Simond, approached them too. Simond himself vested great hopes in his contacts with the German ambassador in Turkey, the former chancellor Franz von Papen, and in the efforts of Hirschmann and the American ambassador Steinhardt. But as was to be expected, the elaborate ballet of this round of meetings and discussions, which gave rise to an intense exchange of correspondence between Geneva, Bucharest, Ankara-Istanbul and marginally Budapest, came to nothing. In mid-July 1944, at a time when deportations had been suspended and the Hungarian government was apparently prepared to contemplate emigration on an unprecedentedly large scale, and when it appeared possible to save the last major Jewish community in Europe, there seemed to be total stalemate since the Reich no more responded to the request concerning the *Tari* than it did for the *Bellacita*. So the only possible avenue left open remained that of small boats and launches, bought or hired, with all the risks involved in unauthorised navigation, and the sordid haggling that it entailed, despite the setting up by the Romanian authorities of an emigration commission headed by Dr Abraham Zissu.

It was not in Kolb's nature to take things lying down. A conversation with Radu Lecca, the Romanian commissioner-general for Jewish affairs, at the beginning of July 1944, suggested another idea to him: perhaps the Nazis' silence was a sign on their part of a lack of interest which could be read in a positive light as an undertaking, albeit tacit, not to block emigration. If that were the case, Berlin's permission was unnecessary and the ICRC, on the strength of this reading of the situation, could grant its protection to ships and content itself with the safe-conduct already given by all other governments, the Soviet Union included.[57]

Even if he was unaware of the profound political reasons behind the Nazis' refusal to allow emigration of any kind, Kolb was not blind, nor was he naïve enough to believe it possible to get the Germans to issue a formal declaration of no interest, and yet without it nothing could be done, particularly since the Romanian government was not willing to make a ship available without the ICRC's protection. So, on reflection, his first suggestion was doomed as impractical, but there remained another, which required the ICRC to make a concession on the issue of principle and recognise the Red Cross flag which the Romanian Red Cross society would fly on the emigrant ships that it took full responsibility for. All the ICRC had to do was notify all the countries concerned, Germany included, that the sailings were taking place, but it meant taking the risk of extending the use of the Red Cross flag to other forms of transport than those envisaged by the Conventions and the agreements covering supplies to POWs and civilian internees, and of taking responsibility for any loss of life if the boats were torpedoed or shipwrecked (as happened for example to the *Struma*, which sank off the Bosporus early in 1942 with over 700 Jews on board, nearly all of whom perished).

The ICRC was hardly predisposed to welcome getting involved in such a venture, but the growing menace hanging over the Hungarian Jews and other pressures led the Bureau to take a fresh look on 3 August 1944 at the whole problem. The meeting was a tense one, since any decision reached would clearly have serious consequences. Since Huber was convalescing, Burckhardt travelled to get his opinion. Not surprisingly, Huber favoured a cautious but scarcely realistic compromise, namely a new distinctive emblem to cover the operation which the ICRC would undertake to have recognised by all the belligerents. That would, however, take time, and probably require the calling of a diplomatic conference, something difficult to envisage at that stage in the conflict.

At the meeting several members pointed out, sensibly enough, that the question was a trifle arcane. Sailors and airmen had testified that the ICRC emblem marking ships carrying parcels for POWs and civilian internees, namely the Red Cross flag with the words 'C. International', was little known, and if it was respected, this was only because of the red cross on white ground; so lending the ICRC's initials made no sense. Besides, they went on, the ICRC was not competent to grant the use of the flag; the most it could do was denounce its abuse. Hence, if the Romanian Red Cross flew the red-on-white flag (which was its flag too) on boats it chartered, this hardly constituted an intolerable abuse. The Bureau agreed unanimously, and decided to send Kolb a telegram authorising the Romanian Red Cross to affix its emblem to the boats in question, asking it to inform the Bureau of the date of sailing and route so that the governments concerned could be informed.[58]

The decision to give this undertaking was a shrewd one in that it allowed intervention which did not undermine traditional decision-making principles or procedures. The shrewdness did not imply insincerity, though it was motivated by caution; it proved that the ICRC now expected to have to take a more active role in emigration matters, and raises the question whether the intervention envisaged would have led to an acceleration or improvement in that area. Romania's withdrawal from the war a few weeks later and the arrival of the Red Army was to alter the situation profoundly, but the problem remained, as did the ICRC's involvement, since the Romanian Jews' wish to get to Palestine after the summer of 1944 continued to encounter obstacles, chiefly British policy in the Mandate.

Chapter 8, devoted to Hungary, goes into some detail about evacuation efforts during the summer and autumn of 1944, so a brief summary suffices at this stage:
1) The ICRC envisaged a major emigration operation for the Hungarian Jews, or at least prepared for such a possibility.
2) The progress of military operations and evident signs of the opening-up of borders on the part of neutral countries like Switzerland, Sweden or Spain, were, for the first time since 1942, to refocus attention on emigration to the West.

3) The USA and the UK had a crucial role to play in this, as the ICRC showed in requesting, on a number of occasions, the cooperation of the authorities in London and Washington. But while the two governments were prepared to increase the number of temporary entry visas slightly (in the hope, essentially, of encouraging neutral nations to take people in), their basic line did not change; the UK in particular continued to the last to subordinate any rescue plan for the Hungarian Jews to policy considerations connected with the Palestine mandate.

4) In any case, whatever the Hungarian authorities planned or intended, the Germans were not ready to let the Hungarian Jews go. Except for a few small groups – mostly saved from deportation as a result of bargains struck between private Jewish organisations and the SS which neither the ICRC nor national governments were prepared to recognise – the Reich was not going to grant enough transit visas for a major operation to get under way. Such was the outcome of hundreds of telegrams, letters and notes and months of discussion.

It is not easy to assess what the ICRC's efforts amounted to in concrete terms since, though important, emigration is a little-understood branch of Holocaust studies. The energy expended was certainly impressive: not only by delegates like Kolb, Simond, Born and Schirmer, but also by Suzanne Ferrière, who throughout the war took a close interest in the question. But as far as the outcome was concerned, it has to be confessed that it amounted to more or less total failure. True, the failure was due in large part to governmental policies; as for the ICRC, it should have abandoned its traditional credentials, kept legal principle at arm's length, and, taking the bull by the horns, should have gone in for untried methods. Everything we know about its attitude on other issues explains why, in the field of emigration, it could do no more than make sadly limited goodwill gestures. Only a few thousand Balkan Jews managed to reach Palestine, mostly on their own initiative and at their own risk.

One-off privileges

'Privilégiés occasionnels' is the phrase used by the ICRC itself. A note of February 1945 defined this category of war victim in the following terms:

Jews of all (ex-)nationalities who have obtained temporary protection in the face of grave danger, such as the risk of execution or deportation. This protection consists of:

a) a promise of inclusion on a list of immigrants to Palestine;
b) an immigration certificate for Palestine;
c) the same, with the promise of naturalisation after a certain period of residence in Palestine;
d) a temporary United States passport (Latin American countries)
e) a transit visa (via Turkey, Sweden, Spain, Portugal or Switzerland) implying hypothetical immigration to a country not necessarily specified.[59]

What these cases had in common was that as a general rule the person concerned was not in possession of the papers that protected him or her, but only of a photocopy or of a notification sometimes issued by an authority which had pushed things to the very limit of what it was juridically competent to do. Nevertheless, even where it was merely symbolic, such a certificate usually afforded sufficient protection, albeit temporary, because being linked to a specific risk it tended to lapse as soon as the risk diminished (no real or definitive status was involved, such as would have been conferred for example by nationality, naturalisation or immigrant visa).

The German–Palestinian exchange

Three civilian internee exchanges took place during the war under the auspices of Switzerland, the Protecting Power for British interests in the Reich; it involved a few hundred Germans interned in the British mandate who were swapped for mandate citizens, chiefly Jews, interned in Germany and the occupied territories. The first exchange took place in December 1941; on that occasion émigrés in Palestine contacted the ICRC in order to get in touch with wives and children left behind in Europe (in Holland and Poland especially); they had managed to get them included on immigration lists because the British agreed without much difficulty to substitute them for people who could not be traced. Although the question of civilian internee exchanges (as the British kept stressing, even where non-Britons were concerned) was a matter for the Protecting Power, the ICRC was led little by little into getting involved, either because people in Europe in possession of a visa for Palestine wished to put their names on an exchange list but could not contact the Swiss legation in Berlin, or because Palestine residents needed an intermediary to inform their relatives that they were on an immigration list and needed to try and call on the British legation in Ankara. In this way the Jewish Agency for Palestine and the Palestine Bureau in Switzerland sought, through the ICRC and the Dutch Red Cross, to convey to Jews in Holland the information they held.[60]

The ICRC was of course never sure of reaching the people concerned in the Reich or in the territories under its control. What is more, most of the time it was aware that the exchange could not take place, since emigration candidates whose names were listed far outnumbered all the Germans resident in Palestine: when negotiations began in 1943 over the third exchange, 900 names were passed on by the Swiss government against nine Germans. But Suzanne Ferrière herself felt that at least for some families inclusion on a list represented the faint hope of avoiding deportation.[61]

That was the reason why, with the connivance of the Swiss authorities, the ICRC ended up agreeing to pass on photocopies of emigration certificates for Palestine (whereas, as we shall see, it was sometimes less keen to do the same over passports and other protection documents). To deal with the many cases of families anxious to avoid internment or deportation by securing a certificate or passport, it set up on 1 December 1943 an *ad hoc* agency, IMPA (Palestine Immigration Service) headed by Flora Daïnow, which until the end of the war did a great deal of work, as shown by the 250,000 individual cards its forty-eight regular staff and forty-one voluntary helpers filled in, the hundreds of lists it drew up, the tens of thousands of messages it sent, and so on. Unfortunately, as Daïnow herself admitted, all that effort achieved next to nothing. Even the enquiries conducted after May 1945 to locate missing persons on the basis of the MCI's index cards of stateless Jews and the files of national agencies for the most part came to nothing even though, for several weeks from July 1945 onwards, the names of surviving escapees were regularly broadcast over the airwaves.

Security considerations were paramount in setting up the IPMA files: no dossier could be put together or list consulted other than by the head of the service or by the archivist. When the balance-sheet was drawn up in 1946 the atmosphere of fear and isolation still persisted: the director felt that it was not desirable to furnish actual statistics of the work done, and in answer to the question 'What has your experience been?' she replied simply: 'It's been deplorable. There's no question about it: we were never able to get any backing at all.'[62]

South American passports and other protection documents
The IMPA service was also put in charge of the cases of people with South American passports. From the outbreak of war onwards, a number of consular representatives of Latin American republics in Europe issued German, Polish and other Jews under threat with identity papers allowing the holders at least to be detained as civilian internees in camps in Germany or France. The consulate general of El Salvador in Geneva, or rather its first secretary, Georges Mantello, was one focus of this traffic, but he was not the only example. It has even been argued

that the Reich itself, at least at the beginning, turned a blind eye to the issuing of phoney passports, since they served to swell the ranks of South American civilian internees in Europe (who otherwise were few in number) that could be exchanged for the many German nationals held by Latin American states.

Whatever the truth of the matter, the Nazis' attitude changed from 1943 onwards, when the countries concerned, who refused in any case to accept foreign Jewish immigrants, began turning down applications to renew papers of doubtful status. With the agreement of the Protecting Power – Switzerland or Spain, depending on the case – the Gestapo carried out checks in civilian internment camps and seized South American passports and similar documents, particularly in the camp at Vittel in France where nearly 300 people, mostly of German or Polish origin, held papers of questionable authenticity.[63]

At first the ICRC took relatively little interest in a problem which fell fairly and squarely within the competence of the nation-states, especially of the Protecting Powers, and potentially of international organisations like the Intergovernmental Committee in London or the International Emigrants Welfare Service in Geneva. It was for this reason that, with the full backing of the Foreign Interests Section in Berne, it refused to pass on to the individuals concerned papers issued by consular officials in Geneva.[64]

In December 1943 Jewish organisations such as HIJEFS (the Swiss Aid Committee for Jewish Refugees Abroad) intervened on behalf of the Vittel internees threatened with deportation to the East. They contacted the nuncio in Berne, the Allies' diplomatic representatives and the ICRC. Burckhardt promised the daughter of the Belgian Chief Rabbi, one of the people at risk, to get in touch with the effective head of the German Red Cross, Ernst Grawitz, and the Latin American states. Schwarzenberg, though, was vehemently opposed to the idea, considering that this whole business of false passports bought by rich Jews was too shady to merit the Red Cross's intervention in Berlin.[65] Burckhardt was probably moved by his correspondent's distress, and his symbolic gesture was but one of a long list of discreet personal démarches he undertook throughout the war on behalf of individuals (mostly well-born or wealthy people, but also writers and artists) with whom he had some connection; he was, after all, a bit of a snob. As for Schwarzenberg, his violent opposition may have been rooted in a narrow legalism, a moralistic tendency, or deep distrust of the rich and influential international Jewish community. The documentary evidence points neither one way nor the other, but it does seem to reflect political and possibly personal antagonisms rarely found elsewhere. In any event,

Burckhardt overrode all objections, maybe in part also because in a separate development the Intergovernmental Committee for Refugees had drawn to the ICRC's attention the existence of a camp at Behrenbostel (presumably Bergen-Belsen) where numerous South American nationals, or people claiming to be such, had been grouped together, perhaps with a view to an exchange. Before contacting the DRK or the German Foreign Ministry as he had promised, Burckhardt thought it advisable to find out through the papal nuncio in Berne, Mgr. Bernardini, whether the countries concerned recognised the disputed passports or not. At the same time, he suggested to the Polish government in exile in London that it should commit itself straightaway to the reinstatement in Poland after the war of the people concerned, because the point at issue seemed less a question of nationality and more one of exchange: that was what the Germans cared about. If the South American republics agreed to recognise the passports, even without undertaking to proceed at once to an exchange, the Vittel internees could at least benefit from a reprieve while the Germans waited for the exchange to take place. Before even getting the assurances he sought – because the negotiations were long drawn out – Burckhardt turned to the DRK's head of external relations, Walter Hartmann, during his fifteenth visit to Geneva, to ask him to get the German authorities to postpone all deportations until the question of the internees' nationality had been resolved.[66]

In the absence of all trace of any written reply that the DRK may have made, it is hard to decide whether the efforts of the ICRC, and of Burckhardt in particular, really contributed to securing the necessary reprieve to allow the Protecting Power to intervene. What is certain, on the other hand, is the two-pronged approach of the War Refugee Board (made in the teeth of State Department opposition) to the South American states, that they take no steps before the end of the war to cancel or revoke the passports, and to Switzerland, as the Protecting Power, to get the Reich to recognise the documents' validity, at least those of bearers held in civilian internee camps in France and Germany, as long as the documents were not formally invalidated by the issuing authority. This démarche, to put it mildly, was met with less than wholehearted enthusiasm by the Swiss foreign minister because it involved Switzerland in a matter of great delicacy that fell outside its competence, but there was no eluding it.[67] As for the South American states, whatever they may have thought at the outset, they too had no alternative but to go along with what was asked of them. In any case by then several hundreds of the German internees that they had earmarked for exchange were being held by the Americans in Texas. So some of the

Vittel internees got the benefit of the doubt, while the rest were deported to Auschwitz. At a later stage the survivors were sent to Bergen-Belsen (by then a camp for prominent people and for potential exchangees), and others were included in the third and last exchange, which took place in the summer of 1944.

The question of protection passports was given new impetus by the events in Hungary. In April 1944 the ICRC was still telling its delegate in Budapest not to get involved in passing on certificates allowing Jews to establish their foreign status in good time for them to benefit from the German–Hungarian agreement of 19 March 1944.[68] In July Switzerland bowed to the wishes of the United States and extended to Hungary the protection measures that it had already had to adopt towards the civilian internment camps in the Reich and its occupied territories; this meant that the Confederation would thenceforth protect any citizen of a country which it represented in Hungary, such as the USA, Chile, Uruguay and El Salvador, whether his or her nationality were attested by a passport, or by another document, even a disputed one, or by an undocumented declaration, until such time as the country concerned had the opportunity to check that the document or declaration was genuine. Moreover British Jews were covered by a blanket protection measure, and the Protecting Power had to get the Hungarian authorities to agree even when a blatantly forged passport was accepted by the country which had supposedly issued it.[69] So there was no longer any reason for the ICRC to hold back, even if the question of protection papers still came under the competence of nation-states, who though not obliged to did keep it informed. The ICRC delegation in Hungary would therefore collaborate with the Swiss legation in this matter,[70] as a little later would the delegation in Slovakia, as long as this traffic seemed under the control of states and was, if not accepted, at least tolerated by the government of the country.

The Hungarian affair, followed by the events in Slovakia, saw the development of yet another kind of protection document, issued by the ICRC itself and consisting of papers or signboards placing their holders or bearers under the delegation's protection. These innovations were in the end tolerated by the ICRC; although they obviously had no recognised legal basis, they did on several occasions serve to impress the representatives of authority and thus to save human lives.

Stretching the Conventions to the limit

This section deals with two different but related issues: the 1929 Conventions and the 1934 Tokyo project on the one hand, and the treatment inflicted on concentration camp prisoners and Jews by the Nazis on the other. The first sub-section examines whether Jewish POWs and civilian internees were or were not discriminated against and how the ICRC reacted to it. The second sub-section looks at the ICRC's response to the proposal frequently put to it to secure for Jews the status of civilian internees or even of prisoners of war.

Jewish POWs and civilian internees

Before the question of what the ICRC knew, and of what it sought to do and managed to achieve, is gone into, it should be borne in mind that it was the neutral countries acting as Protecting Powers who under Article 86 were primarily responsible for overseeing the application of the 1929 Code for Prisoners of War; but the ICRC always considered that, as in the case of the Geneva Convention governing the plight of the sick and the wounded of armies in the field, responsibility for POWs fell squarely within its sphere of competence, both for historical reasons and by virtue of the statutes of the International Red Cross and of the Conventions themselves, Articles 79 and 88 of which established its freedom to carry out humanitarian initiatives, and reaffirmed at the same time its role as the moral if not legal guardian of the Conventional apparatus. The ICRC was not content with just appealing to principles, it discreetly negotiated with the chief Protecting Power, Switzerland, an agreement which laid down the terms under which they would collaborate and settle such differences as might arise, particularly over the right to visit camps, a right exercised by the Protecting Power but one which it was acknowledged the ICRC could exercise too.[71] Moreover, the ICRC took full advantage of its various competencies, particularly where complaints from POWs and civilian internees, their relatives, or national Red Cross societies were concerned. In the case of POWs alone, it carried out more than 11,000 camp visits to seek improvements in conditions of detention, and sent its reports and observations to the country from which the prisoners came as well as to the state holding them.

As has already been noted, Article 4 of the POW code laid down rank, state of health, professional skills and gender as the only criteria for treating prisoners differently; de facto, however, the state holding them established a whole range of situations where detainees were concerned. Between 1939 and 1945 millions of men who had fallen into German hands either were only partially covered, or were not covered at all, by the terms of this agreement. In the first place, there were Russians, the USSR not having ratified by 1941 the 1929 Convention; secondly, there were Poles, Greeks and Yugoslavs whose states had disappeared and who therefore had no Protecting Power; and thirdly, there were in Japanese hands Allied prisoners to whom the Convention (which Japan had not signed either) was only partially applied. The General Report of the ICRC contains a detailed analysis of all these situations – especially of the plight of Soviet prisoners in the Reich – so there is no need to go into them here, any more than into the question of prisoners about whom there was some doubt as to whether the Convention applied, such as partisans or interned Italian soldiers. As for POWs subsequently reclassified as political prisoners, like the French POWs of Spanish Republican origin held at Mauthausen, their situation has already been discussed (see p. 57 above).

On the other hand, the ICRC's Report makes no mention of measures likely to have been taken against Jewish POWs, and records, among violations of the Convention, only one racially inspired instance: the plight of doctors and medical personnel of Jewish origin, who were not repatriated, but transferred systematically to a reserve which also included French, Belgian and Dutch medical personnel.[72]

As in the case of the Poles, until spring 1942 the ICRC's reaction to indications that Jewish POWs were being treated differently was one marked by extreme caution: faced with cases drawn to its attention on the occasion of this or that camp visit, or when questions were raised by external bodies, it seemed willing to cling to a belief in the German commitment to respect the Conventions, if only to discourage any suggestion that a particular agreement was needed for Jews, as that would have undermined the universality of the POW code and would have been impossible to secure anyway because of lack of reciprocity, since German Jews were in theory banned from military service.

On the other hand, the treatment meted out to all Jewish doctors and medical personnel of enemy nationality pointed much more clearly from spring 1941 onwards to a systematic and generalised violation of the Conventions. These prisoners were forbidden to care for their compatriots in the hospitals and camps and were not designated for repatriation either. Instead they were grouped in separate accommodation and the ICRC learned that from summer 1941 onwards the French in particular were being held in Russian POW camps where typhus raged. In spring 1942 it was also clear that sick and wounded Jewish POWs were being removed generally from lists of prisoners eligible for repatriation.

The ICRC's reaction on the issue of principle was firm. Huber and Burckhardt felt that there was only one Convention and that it was therefore appropriate to make a démarche to Berlin either on the subject of doctors and medical personnel, or of Jewish POWs as a whole. But whereas Huber's viewpoint was a strictly legal one, Burckhardt's was political: he cautiously suggested seeing the problem, given its sensitive nature, in the context of the ICRC's activity in general, and taking soundings first.[73] The plight of Russian prisoners was, he felt, if only by virtue of the large numbers involved, even more worrying. The session known as Activities Prioritisation of 15 May 1942 confirmed this twin-track approach. On the basis of the reassertion in principle that where war victims were concerned the ICRC ignored all questions of race, it was decided to press the OKW about medical personnel and badly wounded prisoners, and the Reich government about its position on POWs without Protecting Power and on the responsibility it considered that the ICRC had for them. This latter démarche could have taken on board the racial aspect of the discrimination suffered by prisoners at the mercy of the country holding them; but the notes handed to Maximilian von Engelbrechten did not in the end broach the question of the plight of captives without Protecting Power, and no document in the ICRC's archives establishes for certain whether the OKW was officially approached or whether the démarche, if it was made in confidence, had the slightest success. On the contrary: the reports of visits by delegates mention many instances in 1942 and 1943 of discriminatory treatment (except towards British and American prisoners), even if the topic fell under no special rubric in their enquiries, which dealt with Serbian prisoners, French and Polish officers recaptured after escaping who were transferred to Norway, Polish Jews in the French Foreign Legion taken to Auschwitz where they promptly disappeared,[74] and Yugoslav officers denied all correspondence with their families, who had in fact been deported to the East. Nevertheless the ICRC made no attempt on the basis of the Conventions to press the issue of principle with the authorities in Berlin; it preferred to deal, on a case-by-case basis, with the effects, rather than to enquire into the cause. Only by going through all 11,000 reports of visits would it be possible to say with certainty whether this way of proceeding had any success; but, apart from Oflag VI at Osnabrück, where the delegates were able to ascertain during their two visits in July 1943 and February 1944 that the Yugoslav Jewish officers were still being kept apart from their comrades-in-arms in a special camp, it is probable that the approaches largely failed overall. As is proved by its silence on the racial question in its public appeal of 23 August 1943 to governments on the subject of prisoners of war, the ICRC had several reasons for not changing its mind: the conviction that for the Nazis the Jewish question was taboo; the concern to be able to continue effectively to get at least material aid through; and above all the complexity in many instances of the reasons for the acts of discrimination, which often could not be explained primarily or solely in racial terms. In reply to the World Jewish Congress in spring 1943 Schwarzenberg had no hesitation in writing that the ICRC, when all was said and done, had no information to indicate that Jewish POWs in German captivity were generally being subjected to a treatment different from others because of their race,[75] a conviction shared by Switzerland (as the Protecting Power) in a reply to a telegram from the British government, which stated that 'it has not in general been possible to establish that Jewish and non-Jewish prisoners are treated differently; only exceptionally have German officers and NCOs abused their authority towards certain Jewish POWs'.[76]

The postwar publication of the official orders of the OKW relating to the treatment of prisoners of war supports this conclusion up to the summer of 1944, at least as far as intentions were concerned.[77] In theory, the German High Command did not order the application of the racial laws in the Stalags, Oflags and Marlags, nor did it create camps for the Jews; but it did seek to keep Jews in separate huts and to treat doctors and medical personnel – particularly French – differently, and it did allow certain individual acts of brutality to go unpunished.

The question, then, is whether the ICRC and the Protecting Power were right and the World Jewish Congress – and others – were wrong. It cannot be answered solely from the point of view of what took place, since the absence of systematic discrimination was something the Germans alone should be credited with, however calculating their attitude. As for the ICRC, it stuck to its guns until the end of the war, even when anxiety about a general threat increasingly made itself felt, as the episode of March 1945 proved.

From autumn 1944 onwards there was a noticeable change on the German side in the instructions relating to Jewish POWs. While maintaining the principle of not creating special camps, new measures required Jews to occupy different accommodation in all Oflags and Stalags and, in order to prevent all possibility of contact with the local population, to work in separate commandos outside the camps. Otherwise they were to be treated the same as other prisoners, except that those who, under the racial laws, had lost their nationality would, in the event of their death, be buried without military honours.[78] Many Jewish prisoners were moved around as a result both of this order and of the altered deployment of the Wehrmacht following the Allied landings in June 1944. So Jewish organisations, national Red Cross societies and the Allies themselves feared a worsening of the prisoners' situation. The ICRC collected no hard evidence of this except in a few specific cases, but told its delegates to be extra vigilant and intervene forcibly, as they did for example in the forced transfer of Polish officers held in Hungary.[79] To no avail: at the beginning of 1945, fuelled by the stories which liberated prisoners told, and even more by the terrible news brought by escapees from the concentration and extermination camps, many of which were by then in Soviet hands, talk spread of a possible extermination of POWs, and particularly of Jews, and it galvanised the World Jewish Congress.

In mid-March 1945 many people drew Gerhart Riegner's attention to what was going on in Oflags VIIA and IIC, and he in turn pestered the ICRC to intervene energetically at once in the name of the Conventions.[80] But while confirming the policy of separation of which it was well aware through the reports it received from Marti and his démarches in Berlin, the ICRC declined for the present to go beyond asking the OKW for information, since it did not share fears of unfavourable treatment of Jewish POWs becoming routine and denied that their separation constituted in itself a violation of Article 4, Paragraph 2 of the POW code. Far from reassuring people, this denial breathed new life into the debate in the shape of an exchange of letters of a particularly sharp tone more revelatory perhaps of the feelings of those involved than the generally courteous and circumspect turns of phrase in the correspondence between the ICRC and the World Jewish Congress.[81]

In discussion with Gerhart Riegner and Paul Guggenheim, who reckoned that the separation which had been confirmed constituted 'the most serious violation that had been committed to our knowledge in POWs' treatment',[82] Carl J. Burckhardt cast doubt on the wider significance of reported separations, referring to the visit which he had just made to Germany. He later set out in writing the legal basis of his position and his full commitment to the 1929 Convention.[83]

Riegner brought into play his pressure group (the delegates in Geneva of the Greek, Polish, Yugoslav, Czech and North American Red Cross societies)[84] while vigorously disagreeing with Guggenheim over Burckhardt's legal interpretation of the Convention, and arguing that as the POW code did not preclude action to forestall a breach of its stipulations, the ICRC should not wait until an irreparable violation occurred before intervening.[85]

Fortunately, the German surrender resolved the POW question, before the fears of the World Jewish Congress could be realised. But the ICRC did not budge an inch on the issue of principle. By putting its right of access to all prisoners before the condemning of separation in principle, it believed that it had stuck to its doctrine, even though it had to concede the failure of all attempts at objecting to separation as a fact. It had also stuck to the Convention, Article 9 of which provided for separations that had nothing to do with the treatment of individuals, for example between prisoners of the same nationality or country holding opposing political views. The World Jewish Congress's misgivings, however understandable, did not constitute proof, and they did not deflect the ICRC from its mission.[86] This line of reasoning had no hope of convincing the World Jewish Congress and indeed signally failed to do so, but the problem was given fresh impetus later when the revision of the Conventions came up for discussion.

The civilian internment camps, like the POW camps, contained a certain number of Jews who belonged, at least in theory, to states at war with the Reich. Generally speaking, the ICRC's delegates who regularly visited different Ilags in Germany, for example those of Liebenau and Wurzach, did not observe any particular discrimination towards this category of Jew, but that did not mean, as the Vittel incident showed, that such people were secure from the attentions of the Gestapo, against whom not only the ICRC but even the German Foreign Ministry, which was administratively responsible for the Ilags, could do nothing. But there is no question that the ICRC, by securing in 1939 the extension to civilian internees of several of the provisions of the POW code, contributed to saving Jews, especially British and American ones.

Jews given POW and civilian internee status

As has already been observed, the ICRC's note of 24 September 1942 was aimed not at tackling the problem of racial persecution head on, but at approaching it indirectly, by raising the question of reciprocity over civilian aliens arrested in the occupied territories and either held there or deported to the Reich. In the case of these people the ICRC referred to the POW code and the Tokyo proposals, and asked to be told their names and where they were being held so that they could be visited, sent parcels, and enabled to write to their families, thus *de facto* suggesting an analogy between concentration camp prisoners and civilian internees. It was in this light that Burckhardt presented the démarche to Gerhart Riegner in November, adding that, for the ICRC, it also applied to deported Jewish aliens, and so should satisfy the World Jewish Congress, which was asking the American authorities at the time to give civilian internee status to deportees to the East and to Jews shut up in ghettos, whatever their nationality, so as to obtain at least the exemptions needed to allow aid through the Allied blockade. And since such a classification had to be accepted by the other party too, the World Jewish Congress thought the ICRC should ask the German authorities to grant it.[87] But contrary to the impression Riegner may have gained from his conversation with Burckhardt, the ICRC had no intention of entering into an argument about fundamentals with the Reich, as the content of the note of 24 September, and the decision of 30 December 1942 to give up trying to get an answer to it and concentrate instead on direct aid, both showed. In response to approaches on issues of principle the ICRC set out the *de jure* and the *de facto* position and stressed its wish in very difficult circumstances always to act pragmatically.[88]

This position was not undermined either by a new World Jewish Congress plan to supply, with the assistance of the Allied governments, the national Red Cross societies under the command and control of the ICRC, the refugees, the ghettos and the concentration camps[89] or by the attempt to involve Karl Bruggmann, the Swiss ambassador to Washington, in discussions about the status of the Jews, a clever way of approaching at the same time the Protecting Power for American and British interests in the Reich. The assistance plan and the draft appeal to the governments in Washington and London, both very embarrassing to the ICRC, were taken up again in the autumn of 1943 with a more reassuring partner, the Intergovernmental Committee for Refugees, and discussions with Bruggmann came to an abrupt halt before the Swiss government could get alarmed.[90]

But the World Jewish Congress kept coming back to the issue, seizing every opportunity thrown up by events, such as the adoption by the congress of the National Fascist party in Verona in November 1943 of an article in the new Fascist constitution branding foreign Jews as enemy aliens,[91] or the statement issued in the summer of 1944 by Helmut Sündermann, the deputy Nazi press chief, justifying the Reich's antisemitic policies on the grounds that the Jews had been waging war against Germany since 1939.[92] In August 1944 the World Jewish Congress appealed to the Conference of the Intergovernmental Committee for Refugees begging the ICRC to declare publicly that it considered Jews deprived of freedom of movement to be civilian internees. Finally, in December 1944, the World Jewish Congress Conference, representing some thirty-eight countries, passed unanimously a motion repeating the demand.[93] The American government gave unofficial backing to these efforts, since in spring 1944 the War Refugee Board asked the ICRC to put pressure on the Germans to treat people prosecuted on the grounds of race, religion or politics as civilian internees, or at least to make it possible for them to receive humanitarian aid. The ICRC refused and checked discreetly that the Swiss authorities would adopt the same position if approached.[94]

The World Jewish Congress's arguments hinged on two considerations, one humanitarian, the other jurisprudential. The humanitarian argument was that since the Jews were the war's most ill-treated civilian victims, where aid was concerned they deserved priority treatment. Even if the ICRC's members had been ready to accept the validity of this proposition, they recoiled from its implications in terms of aid priorities, as indeed did all Allied governments, even those in possession of the most reliable intelligence about the reality of the Final Solution.

The legal argument was that in international law any individual deprived of liberty because of war is considered a POW. Indeed, in 1939–40 the ICRC had got the belligerents to agree, if not to bring the Tokyo project into effect, at least to apply the relevant articles of the POW code to alien civilian internees, especially since the Axis powers considered themselves at war with the Jews. From then on the World Jewish Congress turned on its head the ICRC's argument that the Germans considered the Jewish question a purely internal matter, that civilians arrested in occupied territories were not civilian internees, since they were being held to answer charges and not because of their nationality, and that, as a result, only aliens deported to the Reich or to the occupied territories could (as had been established by the note of 24 September 1942) lay claim to be treated on a par with civilian internees. Gerhart Riegner wrote to Max Huber in October 1944 that there was no convincing reason for making a distinction between enemy residents in a belligerent country at the outbreak of hostilities and enemy residents in a country occupied through military conquest. Both groups, he pointed out, were imprisoned for security reasons as much as for their nationality, and unlike people convicted of individual offences, were all being held for the same reason. In these circumstances, the ICRC's refusal to insist on Jews being treated as civilian internees had no basis in law and represented acquiescence pure and simple in the definition the Nazis chose to give of Jewish status.[95]

At the end of the war, when Burckhardt was negotiating with Kaltenbrunner the partial realisation of the list of demands contained in the note of 2 October 1944 in favour of alien deportees held in concentration camps on German territory, a Hebrew Committee of National Liberation, based in the United States, gave the issue of nationality a new twist by pointing out that in international law the Jews were not stateless but citizens of the newly reborn Hebrew nation, and claimed, naturally enough, that they should be treated as POWs and entrusted to a Protecting Power.[96]

The World Jewish Congress stressed furthermore the political rather than the legal weaknesses of the Conventions, however broadly interpreted, in the face of an ideologically motivated war of extermination. This amounted to a demand that Jews should not be seen as second-class victims, concealed within other categories which failed adequately to define them, but that the problem of racial persecution, i.e. the Nazis' aim of hunting down and destroying a human group on the grounds of ethnicity alone, should be challenged on the basis of humanitarian law in time of war.

The ICRC of course stood by the strict interpretation of the 1929 Conventions and by the concessions it had obtained for alien civilian internees and other categories in the Tokyo project (even though not ratified). It did so for legal reasons, since it was not up to the ICRC to decide who was a civilian internee and who was not, or to accept the statements of a press chief or a draft constitution article as the equivalent of an international arrangement to which all parties had agreed. It did so, too, for strategic reasons, since it feared having its activities called into question under the Conventions if it departed from them itself, or if it gave signatories an excuse to do so by taking certain liberties itself with agreed arrangements. Furthermore, it was confirmed in this attitude by the setbacks of 1939 and 1942 and by the failure of attempts to get visiting rights or information about the destination of, or the possibility of providing help for, Jews and others deported to the East. That is why in spring 1944 the ICRC also refused to discuss a World Jewish Congress proposal first to get the Allied powers to make a declaration of co-belligerency for the Jews so that the same could be demanded of the Germans. Burckhardt was singing from the same hymn sheet when he stressed several times in Riegner's presence that Jewish enemy aliens deported to the Reich were quite obviously civilian internees, accompanying this legal recognition with the observation that all attempts to get the Germans to share this point of view had failed.

Following the World Jewish Congress's démarche to the conference of the Intergovernmental Committee for Refugees in August 1944, this line of reasoning showed signs of running out of steam, whilst the ICRC got ready to undertake a new démarche in favour of Allied civilians, chiefly French and Belgians deported to German concentration camps. So in a memorandum shown (to Schwarzenberg's intense annoyance) in draft form to Riegner and Paul Guggenheim,[97] Max Huber endeavoured to clarify the notion of civilian internees. Although, according to Riegner, Huber took some of his comments into account, the text basically repeated what we know already, maintaining the traditional definition of the alien civilian imprisoned by the occupier as a detainee held solely by reason of his or her nationality, and seeking to distinguish between the various forms of internment envisaged in the Tokyo project and the kinds of imprisonment carried out for judicial reasons and excluded from the ICRC's remit, while recognising that it was sometimes difficult to know whether the arrest was carried out for military or political reasons, or arose from a criminal offence.

This interpretation – still, as can be seen, singularly more timid than the thinking developed by the international Red Cross before 1938 over the definition of the concept 'political prisoner' – having been set out, the memorandum conceded that, wherever there was no basis in the Conventions and no possibility of reciprocity, the ICRC should endeavour, without raising an issue of principle, to guarantee everyone imprisoned as an enemy citizen the assistance and legal protection accorded to POWs and, by extension, to civilian internees, that is, if not correspondence then information about their place of incarceration, the possibility of receiving aid, the right to visits by the Red Cross or the Protecting Power, legal representation for detainees charged with criminal offences, and so on. This amounted to seeking the *de facto* application of the Tokyo project and rejecting the principle of any discrimination between victims of war.

Furthermore, in an accompanying letter, Max Huber reiterated the ICRC's doubts and even fears about a public appeal, mentioning the frequent but discreet démarches made in favour of civilian deportees, thereby foreshadowing, without referring directly to it, the note he signed the same day on the subject, addressed to the German foreign minister.[98]

So the ICRC never changed its position, either *de jure* or *de facto*, on the question of racial persecution. Tacitly giving up on attempts to find a basis in common law, such as the Hague jurisprudence, for the treatment of civilians, it persisted, right up to the collapse of the Reich, in believing that to raise this issue would be of no tangible benefit to the persecuted, and could even harm the other categories of victim with which it was concerned. Furthermore, feeling that the legal aspects could not be examined until the war was over, it preferred through actions of a concrete nature and a step-by-step approach to secure *de facto* assimilation of the various categories of internee, thereby confining its cherished prerogative for taking humanitarian initiatives to the sphere of material assistance.

That, clearly, was not quite what the World Jewish Congress was hoping for. But, more than the writing of a memorandum, the fact that a new démarche was being attempted on behalf of the Jews was in itself a small step forward, as Riegner, taking a fair bit of the credit for himself, pointed out to the World Jewish Congress's leaders in October 1944.[99]

Part II

The ICRC and Political and Racial Persecution in Hitler's Europe

Introduction

This part of the book examines, country by country, the intentions and the more significant actions of the ICRC aimed at those suffering from political and racial persecution. The Final Solution, though planned and directed from Berlin, was in practice shaped to some extent by local factors, such as the strength of antisemitic opinion among the population and within the regime or the degree to which national leaders were keen to serve the Nazi cause; the ICRC's efficacy and resolve were therefore also partially influenced in each country by the situation on the ground.

Consideration will not be given here to all the territories that were directly or indirectly dominated by the Reich, since it was only the sending of a delegate, the establishment of an official presence, or the carrying out of an aid mission by the ICRC or by the Joint Aid Commission of the international RC that defined a Red Cross theatre of operations. Little or no mention will therefore be made of countries where the ICRC had no direct involvement, but which nevertheless found themselves centre-stage where the Final Solution was concerned, such as the Soviet Union or (leaving aside Theresienstadt) the Protectorate of Bohemia-Moravia.

The countries are divided into three groups. The first contains the occupied territories under various forms of local adminstration: Poland, France (both the part under German control and the south-central area, the so-called 'free zone', governed by the Vichy regime), Belgium, the Netherlands, Greece, Denmark and Norway. The second consists of two satellite states, Croatia and Slovakia. The third category includes three of Germany's allies, Romania, Bulgaria and Italy. (The size and extent of the ICRC's involvement in a fourth ally, Hungary, was such that a separate chapter is devoted to it in Part III.) The policy followed, both on the ground and at headquarters in Geneva, will be outlined in each case, but no attempt will be made to draw up exhaustive lists of every form of assistance and type of intervention, nor to cover the entirety of aid operations.

5 The occupied countries

Poland (and the Soviet Union)

Contrary to my usual practice, I should here like to look more closely at the plight of prisoners of war. For their Polish and Russian officer POWs the Germans had a treatment in store that, although not comparable to their handling of those persecuted on racial and political grounds, nonetheless formed part of the same policy of racial reorganisation and destruction of national and social institutions which was without equivalent in the campaign fought in the West.

The Russian case is simple. What was launched against the USSR by the Reich on 22 June 1941 was an ideological crusade. The Soviets had signed the 1929 Geneva Convention on improving the lot of sick and wounded soldiers in the field, but had not ratified the POW code, so Russian combatants falling into enemy hands were unable to invoke the protection of international law, let alone of simple humanity; though entry to the camps where the poor wretches were to die in their thousands was barred, the ICRC sought throughout the war to act as go-between in the hope of mitigating their plight.[1] Relations between Moscow and Geneva were not good, however, and the lack of permanent diplomatic contact at governmental level between Switzerland and the Soviet Union made matters worse. In the eyes of some historians, the determining factor where a large part of the ICRC's diplomatic activity during the war is concerned was the effort it deployed in this area; others consider its attempts marginal and not always well coordinated. In any case, they failed. Apart from sending a little aid, the ICRC could do nothing for Soviet POWs in Germany (or for German POWs in the USSR) and this, in terms of the number of people involved, represented its chief failure – and signal weakness – during the Second World War.

The Polish prisoners of war

The Polish case is somewhat different since it was not the absence of the Geneva Conventions that occasioned the particular treatment meted out to POWs but the destruction of the Polish state. From winter 1939 onwards the Germans and Russians drew the conclusion that they could do as they saw fit with the prisoners in their possession. The ICRC could do nothing for Polish POWs in Russian hands, reduced as it was to impotence through lack of contacts.

Half a million prisoners fell into the hands of the Wehrmacht during the September 1939 campaign. The Germans quickly stopped considering as Polish those Poles who came from the General-Government or from the territories annexed by the Reich; they had become stateless, and so had no Protecting Power; Sweden, the Protecting Power concerned, bowed to the inevitable. The Polish Red Cross survived, however, in the General-Government; after being for a while in two minds about suppressing it, the Nazis handed over the task of running it and of conducting its external relations to the DRK, whose first plenipotentiary in Cracow, Dr Sanne, was a member of the RC and not of the SS who before the war had known the people in charge of the Polish RC; but there was also a Polish RC in exile which had fled first to Paris and then to London with the Polish government.

In accordance with its doctrine, the ICRC recognised the *de facto* situation and, using the DRK as intermediary, went on with its work on the ground, but it also kept in touch with the Polish RC in London, chiefly though Prince Radziwill, its Geneva representative.[2]

During the early months following the Polish defeat, visits to POW camps seemed possible, but at the beginning of 1940 prisoner lists stopped arriving at the Agency; in Geneva people wondered why, and by March began to suspect that the Germans were withdrawing POW status from the Poles it held. If, as Burckhardt claimed, he was not informed officially of this by the people he spoke to during his visit to Berlin in March, Junod was able to confirm the truth of it after his third mission in May 1940 and Hartmann discreetly acknowledged the fact in Geneva at the same time.[3]

The ICRC referred the matter to a study group, which meant that it accepted the *fait accompli*.[4] In two and a half years the number of Polish POWs in German hands was to fall from 500,000 to about 55,000, since the absence of protection under the Conventions did not only bring about a worsening of the conditions of detention and make exchanges and repatriation impossible, it also enabled the Germans to use the prisoners as civilian workers in the German war effort and hold them in camps controlled no longer by the army but by the police. This treatment was not confined to the Poles but it was meted out to them, even officers, in an unfettered manner that did not exclude the use of force.

In spring 1942, after a visit by Marti to headquarters, the problem of the altered status of Polish POWs was again brought up and the question asked whether the issue of principle should be raised with the German authorities or whether their point of view should be accepted in order to leave open the possibility of occasional visits and of some aid being sent.[5] It was in the end the second alternative that was adopted since nobody wanted either to pronounce on the German position or give up seeing the Poles and all other citizens of vanished states as victims for whom as much as possible had to be done.

In spite of the alarm expressed by the ICRC on 23 August 1943 to all the belligerents about the spiralling number of violations of the Conventions, the plight of the Polish POWs, whether subjected to forced labour or not, was to remain right up until 1945 worse that that of any other nation fighting Hitler, with the exception of the Russians. The balance sheet in the end was disappointing: a few delegate visits to Germany, the sending of aid (always fraught with difficulty and never in sufficient quantity: 500,000 kg in 1941 as compared with 30,000 tons for the French and 14,000 for the British),[6] and the enquiries made by the Polish Service of the Agency, whose report underlines how very complicated it was to follow things up, given the way Polish people had been scattered by the war.[7]

The Cracow professors

On 6 November 1939, in a lecture theatre at the ancient Jagellon University, Cracow, the professors and lecturers from the university and the school of advanced mining engineering gathered for a lecture on the orders of the Gestapo, but the SS was there, rounded them up and deported them to Sachsenhausen. There the 160-odd prisoners, some very old and sick, suffered intensely from cold and hunger, and several soon died. Such arrests without trial or explanation were part of a general policy of striking terror in the Polish population and of reducing scientists and intellectuals to silence.

The ICRC, with the benefit of precise and accurate information about the round-up, entered into contact with the DRK on the one hand and with the German consulate-general in Geneva on the other, requesting a list of the deportees' names and their place of internment. But in spite of the many appeals made to it from a number of quarters, including the Swiss Federal Political Department,[8] the ICRC remained very circumspect. Carl J. Burckhardt, who had from the outset advised caution, may, as he later gave out, have interceded in high places with the German political police; there is no written record of such a démarche being made during his visit to Berlin in March 1940, which proves nothing one way or the other, but the release on 8 February 1940 of a hundred or so academics does not appear to have resulted from any intervention of his. So the deportation on 3 March 1940 of about forty prisoners to Dachau did not prevent the ICRC agreeing with the DRK that the issue had been resolved, although one last humanitarian démarche was made to the German Foreign Ministry on behalf of the two oldest deportees.[9]

Frédéric Barbey wrote at the end of May 1940 that despite the official instructions they had been given it was unfortunately quite impossible for the ICRC authorities to dispatch parcels to Dachau; even if it were possible, he went on, they could not undertake to send them since – as usual – they were constrained by the international Conventions relating to POWs and to civilian internees of comparable status, and at Dachau it was a case of political prisoners on whose behalf, sadly, they had no legal grounds for taking action.[10] Burckhardt put it more diplomatically when in reference to Junod's last, discreet démarche in Berlin he concluded: 'You can however reassure people writing to you about it that we have done all in our power to improve the lot of these detainees and that in the course of forthcoming missions we shall not fail to bear in mind the information passed on to us.'[11]

Re-establishing contacts

The *Blitzkrieg* against Poland hastened the implementation of measures prepared since the Munich crisis, but it also upset the ICRC's plans. In response to a confidential request from the Polish government and the Polish Red Cross the Committee decided, less than a week after the outbreak of war, to send a delegate to Warsaw, paralleling the missions dispatched to Berlin, London and Paris. Robert Brunel was not, however, able to reach Warsaw but had to make do with Bucharest, from where he did his utmost to coordinate aid activity and organise with the Hungarian and Romanian national societies an agency for locating and for getting news about missing people. Such information-gathering, with particular reference to civilians whether interned or not, was also part of the brief given to Junod when he left on his mission to Berlin, since at the time communications were cut off between invaded Poland and the rest of the world and remained so until the Germans finished reorganising the territories they had conquered.

By early October, with several thousand anxious requests already piling up in its in-tray, the ICRC decided to channel some of its efforts into seeking the whereabouts of civilians, whether individuals or families, Jews or Aryans. Surprisingly neither the German Foreign Ministry nor the DRK objected in principle, so that as the General-Government administration took shape and post-offices reopened the ICRC was able to send on via Geneva short messages of twenty-five words including the address from citizens of other belligerents to civilian internees and others in occupied Poland until such time as postal traffic with neutral countries was fully restored.[12] The ICRC then discontinued this service except for requests for information about missing people, particularly Jews and concentration camp detainees, in which case it continued turning to the DRK in the last analysis.

These activities were bound to give rise to close contact between Agency staff and the WJC in the person of Gerhart Riegner and the standing bureau of the Jewish Agency for Palestine in the person of its secretary Mieczeslaw Kahany; indeed ever since the outbeak of war representatives of the larger Jewish organisations had been turning to the ICRC, and on 4 September the chairman of the WJC executive committee, Nahum Goldmann, placed himself and his network of correspondents at the disposal of the Red Cross to come to the aid of Jewish victims of the conflict,[13] and shortly afterwards Kahany followed suit. Of the 460,000 Jews in Palestine at that time more than half were of Polish origin, so the Jewish Agency for Palestine was prepared to finance the setting up of an information or even an aid bureau with potentially a yet wider role, organised by the ICRC as a neutral institution.[14] First Saly Mayer, president of the Swiss Federation of Jewish Communities, accompanied by Emmanuel Rosen representing the American Jewish Joint Distribution Committee, then Morris S. Tropper, European president of the Joint, put the same request to Mme Frick: the setting up of an information service and the sending of aid which their organisations undertook to finance on conditions laid down by the Red Cross.[15] The Jewish Agency for Palestine even suggested that the ICRC be brought into the negotiations then taking place in Berlin between the Palästina Treuhandstelle der Juden in Deutschland and the German authorities over the extension to Poland of the Haavara agreement signed in 1933 to facilitate the emigration of German Jews to Palestine.

The ICRC made no response to this last proposal, which was undoubtedly beyond its competence and fell outside the usual scope of its activities, even though, it will be remembered, Nazi racial policy at this time was still directed towards making the Jews emigrate through a progressive use of force; but it did not follow up the suggestions just listed, nor, as we saw earlier, did it involve Jewish organisations in schemes for delivering aid to concentration camps in 1943.

The occupation of the country and the sweeping away of the Polish state afforded the Germans fresh opportunities for isolating the Jews, rounding them up and finally locking them away. From mid-October onwards the information reaching Geneva highlighted clearly the worsening situation in racial policy. From Vienna and Bohemia-Moravia, moreover, Jews were being deported by the trainload to Lodz. During his second visit to Germany the ICRC's delegate Marcel Junod expressed his unease over this; then as a guest of the General-Government he met the Nazi 'proconsul', Hans Frank, who was prepared to sanction an aid operation and the sending of medicines. Moving on to Warsaw he saw in the distance the walls of the ghetto, then still only a restricted area, and had talks with the chairman of the Council of Elders of Warsaw's Jewish community, Adam Czerniakow, who later confirmed his request for aid in writing.[16] In the notes he handed to Hartmann during his visit Junod wondered too how the Jews were expected to run their hospital since their bank accounts had been frozen.[17]

So it would not be accurate to say that the Red Cross washed its hands of the Polish Jews, either in showing no awareness of the Nazis' preliminary measures or even of their early intentions, or in refusing to concern itself with this section of the population, or in condoning racial discrimination in its work with military and civilian victims – discrimination not yet explicitly demanded by the Germans in any case, at least insofar as Polish non-internees were concerned.

Nevertheless the events of winter 1939 highlight even more sharply than previously the narrowness of the ICRC's room for manoeuvre and the limits imposed by itself as much as by circumstances on humanitarian action targeted at the victims of political and racial persecution. In mid-December 1939 chairman Huber confided to Hartmann his unease over the 'evacuations', as he put it, of Viennese Jews to Lublin. In his capacity as the DRK's head of external relations Hartmann gave an assurance that the deportations had been suspended for the time being and indicated further that Polish Jewish non-internees would encounter no difficulties in emigrating from the General-Government and that the relevant organisations were free to send material aid through the Reichsvereinigung der Juden in Deutschland, but one activity was still banned: visiting and sending food aid and clothing to concentration and 'evacuees'' camps.[18]

Knowing from experience that this subject was taboo, the ICRC trod warily: Max Huber, while drawing the Central Commission's attention to the critical situation of the Jews in the Lublin region, large numbers of whom were crammed dangerously within a confined area, pointed out that although requests for help had come from many quarters the ICRC had little hope of achieving anything and risked compromising its other activities; he felt that the matter should be looked into nonetheless, noting Hartmann's assurances – confirmed by Junod – that the Jewish exodus from Germany, Austria, Czechoslovakia and Poland to the Lublin region had been halted, and that the Quakers had been authorised to embark on a wide-ranging aid operation in Poland and in the Lublin district in particular.[19]

So continuing and even stepping up investigations into individual cases, a system put in place by the ICRC and the DRK from 1933 onwards, was understandably dictated by prudence as much as by necessity, especially since Hartmann agreed that the cases of Jews deported to the General-Government about whom the ICRC's enquiries had remained unanswered by the RVJD, should as in the past be taken up by the DRK directly with the police authorities. But it was doubtful whether much could be expected of channels that had not been of great help in earlier years, now that systematic segregation had been instituted in the East with the firm intention of cleansing the Reich and its occupied territories by grouping the Jews in a sealed-off area whilst, according to the ACPG itself, 2.5 million Poles were wandering far from home. Even if Hartmann thought he was assisting the ICRC with this offer and bringing a touch of humanity to bear on the situation, he could not fail to be aware that the RVJD was a cog in the Nazi racial machine and that the DRK was held in the party's grip; in any case he had at the end of February 1940 to announce to the ICRC that restrictions had already been placed on the undertaking given in December and that the DRK could no longer provide information on all the Jews about whom enquiries were being made. 'We do not rule out', he said, 'supplying details in important cases, but we cannot give information en bloc as it often gets used for propaganda purposes', adding that he felt that the ICRC's search service passed everything on indiscriminately. His advice was to refer enquirers to the RVJD, which was also the appropriate agency for Jewish emigration, something that as in the past it would seek to facilitate.[20] In March the German authorities closed the Polish Red Cross's Jewish information bureau in Warsaw, thereby further complicating search procedures.

Such was the reality of the situation, but in Mme Frick's opinion the ICRC could not simply leave it at that; she now sought to persuade chairman Huber to send Carl J. Burckhardt to Berlin to clear up a whole range of outstanding issues in relations between the Reich and the Red Cross including aid, the installing of a delegation, and the treatment of political prisoners like the Cracow professors; the latter was an especially delicate question and the ICRC's negotiator would need a completely free hand in dealing with it.[21]

Burckhardt does not seem to have taken up this suggestion when he visited Nazi leaders in March 1940 and August 1941, either where intervention on behalf of political and racial deportees and internees was concerned or over the question of getting permission to send to the General-Government a permanent delegate to work closely with the DRK on aid operations for the benefit of the civilian population; and while it is true that Marti went to the General-Government in summer 1940 for talks with Nazi officers and German and Polish Red Cross officials, no discussion about the deportees was permitted then or later, even in 1942 when there was clear evidence of a policy of persecution on a colossal scale, so Burckhardt's admission of powerlessness at the end of that year, referred to earlier, was based not only on the failure of an aid attempt that I will come to shortly, but also on the extreme meagreness of the results achieved thus far, since it had for some time been quite impossible to conduct an enquiry or carry out a search for a Jew in Poland through the intermediary of the DRK.[22]

Aid to the civilian population

Action sometimes took the place of words: from 1940 onwards humanitarian aid to the General-Government's population grew, with the ICRC, through its Aid Division and from autumn 1941 onwards through the Joint Aid Commission of the international Red Cross, taking an active part alongside other humanitarian organisations. On the ground – that is in the General-Government, since the territory annexed by the Reich as well as the Polish zone now in Soviet hands remained closed – food, pharmaceuticals and clothing were received by the DRK free of customs and delivery charges and shared out via the RGO among the aid organisations serving the country's different nationalities, with acknowledgement slips addressed to donors returning by the same route.

Within the framework of this aid operation it was possible to help Jews, not only those still at liberty but to some extent too those in the ghettos and even it seems in labour camps, though not of course those in concentration and extermination camps. The actual numbers involved are, however, open to question; the reports published by the ICRC after the war are obviously unable to quote precise figures and merely give the breakdown of distribution between different nationalities as agreed with the DRK and the RGO – for instance 61 per cent for the Poles, 22 per cent for the Ukrainians, 16 per cent for the Jews, etc.; this last figure was never constant and indeed, according to the reports, fell to 10 per cent in 1943,[23] being aimed chiefly at the JUS in Cracow and the Warsaw philanthropic and medical association TOZ.

Accurate assessments of the quantities involved are not feasible, even through the files of the Joint Aid Commission, since distribution on the ground could not as a rule be properly checked; on the other hand, through a concrete example, it is possible, if not to answer all the questions raised by this indirect form of assistance to non-interned Jews in the General-Government, at least to arrive at a better understanding of what actually took place.

Thirty-five tons of medicines collected by the American Polish Relief Committee reached Lisbon in autumn 1941. It took months of long negotiations for the Joint Aid Commission of the international Red Cross to get permission to send this aid to Geneva and oversee its distribution in the General-Government and to obtain for its delegate, the sixty-three-year-old Zurich doctor Max von Wyss, special authorisation to visit Cracow; going via Berlin, where he arrived only on 18 August 1942, he reached Cracow on 26 August accompanied by a senior DRK official and six railway wagons containing the thirty-five tons of medicines, together with twelve tons of vaccines and other supplies purchased in Switzerland. Once the stock had been checked, however, Dr von Wyss was unable to proceed with distributing it to the 300 chemists in the country and the ghettos as planned. Customs redtape obliged him to put the whole consignment for the time being into the hands of the RGO and on 1 September, when he was still expecting to be allowed to stay a while longer in the General-Government, he was forced, despite making energetic representations, to return home without being able to carry out the first part of his mission.[24]

It might have been a hitch, or a misunderstanding, but the General-Government authorities certainly did not see it that way, their primary concern being to close as soon as possible the door which had been half-opened to let in medical aid; in this respect their policy was no different towards other humanitarian organisations like the Quakers, the Hoover Committee, the YMCA, and so on. On the other hand, no sooner was Dr von Wyss back in Geneva than Hartmann redoubled his assurances that a new visa could be obtained to allow the ICRC's delegate to undertake another mission in order to check that the supplies had been properly distributed to all the pharmacies designated, including presumably those in the ghettos.

At the only meeting he managed to arrange with JUS officials Dr von Wyss was not able to discover a great deal about the fate of internees and deportees on whose behalf, under his instructions, enquiries could be made, but no direct contact,[25] though he was able to establish that apart from Jews of foreign nationality whose whereabouts had been ascertained by their consular authorities or in the case of civilian internees sometimes by their Protecting Power, the rest had disappeared so that it was impossible to get information about them, let alone make contact with them.[26]

In mid-March 1943 Hartmann's efforts as the DRK's head of external relations finally bore fruit: Dr von Wyss was allowed to return to Cracow to check on the success of his mission of August 1942. This time he spent over a week in the General-Government, from 22 March to 4 April, and although he could not go about unaccompanied, he was able in particular to visit the pharmacies and aid depots in Radom, in Kielce, and in Warsaw (a mere fortnight before the ghetto uprising there), but only to ascertain that, contrary to what had been said and despite a number of acknowledgement slips reaching Switzerland, the Jewish population had not in the meantime received the 16 per cent of the August 1942 shipment allocated to it. The RGO had held back the parcels intended for the Jews whose numbers had in any case declined dramatically over the preceding months for reasons now all too familiar. In Berlin Hartmann implicitly acknowledged the change when he informed von Wyss that the Jews were henceforth not being included in the new breakdown for the distribution of aid to the civilian population. Moreover the JUS had, the previous December, suspended its operations, so von Wyss's report (see Appendix, document V) is pessimistic in the extreme about the situation of the Jews and devoid of illusion over the Jewish question.[27]

And yet, shortly afterwards, the JUS was given permission to resume its activities and its head, Dr Michael Weichert, contacted Jewish organisations to get supplies which, he hoped, could once more be shipped by the ICRC. But a visa application for a third journey by Dr von Wyss came up against so many objections, even on Hartmann's part, that it was clear by summer 1943 that there could no longer be any question of the Germans entertaining the idea of assistance to the Jews in the East (or to such of them as were left) nor even, as André de Pilar noted in September 1943 after a visit from Hartmann, the dispatch of medicines and tonics to the JUS.[28]

In 1944 efforts on behalf of the civilian population were stepped up. Polish Red Cross reports mention among other things a percentage allowance for Jews, permission for the JUS to resume its activities, and shipments to Cracow, but given the number of Jews still alive and able to be reached, little credence can be attached to them. By the time the ICRC sent a delegate to the General-Government first in September and then in November 1944 to help with aid operations on behalf of civilians fleeing the Warsaw uprising, the 'Jewish question' (to use the Nazis' terminology) was to all intents and purposes 'solved' as far as Poland was concerned.[29]

Deportees and internees

It was important to gain access to the camps and provide aid where the victims of racial and political persecution were being held, and that explains for instance the intervention in autumn 1941, repeated a year later, of the Churches' Ecumenical Council in producing, as did Jewish sources, evidence of mass extermination and in demanding that there should be a Red Cross delegate on the spot.

As we saw above, Red Cross chiefs knew that the Germans would never agree to a delegate being posted to the camps or to aid being sent there either, but, as the DRK seemed to indicate in spring 1942 in accepting individual and collective aid parcels for the General-Government ghettos, aid could perhaps be directed to other places of detention by the ICRC in collaboration with the Joint Aid Commission and other international bodies on the lines of what had been done in the refugee camps of southern France; by refusing the request for *navicerts* put to them by Burckhardt during his visit to London, however, the British, not wishing to go beyond the dispensations for lifting the blockade (normally restricted to the shipment of POW parcels) that they had agreed in respect of civilian internees and the French camps, settled that question.[30] So if, for different reasons, both the Germans and the British refused to consider interned Jews as civilian internees, or even to treat them as being on the same footing, it was difficult to imagine on what basis aid operations to the camps in the East could be conducted. As we have seen, ICRC members held differing views on the question, as did the handful of reliable Germans with whom they dared to broach the matter. At the end of spring 1942 during a technical visit to the Agency by an OKW delegation, Captain Wilhelm Clemens slipped Burckhardt the idea of approaching not the political police as suggested by the German consul in Geneva, Wolfgang Krauel, but rather the OKW, since many internees were under joint OKW and police control.[31] It was worth a try, so the Coordinating Committee decided to send aid to all Polish civilians held in concentration camps in the Reich and the General-Government without singling out the Jews, and wrote a letter on these lines to the OKW, c/o Captain Clemens, for Hartmann to deliver when he left Geneva at the end of August 1942.[32]

In what may have been cleverness, naïvety or bluff on the ICRC's part, it is open to question what significance this proposal really had, since the ICRC was well aware that civilian internees came under the German Foreign Ministry and that the OKW was responsible solely for running POW camps; whatever the truth of the matter, Burckhardt immediately informed the Polish Red Cross in London of what he had done in response to their demand for an ICRC initiative on behalf of the Poles held in concentration camps, whereas, with his experience of daily contacts with the Nazis on the ground, Marti reacted with characteristic pessimism when he was told.[33] In any event, of course, there was no follow-up: only the Theresienstadt ghetto-camp was opened up in the same autumn of 1942 to allow in, solely for propaganda reasons, shipments from abroad via the DRK, whilst concentration camp parcels reached camps like Auschwitz only during the closing stages of the war and in small numbers.

The General-Government was not home to the big European Jewish reservation that some leading Nazis had at one time envisaged, but instead became, even more than Russian territory on which the *Einsatzkommandos* operated, the country *par excellence* of the Final Solution with its ghettos, labour camps, concentration camps and extermination camps, all of which as early as March 1943 the Polish Red Cross in London listed with impressive detail and scope. Although unaware of the full extent of the Nazis' determination to wipe out the Polish nation, the ICRC soon learned, from precise examples, of the political and racial persecution that had struck the General-Government, having, through the information network provided by its delegates and by national Red Cross societies, monitored the way the European Jews had been herded together in this part of Poland where, more than anywhere else, the presence of a permanent delegate would have had a genuine humanitarian and political impact, and where, more than anywhere else too, the ICRC's caution betrays its true order of priorities. Since it had no delegate on the ground and there was no local administration it could deal with, the Red Cross had to accept the rules laid down by the occupying power, including the need to operate through the DRK and in close collaboration with it.

France

From reception to internment

In the universal disorder following the French capitulation and the signing of the armistice at Rethondes the fate of alien civilian internees did not immediately attract attention. The Red Cross was preoccupied with the departure of POWs to Germany, the return home of millions of people who had fled the German advance in May–June 1940 and the distress amongst the civilian population. There were, however, many categories of internees now in danger in the camps hurriedly opened by the French government at the beginning of hostilities. Spanish Republicans and former members of the International Brigades, Jewish refugees, German antifascists due to be handed over to the Nazis under Article 19 of the Armistice Convention, stateless people and political detainees formed a very diverse population equally at risk from the Vichy regime and the Germans.

In August 1940, following complaints and questions, the ICRC decided to intervene. It sent Dr Alec Cramer, one of its members, to the unoccupied zone to visit the camps in the south and to try and set in train a number of positive measures such as emigration to Mexico for the Spanish refugees and former members of the International Brigades, the granting of visas to enable certain categories of internees to seek asylum in other countries, and the speeding up of releases begun by *ad hoc* organisations known as screening commissions.

In November 1940 Dr Cramer was allowed to visit and observe closely three important camps, Argelès-sur-Mer, Le Vernet in the Ariège, and Gurs in the Basses-Pyrénées. The latter camp had just admitted more than 6,000 Jews from the Palatinate and Alsace-Lorraine who had been expelled into unoccupied France. Everywhere Cramer was met with more or less the same spectacle: makeshift quarters quite inadequate in view of the approaching winter, groups of all nationalities and in all conditions making in total 12,000 at Argelès, more than 3,000 at Le Vernet and more than 12,000 in Gurs. They represented a staggering mass of physical wretchedness and mental distress, made worse by military attitudes more evocative in general of detention than internment. The overall assessment was distinctly worrying:

Before attempting a description of the camps, I wish to draw your attention to the fact that there are several categories of prisoners that should not be confused. While it may be essential to keep some of them out of harm's way (common criminals, or people representing a danger to the state such as those held at Le Vernet), there are others, indeed the great majority, whose arrest, deportation and internment are in no way justified by any political or military necessity and indeed would shock any right thinking person of decent mind. It is a feature characteristic of the present war that these people who are being deported en masse, old people, women, children, even whole families, share for the most part one crime, that of being Jewish or of Jewish descent. Even now it is not Jews alone who are being pursued, but we are impotent, horror-struck bystanders witnessing the brutal expulsion of whole populations who are being forced to make way for the invader.[34]

What could be done? Obviously the small amount of aid in cash and kind which the delegate took with him was no answer. The numbers of civilian internees needed to be reduced by speeding up releases and facilitating repatriation with the help, for example, of French ships blockaded in the colonies, which with British authorisation could sail under a Red Cross flag to fetch emigrants in return for conveying food supplies to British POWs. But which countries would be prepared to accept these internees, especially the Jews?

Improvements were both necessary and possible in the camps during negotiations and for the people who could not be released, and only the ICRC had the necessary authority to bring this about. Thus despite its hard-hitting nature Dr Cramer's report was sent to the French Foreign Affairs Ministry with three suggestions: the supply of food, medicines and warm clothing, the improvement of detainees' accommodation and the reduction in the number of people held through the release and emigration of women, children and old people in particular.[35]

For its part the ICRC tried to get authorisation for the free movement of aid from the authorities. This was not easy since those in the camps were neither POWs nor civilian internees since their countries were no longer or had never been at war with France (stateless persons, German and Austrian Jews, etc.). It took a whole year's negotiations to arrange that collective aid for camps in the south should cross the British blockade under the supervision of the CMS. The latter was entirely dependent on donations, and so with only limited means it specialised in distributing pharmaceutical products in collaboration with a Unitarian committee whose Marseilles branch was directed by Noel H. Field. An estimate during the summer of 1944 concluded that Jewish internees whose numbers had dwindled rapidly since 1942 through deportation had received in this way aid totalling 90,000 Swiss francs.[36]

When in autumn 1941 he returned to the unoccupied zone Cramer noted both an improvement and a worsening of the situation particularly during his visits to Rieucros (Mende), Rivesaltes (Perpignan), Gurs, etc. The improvement lay in the appointment by Vichy of an inspector-general for the camps throughout France, a former prefect of the department of the Ardèche, Jean Faure, and in the coordination of the efforts of several relief organisations such as the YMCA, the CIMADE, the Service social d'aide aux émigrés, the Quakers and Jewish groups such as the OSE and Relico, along with those of the French Red Cross. The worsening came from the diminution in emigration possibilities, notably for Jews to reach America. On 1 July 1941 the USA had introduced a new procedure aimed at discouraging Jews from embarking for the New World. In order to slow down departures from unoccupied

France the North American consulates, except those in Lyons and Marseilles, were closed. As a result the efforts of the Joint in providing financial help for Jews originating from Germany and occupied countries to leave via Spain and Portugal were in vain. By their refusal from October onwards to authorise any Jew to emigrate the Nazis put the finishing touches to a blockade of Jews within Europe. The internees in the southern French camps therefore had no further hope of being able to leave either. If the ICRC was to do anything to help them, the only thing left was to improve their conditions of housing, hygiene and board although, as Burckhardt explained to the leaders of the Intergovernmental Committee for Refugees in December 1941, 'the problem of aid to the refugees in the unoccupied zone of France is only of relatively peripheral importance to the Red Cross'.[37]

In late 1941 the situation was broadly similar in occupied France after a year that had seen the setting up of makeshift camps according to the movement of various groups: French colonial troops (white French POWs had been taken to Germany), civilian internees (British in particular), political suspects and Jews. At the time, the two camps reserved for Jews at Beaune-la-Rolande and Pithiviers seemed adequate to Dr Marti and Dr de Morsier. The latter, a doctor attached to the Swiss legation in Paris, and serving there temporarily as ICRC correspondent, was awaiting his appointment as delegate for France reporting to Marti in Berlin. These two representatives of the ICRC made a general tour of the occupied zone and noted:

We have continued our visits within occupied France, seeing two camps of non-French Jews, about 4,000 men in all, who were arrested and placed in these camps in the Loiret, 2,000 men in each camp. They have POW status. The Germans ordered their arrest but had them placed under French authority. They are all right. Their families can visit them every two months and they can receive parcels and letters. They are mostly Jews of Polish nationality.[38]

In autumn 1941 more disturbing news reached Geneva.[39] In particular they concerned Drancy, near Paris, where in August 5,000 Jews had replaced the British internees who had been decently housed when Marti and de Morsier had seen them. In the course of a new tour of inspection the two delegates were able to confirm the rumours during an interview with Dr Tisne, the camp doctor.[40] There was need therefore for a more detailed inspection. The French Red Cross requested this in order to strengthen its hand with the French authorities. In Geneva, however, opinions were sharply divided over whether the ICRC was meddling where it had no business to.[41] Surely the internment camps, even Drancy which was a matter for the French Ministry of the Interior, were under the jurisdiction of the police? If they were to send a committee member, as they had sent Dr Cramer in 1940 and 1941 to the unoccupied zone, would not the whole affair assume an importance that could prove disagreeable? The events of spring 1942 were to provide an answer and confirm the dramatic change in the fortunes of the Jews.

From detention to deportation

In October 1940 the Vichy regime promulgated the statute of the Jews and authorised prefects to intern foreign Jews in special camps. A year later in December 1941 the third large round-up took place, following those of May and August of the same year. Using the pretext of their racial responsibility for the entry of America into the war, these new-type hostages were sent to camps at Beaune-la-Rolande, Pithiviers and Drancy. In March 1942 deportations began from Drancy and Com-piègne to Auschwitz. These were followed, according to an arrangement between the Germans and Laval, by the implementation of a full-scale deportation plan which culminated in the great 'rafle du Vél d'hiv', the round-up on 16 and 17 July,[42] and the round-up in the free zone on 26 August.

At the same time resistance towards the German occupation troops was building up and from summer 1941 attacks were made against personnel and military equipment. The Germans retaliated, taking hostages and carrying out savage reprisals. In December with the introduction of the 'Night and Fog' decree there was a rapid rise in the deportation of resistants and suspects of all kinds to concentration camps. Inevitably it may be imagined that news of events in France spread to French-speaking Switzerland. The ICRC, better informed about these events than about others anywhere else, was particularly concerned. During 1941 the Committee adopted a two-pronged ap-proach in the face of antisemitic measures and police repression: they supplied aid through the CMS to the camps in the south of France where there were also Jewish prisoners, and gave support in general, especially in the Jewish camps in the north, to the aid and information programme run by the French Red Cross and its civilian internees agency. In this respect it seems that it was broadly in agreement with the views of the Vichy regime, at least until Laval's return to power as premier and the devil's pact which he made with the Nazis to press ahead with the implementation of the programme decided at Wannsee.

Could more have been done? In March 1942 the French Red Cross alerted the ICRC in Geneva that it was being denied access to the Jewish camps, irrespective of whether the inmates were French or foreign nationals. Only the ICRC was in a position to do something. The French Red Cross repeated this warning at the end of April:

A large number of Jews, chiefly of French nationality, have been moved from German internment camps at Compiègne and Drancy to Eastern Europe.

They seem to have been sent in two trainloads of about a thousand each and to be working in Silesia. The French Red Cross is neither authorised nor able to bring humanitarian aid to these internees who are no longer held on French territory: they are therefore entirely dependent on the charity of the ICRC. In particular we wish to draw your attention to the fact that those internees who were arrested in December had no contact with their families the whole time they were in France. It is therefore solely up to the ICRC to organise this correspondence along lines to be agreed with the authorities.[43]

The French Red Cross thought the ICRC should request the right to visit internees in both zones of France irrespective of whether the camps were under German or French control, and that it should also act on behalf of French people, whether Jewish or not, who had been deported from French territory:

Only the ICRC can intervene. There is no need for Jews to be mentioned: the fact that Aryans have been taken to camps in Germany means that the deportees' racial origin can be glossed over.

If the German authorities reply that these French people are being moved to Germany for activities that threaten the security of the army of occupation this cannot be considered pertinent unless details are given. A refutation is immediately forthcoming, since such activities are summarily tried and punished by German tribunals . . .

The only recourse for the French Red Cross is to entrust the ICRC with the protection of its nationals of all races and it is to the ICRC that it is now sending the requests from families without news of their relations for the past six months and with no means of sending them food parcels.[44]

Action. Of what kind? Through whom?

The information it possessed and the requests for help that it received made the ICRC look carefully at the whole range of its activities so as to determine the respective importance of each and to make sure that it was remaining faithful to its essential purpose without neglecting its humanitarian duties. At the end of April, with this in mind and still on the subject of France, Chenevière, Huber and Burckhardt opposed Dr Alec Cramer's suggestion that he should visit the camps for civilian workers in the Haute-Savoie, a stone's throw from Geneva:

Monsieur Huber believes that in the main the ICRC is a go-between between two warring powers and that it should only intervene in cases falling into this category. As a consequence these questions concerning the internal regime of a country while obviously interesting from a humanitarian point of view are not the specific responsibility of the Red Cross.[45]

In June Schwarzenberg reacted similarly to requests for help from the French Red Cross, since the prisoners involved could not in his opinion be viewed as civilian internees according to the definition in the first part of the Tokyo draft:

> We should first of all decide whether the ICRC wants to take on this problem and indeed if it *can* do so without jeopardising many other issues which are far from being resolved [Marti's visits to the POWs and civilian internees in Europe] and without risking being accused of a lack of impartiality since it has not intervened in the other occupied countries.[46]

And at the end of summer 1942, when news of the deportation of French Jews and of the closure of the Swiss frontier to would-be refugees shook the conscience of many in Switzerland, Huber maintained his stand on the principle of restraint when he met the delegate of the Swiss Federal Council for Humanitarian Aid.[47]

This caution did not, however, mean inaction. On 30 March in a confidential letter signed by a member of the ICRC, Frédéric Barbey, Marti was entrusted with the job of making a discreet approach to the most appropriate Berlin authority, the DRK or the Foreign Ministry, to find out if it would be possible to send aid to the Jewish camp in Compiègne, and if the ICRC could be sure that it would be distributed to the most needy. He was given a free hand to enquire about the possibility of such a delicate approach.[48] That was not all, however. On 16 April the head of the Berlin delegation was asked by Roger Gallopin to find out if possible about the places where the Jews from Compiègne and Drancy were being held and to get permission to send them aid.[49]

Marti typically went straight to the point: he approached the Foreign Ministry as soon as he received Barbey's letter. He subtly cloaked his request in a general approach, enquiring about aid for all the Compiègne internees from a strictly humanitarian viewpoint. There was in fact also a POW camp (Frontstalag 220) at Compiègne and a camp of American, Yugoslav and Russian civilian internees from amongst whom the Germans were to remove the able-bodied Jews under fifty-five years of age in order to deport them. But Marti's usual contact, *Legationsrat* Sethe, seems not to have seen through Marti's request at once; he gave him to understand a favourable reply would be forthcoming and asked for time,[50] only to end up replying in the summer that the French Red Cross was being asked to get involved from time to time and that the occupying forces were providing the camp with the necessary medical supplies.[51]

It came as no surprise to Marti, but the second request of 16 April had obviously even less chance of being considered seriously:

Dr Sethe regrets that he has to give a negative reply. These Jews were deported since they threatened German army security and are therefore considered to be criminals, not internees. Thus they are not under our control.
We could have given you this reply right away.[52]

In the meantime a top-level meeting decided upon a certain number of priorities. So on the very day that Marti informed headquarters that he had failed, a fresh letter signed by Gallopin and written by Schwarzenberg was sent to the German Foreign Ministry:

We have heard through internees in occupied countries that civilian internees in the north of France and especially those in the camps at Drancy and Compiègne, of different nationalities, among them French, Yugoslavs, Poles and so-called White Russians, etc., have been removed to Germany. In view of this change in the composition of the camps we should be grateful to be able to be provided as soon as possible with lists of the civilian internees and their place of detention. We should also be grateful to know whether and to what address we could send aid parcels and whether the people concerned can correspond with their families.[53]

In spite of Marti's efforts[54] no reply to this request had reached Geneva by the end of the summer. These failures therefore played a large part in the elaboration of the note of 24 September 1942, the origin, impact and failure of which have been examined in some detail.

Meanwhile two new attempts were initiated. One was the sending, with the help of the French Red Cross and American organisations, of 500 parcels to French internees in occupied France (a similar attempt was made in Greece) in the hope of establishing, in the field of aid, treatment at least analogous to that allowed for civilian internees.[55] The other initiative was an approach to the Vichy foreign affairs minister for information about the names and destinations of the unoccupied zone internees who had been sent to Germany without, as caution dictated, mention being made of the political detainees or of the right of asylum. This letter began by noting that through the return of mail marked 'unknown' or 'gone away' and news from families, the ICRC had understood that internees from camps in the south had been deported to Germany, and that it had learned from various sources that many Jews, too, had been arrested in the unoccupied zone and put into internment camps or sent to Germany. It was his responsibility, the ICRC reminded the foreign minister, to look after all categories of internees, and it felt that its delegates' two visits to camps in the south allowed by the French authorities had been useful. It was therefore asking the minister, in view of the trust placed in it by the warring parties and its duty of care towards the victims of the conflict, to provide information about names and places of detention of any prisoner sent to Germany, so that it could reassure the families and carry out the task undertaken since the beginning of hostilities by the central POW bureau.[56]

This letter was never to receive a reply, or even an acknowledgement. Before the year was out the CMS decided to let it drop, concentrating its efforts instead on the camps in the south.[57] It had already in early autumn proposed that Dr Cramer, then on a mission in the occupied zone, should be allowed to repeat the visits he made to these camps in 1940 and 1941. Chenevière, however, opposed this suggestion in the belief that the ICRC should stick to its traditional activities, taking care especially of POWs and civilian internees, and should not risk jeopardising them by acting on behalf of other categories of victims with somewhat uncertain results.[58]

The general impression was thus one of helpless resignation, whether in the case of Pasteur Boegner's questions or the individual requests for information which were ever increasing. The stock reply to these was that the ICRC had made many approaches to the authorities involved, whether French or German, but up till then the amount of effort deployed had led to no tangible results to speak of. The ICRC had until recently undertaken some individual enquiries but this channel was no longer open. The only possibility was to note all requests without being able to say when or whether an answer could be given.[59]

Similar replies were made to the High Commission for Refugees, which was also seeking in vain the addresses of German, Austrian and Czech Jews who had been deported from unoccupied France, and which suggested that the ICRC might undertake a campaign on behalf of the children of Jews deported from unoccupied France.[60] Once more the ICRC had to confess that it was powerless to check that aid supplies sent by the Quakers and other organisations were correctly delivered, and this ruled out any relaxation of the rules of the blockade.[61]

Nonetheless requests for information continued to flood in. With the help of Jewish organisations and the Social Service for Aid to Emigrants, the civilian services of the ACPG drew up lists of missing people, first of all Jews and then Aryans when the DRK refused in principle to accept enquiries about the former. For example, a statistical survey from spring 1943 casts light on the search activities which were proceeding slowly but discreetly and the current state of the file of requests concerning deported and detained people which had been placed in the hands of the civilian section of the French branch of the Agency.[62]

The register of missing persons

The figures in the note of 30 April are obviously derisory compared with reality. In the course of 1943 the numbers of people arrested and deported to Germany had risen steadily. According to the French Red Cross, there were by the autumn most likely 150,000 French civilian internees and political deportees in France and Germany[63] for whom nothing could be done by Switzerland, the Protecting Power for the French civilian internees, the POWs coming under the jurisdiction of the Scapini mission through a direct agreement between Vichy and Berlin. As a result, the French Red Cross, the humanitarian organisations and even the Vichy government placed all their hopes in the ICRC. Was it not possible, they wondered, to tackle Berlin again with a view to obtaining information about individuals and to sending aid? In November 1943 the CPI asked Burckhardt and Bachmann to raise the problem again during their visit to Berlin.[64] There is nothing in the files to confirm that such a démarche was undertaken: in any case it could only have been discreet and without tangible outcome.

Indeed for the Germans the insistence of the French Red Cross and the French government was proof of the efficacity of the 'Night and Fog' decree and was thus an encouragement to persevere with the use of silence as a method of repression as is indicated in a German note which, of course, the ICRC only saw after the war:

i) The repeated requests from the French delegation [to the Commission of the Rethondes Armistice] along with the constant efforts of the ICRC prove that the fate of people arrested and sent to Germany preoccupies a great number of people in the occupied territories.

This is precisely what the Führer expected and desired. He believes that the only effective way to combat attacks on the occupying power is to condemn those guilty to death or to deal with them in such a way that their families and the population in general are completely without knowledge of their fate and whereabouts.

ii) This order from the Führer, which was the subject of much reflection, does not mean that after their execution the OKW should not give information on one or other of the condemned men if this were to give rise to internal political measures in France. But this should only happen in a few cases since if the French were informed of all the executions they would reason, rightly, that the other guilty men had only been condemned to detention.

A demurrer should therefore be made to all the demands of the French delegation unless it seems necessary to pass them on to the OKW (WR) for reasons of external politics. Paragraph ix of the order of enforcement no. 2 of 16/4/1942 (draft) provides for the following reply: 'The guilty party has been arrested. No further details can be given.'[65]

This gives an idea of how important also the Concentration Camp

Parcels Scheme was to be in probing the darkness of the concentration camps. But the lists from the camps would not be enough. It was still necessary to have the names and addresses of those detained (the main difficulty) and funds to make up standard parcels. More than once the ICRC turned to the French Red Cross for help with this. In spring 1944 it appealed in the same vein to the French Committee for National Liberation which, writing from Algiers, had asked it to act on behalf of the French deportees. The ICRC pointed out that it had sent thousands of standard parcels of nutritious food to civilian deportees, French people among them. They could only send parcels to individuals in concentration camps, collective supplies not being authorised. They, therefore, needed more names of French detainees. The main obstacle to further similar activities was the need for funds in Swiss currency in Geneva, and this along with aid supplies would not be able to pass through the blockade given the non-POW status of the would-be recipients. Whilst hoping that the Committee in Algiers would be able to find a way of making a contribution, the ICRC recommended great discretion since the detainees were not protected by international conventions.[66]

In France itself Jacques de Morsier was trying to gather together as much information as possible on the camps of administrative internees, especially on Compiègne where most deportation convoys left from, and on Drancy. Until they were opened up at the Liberation, however, these camps remained virtually closed to inspection by the ICRC although this does not mean that they had no information about them. Indirect information was received via the French Red Cross, the social services and through witnesses such as Mme Strauss-Meyer, a Swiss citizen, who had worked as a secretary for a year at Drancy and whose testimony was received on 30 May 1944.[67] In the former unoccupied zone, where the ICRC delegate found it more difficult to penetrate, the representatives of the CMS, who were going about their work as best they could, remained in contact with the camps of refugees and political prisoners.

In summer 1944, however much effort had been expended, the final total of aid provided was not high. Once established on French soil, the provisional government was worried by this and hoped, as will be seen, that the ICRC would now make a major contribution towards saving tens of thousands of French deportees from the hands of a power determined to hold out to the bitter end.

Belgium

There are two main points of interest in the study of the ICRC's activities in Belgium on behalf of political and Jewish prisoners. It underlines, on the one hand, what has already been observed in the case of Poland, that the efficacy, however relative, of the efforts made was commensurate also with the means which the national Red Cross had at its disposal and the presence of an ICRC delegate on the ground; and on the other, it shows how the documents in this file, although limited in number, exemplify the difficulty of interpretation which pervades this whole enquiry.

Hostages or political prisoners?

The increase in the arrests of hostages and members of the resistance during 1942 occasioned several requests for help and intervention from the ICRC. The issue came to a head because the authorities in the Belgian Congo were holding a certain number of German civilian internees. If they were visited by an ICRC delegate this could lead to a reciprocal gesture, as had been the case in 1940 for the Dutch hostages held at Buchenwald. The intervention on behalf of the Belgians interned in Germany was thus one of the concrete attempts at a breakthrough undertaken by the ICRC at the same time as it sent the note of 24 September 1942. However, the German Foreign Affairs Ministry gave a categorical refusal,[68] a position which was not to alter during the following months. Unlike the Dutch case, the Germans cast doubt on the existence of Belgian hostages, and they maintained that the Belgian citizens who had been deported were criminals, convicted of attacks on the Wehrmacht.[69] Marti's insistence, based on an enumeration of the camps which contained administrative internees in Belgium itself, like the citadel at Huy, Breendonk and in Germany Neuengamme, did not shake the Germans' position. Thus in mid-May 1943 the ICRC gave up its démarches.[70]

There only remained the possibility of parcels for the concentration camps. With funding finally sent by the authorities via the Belgian legation in Berne and thanks to the parallel action of the Belgian Red Cross, this aid, after a very slow start due to the slender means and the lack of known names among the prisoners, gathered pace in spring 1944.

In September 1944 the political prisoners who had remained on Belgian soil were liberated by the advancing Allied troops, but there remained 8,000 Belgians in concentration camps in the Reich and the names of only a few hundred were known.[71] It seemed that some reciprocal arrangement could be reached, gaining the right to visit them either in return for inspections of camps where German POWs were being held, as suggested by the ICRC delegate in Belgium or, as the

ICRC president proposed to the French and Belgian Red Cross, by obtaining from the French and Belgian authorities the acceptance of a similar gesture from the ICRC on behalf of the German civilians whom they were or would soon be holding on French, Belgian and German soil.[72]

The deported Jews remain beyond reach

The appalling fate of the deported Jews was, of course, closely followed by the ICRC, helped by the information provided by amongst others the Belgian Red Cross. The ICRC could only acknowledge its impotence as in the case of the Luxembourg Jews.

In summer 1944, the Allied landings and in particular the action on behalf of the Jews in Hungary naturally gave rise to considerable hope amongst the organisations concerned with the Jewish question. The World Jewish Congress, through the intermediary of the Belgian government in London, the War Refugee Board and the ICRC delegation in Washington, called on the ICRC to get the Germans to allow entry into the Belgian Jewish camps, hoping that this time the Nazis would pay more attention, given the increasing numbers of German POWs falling into Allied hands.[73] In any case the World Jewish Congress thought that if only for the sake of conscience the ICRC should continue to knock indefatigably on the door that remained stubbornly closed. The ICRC did not share their view. It wrote that to its great regret it could not undertake another démarche with the German authorities who had arrested Jews for political reasons, and who were of the opinion that the question was an internal one, and so would not tolerate any ICRC intervention. All that it had been able to do for the Jews in Germany and German-occupied territories up to now was to send food parcels to the camps where this was judged feasible. This action had been undertaken for purely humanitarian reasons, not based on international conventions, which the Germans in any case considered inapplicable to this category of detainee. It was thus able to alleviate to some small degree the suffering of these people and would continue in like vein where possible. It did not wish, however, to jeopardise the success of this action by an approach which the Germans would judge misplaced and which had no hope of succeeding. These were the reasons why it felt constrained to reply in the negative to all requests for a visit by an ICRC delegate to Jewish detainees.[74]

The Allied advance, and the liberation of the Belgian camps which it brought about, obviously invalidated the World Jewish Congress's démarche, but not the view of the ICRC. On 17 October, in approving the

Washington ICRC delegation's reply to the WJC, Suzanne Ferrière wrote that private organisations had to understand the ICRC's position, so often repeated. The German authorities met every request to visit the camps where Jews were held with a blunt refusal in principle.[75] Thus at a time when it was preparing, both in France and Belgium, on behalf of those in concentration camps, new efforts which might be equally helpful to the Jews, the ICRC maintained in the case of the latter a prudent principle of *non possumus*. So obvious was this that the Washington delegation did not even bother to acknowledge receipt of this message until March 1945.[76]

Ways and means

The ICRC had thus been able to undertake only limited action in Belgium on behalf of political prisoners and Jews. Its impotence was partly due to the situation of the national Red Cross and partly to its representation on the ground.

After the defeat in 1940 the Belgian Red Cross stayed in Belgium and only a splinter group was created in London to cater for the needs of the thousands of Belgians resident in the British capital. Soon the Germans made their presence felt. In fact, the Belgian Red Cross which had already been sidelined with regard to POWs who, as in the French case, were under the jurisdiction of a special mission, was blocked from any action on behalf of political prisoners, hostages and of course Jews. Its correspondence, even with the ICRC, had to pass through the DRK. Finally its director, Edmond Dronsart, who was arrested for a short period in 1942, was removed from his post on 1 May 1943, only to be reinstated at the Liberation. In spite of the continued presidency of Pierre Nolf the Belgian Red Cross had only the appearance of independence and was incapable of autonomous action without the approval of the occupying power.

Moreover the ICRC only retained the rump of a representation in Belgium. At the end of 1942 they had indeed obtained the accreditation by Germany of a delegate on the spot in the person of M. William Schmid-Koechlin, a Swiss living in Brussels and president of a society for aid to Swiss people living in the Belgian capital. But this representative had only a temporary mission limited to the distribution of the medical supplies sent by the American Quakers in autumn 1941 (Caritas I). His powers were in no way equivalent to those of an ICRC delegate whom the Belgian Red Cross in Geneva secretly insisted be sent. Admittedly Schmid-Koechlin stayed in the post until the Liberation, but he acted prudently and confined his efforts, as the Germans had agreed, to distributing a large amount of aid to the civilian population.[77] Thus in this country under the direct command of the *Militärbefehlshaber*, in spite of visits by delegates on mission, the ICRC found no way of carrying out activities on the spot as was the case in other occupied territories.

The Netherlands

From the Dutch East Indies to Buchenwald

In July 1940, following the arrest of German nationals in the Dutch East Indies, some 200 Dutch civilians, mostly of Asian descent, were deported to Buchenwald in retaliation. In spring 1941 about 700 more Dutch civilian internees joined them, but were not held within the concentration camp proper. Sweden, the Protecting Power for Holland, was given permission to visit the latter detainees but not the former. In contrast, through the cooperation of Dr Sethe of the German Foreign Ministry, the ICRC gained access to the camp which then housed more than 7,000 prisoners.

As we saw above (p. 34), on 14 August Pierre Descoeudres and Roland Marti arrived at Buchenwald. They were met by the commandant, *Obersturmbannführer* Rödl, who was obviously proud to show them round.

The camp is situated in the middle of a large beech forest which covers a vast hillside near Weimar. The approach is along a concrete road which passes through several successive guard posts with sentries, barbed wire, etc. The camp is planned on a vast scale: on one side there are villas for the officers, constructed down to the last detail by the internees, and on another vast barracks for the German troops, and finally the largest area, the actual camp with its many huts, some temporary, built of wood, and others more permanent, built of brick. Many are still in the course of construction, with others being planned since the whole camp is being extended.

We visited a hut of each type: they all follow the same pattern and are impeccably clean. At each end there are dormitories with bunk beds two or three high with a straw mattress and two or three blankets for each man. There are small cupboards in which the men keep their mess tin, their spoon and their clothing, etc. Adjacent to each dormitory there is a refectory where they eat, and in the middle of each hut there are extremely modern showers, with plentiful cold water, and WCs. There are about forty men to each dormitory.

Then we visited the medical block under the guidance of its director, a German doctor. This is a fully equipped, ultra-modern set-up with sterile and non-sterile operating theatres, all that is needed for a small, completely independent hospital with X-rays, diathermy, etc. Everything is sparklingly clean and the number of successful operations carried out is, according to the director, highly satisfactory. He later took us to the wards and showed us a man who had undergone surgery for a perforated stomach ten days before and who was now fine. He also showed us a patient operated on for emphysema by costal resection, and a prisoner whose leg had been amputated. There are 600 beds in the medical block where there are at the moment 340 cases, some serious with illnesses such as meningitis and nephritis. We visited the wards where the patients were fairly crowded: we saw no isolation bays even for the most serious cases. On the other hand everything was meticulously clean, the staff were well trained and the standards of hygiene were outstanding, with bathroom with bathtub, rooms for applying dressings, a pharmacy and laboratories with a microscope. Thus there is a dental department with two chairs and perfect facilities where the German dentist and his assistants carry out all manner of dental operations including prostheses, X-rays, etc.

We then saw the equally modern kitchens with twelve large vats for cooking and a huge adjoining refrigerator in which hung twenty-five sides of beef: the laundry room was amazingly well equipped with washing machines, driers, irons, etc. Nothing could be better or more up to date.

The staff are dressed in white and their heads are shaved. Everything is scrupulously clean whether in the kitchen, the utility room or any other place.

Our visit continued with the inspection of vast rooms where the detainees' civilian clothes are kept. Each individual has a large bag containing all the belongings he brought with him to the camp: everything is recorded on a form in a large file, signed by the detainee and the German authorities, and everything is given back when the owner leaves the camp.

Our next stop was one of the huts where men were working at their trade: the wood-turner, the sculptor, the porcelain figurine-maker, the miniature boat-maker, all were working with modern, specialist equipment.

The library with its 3,500 volumes is in another hut near to a small infirmary. The prisoners can read when they are free in the evenings. All the huts are surrounded by flower beds and lawns. Lower down is a very large kitchen garden and a whole area devoted to horticulture, and multi-coloured borders of flowers lend a bright touch.

Just near there is a sports area where the prisoners exercise. Beyond the barbed wire and the watch towers there is a beech forest through which one occasionally gets a glimpse of the Thuringian plain in the distance.

The camp officials also showed us the establishment's annexes. We saw the reception house, a splendid construction with a superb interior with wood panelling, solid wood furniture, wrought-iron work, chandeliers, and much more. The house and its contents were built entirely by prisoners with no outside help. This is also the case with the flower gardens, etc., and the ten villas where the officers live, constructed by the detainees from local wood and stone. Only a minute or so away from the camp we found ourselves transported, with all these charming houses set amid the beech woods, into a most agreeable, pleasant world.

Finally to round off our visit we saw the animal detainees' camp: monkeys, birds of prey and four bears.

Now to the prisoners themselves. As I have said, they number about 7,000 and are put into various categories: Jews, political prisoners, so-called 'antisocial' people who need to be taught to work again, etc. They are all dressed alike, a fact which strikes one as soon as one enters. Each man wears blue-and-white striped trousers and jacket, and a blue cap. They look like classic convicts and we saw them working everywhere, on the roads, carrying stones, cleaning paths, in various buildings. They all have closely shaven heads and look amazingly indistinguishable.

During this visit to the camp we saw most of the men carrying an enormous stone towards a road under construction. We watched them go by, one behind the other in rows of four, raising their berets in a brisk, mechanical gesture as they neared the Commandant, an endless line of stupefied creatures, indifferent to all that surrounded them, resigned, obeying the orders broadcast over the camp loudspeaker like automata.

A little later we saw them all gathered on the main square of the camp in separate groups according to their status, and we asked the German officials to explain the different categories, recognisable from a distinctive sign on their clothing: Poles, Czechs, Jews (wearing the star of David), etc. From the rostrum in front of all the lined-up and motionless prisoners, the German officials gave succinct orders by loudspeaker, and soon the camp orchestra played a piece of music for us. This was a poignant, never-to-be-forgotten spectacle which our hosts seemed to find perfectly normal but which we found hauntingly sad.[78]

The ICRC's protégés were different from other detainees. They were under the control of the Foreign Ministry, not that of the police or the SS. Their conditions of detention, given the circumstances, were not greatly different from those of prisoners of war, and therefore those of civilian internees. The conclusions drawn from the visit on 14 August 1940 were thus not negative where they were concerned.

The following winter the Dutch authorities were disturbed by the deaths of several prisoners. The ICRC was alerted and obtained permission for a further visit in June 1941, which reinforced its previous judgement at least as far as material conditions were concerned.[79] The main question raised by the detention of these prisoners was that of their legal status. Were they civilian internees or were they hostages? Should the ICRC try to obtain their release through some reciprocal arrangement regarding those Germans held by the Allies, or should it only attempt to improve their conditions of detention through the good offices of the German Red Cross? When writing to the Dutch government to impart the information it held, the ICRC opted for the latter solution and asked for prisoners to be transferred to the Netherlands: they drew the attention of the German Foreign Ministry to the harsh Thuringian climate and the proximity of the concentration camp.[80] In 1941 at the beginning of winter they were granted their request.[81] The Dutch 'hostages' were returned from Buchenwald to a camp near to s'Hertogenbosch which Marti visited in December.

The hostage question

In spring 1942 the situation in Holland took a turn for the worse. The 'hostages' who had been returned from Buchenwald were moved again in March to the seminary at Beekvliet, near to St Michielsgestel, and their numbers were swollen by hundreds of civilians, members of the resistance, Jews, suspects, and in particular hostages who were no longer being arrested as a reprisal but rather as a precautionary measure. They were held in various camps and prisons in Holland, then they were often deported to concentration camps in Germany. More than 2,000 de-mobbed reserve officers from the former army were also arrested, transferred first to a POW camp in Germany, then to Stanislau in the General-Government where they were joined by Dutch POWs brought from the Oflags at Colditz and Linz. The scale of these arrests and deportations was obviously designed to break the passive resistance of the Dutch population.

What, then, could be done? The problem was all the more pressing for the ICRC since it could not visit the places of detention in Germany or even Holland, with the exception of the location where the former internees of Buchenwald were being held. The efforts of its delegate in the Far East towards obtaining an improvement in their conditions or even the release of the interned German civilians would surely be helped if the ICRC obtained some concession from the Germans. Marti took up this idea in Berlin and in Holland and Schwarzenberg in Geneva, all the more so since the position of the hostages brought from Buchenwald seemed to have worsened since their transfer from s'Hertogenbosch to St Michielsgestel. The pressure of Marti's efforts and Schwarzenberg's arguments finally swayed Carl J. Burckhardt. He prudently decided, however, not to approach the Foreign Ministry but to appeal to Ernst Grawitz, the acting president of the German Red Cross.

In his letter, Burckhardt began by saying he hoped that by making a personal approach to the president he could rely on the latter's under-standing of the ICRC's position. He was worried by reports in the press of the arrest of even more hostages in Holland and also by the fact that the s'Hertogenbosch prisoners were to be moved again. The ICRC was concerned by this. Burckhardt was sure that the German authorities only undertook such serious measures when the attacks on them demanded it. He referred his correspondent to the Tokyo project of the fifteenth International Red Cross Conference in 1934 inspired by Article 50 of the Hague Rules which insisted on humane treatment for hostages and the banning of any collective punishment of a population as a consequence of the action of individuals.

He then wished only to address the Dutch case in a manner that might be beneficial to the overseas Germans. The ICRC had kept the German authorities informed of the results obtained by their delegate, Robert Moll, on behalf of the detained Germans in Dutch Guyana, but there would be no lasting improvement unless some reciprocal arrangement could be made for enemy detainees in the hands of the Germans. The work of Professor Moll and others would be put in question if there was no reciprocal improvement, for example for the benefit of the hostages. The ICRC was facing a difficult task on behalf of the many Germans in Latin America, especially those in Brazil about whom the Foreign Ministry had made a proposal. There was, however, no hope of continuing to achieve all it could on behalf of non-combatant war victims if the powers holding the detainees could see no likelihood of a similar gesture forthcoming from the German side.

He begged the president to understand the difficulties and demands of reciprocity and to explain this to the competent authorities so that they might avoid any action detrimental to this process.[82] Grawitz, however, did not accept that hostages and civilian internees could be placed on the same footing and thus benefit in the name of reciprocity from similar treatment.[83]

Following this attempt the question of the hostages, internees and deportees advanced little in the years that followed, at least on the legal plane. The problem of the Dutch officer POWs reduced to the status of hostages and thus considered as civilians, as well as the execution of three reserve officers from Stanislau who were accused of spying,[84] were to be transferred to the file of violations of the Geneva Convention which was to lead the ICRC to launch a public appeal on 23 August 1943 to all the warring parties that they should respect the POW code.

In Holland itself camps and prisons multiplied as the spirit of resistance grew firmer. Thousands of Dutch people were detained in 1943 and 1944 in concentration camps and the political prisons in Amersfoort (this was also used as a transit camp for Jews being deported), Haaren (s'Hertogenbosch), Scheveningen, Vught, Amsterdam, Utrecht and Rotterdam. No visits by ICRC delegates were possible with the exception of Beekvliet and Ruwenberg (St Michielsgestel). When he visited Holland from 29 November to 4 December 1943 Eric Mayer wrote:

The German authorities consider these internees to be a danger to the regime and think that this is a question of internal politics. They thus refuse any aid from abroad. Unfortunately we have no choice but to accept this state of affairs. There seems no point in trying to insist on sending anything or anyone into these camps.[85]

There remained the question of the concentration camps. In parallel to the individual parcels sent to the Dutch deportees whose names were known, in particular at Oranienburg, in spring 1943 personal parcels reached foreign nationals interned at Westerbork. The Dutch detained on home ground ended up receiving if not aid from the ICRC, at least the support of a person who was acceptable to the SS as well as to the Dutch Red Cross, Mme van Obereem. This woman was mentioned by Marti in a note of 17 March 1944 on the concentration camps in Holland. He remarked that the conditions in the camps had improved over the last four months, seemingly because of the execution of two camp commandants who had subjected internees to extremely harsh treatment. For six months Mme van Obereem had enjoyed the trust of the Dutch Red Cross and the Deutsche Sicherheitspolizei and had worked in the concentration camps and other prisons, distributing Red Cross and private parcels. Mme van Obereem would have liked a further person from the Red Cross to be designated for each camp but the German police would not allow this, so she was forced to work alone. In all 26,000 parcels, varying in weight from between 2 and 4.5 kilos, were sent during the war to Dutch detainees and deported civilians by the ICRC.[86]

Mass deportation

The ICRC was informed very early on about the fate of the Jews. From June 1941 they knew that there were many of them in Buchenwald and Mauthausen, but even worse, by the following November they knew that the majority of those deported to the latter camp had died. This knowledge prompted Marti to put in an official request to visit Mauthausen:

I believe you know about this notorious camp: it is where the Dutch Jews are taken. There are extraordinary, tragic rumours rife: it is said that over 95 per cent of them have died. Worse still, it is said that out of the 700 Dutch people who are thought to have been taken there, only fourteen are still alive. I told Dr Sethe that wherever we went we heard this camp referred to as worse than anything invented by the Inquisition.

Dr Sethe replied that 'people could say what they liked'; it was out of the question for any visit to take place even by a delegate of the German Foreign Ministry, which was not in any case involved.[87]

Further information on the fate of the Dutch Jews was given when Dr Masset visited the Dutch Red Cross at the end of 1942, and then a year later when Dr Eric Mayer undertook his visit and estimated that some 250,000 Jews living in the Netherlands in 1939 had been deported and that only some 30,000 of mixed race or in hiding were left.[88] The ICRC's main sentiment at that time was one of impotence: it was unable to obtain information and incapable of sending aid. On two occasions, however, the CMS managed to send medical and pharmaceutical supplies worth several thousand francs via the DRK, firstly in December 1942 to the Jewish Council in Amsterdam and secondly in September 1943 to the camps in Westerbork and Vught. In spring 1944 the visit to Geneva of a German Jew, a naturalised Dutchman, who had managed to escape from the Westerbork transit camp, rekindled interest in an aid operation, particularly since it seemed that the camp would close once the last inmates had left for the East. The ICRC decided on the one hand to approach the commandant of the camp himself and on the other to send parcels. This initiative was, however, overtaken by events in the military domain,[89] and in autumn 1944 the advance of the Allied armies precipitated the removal of prisoners from the Dutch concentration camps to those in the Reich. Thus in November detainees, hostages, political prisoners and probably even Jews were sent to Sachsenhausen, Buchenwald, Dachau and Neuengamme, and the women were sent to Ravensbrück. As soon as it was alerted to this the Berlin delegation of the ICRC tried through supplementary aid to come to the help of these civilians whose lot worsened gradually as the Allied victory drew nearer.

Greece

In spring 1941 Greece succumbed to the assault of the Wehrmacht which had come to reinforce the Italian army. A puppet government was installed in Athens and the occupying powers divided up the country. The Italians took three-quarters of the territory, ancient Greece and a large part of the islands, the Germans essentially took Macedonia and Crete and finally the Bulgarians took control of northern Macedonia and eastern Thrace. The military effort had totally upset the Greek economy which was already weak. The winter of 1941–2 was marked by appalling poverty and in the capital alone several thousand people died of hunger. The effect of the mainly German requisitions was made worse by the partisan conflict which began fairly soon after the summer of 1941. Following a request from its delegation in Athens and the Greek Red Cross the ICRC initiated an aid operation for the civilian population which was to last until spring 1945 and was to be one of the most extensive humanitarian undertakings of the Red Cross during the Second World War. There is no need to dwell on this now since the final report on aid activities in Greece and the third volume of the General

Report of 1948 both give details of it.[90] This action, which required the collaboration of the occupying powers, the British and the Americans, the Greek authorities, the Swedish government and the national Red Cross societies of all these different countries, posed a series of diplomatic problems for the ICRC which were both delicate and complex. In this single instance the ICRC allowed its name and its emblem to be used for an aid undertaking which it did not wholly control or have responsibility for. The action was also of considerable proportions since in summer 1942 about 500 people were employed while early in 1945 the number had reached nearly 5,000. Mostly it was politically risky. Permission was needed from Great Britain to cross the blockade and the British were afraid of seeming to act to the advantage of the occupying forces and played the Swedish card since Sweden was making available the necessary boats. The Germans, and therefore the Italians as well, set as a condition for their participation the presence of the ICRC and they insisted that the ICRC should be the guarantor of the neutrality of the supplies. Whereas the Swedish government backed up its national Red Cross and the Swiss Red Cross intervened on behalf of Greek children with backing from Berne, the ICRC had at one and the same time to defend its own neutrality, to resist its Swedish rivals and to make sure it was not restricted by the support of the Axis whose political manoeuvring was ill disguised by the flag of the Red Cross.

Political detainees and deportees

The action undertaken on behalf of the political detainees and the Jews should be considered against the backdrop of the humanitarian aid for the civilian population. Because of the latter the ICRC benefited on the ground from an infrastructure and unusually extensive material means even if the use of these had to be agreed by its partner, the Stockholm Royal Government. There was permanent contact with the occupying powers and sustained diplomatic relations with all the capitals. Surely this gave them an opportunity to carry out aid operations on a wide scale to help the victims of racial and political persecution who were indeed part of the civilian population?

In fact political repression was gaining strength. Thousands of Greek civilians were imprisoned as members of the resistance or as hostages in concentration camps and in prisons. In addition to the installations throughout the Cyclades where communists arrested during the dictatorship of Metaxas were imprisoned, new names began to appear regularly in the reports from the ICRC delegation in Athens: Larissa, Thebes, Tatoï, Haïdari, Houdhi, Avéroff, the prison in Athens. According to the Greek Red Cross there were 5,000 political prisoners in autumn 1941 and 15,000 a year later in the Italian zone alone, without counting individual groups such as the British soldiers who were taken prisoner in civilian dress after the armistice in April 1941, or the Serbs and the Jews. Most of the camps were in an appalling state. There was widespread famine, cold in winter, neglect, harsh treatment and even assassinations which were more spontaneous in the camps under Greek control than in those under German and Italian. The Germans, however, executed more hostages or deported them to the Reich. After September 1943 they took control of the whole country following the collapse of Italy, which led to increased repression. Unlike in other occupied territories, the delegates from the ICRC were allowed, briefly admittedly, to visit several of these camps, particularly in the Italian zone, which contained together political detainees and hostages when they were not simple internees.[91] The term 'inspection' could not be applied to all such contacts, but they were surely contrary to the instructions issued to delegates since they did not concern the categories of detainees defined by the Conventions. It is interesting to note that the reply is not easy in all cases and that the ICRC had to clarify matters for their representative in Athens, Jean d'Amman, early in 1943, telling him that the circumstances of the war had given rise to differing situations which did not always make a precise definition of the status of the victims possible: the ICRC therefore considered all interned foreign nationals to be enemy subjects in the hands of a warring party, thus similar to civilian internees, and any interned soldier to be a POW.[92] Using this as a principle, all foreign detainees were thus included in the aid supplies provided by the Red Cross for the civilian population and they received, wherever possible, a double ration of food each day. (There were 12,000 such people in spring 1943 in the seven concentration camps and the thirty-seven prisons in Athens.[93])

Nineteen forty-four was a particularly awful year. Not only was the list of prisons and camps growing longer and the number of detainees increasing, but also the material situation of the latter was worsening. There was a lack of everything: clothes, food and soap. The executions of hostages were increasing along with the rounding up of workers. Carl J. Burckhardt was told in July 1943 that they had not yet been able to get into Haïdari or Houdhi even though the ICRC delegate Beat de Glutz had lodged a request with General Schimana, the commander of the SS in Greece. They realised that awful atrocities were taking place in the prison at Haïdari. These prisons contained mostly hostages who, when a bomb attack took place, were sometimes executed in groups or sent to concentration labour camps or even to certain camps in Germany. All the Jews had been imprisoned in Haïdari and were then loaded into cattle trucks, eighty of them in each, which were then firmly secured. The delegation, as well as the Greek Red Cross, had managed on a few occasions to distribute food through the bars of these rail wagons.[94]

The only humanitarian gestures that were still possible were being present as the trains left, the distribution of some supplies and the sending of parcels to the concentration camps. Apart from this, those who were taken away disappeared without trace and Marti received nothing but evasive or deceitful replies when he questioned the German Foreign Ministry about their fate.[95]

The Jews

Unfortunately for them, most of the Greek Jews after the armistice of April 1941 found themselves in the German occupation zone, that is 55,000 of them, with 53,000 in Salonika alone, as against 13,000 in the Italian zone and 5,600 in Thrace under Bulgarian control. Thus Dr René Burkhardt, the assistant delegate in Salonika, who was in charge of the distribution of aid to the civilian population, was to witness the racial policy from summer 1942 and to see the arrival six months later of Dieter Wisliceny, one of Eichmann's deputies. Early on Burkhardt scrupulously informed the ICRC of the measures of concentration, segregation and deportation being carried out, saying that at the beginning of 1943 the occupying authorities had decided on the mass deportation of all the Jews in the Greek areas occupied by German forces. The Jews were first forced to wear a yellow star of David, eight centimetres across, and then were gradually banned from trams, the main streets and shops. They were then confined to certain areas and could not leave them to go to work: their shops were requisitioned and then the comfortable Jewish houses. Two families had to live in one room. Once the deportations started (on 15 March, Burkhardt thought) a concentration camp was set up near the station, complete with flood-lighting, searchlights and machine gun turrets. This camp was normally meant to hold 2,500 people, but at times there were about 12,000 Jews packed into it. In one period of eight weeks 43,800 Jews passed through this camp before being sent to Germany by train in trucks that were sealed externally, each truck holding between seventy and a hundred deportees. The camp was quite clean and contained a medical wing, although this was not in service. The food was to a large extent provided by the ICRC – for example, bread, milk and beans – and the rest was bought on the black market by the Jews. Medical supplies were also provided. The ration per person was the same as in the town. Burkhardt added that by the time he left all the Greek Jews had been deported and those of other nationalities were due to leave Macedonia before 1 July.[96]

However, as the ICRC's assistant delegate in Salonika he was not content with sending reports and arranging food supplies, he protested. On 13 March, as the first trains left for Auschwitz, he sent to his collaborator, the head of the German administration for food supplies to Macedonia, a telegram for Geneva, which he trusted would be forwarded via the German Red Cross. It read: 'Please telegraph the ICRC at Geneva headquarters. Start of deportation of 45,000 Jews from Salonika almost decided. Urgent examination needed with governments involved. Deportation [sic] women and children to Palestine indispensable.'[97]

This démarche was brought to the knowledge of the German plenipotentiary for Greece, Ambassador Altenburg, and resulted in German insistence on the recall of Burkhardt to Geneva. This was only to be expected since the occupying forces had already closed down the Swiss consulate in Salonika and had thus removed the other active, embarrassing witness to the persecution of the Jews, the consul Fridolin Jenny from Zurich.[98] In spite of a démarche by the Swiss chargé d'affaires in Athens to the German plenipotentiary, in which he tried to make light of the affair, the Germans remained inflexible and the ICRC had to ask its assistant delegate to return home. The Swiss chargé d'affaires concluded that the distressing incident proved yet again how delicate the choice of ICRC delegates was, particularly in occupied countries. He added that the delegates, who sometimes allowed themselves to be dazzled by the privileges and advantages occasioned by the mission entrusted to them, should be careful to follow to the letter the instructions given them by the ICRC and not to concern themselves maladroitly with questions that did not concern them directly, however interesting they might seem.[99]

This opinion was all the better informed since the chargé d'affaires' brother was himself an ICRC delegate; a note from Schwarzenberg to the Secretariat is, however, more interesting in its statement of the policy of the ICRC. He said that they were aware of the situation of the Jews in Salonika: mass deportations as in all the occupied countries (France, Belgium, Holland, etc.). Unfortunately they no longer had any way of stopping these deportations, or rather the ICRC did not wish to make any move over this. He quoted the last line of a memo from the Greek delegation in which they said that the ICRC had a very clear task: it was up to it not to allow to die from hunger those 50,000 human beings who were stretching their arms towards them in entreaty. M. de Glutz added that the Greek Jews should have the same right to Greek Red Cross food supplies as the other Greek nationals, but he felt that they could do no more for the present. Schwarzenberg wondered whether this should be the directive given to the ICRC delegation and whether money should be sought from Jewish organisations in Geneva. He recommended caution, however, since Carl J. Burckhardt had not seemed to want to extend their work on behalf of the Jews beyond the meagre limits fixed at the last meeting of the Bureau.[100]

Writing from Athens a month later, Jean d'Amman returned to the subject from a different angle whilst noting the impossibility of preventing the inevitable. He said that the exodus of Jews from Salonika was complete, the last trains having left the week before. Nearly 50,000 Jews had been evacuated, representing the quasi-totality of the Sephardic community in Salonika who had taken refuge there when the Jews had been expelled from Spain by the Catholic kings. Several thousand men had been enrolled in the Todt organisation and were working on two sites with minimum food and hygiene. Many of those expelled had relations in Athens and other parts of Greece, who were very concerned over their fate and kept begging the ICRC to find out whether the prisoners would be able to send messages to them via the DRK following the 'civilian messages twenty-five words' formula. He asked the ICRC to throw some light on this.[101]

The ICRC's recognition of its impotence fell like a hammer-blow. It replied that the DRK did not accept PMS forms for Jews, and it could see no other way of ensuring contact between Jews moved to Germany or to other countries and their relatives in Greece. Nor would any enquiries be allowed concerning deported Jews.[102]

By autumn 1943 the Germans occupied all of Greece. The fate of other Greek Jewish communities, hitherto largely left alone, was sealed. The Foreign Interests Division of the Swiss legation in Athens tried hard to stop the deportation of the Jews under its protection,[103] but the ICRC had to admit its own impotence, saying that they were well aware of what had happened to the Jews in Salonika but that they had no further means of intervention than they had in the deportations from France, Holland and Belgium. The Jewish problem was considered by the occupying power to be purely internal and no external intervention would be tolerated.[104]

By a curious twist, however, some Jews from Greece did survive. In a letter of June 1943 to the ICRC Jean d'Amman said that the German occupation authorities had asked the Spanish government to repatriate from Salonika those Jews who held a Spanish passport. A special train would convey them, about 600 in all, from Salonika to the Spanish frontier under German escort before 15 June 1943. The Spanish minister in Athens had expressed a wish to see an ICRC delegate accompany the train, but the German authorities refused, making it clear that the ICRC had no right to interfere in the Jewish question. Madrid and Berlin negotiated over the nature of the repatriation during the whole of 1943. General Franco did not want to see a massive return of Jews to Spain but he wished no harm to be done to them by the Germans either. The German Foreign Ministry thought hard about the priority to be given to passport as opposed to race and those responsible for the Jewish question did not want enemy propaganda to be able to score a point. In the end these Spanish Jews were sent to Bergen-Belsen, where about two-thirds of the group survived and returned to Spain after the Liberation.[105]

Norway (Scandinavia)

When in early July 1942 the ICRC turned its attention to the situation of the civilians interned by the German occupying troops in Norway, following a request from the Norwegian minister in Berne, it was embarking upon nothing unique but, as Mme Frick underlined, the same general problem as in the rest of occupied Europe, namely requests for the ICRC to send supplies and to visit the prisons and the camps.

However, the Norwegian case seemed interesting to the Coordinating Committee. On the one hand the civilians seemed like hostages for which there was the precedent of the Dutch in Buchenwald and s'Hertogensbosch, and at that time Carl J. Burckhardt had not yet received a reply from the acting president of the DRK to his letter of 1 June 1942. On the other hand the situation was interesting because there was the possibility of a reciprocal arrangement: the British had interned on the Isle of Man some Norwegians who supported the Axis powers and they had been visited the previous June by two delegates from the ICRC, Rodolphe Haccius and Nicolas Burckhardt. The Committee therefore decided to ask Schwarzenberg to look into the matter whilst making clear in advance the confines of any future action the ICRC might undertake. Carl J. Burckhardt, who considered at the time that it might be possible to approach the Gestapo via the German Foreign Ministry, was thinking only of infrequent visits and could not envisage for these internees a regime similar to that of the POWs. For his part Jacques Chenevière gave a warning about the consequences of any future extension of Red Cross activities: it should not be thought that the ICRC could undertake regular aid work, nor that it could oversee such work. This warning concerned the general activities of the Aid Division whose concrete initiatives had to remain subject to the political decisions of the ICRC.[106]

The request, based on the Dutch precedent and the argument of reciprocity, was not refused in principle by the German Foreign Ministry in November 1942, but the ICRC was invited to return to the attack later on, since the reorganisation which was then taking place in the camps precluded at that moment any action which might satisfy the Committee.[107] Although the note of 24 September 1942 had still received no reply despite Marti's urgent approaches to Dr Sethe, this attitude, positive as it was in principle, could be considered a small triumph for the ICRC, although it was essentially procrastinating. In fact this opening was never realised, either for the Norwegians interned in concentration camps and prisons on home ground, or for the hundreds of their compatriots who had been deported to Germany, mainly since winter 1942–3.

From 12 August to 15 September 1943 Marti went on a long tour of Norway. He had suggested this to the Germans from early 1942 on. His main object was not the civilian internees but the supervision of the aid sent by the CMS to the civilian population and the condition of a number of Polish and chiefly Yugoslav POWs, who had been deemed to be civilian workers and had been transferred to the Todt camps in the north. Marti also hoped, however, to make the most of his visit and to obtain a concrete follow-up to their opening of November 1942 from the Foreign Ministry, to whom he had renewed his request several times. There was another negative response on the eve of his departure for Oslo, but once there he tried hard to wheedle permission to enter the main concentration camp at Grini near the capital and to visit the prisons or camps in Oslo, Trondheim, Bergen, Tromsö and Narvik. However, in spite of the backing of the Norwegian Red Cross which was sending supplies regularly to the Norwegians in Oranienburg, his interventions at the headquarters of the Gestapo in Victoria Terrace and via the representative of the DRK in Norway met with a blank refusal.[108]

Marti did not, however, return completely empty-handed, even where interned or deported civilians were concerned. He gathered information about the camps, especially Grini. He learnt that there remained only a handful of Jews – married couples of differing faiths – in the camp at Tönsberg, the rest having been deported to Germany. He collected both in Oslo and Stockholm hundreds of names of Norwegians detained in Oranienburg.[109]

The concentration camps in Norway were to remain closed to any visit from the ICRC until the end of the war, in spite of renewed efforts by Luc Thudicum during his summer 1944 mission and by Georg Hoffmann, the Red Cross delegate in Stockholm, during a visit to the

Norwegian Red Cross in autumn 1944.[110] There was no success either when, in autumn 1943, the ICRC tried, through the DRK, to obtain information about some Norwegian sailors who had been transferred from a prison camp (Milag Nord) to a concentration camp. Nonetheless the démarche by Schwarzenberg corresponded with the spoken undertaking made by Hartmann, head of foreign relations at the DRK, during his last stay in Geneva, to send to the competent authority requests for information about the whereabouts of individual Aryans who had been deported from occupied territories to Germany. Hartmann could not honour his word in this instance, writing that the DRK could obtain no further information on the Norwegians who had been taken from Marlag-Milag Nord to another place. In the circumstances it turned out to be an action that the competent German authorities considered necessary for precise reasons that could not be divulged. The DRK was still willing to try to obtain, if at all possible, information on the whereabouts and condition of Aryan people arrested in occupied territories. But, as facts showed, the percentage of positive replies was likely to be low. In general it was not possible to predict whether a response would be obtained in a particular case, so he was unfortunately not able to say which groups of missing people (apart from the non-Aryans) should *a priori* be excluded.[111]

The Norwegians deported to Oranienburg played a central role in setting up the dispatch of aid parcels to concentration camps. Through the contacts that it had in Germany with Norwegians there, some of them former deportees or parents of deportees, the ICRC delegation in Germany knew the names and roll numbers of prisoners to whom the ICRC could send individual parcels, as the German authorities allowed from early 1943 on. The Norwegians were, therefore, the nationality with the highest representation in the list of those who received the fifty parcels weighing two kilos which the Swiss federal authorities allowed the ICRC to send from Switzerland to the concentration camps as an experiment. But the parcels could not be acknowledged and the dispatch could not continue since the ICRC needed the assurance of safe arrival of the parcels which was the only thing that would gain the confidence of the warring party, a confidence that was necessary for it to be able to continue its work on behalf of both POWs and civilian internees. Marti, who was well aware of the relatively favourable regime allowed for the Norwegians at Oranienburg – with the benefit of racial elitism – undertook to try to lengthen the list of people found and of their needs, and also to try to establish contact with the camp authorities. Through the year he widened the circle of his contacts to other camps, prisons and commandos in the Hamburg area. By May 1944 he had made contact with the authorities of all the large camps in which were imprisoned Norwegian men and women (and more generally Scandinavians and Dutch people), i.e. Ravensbrück, Oranienburg, Dachau, Natzweiler and Buchenwald.[112] Even though he was not allowed entry into the camps, his contacts enabled him to ascertain more or less exactly the number of prisoners of Nordic nationality, to get an idea, quite often positive, of their state, and to question those in charge about the prisoners' needs and to make sure that the aid supplies, the collective ones included, reached their destination for the most part. He was also able to trace certain groups, such as the 200 sailors from Marlag-Milag Nord who had been transported to Rendsburg, or the 300 students deported to Buchenwald and Natzweiler during the winter of 1942–3 whose fate had so perturbed Swiss university milieux that the Federal Council had undertaken on their behalf several démarches in vain.[113] Finally when in autumn 1943 the Norwegian and Swedish Red Cross were banned from sending aid to Oranienburg the ICRC obtained permission to substitute their own aid supplies.

This last remark allows me to draw certain conclusions about the relations between the ICRC and Sweden during the war. From autumn 1943 the ICRC maintained a delegation in Stockholm, headed by Georg Hoffmann, a thirty-six-year-old university lecturer from Zurich, whose mission, unlike all the others, was primarily politico-diplomatic.[114] Scandinavia was, for the Swedish Red Cross as for the Swedish government, a privileged zone of action. That is to say that here, as in other theatres of operation, the ICRC and the Swedish Red Cross maintained relations consisting at one and the same time of collaboration, rivalry and competition.[115] In aiding the Danish and Norwegian Jews, Sweden, its leaders, its national Red Cross society and its people played an essential role. The ICRC was hardly involved in this problem, but where action on behalf of the deported Norwegians at home and in Germany was concerned it acted on its own authority: it even made up for the impotence of the Swedish Red Cross. Finally, the rescue of those interned in the concentration camps at the end of the war was to constitute a new episode in the ambiguous relations between Geneva and Stockholm.

6   The satellites

Croatia

The search for dialogue

In April 1941 the independent state of Croatia was created and consequently a new national Red Cross. In autumn 1942 relations between the ICRC and the Croat authorities, both the state and the Red Cross, were still at a standstill. The ICRC had made every effort to try to establish contact with Zagreb. It hoped that the fate of Croatian POWs and especially that of the hundreds of thousands of Croats in the New World could be balanced against the new State signing up to the Geneva Conventions, the exchange of lists of prisoners, the dispatch of correspondence and the establishment of a delegate on the ground. Mainly through the intermediary of the Croatian consul in Zurich and the support of the Swiss consul in Zagreb, via letters addressed directly to the Foreign Ministry and the national society, the ICRC brought to the fore the argument of reciprocity. In its patient insistence how much weight was given to the fate of political prisoners and Jews? From autumn 1941 it received matching information that was increasingly precise about the atrocities committed by the Pavelitch regime.[1] At the same time, however, the requests for information sent by the civilian Yugoslavian service of the ACPG (central POW bureau) to the local Red Cross remained unanswered. It was through the intermediary of the DRK that the ICRC asked the OKW to suspend the return of the Yugoslav POWs and internees who belonged to the Croatian state when it became obvious that the latter were being killed on their return if they were Jewish, Serb or Orthodox. In spring 1942 the ICRC's liaison agent in Belgrade, Rudolf Voegeli, got in direct touch with the Croatian Red Cross. His mission was no more successful. His reports confirmed the gravity of the situation and the need for energetic intervention. For the persecuted ethnic and religious groups, certain well-informed sources estimated in summer 1942 that it was perhaps already too late.[2]

175

A visit on the spot, however, managed to resolve the situation, to the relief not only of the ICRC but also the Swiss consular mission in Zagreb which looked for much from the presence of the ICRC, especially for help in its activities as Protecting Power and in its humanitarian efforts.[3] In December 1942, Robert Schirmer from Berlin went to Croatia where he was received by the minister of foreign affairs, Lorkovic, among others. He obtained from the Croatian government the recognition of the Geneva Convention, the application of the code concerning POWs and the installation of a Red Cross delegate in Zagreb. He established with the Croatian Red Cross *de facto* relations, in conformity with the doctrine of the ICRC for wartime. The new national Red Cross, which was very hedged about by the government, wanted for everything – materials, executives, personnel and most of all moral authority. It declared itself ready to take on board the ICRC's wishes, to distribute even to the Jewish community the supplies that the ICRC and the CMS could send exempt of customs duty.[4]

There was no longer any obstacle to the installation of a delegate on the ground: the man chosen was Julius Schmidlin Jr, son of the first Swiss consul in Zagreb. In March 1943, after a series of meetings at headquarters, the ICRC representative returned to the capital of a country that he knew well and whose language he spoke fluently. But did the concessions obtained by Schirmer, in particular the application of the Geneva Conventions, correspond to the actual situation? Croatia was surely above all a country ripe for civil war and revolutionary and social troubles. It was interesting that even before the appointment of Schmidlin, Schwarzenberg drew the attention of the Coordinating Committee to this. He felt that the oral and written reports, especially the confidential report from its delegate Schirmer on his experiences in Croatia, seemed to raise the following problem: did not the situation that Croatia found itself in at that time resemble a state of civil war? He felt that the accounts of M. Schirmer deserved scrutiny in the light of the resolutions taken at the Tenth International Conference of the Red Cross in Geneva (1921), when the Red Cross affirmed its right and its duty to bring aid in the event of civil war and 'social and revolutionary troubles'. The movements in Croatia could indeed be described as 'revolutionary'. These resolutions equally foresaw the case of a national Red Cross which could not, 'of its own admission, cope alone with all the needs for aid'.[5] If this national Red Cross wanted help, it should approach the ICRC.

On the other hand, Schwarzenberg went on, the resolutions suggested that if through impotence or unwillingness on the part of this society which did not ask for outside help or did not accept an offer of help through the intermediary of the ICRC, unaided suffering caused by civil war would require urgent assistance. The ICRC would have the ability and the duty to insist, or to delegate a national Red Cross society to insist, that the authorities of the country concerned should accept necessary aid and allow it to be freely distributed. If the authorities of the country refused to allow this assistance to be provided, the ICRC should make public the facts, with evidence from the relevant documents.

Schwarzenberg declared himself unable to support this idea, but allowed himself to draw the attention of the members of the Coordinating Committee to the text of the resolutions of the International Conference in Geneva, already mentioned, once they had studied the question of the imminent appointment of a delegate in Croatia. Given the special task assigned in particular to the ICRC by that Conference, the work of this future delegate would take on an especially important aspect and the aid work to be undertaken by the ICRC in this country should, he felt, be organised on a larger and more detailed scale than usual. Even if the situation in Croatia were not considered a state of civil war or seen as 'social and revolutionary troubles', the spirit, if not the letter, of the resolutions of this International Conference would seem to justify the above conclusion.[6]

In his first, long report to the ICRC on the political and military situation, Schmidlin, writing still from Geneva, confirmed Schwarzenberg's analysis, saying that after the Yugoslav defeat in 1941 and the establishment of the new Croat Free State, or rather its authoritarian regime, the passions of a small minority of extremists and of former native inhabitants were unleashed; civil war broke out, encouraged by external elements, the country's western neighbours. The consequences of this civil war were disastrous. Whole regions were depopulated, either through war, executions, murders, disease or mass deportations. In fact this depopulation represented an advantage for certain foreign political elements. It was certain that the great majority of Croats were forced to remain passive in the face of all these hardships. There were only two organisations that could provide aid. The first was the Catholic church which until then had taken on this role in an effective way. The other was the ICRC, whose aid would be all the more effective given its neutral origin.

He affirmed that from his previous experience he knew that the ICRC was held in great esteem in Croatia. This had been most evident in the last few weeks since it was generally known that Croatia had signed the Geneva Convention. He was able to confirm that the ICRC was seen as providential. Unfortunately some of the authorities, in particular a large section of the Ustachi party who occupied prominent positions in the Interior Ministry, lacked understanding, mainly through ignorance. The officials in the other ministries were better disposed. He had noticed that as a result of general internal opposition the remaining boorish, violent elements were being replaced. It seemed probable, however, that this process was taking time.[7] The new delegate judged that in this situation, in spite of its lack of political independence and its embryonic nature, the Croatian Red Cross could play a crucial role, once it was reformed from within, if the ICRC gave active support to those people in it who were already working according to the ideals of the Red Cross.

The list of problems highlighted by Schmidlin during his meetings at the ICRC headquarters was a long one, the depiction of the situation of certain categories of victims was dramatic, and the material supplies and political or moral support were described as derisory. The reply and conclusions of the ICRC seemed, in comparison, circumspect and feeble, even if they pointed at real impasses. The following extracts from the minutes of the meeting of 25 March bear witness to this. Those present included M. Schmidlin, Mme Frick, Carl J. Burckhardt, Jacques Chenevière, Jean-Etienne Schwarzenberg, and the director of the CMS, Robert Boehringer.

Comments and special questions put by M. Schmidlin:

3) Persecution of the Serbs by the Ustachis. – Not discussed.

4b) Could we obtain lists of the Jewish people interned in Germany or the occupied territories? – No, there is no hope of obtaining them.

c) Could we obtain the lists of the Croats interned in Germany for political reasons? No. These are not really civilian internees but rather political detainees on whose behalf it is very difficult to act. . .

5) Is it possible to send parcels and letters from Croatia:

a) to Croatian Jews interned in Germany? – No, except to Theresienstadt, if the names of the prisoners concerned are known.

b) to Croatian Jews interned in Italy? Yes, if we know of them and where they are.

c) to Croats interned in Italy? Idem.

d) to Croats interned in Germany for political reasons? – No, only to detainees in certain concentration camps if their names and addresses are known.

e) to Croats interned in Allied territories? – Yes.

6) Can the ICRC intervene on behalf of the civilian Croatian internees in camps in Croatia? – M. Schmidlin should try to act on his own initiative. He should contact M. Graz who will inform him of the activities of the ICRC during the Spanish Civil War.

7) Can the ICRC intervene on behalf of the Serbs deported from Croatia to Serbia and thence on to Germany? – It would be better if the Croatian Red Cross approached the German Red Cross directly.

At the end of the meeting when M. Schmidlin asked how the ICRC could help and morally assist the Croatian Red Cross in its task, the reply was given that M. Pictet would look into the statutes of this Red Cross to see whether, in general, these conformed to the stipulations concerning the statutes of national societies.

In answer to his question about help from the ICRC if the Croatian Red Cross ran into difficulties, it was suggested that the latter could consult the former in any given case. The ICRC would then send a letter of advice that the Croatian Red Cross could put forward to its own authorities; that would be in the nature of a consultation. This decision was taken with the idea of giving a new national society all the back-up possible to its action and also so as not to disappoint *a priori* a society which saw the ICRC as an authority which could enable it to accomplish its task.[8]

A delegate on all fronts

Dynamic and well informed, Julius Schmidlin set to work in the Croatian capital from April 1943 onwards. Only his work in the field of racial and political persecution, including his relations with the Croatian Red Cross, will be discussed here. Schmidlin tried hard not only to strengthen the ties with the national society and to reinforce his collaboration with it, but also to push through reforms and changes of personnel at the heart of the society. He realised immediately that it was to be a very difficult and delicate task which could only be carried out slowly and with a great deal of patience, and which was indeed outside his brief.

On a formal level, relations between the ICRC and the Croatian Red Cross gathered momentum. In March 1944 the president of the latter, Dr Kurt Hühn, made a three-day visit to Geneva, to the ACPG, the CMS and the LSCR. But at home the society did not seem to increase in efficiency, independence or credibility. Schmidlin therefore continued his obstinate efforts in the background to bring about a change at the head of the local Red Cross, which did not seem equal to what was required of it. They were in vain. In the end he only succeeded in arousing the anger of the management who sought indirectly to obtain his recall. The tension which finally seemed to have taken root between the ICRC and the Croatian society was to play a considerable role in the turbulent end of Schmidlin's mission to Zagreb which will be examined later.

There were roughly 35,000 Croatian Jews and their lot soon became one of the worst. By spring 1943 both the ICRC and Schmidlin were aware of this as well as of the fact that political and racial persecution by the regime extended to other sections of the population such as the Orthodox Serbs. Schmidlin endeavoured to intervene on behalf of the Jews on three fronts.

First of all he established contact with the large Jewish cultural community in the capital, and in particular with its president Dr Hugo Kohn just before he was deported. With the creation of the independent state of Croatia the Jewish communities which were freely organised according to the law became instruments of the antisemitic policy. Their goods and those of their members were seized, then leaders were forced to maintain control and order within them, and yet they were still the final, derisory refuge for the persecuted. From winter 1941 transfers to concentration camps and then deportations to Germany gradually caused their populations to dwindle. In spring 1943 the Jewish cultural community in Zagreb was still hanging on and made efforts to help not only its members but also those Jews still at large and those they could reach in the camps. Schmidlin's first task was to notify the representatives of the Jewish charity organisations in Switzerland, like Saly Mayer (Joint) or Adolf Silberschein (Relico), of the need for food and medical supplies and for money, particularly because of the increasing number of deportations. He also offered his services to oversee the safe passage of the supplies via the Croatian Red Cross.[9] Until the community ceased to exist, Schmidlin acted as intermediary between Zagreb and Switzerland in order to try despite all the problems to keep alive an indispensable supply.

In 1943 the intensification of persecution led him to intercede with the authorities although this represented a risk that had not been specifically written into his mission by the ICRC. On May 7 the ICRC delegate asked for an audience with the new minister of the interior, Andrija Artukovic, whom he knew well personally. He received no reply it seems, unless it was that concessions might be possible in certain cases.[10]

Finally, he tried to organise collaboration with the church which was so powerful in the country and so divided vis-à-vis the regime. The threat of the complete disappearance of the Jewish community took him to the Archbishop of Zagreb, Mgr. Stepinac, the metropolitan of the national church, to consider with him the possibility of Caritas taking on the supply of aid to the concentration camps.[11] At the end of spring 1943 Edouard Chapuisat and David de Traz raised the Jewish question with the prelate who according to Chapuisat later delivered a very courageous sermon on the subject.[12]

These were Schmidlin's actions, both *ad hoc* and permanent, throughout the year on behalf of the persecuted. They allowed him to provide the ICRC with precise information on both the existence and location of camps and the destination of certain deportation convoys. In April 1943 the Jews deported the previous summer were able to send cards from Birkenau to their relatives in Croatia.

Another group then became the object of the delegate's efforts and attracted the attention of the ICRC, that of the partisans imprisoned by the Wehrmacht and the Ustachis. This is mentioned only for the record. Even if in summer 1943 the OKW declared itself prepared to consider, in principle at least, these partisans as POWs, the troops on the ground and the Croats in particular were far from doing so.

New risks

Until spring 1944, Schmidlin limited his activities on behalf of politically and racially persecuted people to the Jewish population at large (the Jewish cultural community in Zagreb). It was to these people that the CMS sent medical and nutritional supplies (tonics) in 1942, and Schmidlin sent, in 1943, clothes and shoes.[13]

It was through this agency that he tried hard to maintain an aid movement in the camps. However, in the case of the camps on Croatian soil and in general where political prisoners were concerned he was only able to intervene on a case-by-case basis by sending the ICRC requests for aid.

Any large-scale dispatch by the international Red Cross itself supposed that the Committee could ensure the arrival of the parcels and thus supply the blockade authorities with the guarantee that the aid was being correctly forwarded. By spring 1944, the condition of the Jewish population and also the hardening of the struggle between the Pavelitch regime and its adversaries in the face of the probable defeat of the Axis, stirred the ICRC to new efforts. These were such that by the end of January the Croatian government, following many approaches by the ICRC, finally accepted the principle of considering interned enemy civilians on the same terms as POWs. By then of the 35,000 Jews that had been in the country, about 10,000 had found temporary shelter in Hungary or Italy, and 1,200 were imprisoned in the camps at Jasenovac, Stara Gradiska and Gredjani Salas. A few were in hiding. All the rest had disappeared in the deportations directed at all enemies of the state.[14]

The ICRC therefore approached the foreign affairs minister, Stiepo Peric, to ask him to give its delegate authorisation to enter the three camps just mentioned to check the arrival of parcels and the list of supplies needed.[15] Schmidlin on his side was told to do everything possible to help the Jews in Croatia and to extend his efforts, for reasons of principle and tactics, to all political detainees.[16]

On the one hand he approached the Foreign Ministry with great determination, both personally and by letter, and on the other he tackled the general management of Public Security and Order, demanding the right to visit for himself and of humane treatment for the detainees, in the name of humanitarian principles but also through the argument of reciprocity.[17] The people he approached, even when they gave assurances of their understanding, either prevaricated or shied away. Schmidlin tried to use Mgr. Stepinac's influence with no obvious success. He then undertook, through intermediaries, an approach to the all-powerful commander of the concentration camps, Luburic, who was said to be more determined and awesome than Pavelitch himself, and tried, as he was to record in 1946, to bribe him.[18] This was also fruitless. He was, however, allowed in the middle of July 1944 to visit the concentration camps in Jasenovac, Stara Gradiska and Gredjani Salas, accompanied by several top security officials. It seems to have been a thorough visit, taking, as it did, three days. At the beginning of August he sent the ICRC a twelve-page report which described in detail the men and the installations. In general the impression was not unfavourable, given the extreme poverty in the country. At the end of the war Schmidlin was to record that he had deliberately played down the facts in the hope of securing improvements, but that he had suspected his visit had received careful preparation and beneath what he saw lay a much worse state of affairs. His conversations with the accompanying officials had in any case put him in the picture.[19]

Did all the efforts he made along with the visit in July 1944 bring about any improvement in the situation of the detainees? Schmidlin thought so when he looked back on his activities after the war. At the same time as authorising the ICRC delegate to enter the three camps, the head of Public Order and Security claimed that he wanted to grant the Jewish detainees the same treatment as all other internees, that is twice-monthly letters and parcels and the provision for the ICRC of a list of names of all imprisoned persons and permission for visits. For in a letter sent on 12 June 1944 to the Ministry of Foreign Affairs Schmidlin had set out the supervision needed if the ICRC was allowed to help the Jews in Croatian camps. He suggested lists of names and whereabouts, speedy information about deaths, changes of location and hospitalisation and above all the designation of trustworthy men from among the Jews in the camps who would supervise the distribution of mail and aid and channel Jewish prisoners' requests to the ICRC. He also asked for regular visits to the camps by himself and contact with the Jews on these occasions.[20]

But did the response in principle to the requests in the letter of 12 June constituted by the July visit have any lasting foundation in reality? The answer would seem to be no when one realises that, a few weeks later, in September, the plight of the detainees in the concentration camps took a sudden turn for the worse, as Schmidlin himself confirmed, following a visit to Zagreb by Kaltenbrunner, who was in charge of the Reich central security bureau, and also as a result of the takeover of Croatian security by the SS. Many of the people with whom the ICRC delegate had held talks or had at least had dealings for several months were themselves thrown into prison and any humanitarian move became illusory. It was probably for this reason that, admittedly very late on, at the end of November 1944, the ICRC stopped taking the Croatian authorities at their word and ceased asking them to collaborate with the help of the Jewish community in Zagreb in the CMS's dispatch of 1,200 parcels for the Jews in the camps.

Nonetheless some efforts continued during the interval. At the end of September the ICRC wrote directly, but not publicly, to the head of state, Ante Pavelitch, to request that he renounce the hostage-taking which was worsening the suffering of the civilian population and that he avoid at the very least inflicting on imprisoned people treatment that was contrary to human rights.[21] This discreet appeal was repeated on 21 March 1945 but its receipt does not seem even to have been acknowledged.[22] In the Croatian capital Schmidlin himself was not idle. In October 1944 the leaders of the Zagreb Jewish community, or rather what was left of it, were arrested for having registered two fugitives under false names. Schmidlin took up the case. On five occasions he went to the Ministry of the Interior and finally obtained the release of the community leaders on 26 October. On the other hand the two fugitives were hanged.[23]

The delegate had, however, put many people's backs up, in particular the leadership of the Croatian Red Cross. After Kaltenbrunner's visit, the Red Cross tried indirectly to obtain his recall. They did not succeed, but he received more and more death threats. These became the more worrying when, in early 1945, many of his 1943 and 1944 contacts were assassinated by the Ustachis. In February 1945 in the dying Croat state, only the German presence still ensured a minimum of order. The Swiss consul himself was isolated. On 5 March, realizing that his life was from then on directly threatened and that there was nothing more for him to do, Schmidlin hastily left Zagreb to return to Switzerland.[24]

Slovakia

The case of Slovakia occupies a special position in this account; not that Mgr. Tiso's clerico-fascist dictatorship showed any more humanity to Jews, or to its political enemies, whatever the dignitaries of the regime may have maintained. The antisemitic policies from 1942 onwards were motivated by the same considerations of class resentment, racial hatred and opportunism as were those of the other avowed or *de facto* satellites of the Third Reich. And the German deportations beginning in October 1944 were only the last act in a drama which started with the Slovak convoys of 1942–43. However, the date of this last act and the personality of the ICRC delegate, Georges Dunand, lend the story particular importance. At the time when the Germans were intervening in a direct and brutal manner in Jewish affairs in Slovakia in August 1944, the ICRC was extensively committed in Hungary. As the defeat of the Axis became inevitable, a new initiative started in Geneva to tackle the whole problem of political, if not racial, persecution. It is within the context of this initiative, the subject of the next chapter, that must be situated the special effort which Schwarzenberg recommended that Dunand should make as soon as he was installed in Bratislava.

On reading the documents, one might be forgiven for thinking that Georges Dunand was more deeply committed to the Jewish question than other delegates. This impression is certainly not a false one, corresponding as it does to the instructions which he received as he left Geneva. In all justice, however, one should not ignore three factors which may disproportionately increase the volume of documentation at our disposal. In contrast to the other delegates, once Dunand took up his post he had very little else to attend to besides political prisoners and Jews, since neither POWs nor civilian internees constituted large populations within the Slovak state, and the partisans were in the hands of the Germans. Secondly, unlike Julius Schmidlin in Zagreb, or even Roland Marti in Berlin, he could not easily speak to Geneva by telephone or come to headquarters in person to explain his actions. The military operations made communication slow, even using the Swiss diplomatic bag. In order to explain his actions, he therefore had to write, returning regularly to the attack. This gives rise to a varied and copious correspondence, which also expresses the third factor, the delegate's character. He was one of the few to publish his memoirs after the war, under the title *Ne perdez pas leur trace!* ['Don't lose track of them'] (Geneva, 1950). All these things serve as reminders of how difficult it is, using written documentation or even eyewitness accounts, to evaluate the part played by each person in what happened.

The events of 1942–1943

The ICRC maintained *de facto* relations with the Slovak Red Cross from the time of its inception in the spring of 1940, as it did with the government of the new state once the war started on the Eastern Front. These relations remained somewhat distant, however, and until the spring of 1943 no envoy was sent from Geneva to Bratislava, nor was there a resident delegate. This did not prevent the Committee from being aware of much of what was going on; nor from hearing, via Budapest, of the persecution to which the Jewish community was subjected following the deportation decision taken by Tiso's government in March 1942.[25] After the eyewitness accounts, which record among other things the unbelievable brutality with which the local police treated women and children as they took them away, comes the information provided by the Slovakian Red Cross itself. There are precise details of the government decrees, of the numbers of people concerned, of the destinations of the convoys (the district of Lublin (Chelm) and Auschwitz, in particular) and of the existence of a list of the names of the deportees, held by a central bureau of Slovak Jews.[26]

In contrast to its Croatian counterpart, which was completely under the thumb of the regime, the Slovak Red Cross was not content merely to notify Geneva of the events taking place. Faced with its own inability to help the victims of persecution, it decided to request that the International Committee should intervene. This appeal inevitably placed the ICRC in a difficult position. It was now July 1942, and for some weeks information had been accumulating and converging which made it clear to the organisation that racial persecution was becoming more extensive, and that the measures taken by the Germans against civilians were escalating. The PIC Commission therefore clung to a legal fiction, stating that 'it is the responsibility of the Slovak authorities themselves in the first instance to ensure the protection of their nationals who fell under the jurisdiction of a government with whom the Slovak authorities maintain normal diplomatic relations'. For once, the Coordinating Committee appeared to be shrewder, in judging that the very fact that the Slovak Red Cross had appealed to Geneva demonstrated that the reality of the situation was at odds with the position adopted by the PIC Commission: which was that the national Red Cross was unable to intervene despite wishing to do so. But it did not depart from its usual cautious procedure, deciding to look into the matter with the Slovak chargé d'affaires in Berne, who was due to pay a courtesy visit to the organisation in the near future.[27]

This visit was slow to materialise. In the interim, Mlle Ferrière discussed the problem with Walter Hartmann, head of external relations of the DRK, during his stay in Geneva at the end of August. The assessment of the situation left no room for hope: the DRK was not in a position to get involved in the case of the Slovak deportees. The International Committee's reply to the Slovak Red Cross, therefore, was negative, more for practical than for legal reasons:

You have requested that the International Committee of the Red Cross should intervene on behalf of these people, but we must point out that it is difficult for us to do so in the way that you wish. Our role is normally to act as a neutral intermediary between one or more warring parties, whereas in the present case there seems no reason why the authorities concerned should not communicate directly with one another. However, we would intervene nonetheless, if there seemed to be any hope of our intervention yielding some result. Unfortunately, this is not the case, since in the present circumstances we could do no more than draw the problem to the attention of the German Red Cross, and this organisation has recently informed us that such cases lie outside its remit.

You were kind enough to inform us of the existence in Bratislava of a central bureau of Slovak Jews, which has in its possession a comprehensive list of the names of all of those who have been handed over to the German authorities. We are grateful for this information, but would like to know whether it would be possible for this bureau to take responsibility for relaying messages which we have received on behalf of the Jews concerned, who are now in the General-Government. It seems that, prior to their departure, these people were allowed to write civilian messages, which the Slovak Red Cross has kindly passed on to us. These messages requested that their relatives living in countries at war with one another should write to them via another such bureau in Krakow. We estimate that these messages would be better guaranteed to reach their destination were they to be forwarded through the bureau in Bratislava that you have told us about.[28]

A long-awaited delegate

A year after these dramatic deportations, Edouard Chapuisat and David de Traz stopped in Bratislava in the course of their general information-gathering mission through south-east Europe. There they learnt that, of the 90,000 Jews resident in the country, only 5,000 remained, 1,500 of whom were in labour camps in Szered, Novaki, Vyhne and Ilava. The Slovak Red Cross had access to these camps and could come to the assistance of the inmates, but its sphere of action did not extend to include the hundreds of thousands of deportees who had disappeared in Poland or Germany. The International Committee seems to have been satisfied with this information, of which it duly notified the Joint and the World Jewish Congress.[29]

More than a year went by before the Committee returned to the idea of installing a resident delegate, a move which had been called for in many quarters (the Joint included), and which Jean-Etienne Schwarzenberg had advocated as a means of facilitating the aid operations in Poland. For there was a certain significance attached to the posting of a delegate, even one from the Red Cross. Once the matter was decided, the Slovak government was eager to help in its realisation, not for humanitarian reasons, but in order to benefit from any sign of international recognition and even to justify itself before an independent tribunal, whereas the exiled Czechoslovakian government naturally deplored the decision taken in Geneva.

The crushing of the maquis uprising of September and October 1944 by the Wehrmacht toppled the country into the horror of complete subjection to the Third Reich. In addition to the camp inmates and the POWs, who were few in number, there were now much larger categories of victims in need of assistance who clearly lay beyond the framework of the Conventions. These included the partisans, for whom it was appropriate to secure POW status, and those Jews remaining at liberty, since from September onwards the Germans started to round them up with a view to deportation. This time foreign nationals were targeted as well. Around 150 Jews carrying passports or papers from the United States and other American republics were assembled in the manor house at Marianka in makeshift circumstances.[30]

At the beginning of September, Georges Dunand, until then the attaché at the Swiss Federal War Office for Industry and Labour, accepted the mission which was offered him. It was a difficult and delicate assignment, since for the most part it fell outside the CICR's traditional activities. Consequently, despite impatient appeals from the Slovak Red Cross, he made a point of having a meeting with Saly Mayer, who gave him the names of correspondents with whom he could make contact and granted him an initial credit of 200,000 francs to be used to help the Jews.[31]

At the end of October 1944, Georges Dunand finally took up his post in Bratislava. But although he started immediately to collaborate with the Slovak Red Cross, he had some reservations at the start. He had arrived too late, and the diplomatic circumstances were catastrophic, as a result of the rebuff which the Swiss Federal Council had received from the Soviet Union, who had refused to re-establish diplomatic links, while its armies were nearing Slovakia. Dunand felt it hardly seemed worth persevering with an impossible task under such conditions.

. . . in conclusion, *my mission has obviously come too late*, and I do not have the necessary experience. In any case, no preparation has been made here for my arrival, except insofar as they wished to use me as a witness for the defence. The only idea in anyone's head was and remains that of trailing me around the East in order to show me the 'atrocities' committed by the partisans.

This lack of preparedness is steadily being remedied, admittedly, but it would take several months yet.

If I were confident of having that much time at my disposal, it would be a different matter; and if, contrary to all expectation, things were to stabilise on the Hungarian Front, I would certainly wish to qualify or even to alter the above.

But, assuming a rapid advance, the tension between Russia and Switzerland fundamentally alters my own position and the possibilities for preparation. In this situation, the risks arising in the course of the mission would, in my opinion, outweigh the benefits. It is true that I am not a representative of the Swiss government, but the Russian authorities will view me primarily in the light of my Swiss passport, which is, moreover, a diplomatic one . . .

However, as I said in my third telegram, it is difficult to make a judgement from here. I retain a great desire to wait and see, and to try to achieve something in the several areas already close to me heart. Whatever happens, my inclination is to stay here as long as possible.[32]

Geneva left the delegate to be sole judge as to the date of his return, whether in his own interests or in those of the Red Cross, but, in the last analysis, they agreed with this conclusion on grounds of principle:

Now more than ever, we believe that the CICR should maintain a presence in each of the warring countries, in order to establish contact with the various Red Cross authorities and institutions, regardless of their nature, and to place itself at the disposal of these authorities and institutions for all humanitarian activities in accordance with CICR traditions.[33]

Concentration and deportation

As he left Geneva, Dunand had learned that those Jews who had remained at liberty since 1942 were being crammed by the SS into the Szered camp, under inhuman conditions. On his arrival, he found that the situation was in fact even worse. The object of the measures taken was to eradicate the Jews from Slovakia completely, and Szered was merely a transit camp from where weekly deportation convoys departed. Consequently, during the audiences of welcome accorded to him by the ministers and the head of state, he demanded to be allowed to visit the camp. But his interlocutors declined. The camp was under military control: permission could only be granted by the OKW. Through Geneva, the question of the visit was taken up by Roland Marti with Berlin, but of course without success.

On the Jewish question, the head of state and his ministers had again pleaded incompetence, claiming that they were unable to oppose

German orders; neither, however, were they collaborating with the antisemitic measures taken since the crushing of the 'putsch' that summer. In direct contradiction of this affirmation, on 16 November, the municipality of Bratislava ordered all Jews resident in the city to assemble in order to be taken to the Szered labour camp. In addition, all exceptional clauses of the law of 1942, exempting certain groups (such as a number of protégés of the president of the republic, people of mixed race and mixed-race couples) from the racial policies, were revoked.

Both the ICRC delegate and the Swiss consul-general immediately interceded with the Slovak authorities, who responded evasively. The obvious failure of the round-up, which Dunand watched in person at the town hall, encouraged him to persevere in his efforts. He thus finally succeeded in obtaining interviews with various ministers, with the head of the regime's praetorian guard, the famous Hlinka guard, and with the SS officer in charge of the town, *Hauptsturmführer* Lehmann. To the latter, as well as to the Hlinka guard, he submitted a questionnaire which concerned, in particular, the fate of mixed couples and their children. This was a means of suggesting certain ways in which leniency could be shown towards them, for example by granting them exemption from deportation to Szered and the right to receive parcels and to correspond with their relatives. The response from the Slovak side appears to have been one of readiness to discuss the matter, while emphasising that the unfortunate experience of the 'putsch' had demonstrated the necessity of antisemitic measures, which the current circumstances rendered implacable. The Germans, on the other hand, replied in unequivocal terms. *Hauptsturmführer* Aloïs Brunner, the commandant of the Szered camp – who eventually managed to avoid prosecution for war crimes by gaining asylum in Syria – spoke to Dunand to confirm their negative attitude and their refusal to compromise in any way.[34]

At the beginning of 1945, Dunand once again had the opportunity to speak to the head of state about the deportation problem, while handing over to him the letter from President Huber, who will be mentioned later. On this occasion, the prelate rehearsed for his benefit the official Slovak position:

Up until this summer, the Jews continued to work and to prosper in Slovakia, in the camps or in their own homes. This prosperity was demonstrated particularly by the fact that they made large donations to the partisans. For his part, Mgr. Tiso had hoped that the Jewish situation would remain stable, but there was an open Jewish revolt at the time of the putsch. When Mgr. Tiso requested the PP [the Tiso regime's Protecting Power, i.e. the Reich] to suppress the putsch, the

Germans quite naturally wished to have a free hand, in order to protect their rear. Nonetheless, it was originally intended that Slovak law would remain in force, and that the measures necessary to ensure order would be taken by the Slovak authorities. However, the circumstances became more and more difficult, and it became necessary to leave the Germans complete freedom. Thus it was that all of the Jews were taken into custody under Mgr. Tiso's nose. In fact, he had thought that this would be a faster process.[35]

Having duly obtaining the prelate's permission, the ICRC delegate approached the minister for foreign affairs that same day, suggesting that women, children and invalids should be exempt from deportation and given shelter somewhere, under his protection. This request was transmitted to the German embassy in Bratislava, and met with an absolute refusal. When Dunand visited the councillor of the legation in person, he received confirmation that 'the German security services in Bratislava refused to make the slightest concession, and remained determined to liquidate completely the Jewish problem in Slovakia'.[36]

Thus, every move to halt the deportations or to gain access to the camp at Szered, made in writing or by the delegate in person, came up against a brick wall. Even the destination of the convoys remained officially a secret. But Dunand managed to find out in mid-December that one train which had just left was destined partly for Ravensbrück and partly for Sachsenhausen.

Marianka and the Jews of foreign nationality

This camp, or rather refuge, was set up in mid-September 1944, as we have seen, for 164 Jews holding passports or papers from American countries. It was not so much a camp as a sort of safe haven. It was a dilapidated old manor house, in which the internees were allowed to install their own furniture and belongings, one family to a room, and to live at their own expense, in very precarious circumstances.

The Germans lost no time in going back on the degree of tolerance thus shown by the Slovak authorities. On 11 October, they intervened directly and inspected everyone's papers; only three sets were recognised as being valid, and 161 people were taken to Szered, from where they were deported to the Reich or to the occupied territories. While, as Dunand recognised, doubts concerning the validity of the documents may have been permissible, especially of those which had been bought from certain Central American countries, it was nevertheless scandalous that the Germans should treat innocent civilians in this way. He therefore made several attempts to intervene. From the Slovak Red Cross, he obtained a list of those who had been taken away, and sent a copy to

Geneva. He twice visited Marianka in person, and gave money to the few internees still haunting the premises. In addition, he witnessed two attempts by the Nazis to remove or intimidate people, and made emphatic protests both to the local authorities and to the Ministry for Foreign Affairs.[37] His efforts were all to no avail, and the manor house was eventually emptied of all its inhabitants. The last of these, considered to be North American citizens, also left, but were interned in Bergen-Belsen, with a view to a possible exchange. This was despite some very imaginative efforts on Dunand's part to prevent their departure: he advanced, one after the other, claims that they had civilian internee status, that the ICRC delegation in Berlin, or the Protecting Power, should be informed, and that their nationality, not their race, should be considered paramount in attempts to arrange an exchange. Geneva remained more circumspect. It would be pointless to send the list of Jews holding American citizenship to Berlin, since the German authorities had forbidden all enquiries concerning Jews detained within the Reich. It was meaningless to consider them as civilian internees, since the Reich did not recognise them as such. Nothing definitive, then, could be done to help the guests at Marianka.

Emigration, protection documents and bargaining

During this phase of persecution in the autumn and winter of 1944–5, the Jews of Slovakia did not, of course, have any hope of being allowed to emigrate. Some nonetheless managed, using either money or ingenuity, to obtain certificates of immigration to Palestine or Swiss entry visas, not to mention passports and papers which a number of American countries were willing to connive in issuing, as mentioned above in connection with Marianka. Unfortunately, even when the Slovak authorities allowed the holders of such papers to leave the country, the Germans, furiously intent as they were on rounding up and exterminating the Jews, would never accord them safe passage through German territory:

We refer you to your letter number 18 of 18 November 1944, in which you expound to us the difficulties inherent in placing the two to three thousand Jews remaining in Slovakia under the protection of the ICRC. It seems to us that such protection would indeed be absolutely impracticable, and would in any case have no practical consequences in the circumstances which you have described.

As far as the emigration of Slovak Jews is concerned, it seems probable that the Swiss Federal Political Department would be willing to consider the possibility that they might come to Switzerland, and could perhaps issue them with entry visas. However, in the case of those holding Swiss visas as in that of persons in possession of certificates of immigration for Palestine and the United States, it is likely that the German authorities would refuse to grant them exit and transit visas, without which they cannot leave Slovakia. Consequently, we see no point in approaching the Federal Political Department on their behalf, at least for the time being.[38]

One might be forgiven for wondering why Dunand, who was on the spot, did not distribute protection documents to the remaining free Jews on his own initiative, as Frédéric Born was doing at the time in Hungary. Dunand did not really believe that this would have any effect, since there was no hope that the government in Bratislava, in contrast to the one in Budapest, would show any leniency towards the Jews. Nevertheless, encouraged by Robert Schirmer (who, together with Luc Thudicum and Maurice Rossel, passed through Bratislava in mid-December), he issued four letters of protection, in the hope that these documents would give the bearer a sense of confidence, cause some junior policeman to act with restraint, or at least prevent extremes of brutality. Geneva did not disclaim this initiative, but, feigning ignorance, did not interfere:

We do not know under what circumstances M. Born issued 'Schutzbriefe', but we emphasise that great prudence is called for in Bratislava at the moment, as it was in Budapest. We leave you to judge what can be done on the spot. In any event, these documents should be issued only in exceptional circumstances, to people personally known to you. Moreover, the delivery of such documents does not entail the responsibility of the International Committee of the Red Cross with respect to the identity of the beneficiaries.[39]

However, Dunand refers several times in his correspondence and reports to another possible solution, namely the exchange of people for goods or currency. In November, the central Jewish organisation Ustredna Zidov was in touch with the commandant of the Szered camp to discuss this. But whereas similar negotiations in the case of 12,000 Hungarian Jews had resulted in their being 'bought' by the Union of Orthodox Rabbis, via the former Swiss federal councillor Jean-Marie Musy, the proceedings in Bratislava were stalled. In any case, the ICRC was not interested in such dealings, limiting itself to relaying its delegate's communications on the subject to the Joint.

All in all, none of the measures considered or suggested by Dunand came anywhere near realisation, since the intransigence of the Nazis and the wiilingness of the Slovakians to collaborate in the persecutions stood in the way of any attempt at a solution, even for Jews of foreign nationality.

Life in hiding

In mid-November, Dunand wrote:

A provisional solution, and the only one possible, although it is extremely
uncertain and gives rise to genuine suffering in the long term, is for the Jews to
go into hiding, and to keep changing their hiding place. In order to do so, they
need money, to pay for their entry to the bunker or for information concerning
the location of such a shelter (often a cellar, or the ruins of a bombed-out
house), not to mention the food which they have to buy in the evening or on the
black market.[40]

Thus the only real assistance which Dunand was able to offer the Jews
was that of concealing them in bunkers and aiding them while they were
in hiding. This is something of a historical irony: if helping the persecuted in their own country is an activity which lies outside the Geneva
Conventions, what then if this activity is carried out in secrecy and in
violation of the laws of the land?

Ever since his arrival in Slovakia, Dunand had been upset by his
inability to exert more influence over the events that he was being
forced to watch. Thus, the bunker operation allowed him to be of use,
to do something, while being as cautious as his own security, as well as
that of the Committee, demanded. Seen from Geneva, there were
evidently grounds for concern. For this reason, without formally condemning the initiatives which the delegate had taken, Jean-Etienne
Schwarzenberg reminded him to be careful, in a letter thanking him for
his efforts:

We take this opportunity to advise you to adopt as circumspect an approach as
your very delicate circumstances require. We do not think that you may give
advice, even in a simple fashion, to persons who are in an irregular situation. It
would be most unfortunate were you to risk compromising your position as the
representative of our institution by acts of this nature. If help must be given to
persons in this category, it should not be given directly by you.[41]

In reply to this, Dunand observed that if he acted strictly in accordance
with the recommendations given to him, he would do nothing at all,
since there was in principle nothing which could be done to help the
Jews.[42] As the weeks went by, clandestine action became more and more
difficult. New bunkers were discovered, and arrests made, every day. In
October, Saly Mayer had not only granted Dunand a substantial credit
and made him a cash advance, but had also given him the names of
some trustworthy people whom he could approach. But, once in
Bratislava, the delegate discovered that the Joint's guarantors had fallen
into the hands of the Gestapo, and the new intermediaries which the
Joint proceeded to designate in replacement disappeared in their turn,

one after the other. It became so complicated to identify correspondents that the Joint eventually agreed that money could be distributed without direct supervision, despite the fact that the ICRC itself could not always exercise much control over the transactions into which its delegates were forced to enter in order to change money or to make emergency purchases. The risks which sometimes had to be taken on the spot, even when they did not contravene existing regulations, did not always accord with the administrative directions from headquarters, to the detriment of the patience and of the willingness to cooperate of all concerned.

Throughout the winter of 1944–5, therefore, the delegate continued to make both oral and written protests to a wide variety of authorities, and to keep Geneva informed down to the last detail. Meanwhile, he pursued a course of concrete action on a day-to-day basis: meeting people in secret; acting as a depository for pieces of baggage, perhaps containing the wherewithal to make false papers, without asking any questions; giving children a few nights' shelter under his roof; continuing to employ a servant despite her Jewishness; sending parcels to deportees in Germany in response to letters which, now and again, somehow managed to get through; giving material assistance and, sometimes most important of all, giving moral support.

The action taken by Geneva

The decision to establish a delegation in Bratislava in the summer of 1944 was a gesture with unquestionable political significance. Insofar as the new delegate was, for the most part, to devote himself strictly to humanitarian work, not covered by the Conventions, he bore witness to the changes taking place within the ICRC at that time. But as time goes on, a gulf becomes discernible between Geneva and Bratislava, as the warnings sent to the delegate by the Committee testify, subtle as they may be. One has a sense that Geneva lagged behind Dunand and his initiatives. This impression is reinforced by his demand, made soon after he took up his post, that the ICRC or Switzerland, or both, should take rapid steps to give the Jews at least a chance of survival.[43] Nonetheless, the Committee was eventually roused to direct action by the information that it was receiving, although there is no way of knowing their reasons, as the PIC Committee documents do not mention the measures which were taken.

On 21 November, an initial request for information concerning the fate of the deportees from Szered and Marianka was addressed to the Slovak legation in Berne. It is interesting that the letter is not signed by

Jean-Etienne Schwarzenberg, as had originally been intended, but by a member of the Committee, namely Mme Frick-Cramer.[44] However, apart from an acknowledgement of receipt, the letter went unanswered. In mid December, the Committee returned to the attack, this time in a more formal manner. Max Huber wrote to the head of the Slovak state, Mgr. Tiso himself, a letter very similar to the one that he had sent to the Hungarian head of state six months previously:

> Your Excellency,
> The International Committee of the Red Cross is in receipt of queries and protests from many quarters concerning the coercive measures taken against the Jews in Slovakia, in particular a large number of deportations.
> What we have been told runs so counter to the Christian principles of the Slovak people that we find the information impossible to believe.
> In the name of the International Committee of the Red Cross, I would like to ask that your Excellency should give instructions which would enable us to refute these rumours and accusations. In particular, we would like to hear that deportations out of the country have now ceased, should any in fact have taken place.
> I would especially like to know whether the International Committee of the Red Cross should make public this appeal, or whether you would prefer it to be treated in confidence.[45]

Dunand was given the task of delivering the letter to the prelate-cum-dictator, should he consider the move to be appropriate, and the Committee informed him that, if there were no reply, they were prepared to make public the fact that an appeal had been made to the president on behalf of the Jews of Slovakia. This proved to be unnecessary, however, at least in formal terms. During the audience which he accorded to the delegate, as well as in his lengthy reply to Max Huber, (reproduced in full in the Appendix, pp. 300–1 below), Mgr. Tiso claimed that the antisemitism of his regime was justified on purely social and economic grounds. The Jews had occupied a privileged socio-economic position, to the detriment of the native Slovaks. They had also exerted a significant political influence, favouring Hungarian-, Czech- or German-led governments with an anti-Slovak bias, demonstrating their reluctance to assimilate to the Slovak people. After 1939, the Slovakian state had needed to put an end to Slovak emigration, by guaranteeing an adequate standard of living: this was necessarily done at the expense of the Jews. The exclusion of the Jews had taken a number of forms, primarily that of granting them permission to emigrate (many were, in any case, recent immigrants). Those who remained Slovakian citizens were largely left to continue as before, but some had their activities restricted by law. Mgr. Tiso firmly denied the accusations made against him, blaming instead the German suppression of the 'putsch' of 1944 and the social, political and economic problems arising inevitably in conditions of war. He asserted that his government were making every effort to act humanely towards the Jews, under difficult circumstances, and requested that the contents of his letter should be treated as confidential.[46] The tone of the document, even more than the fact that it was completely negative, stunned even a career diplomat like Jean-Etienne Schwarzenberg. There was therefore no reply, no duplex, and no publication of the documents by the Red Cross.[47]

The question arises as to whether the committee's intervention would have been more effective if it had been made in November, as Dunand had requested. It is very difficult to say, although there seems no reason why this should have been the case.

A highly committed consul-general

Dunand's work in helping the Jews was very much supported by Max Grässli, the Swiss consul-general in Bratislava. In contrast to the majority of his colleagues, this diplomat had been making courageous efforts since 1942 to come to the assistance of the victims, with the help of the staff at the consulate, and had managed to save many lives 'by invoking Swiss economic interests, in the widest sense of the term', in the words of Dunand himself.[48] On 24 October 1944, probably as a result of warnings and promptings on his part, he was given the task by the Swiss Federal Council of drawing the attention of the Slovak government to the inevitable negative foreign repercussions of their anti-Jewish measures, and of demanding that the deportations should be suspended and permission granted for delegates either from neutral countries or from the ICRC to visit the camps. The reply from the Slovak government, a few weeks later, went no further than to justify the policies on security grounds.[49]

It did not take long for the contact established between Dunand and Grässli to develop into sustained cooperative efforts, when it came to seeking a direct intervention from the Committee in early November, for example, and in responding to the assembly order issued to the Jews of Bratislava on 16 November. Their shared concerns also united them in undercover activities. The Grässlis hid Jews under their roof, and when they left for Switzerland in December, Dunand moved into their apartment-cum-shelter until the arrival of the vice-consul, Adolphe Keller. When the German police began to make their presence felt, as a result of the Grässlis' departure, it also fell to Dunand to empty this unusual refuge of its occupants, with the help of his colleagues from the

Berlin delegation, who happened most opportunely to be passing through Bratislava at the time.[50]

Such activities obviously lay outside the remit both of ICRC delegates and of Swiss diplomats. They represented, however, the only real way in which either could take action in order to save a few Jewish lives.

7   The Axis allies

Romania

The difficult decision to send a delegate

The German attack of 22 June 1941 on the Soviet Union marked the first important development in the relations between the ICRC and Romania since Robert Brunel's impromptu stay in Bucharest in the autumn of 1939. At the start of the winter of 1941, the Romanian Red Cross asked the International Committee to send a delegate to help them in fulfilling their mission. This appeal, unusually, was paralleled by a direct personal intervention from the Swiss minister in Bucharest, René de Weck. Still more unusually, this intervention was made on the grounds of the plight of Romania's Jews:

Dear Chenevière,
    As I am sure you are aware, the Jews of Romania have for some time, particularly since the country's declaration of war against the USSR, been the object of systematic persecution, compared to which the massacres in Armenia which aroused such indignation in Europe at the dawn of our century seem as harmless as children's games.
    I will not go into detail here concerning the inhuman acts of violence, despoilments of every kind, deportations, executions and massacres which have taken place. I am keeping our government as accurately informed as possible, but I cannot hope for it to lodge an official protest under the current circumstances.
    I am writing to you in a purely personal capacity, man to man. I would like you to investigate, while avoiding any reference to me, what possibilities exist for the International Committee of the Red Cross to take action, without stepping outside its sphere of activity, in order to alleviate the victims' sufferings, at least to some degree . . .
    What, then, might be done?
    The most effective step that could be taken would be the posting of an ICRC delegate in Romania, with an official mission unrelated to that of taking a special interest in the Jews (this precaution would enable him to obtain his passport visas). The prestige of the 'Geneva Cross', as it is known here, is great enough to

ensure that, once in Bucharest, your representative would gain authorisation to gather all relevant information and give any necessary advice. It goes without saying that I would assist him in this. The government could not ignore his recommendations, since these would be, in the eyes of all Romanians, an expression of the views of a respected, impartial international organisation with a legitimate concern in these matters. Thousands of lives now under threat could thus be saved. The president of the Romanian Red Cross Organisation is a friend of mine, and would certainly lend his support.

I may add that the official motivation for the posting of a delegate could be provided by other tasks to be carried out, the importance and usefulness of which are, moreover, obvious: these include the prevention of epidemics, aid to Polish refugees, visits to POWs and so on. A rapid decision in this matter would be eminently desirable.

Unless such a decision can be made very quickly indeed, the Committee ought at least, on the grounds of the preceding information (though without revealing its source), request that I should deliver notes in its name to the Romanian Red Cross and to the Ministry for Foreign Affairs, with the aim of obtaining minimum guarantees for the Romanian Jews concerning medical assistance and hospitals.[1]

The recipient of this letter, Jacques Chenevière, replied in what seems to be a more distant tone. His reply is also worth quoting at some length, especially as René de Weck was not slow to repeat his suggestion, referring to the wretched situation of Polish refugees in Romania, which should also receive the attention of a future delegate from the International Red Cross:

Dear de Weck,

I have been slow in replying to your personal note of 29 November 1941, because we do not feel able to resolve the question which you put to me in the way in which you ask, although the matter is receiving our continual attention.

We are not unaware of the fact that the persons in the category of which you wrote are in a truly deplorable situation. The information which you sent us is nonetheless very valuable, but we do not see any way in which we can provide an effective solution to the current state of affairs. Nevertheless, we perceive very well the indirect advantages which would accrue from the posting of a representative of our organisation, despite the restraint which he would, of course, have to show in this matter. Just as you yourself suggest, if we were to have such a person at our disposal today, his activities would have to have a more precise objective, and one whose position within our mandate was less open to dispute. The various topics which you have enumerated, such as epidemics, assistance to certain refugees and visits to certain POWs, are undoubtedly of the greatest importance, but the setting up of a delegation is, on the other hand, not an easy matter at the present time.

It does, however, continue to receive our constant attention, and you will certainly be among the first to be informed should we succeed.

Let me assure you, both in your capacity as a representative of our country and as a friend, that I myself am very conscious of the mark of respect which your letter represents, and that we are grateful for the interest which you have shown in the ever weightier and more complex task of the International Committee of the Red Cross. I was already sure that we could count on your full support if ever we needed it, but your letter has given us renewed proof of it, and for this you have my sincere thanks.[2]

This exchange of letters should not be confused with the steps being taken in early 1942 to obtain accreditation as the Romanian delegate for Mr Edouard Zamboni, who had visited the Balkans once already, in 1941, on behalf of the Swiss Federal Department of the Public Economy. For the mission envisaged by the ICRC would involve mainly the CMS, particularly as there were thirty-six tons of medical supplies sent by the Polish Relief Committee waiting in Lisbon for distribution, and it was felt that this could better be organised from the Romanian capital than within the occupied General-Government itself. Since the Romanian government made its agreement conditional upon the estab-lishment of an ICRC delegation in Moscow, Edouard Zamboni never actually left for Bucharest.[3]

In the autumn of 1942 a second attempt was made, and this time was crowned with success. The CMS sent Vladimir de Steiger on a pur-chasing mission to Budapest, Bucharest, Sofia, Istanbul and Ankara, as part of the action undertaken in aid of the Belgian civilian population. At the end of his tour, he installed himself in the Romanian capital, where he continued his commercial and technical negotiations, still in the name of the CMS. However, his work was no longer exactly that which had been envisaged when the first steps were taken in early 1942. The Jewish question now figured explicitly among his concerns. As he left Geneva, the CID service requested that the delegate should make enquiries regarding the fate of the Jews in Hungary (particularly those who had been deported to the Ukraine) and in Romania (including those who had been deported to the area of the Ukraine known as Transnistria), and asked him to obtain information concerning the attitude of the governments of the two countries towards those of their Jewish citizens who had been deported abroad.[4] The Committee had in fact received some alarming and very detailed information about events in the new Romanian territories in Transnistria. The recapture of Bukovina and Bessarabia had been accompanied by the massacre of more than 100,000 Jews. Then, in the autumn of 1941, 140,000 more, the majority of whom originated from these two provinces, were deported to Transnistria. The report from France which reached Geneva via the CMS, as well as three accounts from Romanian Jews sent by Gerhart Riegner in early 1943, all described the disastrous plight of the deportees, more than half of whom were estimated already to have died from hunger, cold, typhus and ill treatment. The survivors, in ghettos, villages and labour camps, were all urgently in need of assistance on a massive scale.[5]

Despite the precise nature of the information received, the instructions sent to Vladimir de Steiger remained very cautious:

We have repeatedly been called upon to come to the assistance of the Jewish populations of countries under occupation, particularly the deportees. You are well aware of the enormous obstacles standing in the way of attempts by the International Committee of the Red Cross to take action in their favour. Despite these difficulties, which are largely of a political nature, the CMS has succeeded in carrying out certain missions of limited scope, consisting of sending parcels of food and medical supplies to the ghettos.

Our attention has recently been drawn to the Jews deported from Romania to Transnistria. Their circumstances were described to us by someone who seems fairly well informed, having been the recipient of several accounts from Romanian sources. [This is a reference to the letter from Gerhart Riegner of 28 January 1943 mentioned above.] . . .The Jewish organisations in Romania are requesting substantial financial assistance. This would be very difficult, since it is impossible to transfer large sums of money from Great Britain or the United States. These countries have, as you know, imposed a very strict blockade which covers not only the shipment of food to Europe, but also the movement of money.

Nonetheless, we could perhaps envisage a mission of assistance similar to the one being undertaken in Poland and other occupied countries. However, it would be necessary to proceed step by step, on a small scale. Before we start to approach the organisations which might be willing to contribute to the consignments, we would be grateful if you could make discreet enquiries regarding the conditions under which such a mission might be accomplished. These conditions will be imposed on the one hand by the Romanian authorities, and on the other hand, they will have to conform to the requirements of the Allied countries concerning the blockade:

1) Do you think that it would be possible for a representative of the international Red Cross to visit the parts of Transnistria where the Jews are to be found?

2) Could you tell us of any organisations or persons with an interest in the Jewish deportees whom we could contact for help in organising a possible aid mission? Could these organisations or persons be entrusted with the money which we are likely to receive for this purpose?

3) Can you see any possible way of supervising the distribution of any aid provided (e.g. ghetto elders, the use of receipts, etc.)?

4) Finally, could we possibly be sent lists of the Jews living in these places in Transnistria? Could they, in that case, receive individual parcels?

These few questions are in no sense exhaustive, and we would be grateful for any information which might tell us more about the possible ways of providing assistance, and which might be of use to us in drawing up a plan of action which we could then discuss with the authorities and circles concerned.

We would, however, ask that you proceed with all possible caution and discretion. What we wish at all costs to avoid is alerting public opinion or the authorities and encouraging speculation about a great action to be undertaken by the International Committee of the Red Cross on behalf of the Jews. Such speculation would have very adverse consequences and would be liable to jeopardise our aim, which is simply the inclusion of the Jews in the activities organised by the CMS for the benefit of the civilian population of the occupied countries, within the bounds of feasibility and with the consent of the governments concerned.

We would like to thank you in advance for your work, which, we must repeat, should be carried out with the utmost discretion. We would likewise ask you to avoid raising the hopes of the Jewish organisations, and to ensure that they do not take for granted this action on the part of the International Committee, which is far from certain to succeed. At the moment, in fact, we are still only at the stage of a preliminary enquiry, which is, however, urgent and necessary in view of the very uncertain situation of these deportees.[6]

This cautiousness is not in itself surprising. It is underlined here by the fears of those in charge of the CMS that the delegate's work might be slowed, impeded or even made impossible if he showed too marked an interest in the racial persecutions. When they insisted, following the instructions given above, that Vladimir de Steiger should not make any approach to the authorities and should give Geneva his own personal opinion only,[7] the CMS was confirming the cautious approach adopted by the ICRC, along the lines of Carl J. Burckhardt's warning to the Bureau on 22 March 1943 against any slide of ICRC activity beyond its main traditional domain.[8] And the delegate of the Swiss Federal Council for International Cooperation was not a man to adopt a different stance on the matter.[9]

The journey to Transnistria

The completion of the first stage of Steiger's mission for the CMS, and most of all the decision of the Romanian government to authorise in principle the emigration of Jews, opened up a new perspective for the ICRC which made Schwarzenberg's intended large-scale operation on behalf of the Jews seem more feasible. The ICRC was not alone in noting this change. Observant witnesses as they were, the Swiss minister René de Weck and the papal nuncio Mgr. Cassulo came to the same conclusion. Initiatives seemed possible in this region, whether charitable or with an ulterior motive. The mission of the ICRC delegate in Bucharest was, therefore, modified in June 1943 so that he should thenceforth balance his work between the CMS and his protection activities, among which figured the search for emigration possibilities for the Jews, overland, via Bulgaria and by sea.[10] For their part, Chapuisat and de Traz, who, in spring 1943, had been sent to south-eastern European capitals to strengthen links with the national Red Cross societies, to ascertain their needs and the conditions in the field, including their work with the Jews, met the leaders of the Romanian Red Cross and the minister of foreign affairs, the vice-president (and acting president) of the Council of Ministers, Mihaï Antonescu, who confirmed his policy of emigration for the Jews with the help of the national Red Cross and, hopefully, the ICRC. They also met Wilhelm Fildermann, ex-president of the Union of Romanian Jews and historic head of that community whose existence he defended in 1919 at the Peace Conference. They supported his release, since his public protestation over the tax of four thousand million lei imposed on the Jews by the government for the war effort had occasioned his brief relegation to Transnistria. They finally obtained permission to go to that region where, on 22 and 23 May, they visited without illusions the model ghettos of Tiraspol and Odessa, in the wake of many other foreign diplomats.[11]

The talks they held during their mission were carefully prepared by the Swiss minister and these, along with the supplementary information he was able to send on the persecution in Transnistria, made the ICRC feel that it was both necessary and possible to make some attempt on behalf of the Jews in Romania. At the end of June, Schwarzenberg wrote to Burckhardt with an assessment of the situation and a concrete proposal to send an *ad hoc* delegate to Bucharest. He felt that there were plenty of possibilities for action in Romania, but first of all they must appoint a permanent delegate. He wanted someone on the spot since the reports they received via Jewish organisations were contradictory. From their own delegate they would learn of the needs and possibilities such as funding, supervision of distribution, and so on. He also wrote of the evacuation of Jews towards Palestine to which the Romanian government was favourable. The land frontier with Bulgaria had been closed and in consequence the only way out was by sea. The Romanian Red Cross hoped that the emigration by sea could take place under the aegis of the ICRC which would facilitate the obtaining of German and Russian safe-conducts. There was the suggestion that if an ICRC delegate was not likely to be nominated soon, then a certain M. Kolb could be sent since he was an expert in maritime affairs and would be able to ascertain availability of ships, cost, navigation problems, and so on.[12]

However the Bureau, the decision-making political organ of the ICRC, hesitated to take the plunge. It obviously hoped to play for time before taking decisions which could be interpreted as changes in objectives or means.[13] It drew strength from the idea that de Steiger could take on a further task, that of a mandate concerning the Jews. The Bureau thought that a collaboration with the national Red Cross might allow sufficient opportunities for action. It decided to put this to the test. At the instigation of the Swiss legation, following a suggestion from the Romanian Red Cross, president Huber asked the president of the latter, Jean Costinescu, to intercede with the Romanian authorities, requesting their help in the efforts being made by the ICRC through the Romanian Red Cross, to trace people deported to Transnistria who were being sought by their families. This request was crowned with success, at least in so far as it was greeted positively by the vice-president of the Council of Ministers, Mihaï Antonescu.

By mid-August the decision to send a second delegate to Bucharest was at last taken, perhaps only because of the burdens already placed on de Steiger.[14] The Romanian authorities were asked to approve Karl Kolb, a fifty-eight-year-old businessman, originally from Thurgau, who was well acquainted with south-eastern Europe, Romania in particular, since he had worked there for ten years in a local oil company.

In principle, there was no obstacle to this decision except for the problem of protocol raised by the organisation of a delegation whose two members would not be subordinate one to the other but would collaborate on an equal footing with different areas of competence. De Steiger, the ICRC's delegate for the CMS with its headquarters in Bucharest, was given the more technical job of purchase and transport of aid supplies, which led him to travel in the Balkans. Kolb, the delegate for Romania alone, was entrusted with a mission essentially defined by the Conventions of 1929 and the arrangements concerning civilian internees. Action on behalf of Jews did not figure in the written order of his mission. On the other hand, before his departure the new delegate received spoken instructions which emphasised the importance of the task before him, in particular where the Jews of Transnistria were concerned. 'It is important for people to be able to realise that the ICRC has done all it can in this respect' record the minutes of the interview.[15]

This last remark is particularly important in the light of the intentions shown by the Bucharest authorities or at least certain among them. At the end of September 1943, the vice-president of the Council of Ministers, Mihaï Antonescu, at the prompting of the Swiss minister and de Steiger over the Jewish problem, expressed his wish that the ICRC should investigate with total impartiality the situation on the ground in Transnistria. As proof of his good faith he gave orders for the repatriation from Transnistria of certain categories of Jewish people, widows, invalids, people who had been decorated and former civil servants, and for the assembly at Odessa, with a view to emigration to Palestine, of several thousand children orphaned as a result of the deportations.[16] Was Mihaï Antonescu, a young professor of international public law, vice-president and acting president of the Council of Ministers and minister of foreign affairs (no relation for all that of the man of the same name, the marshal and *Conducator* of Romania), really trying to save his country's Jews from death, or was he merely trying to ensure for himself a way out, six months after the German disaster at Stalingrad? Was there any hope of success for such a policy over that of the Germans who were present in the country in various capacities? In any case the ICRC replied with great caution to this invitation. Saly Mayer having made available for Transnistria an initial credit of 100,000 Swiss francs, the ICRC accepted that the supplies should be distributed on the ground by the national Red Cross, under the general supervision of its own delegate. It still had, however, great reservations about emigration by sea. It wrote that it would be delighted to see the rapid implementation of the emigration projects that it was familiar with and it had sent de Steiger on 15 September 1943, as proof of its interest, a letter addressed to the president of the Romanian Red Cross. On mature reflection, however, the ICRC did not feel that it could take on a task so different from its normal responsibilities and it was delighted to learn that the Romanian Red Cross was willing to shoulder the organisation of the emigration on the lines established in the conversations with Messrs Chapuisat and de Traz in Bucharest. Whilst using its influence to encourage the present tendencies in Romania towards implementing the departure of the number of Jews admissible to Palestine, the ICRC wished to limit its own activity to the granting of its flag to those boats in which the emigrants would travel. The ICRC could not hide its disappointment when it read the information sent, and it hesitated to send it on to the national Red Cross associations and other groups in Allied countries and especially to the USA and London who were keenly interested in the emigration of Romanian Jews. While maintaining its position that it could not become involved in the practicalities of the problem that the Romanian groups concerned would have to solve, it recommended that de Steiger should take such steps as he saw fit to bring about the successful resolution of the Romanian Red Cross's efforts.[17]

Whereas de Steiger seemed to share these reservations, Kolb gave the impression on his arrival in the Romanian capital at the beginning of November of wishing to seize any opportunity that was offered, with or without ulterior motive, by Mihaï Antonescu. From 11 to 21 December he visited Transnistria, in the company in particular of Colonel Stefan

Radulescu, the premier's head of bureau for Bessarabia and Transnistria. He visited the province extensively within the limits imposed on communications by the state of war and made stops in the towns of Tiraspol, Tulcin, Cernauti, Moghilev and Odessa. He was therefore able to ascertain that some of the Jews from the old kingdom and from the Dorohoï district had been repatriated according to the promise made by Antonescu; on the other hand the orphans had not yet been assembled for possible emigration, and finally extreme poverty was rife amongst the deportees and the Jews in Transnistria. The report which he submitted to the ICRC, with a copy to Mihaï Antonescu, was distributed in confidence to Jewish organisations, but they only knew the broad outlines. The text was indeed very political insofar as it drew a blank with respect to the dramatic events of earlier years and was content to present demographic statistics on this subject which indicated the disappearance of 250,000 people out of 300,000. Essentially it proposed a programme of action: immediate aid taking the form of fuel, shoes, clothes and food using funds from the Joint, and then the fulfilment of the promise of Mihaï Antonescu to bring the Jews from the old kingdom back, to make provision for the 4,500 orphans and to repatriate the remaining deportees from Bessarabia and Bukovina.[18] In the very firm letter which he wrote to the vice-president of the Council of Ministers, on the occasion of the audience following his return, the delegate of the ICRC, still supported by René de Weck, clearly reaffirmed his intentions and his conviction that these could be achieved with the help of the national leaders.

The repatriation of those who had been deported

In the weeks following his return from Transnistria, the delegate, often accompanied by the Swiss minister, besieged the vice-president of the Council of Ministers asking for fulfilment of his promises, especially those concerning repatriation. However, even though the welcome he received was always cordial and the talk open, it has to be conceded that the notes he wrote were not followed up and except in very limited respects the promises were not kept. Kolb blamed the Germans and their henchmen. He wrote to headquarters saying that in a letter to Mihaï Antonescu he urged him to set out clearly all the difficulties that he encountered in trying to implement his ideas. There was an influential element in the government itself which was seeking to prevent the return of the deportees to Romania. The head of the antisemitic party, Alexandru Cuza, protested to Marshal Ion Antonescu against the plan to bring back the deportees, and because of this intervention the order

The Axis allies

207

given towards the end of November to bring back those deported was withdrawn and only the 6,000 Jews from Dorohoï were able to return. Moreover the section of the German embassy which oversaw Jewish concerns was opposed to both the repatriation and the emigration. Mihaï Antonescu himself did not doubt that it was necessary to repatriate the Jews and he assured Kolb that he would do his utmost, although patience was necessary as they advanced step by step. It was evident that the deported Jews could not expect to be better treated than the Romanian population on the ground, and since the latter's evacuation had not yet been decreed, there was no question of demanding from the Romanian government the immediate return of those who had been deported.[19]

Thus it was to the vice-president of the Council of Ministers and not to the marshal, head of the regime, that President Huber wrote when M. Kolb asked him to support his initiatives. He assured Mihaï Antonescu that the ICRC was grateful for the support that it had received from him and the Romanian leadership, and he thanked the government for allowing its delegation to distribute aid to the interned Jews in Transnistria. He permitted himself to indicate the gratitude the ICRC would feel on learning that the Jews in Transnistria were sheltered in less exposed areas where its delegates could continue to help them with the backing of the Romanian authorities. He felt certain that the vice-president would share the ICRC's feelings, which were prompted by the concern it felt over the fate of the internees.[20]

A few days after the sending of this message, an incident reinforced Kolb's belief that the surest means of getting backing for his actions on behalf of the Jews was indeed the vice-president of the Council of Ministers. Three of the Jewish community's leaders, Misu Benvenisti, Samuel Enzer and Wilhelm Fischer, who were working with him on the distribution of aid and the preparations for emigration, were arrested and accused in particular of violating the law on foreign currency exchange. The affair was blatantly set up by the antisemitic groups and the Gestapo. Mihaï Antonescu appealed to Karl Kolb who, like René de Weck, had in any case immediately interceded with him, asking him to investigate in his name all the charges made against the accused. Their intervention resulted in the men's liberation which, in turn, led two days later to the sidelining by the interior minister of the chief of police who had given in to the orders of the vice-president, concealed behind the ICRC delegate, unless the reverse was the case; this liberation made possible the pursuit of the emigration projects which Mihaï Antonescu said he was particularly keen on.

In the long run, however, Karl Kolb did not achieve much in the field of repatriations in spite of his efforts and those of the Swiss minister. The *Conducator* was to remain deaf to the requests of his namesake except in the case of the children.[21] And then the Russian advance brought about in its own way a solution to the problem. With the approach of the frontline and the bitter fighting in which civilians were caught up, repatriation turned into mass exodus. The ICRC delegate managed at least to gather together in Moldavia about 2,000 orphans and to avoid the Jews being kept in ghettos when they returned to Romania and especially, no mean feat, to prevent the enforcement of a decree of 29 May 1944 providing for the death penalty for Hungarian Jews who might try to seek illegal refuge in Romania, this latter also thanks to the intervention of Mihaï Antonescu. Kolb wrote that the protest that the vice-president of the Council of Ministers, Antonescu, made to Marshal Antonescu, the state *Conducator*, over his having promulgated the decree in question without previous consultation with him seemed successful mainly because it apparently mentioned the fact that this law would expose former Romanian citizens, that is Jews living in the part of Transylvania that had been ceded to Hungary after the Vienna arbitration, to the death penalty if they tried to return to their former motherland, whereas the Christian Hungarians from the other Hungarian regions, even mortal enemies of Romania, would be welcomed with open arms.[22]

Aid

At the same time as he authorised and even urged the ICRC delegate to visit Transnistria, the vice-president of the Romanian Council of Ministers had agreed to the setting up of a vast aid operation for the deportees. Briefly summed up, this action, which was to absorb much of the energy of Karl Kolb, who had recently acquired a deputy, was chiefly concerned with clothing, shoes, food and medicines. At the end of hostilities in Romania the action was taken over by the CMS.

As far as the Jews were concerned, during the period of racial persecution, the funds for the most part were to come from three sources. Saly Mayer first gave a sum of 100,000 Swiss francs in the name of the Joint to the ICRC which transferred it to Romania where the Romanian Red Cross made up from its own funds the loss caused by the official rate of exchange of the lei. The national society also took upon itself the purchase and distribution under the general supervision of the ICRC delegate. In spring 1944 a second sum of 100,000 francs, taken from a gift of 100,000 dollars from the Joint, was made available to Kolb, through the intervention of the War Refugee Board. This time the money did not follow official channels. An account was opened in Kolb's name at the Société de Banque Suisse in Geneva and the transfer, with the tacit agreement of the Romanian authorities, was enabled to be made not at the rate of 45 lei for one franc, but this time at 330 lei to one franc. On the ground the money was given to trustworthy men from the Joint, the ICRC delegate once more only acting in a general supervisory capacity.[23] This manner of proceeding, although it was financially advantageous and suitable for the circumstances, was obviously contrary to the practice of the ICRC and a source of much embarrassment in Geneva because Kolb could only give the donors rather vague indications of the use the funds were put to. Albert Lombard wrote to him that the ICRC presumed that his next report would indicate who was responsible for the purchase of the goods that were to be sent to the needy Jews. They felt that the buyers must once more have been the trustworthy men from the Joint (including Fildermann) and that he (Kolb) had not been part of the operation. Furthermore, since they did not wish to carry any responsibility in this matter, even in the future it was essential for him to be given – when the funds had passed through his hands – not only receipts from the people he gave the money to but also a signed discharge from these same people, witnessing that he had no part in determining the use these funds were put to. The originals of the receipts and the witness statements should be sent to the ICRC. If, on the other hand, reports were required on the actions undertaken thanks to the funds sent by the ICRC or through its intervention with the competent American agencies, the possible conclusion that the ICRC was in any way responsible either for the organisation of the action or for the purchases and expenditure undertaken had to be avoided at all costs. The ICRC would only intervene to facilitate the transfer and could in no way be seen as the fiduciary agent, responsible for the way in which the people who received the funds made use of them.[24]

The Joint itself, however, felt that wealthy Romanian Jews, especially in Bucharest, could also aid their fellow Jews who had been deported to Transnistria or who were awaiting emigration. Here too Kolb, taking responsibility into his own hands, acted as go-between with the Romanian Jewish charities who collected into the summer the sum of 847 million lei. Taking his cue from donations agreed by certain wealthy Jews in the form of advances that would be reimbursed at the end of the war, he backed the proposal for a sort of compensation system, similar to an arrangement known as the Haavara agreement, signed before the war between the Nazis and the Jewish Agency, which thanks to a certificate signed by the ICRC delegate permitted through the bank accounts of Jewish organisations the Jews who wished to emigrate to have access on their arrival in Palestine to the sums that on their departure from Romania they had left behind for the benefit of the needy and the deportees. This proposal was not, however, accepted by Geneva and the changing fortunes of the battlefield were soon to make it obsolete. On the other hand the 'clearing' system between donations in Swiss francs in Switzerland, given via the ICRC, and the gifts of the Jews on the ground in lei which were passed on to the charities through the intermediary of the delegate, continued with the agreement of the Swiss compensation office during winter 1944–5.

Emigration

Since the events in Romania have been described in the general chapter on emigration, there will be no discussion here of the central role played by Romania because of its strategic geographical position and because of the intention of certain Romanian leaders to settle the Jewish question 'gently' and thus facilitate a separate armistice with the Allies. However, Kolb and even his colleague, Vladimir de Steiger, devoted too much energy to the emigration project for it to be passed over in silence. An examination should be made of the delicate and sometimes difficult situation of the ICRC delegates on the ground.

Without doubt Kolb played a most important part in the projects of spring 1944. He had access to Mihaï Antonescu and enjoyed the seemingly resolute, if sometimes unofficial, support of the Swiss minister René de Weck. He could also count on the president of the Romanian Red Cross, Jean Costinescu. Finally he managed to gain the confidence of the Jewish organisations, which was no mean feat given the rivalries and conflicts between people within them. At the centre of a network on the ground of people of not inconsiderable influence, Kolb had derived a further stock of authority from the prestige of the ICRC, from the information that he received from his colleague Gilbert Simond in Ankara, who was himself in constant touch with the representative of the War Refugee Board, Ira Hirschmann, and from the means that the Joint made available to him for Jewish organisations. In spite of all this, it would be wrong to conclude that he was in any way in control of the situation, whether the Romanian authorities, the Protecting Power or even the Jewish milieux were concerned, as is proved by his inability to prevent the unauthorised departures of the *Milka* and the *Maritza*. In this game of life and death where political or commercial interest dictated the attitude of the players more often than charity did, the ICRC delegate had to be prepared to take calculated risks and to take them alone or in concert with the Swiss minister, since the slowness of communications often made the desired consultation with Geneva illusory. In this situation, which although not unique was particularly noticeable in the case of affairs of emigration in Romania, the delegate was obviously tempted to overestimate his own efforts, to hear the words only of those he was talking to and to lack the necessary time and hindsight for a lucid appreciation of the situation. This was all the more true in the problem of emigration since he had no Conventions or precise instructions to provide a framework for his mission.

So it is noticeable that the record of the emigration of spring 1944 is shot through with a certain tension between the ICRC and the men on the ground. This did not concern the conditions that the ICRC set on the protection that it would give to boats which might carry Jewish emigrants to Turkey or to Palestine, but rather the appreciation of possible action outcomes which were sometimes underestimated in Geneva and exaggerated in Bucharest. There was, because of this, a permanent fear in Geneva that the risk taken in Bucharest, and to a lesser extent in Ankara, might become a dangerous mistake. In mid-May 1944, for example, Kolb, who had issued a sort of certificate and was asked by the Jewish organisations to choose which emigrants could leave, or at least to supervise this choice, was reminded by Schwarzenberg of the need, given the disputes between the Jewish organisations, for caution, disengagement and neutrality. At the same time the attention of Gilbert Simond, who was negotiating with Hirschmann over the eventual handing over of two ships to the ICRC, and was battling to bring about the departure of the *Tari* for Constantza, was drawn to the same rules of caution, circumspection and neutrality by Walter Füllemann, head of the Transport and Communications Division.[25]

This reminder was not enough and the ICRC was alarmed to see Kolb involved in the quarrels between the Jewish organisations and going beyond his brief. A clear warning was eventually sent to him by the Delegations' Committee:

None of the Conventions concerning the ICRC mentions Jews amongst the categories of people on whose behalf the Committee may act.

On the purely humanitarian plane of its activities, once people enter one of the categories of war victims on whose behalf it can act either following the Conventions or established practice the ICRC does not distinguish between Jews and non-Jews.

When, in certain states, because of their race, the Jews are subject to a particular status determined by the country's internal legislation, the ICRC must not take up a position with regard to this legislation. At the same time it must take account of it.

You must never forget, if you intervene at any time on behalf of Jews as well as non-Jews, that the ICRC's principle of strict political neutrality determines the extent of your activity. You must avoid undertaking actions that could be seen as more political than humanitarian.

We feel that your action with regard to the special permits that are requisite for Jews and foreigners who wish to leave Bucharest is a step too far, going beyond the remit of the ICRC and which, moreover, could be considered to be of a political nature (you only mentioned the Jews, ignoring foreigners, in your letter to the vice-president of the Council of Ministers).[26]

Kolb's reply was interesting in that it was at one and the same time a declaration and assessment of his activity:

The ICRC's position over the problems of the Jews in South-Eastern Europe is well known to me. I know that my activities on behalf of the oppressed Jewish population in Romania cannot be based on Conventions. All that I have done in this respect has been based on an agreement with Mihaï Antonescu, vice-president of the Council of Ministers, who had entrusted me with the task of studying the situation of the Romanian Jews who had been deported to Transnistria, and of making concrete proposals to him. This request prompted me to look more closely into the problems of the Jews in Romania and Mihaï Antonescu thereafter often addressed me as 'Geneva's representative for minorities'. All the proposals and requests that I addressed to him were warmly welcomed and more than once he asked me to give him the details of the sufferings of the Jewish population so that he might, if possible, remedy the potential wrongs and overzealous excesses that some government departments and civil servants might commit. My position vis-à-vis the present government is quite clear: I base my actions on the intentions of Mihaï Antonescu and on the humanitarian sentiments of the ICRC. You can see from M. Antonescu's letter of 6 June which I have sent you that he conveys his thanks for my action in Romania. If he does not expressly mention Jewish affairs, one can well understand why, but his phrase 'for the humane task that you are carrying out in Romania' refers to these actions as well.

You can be sure that I would have put a brake on my undertakings on behalf of the Jews had I noticed on a single occasion that an action would be ill received or could have caused the slightest harm to the ICRC's other humanitarian work. I have the distinct impression that, through my actions, the reputation and the prestige of the ICRC have risen enormously in Romania, which fact was proved, amongst others, by an exclamation of the vice-president of the Council of Ministers towards a civil servant who was too inclined to submit to certain foreign demands: 'by such actions you are acting counter to the ICRC – and do you know what standing it has, this ICRC?'

If I have been led into actions concerning the Jews to a greater extent than I expected at the start, it has only been in order to pursue the humanitarian aims of our institution. I would do the same and more for any other minority, as I have assured M. Mihaï Antonescu to his great satisfaction.

The special case that you mention – to have alluded only to Jews and not to all foreigners – was such that I did not need to concern myself with the latter who depended on their respective legations. M. de Weck, the Swiss minister, had at the start of the antisemitic legislation obtained that the Swiss Jews should not be subject to the clauses of the various special laws, since Switzerland did not allow the differentiation of its nationals according to race and religion. M. de Weck managed to have this exemption extended to the Jews of nations for whom Switzerland acts as Protecting Power. The same is true for foreign Jews under the aegis of the legations of Sweden and Spain. Thus all the Jews who come from neutral and enemy countries are not subject to this special legislation and need not be mentioned. I cannot concern myself with Jews who are nationals of the Axis powers since their respective governments would certainly allow no such intervention. Because of this I have had to limit my activities to the Romanian Jews, treating them as a hard-hit minority, with hostage-taking and posting of notices of which only the Jews were the subject.

These explanations should have shown you that all my humanitarian actions on behalf of the Jewish population were seeking to improve their situation, actions that do credit to the ICRC delegation in Romania and which have not and cannot compromise other countries. Nonetheless I take note of your instructions and will bear them in mind as far as the situation will allow without damaging the interests of people suffering, of the state and not least of the ICRC on whose intervention the lives and happiness of the wretched and the persecuted often depend.[27]

As for Simond, who took Füllemann's remarks very badly indeed,[28] he received a clarification which insisted on the need for the ICRC to integrate its action on behalf of the Jews in an ensemble and also to link together in some way the various actions of its delegates in different arenas. Schwarzenberg was keen to point out to him that the instructions were meant as indications for the future and not as blame. Even if to the man on the ground their position seemed wrong, they formed part of an overall plan into which they fitted. Thus they could not attach importance to the fact that the Jewish institutions in Bucharest and the Swiss legation in that city approved of the protest over the departure of the *Milka*. These organisations were not faced with the same problem as the ICRC and had a different purpose from theirs: their responsibilities were of a totally different order. Care had to be taken, Schwarzenberg went on, that the ICRC's interventions on behalf of the Jews, although entirely of a humanitarian nature, were not considered, wrongly of course, as taking up a position vis-à-vis the internal legislation in certain states and thus assuming a political character incompatible with the principle of neutrality which lies at the heart of all ICRC action.[29]

Means and limitations of the action

Romania was incontestably one of the strong points of actions undertaken by the Red Cross in 1943 and 1944, particularly on behalf of the persecuted Jews. However, without underestimating the work accomplished by Kolb, with the support of his colleague Vladimir de Steiger, and by the Swiss minister, René de Weck, one has to recognise that the operations which were partly successful – the Transnistria orphans, the distribution of aid, the help given to many individuals – were essentially carried out on the margins of Romanian politics, thanks to the intervention of certain leaders foremost among whom was the vice-president of the Council of Ministers, Mihaï Antonescu. These interventions were not, evidently, without ulterior motive: Antonescu wanted to negotiate with tomorrow's victors. Both for history and for his own future he needed undeniable witnesses of his battle against antisemitic persecution, witnesses who could equally observe the aerial attacks launched by the Allies against the civilian Romanian population and even more who, as citizens of a neutral country, could promote the withdrawal to the West of the country's elite who were under threat from the Soviet advance.

In the last months of the conflict all the ICRC delegates, including those in Germany, found themselves more or less involved in this type of calculation. In Romania the exchange of favours went particularly far, mainly because of the evolution of the front and because, as in Hungary, the regime enjoyed a relatively large margin of manoeuvre vis-à-vis the Reich, but also because of the fact that the ICRC delegate knew how to take risks often against the advice of the ICRC, with the close support of the Swiss minister and, more distantly but effectively, with that of his colleague Simond and the WRB. The combination of these factors meant that the results obviously never equalled the hopes that, given the possibilities offered by the situation in Romania, were nourished. In the case of emigration, for example, hundreds of letters and telegrams, dozens of hours of discussions, only resulted in the permission given to the local Red Cross society to use the ICRC emblem at the very moment when the evolution of the conflict made the decision useless. For all the people involved, except Kolb in Bucharest, Simond and Hirschmann in Ankara and, of course, all the organisations concerned, the Jewish problem remained marginal, depending completely on other issues at stake. Kolb was less taken up with Conventional work than some of his colleagues since the war on the Eastern Front did not permit the regular application of the Conventions: he had thus more time and more liberty to spend on the victims of racial persecution and he had the courage and imagination to do this.

Kolb and de Steiger were to stay in Romania after the *coup d'état* of 23 August 1944, the arrival of the Soviets and the September armistice. They pursued their work on behalf of the civilian population, including the Jews whose emigration still proved difficult, even impossible, because of British policy in Palestine. Since the CMS gave rise to even greater suspicion amongst the Russians than did the ICRC, the delegation, in collaboration in particular with the government and the

Romanian Red Cross and with the Joint, established an aid charity for those who had suffered in the war in Eastern and Central Europe, the costs of which were met by the Joint which regularly gave to it 5 per cent of the donations received. Then the charity was wound up and at the end of 1945 Kolb and de Steiger were recalled to Geneva. There was conflict between Kolb and the assistant who succeeded him which made him resign and leave the ICRC, a rather bitter man, on 30 June 1946: he resented its apparent indifference and the decisions taken to ensure the continuation of his work. Later he was to try in vain to get the ICRC to defend him officially against rumours concerning his financial management in Bucharest, especially his handling of the funds from the Joint. The work that he carried out for the Red Cross was to be forgotten.[30]

Bulgaria

In 1948 the Jewish Scientific Institute, specialising in the history of Judaism in Bulgaria, wrote to the ICRC asking what it had done during the war to save the Jewish nationals from deportation in 1943. The letter explained that rumours were circulating in the Jewish community that the ICRC had undertaken such an intervention which had had some success. Replying in the name of the ICRC, Edouard Chapuisat recalled the meetings he had, along with David de Traz, in 1943, with the Archbishop of Sofia, Mgr. Stefan, several ministers and the king himself. He asked all of them not to persecute the Jews and managed to get them to agree that deportation beyond the national frontier would only be inflicted on foreign Jews, in particular on the Polish Jews who were sent back home, but not on Jews of Bulgarian nationality who were merely made to leave Sofia for camps not far from the city.[31]

The sending of a delegate

The visit made by Edouard Chapuisat and David de Traz from 30 May to 8 June 1943 was really the high point of the ICRC's action in Bulgaria, not only for the reasons given above but because until then relations between the ICRC and Bulgaria had remained in an impasse. The numbers of enemy, Greek and Yugoslav, POWs were not very high but Sofia had not even replied to the ICRC's proposal to allow civilian enemy internees to benefit from the provisions of the code for POWs. In autumn 1942, in response to the repeated demand of the Greek Red Cross, the ICRC sent to the Bulgarian sister society two memoranda concerning the bad treatment to which the Greek populations of the recently annexed provinces of Thrace and Macedonia were being subjected. However, the ICRC received no reply and in the following February its assistant delegate in northern Greece, René Burkhardt, was denied access to the two provinces. A few weeks after this last incident, the neutralisation forced on the Greeks of Thrace and Macedonia deprived the ICRC of a powerful argument in its appeals to the Bulgarian Red Cross. Thus in spring 1943 the task before Chapuisat and de Traz was difficult and the points for discussion were numerous.

The conversations in Sofia were conducted at a very high level: a meeting with the president of the Council of Ministers and minister of foreign affairs, Bodjan Filov, with the ministers of the interior and of war and with the Archbishop of Sofia, Mgr. Stefan. On 7 June, Boris III, anxious to meet him, received Edouard Chapuisat most warmly and talked to him for an hour and a half. This discussion centred on the establishment of a permanent Red Cross delegation in Sofia, the Jewish problem and the situation of the Greek populations of Thrace and Macedonia.

The goodwill encountered by Chapuisat and de Traz was slow to lead to concrete decisions. Indeed, it was only at the end of 1943 that René Henry was able to settle in the Bulgarian capital. By then the Jews of foreign nationality, numbering about 10,000, had already long since been deported. On the other hand, the fate of the Bulgarian Jews was not clear. The national authorities were applying antisemitic legislation similar to that of Hitler but at the same time they refused to allow the Germans to get mixed up in their racial policy or to touch their Jewish compatriots. Apart from the traditional tasks, the instructions given to René Henry were limited to a request to study the possibility of action with regard to emigration and any aid that could be supplied to the Jews.

Emigration

Emigration concerned Bulgaria in two ways. On the one hand it was a transit country between Balkan Europe and neutral Turkey, although the German forces controlled the southern frontier from the Aegean Sea to Svilengrad. On the other hand there was the question of the Bulgarian Jews. In spring 1942, in the wake of the plans of the Jewish Agency for Palestine, the ICRC intervened to obtain transit visas needed to send 270 Jewish Romanian and Hungarian children by train to Istanbul. But months passed, telegrams increased between Ankara, Sofia, Bucharest and Geneva, and still no convoy moved off. In March 1943 during the transit of seventy-five Romanian Jewish children to Svilengrad, the Germans seized three adolescents and deported them to Poland. Following this incident the Bulgarian authorities suspended all transport across their territory. In spite of all the approaches made by Switzerland, the Protecting Power, the Sofia government remained firm and the two representatives of the ICRC made no démarche on this subject during their visit.[32]

On his return to Geneva in summer 1943, Edouard Chapuisat finally decided to try a personal gesture to reactivate the process of negotiation, writing directly to the director of political affairs at the Foreign Ministry (there is no reply to this letter to be found in the files of the ICRC):

Mindful of the warm welcome you gave to me and my collaborator, Mr David de Traz, I take the liberty of asking how the emigration of Jews from Bulgaria is progressing.

If such emigration has not yet taken place, may I ask you, Sir, to advise me: do you think the ICRC should write to the Bulgarian government or make its view known by whatever other procedure you think suitable and rapid? Perhaps it would be good for you to be completely *au fait* – if our conversations did not give you sufficient information – with what has happened regarding the plan for the emigration of a thousand Jews from Bulgaria.

On 2 July 1943 the ICRC delegate in Ankara, Mr Simond, informed us that he had learnt of an official notice from the Bulgarian Ministry of the Interior giving its agreement to the emigration of 1,000 Jewish men, with the exception of those aged eighteen to thirty, to Palestine via Turkey on condition that the departure takes place before the end of July 1943. Their entry visas for Palestine were assured since the British Embassy in Turkey had been authorised to issue them.

Given these favourable conditions we have asked our delegation in Turkey to obtain from the embassies concerned in Ankara an agreement in principle to grant German, British, American and Italian safe-conducts for the ships which are to transport these emigrants and at the same time we have asked our delegation to notify the same embassies of the departure date as soon as it is known. Finally, we have reminded them that the ICRC emblem can only be carried or affixed when all the safe-conducts have been granted.

Then another thing cropped up. We were informed that the exit visas for the Jews involved had not been granted. This, Sir, is as far as we have gone. You can easily understand that, given the uncertainty surrounding us, we should like to have a duly authorised opinion.[33]

The posting of a permanent delegate at the end of 1943 brought no difference to this state of affairs. Did the blame lie with the person of the delegate or with the conditions on the ground, the size of the Conventional tasks or the relatively moderate antisemitic persecution? In May 1944 Schwarzenberg sent to René Henry a sort of assessment of his action on behalf of the Jews which, in the framework of the effort that the ICRC intended to undertake, sounds rather like an encouragement to do more or better. He pointed out that before Henry's departure the ICRC had outlined what it hoped he might achieve in furthering Jewish emigration to Palestine and helping Jews in Bulgaria. He wanted to know whether the Bulgarians would let resident Jews leave and whether they would allow the transit of Hungarian and Romanian Jews. The ICRC realised how delicate the task was but hoped he would be able to follow up the contacts that Chapuisat had made.

He was interested to hear Henry's suggestions about helping Jews in Bulgaria, pointing out the success of the similar operation in Romania. He suggested using the Swiss chargé d'affaires to send messages as he could do so telegraphically. He warned him to use extreme care and to make sure that any action would be seen as humanitarian. Groups of Jews were to be found in Sofia, Plovdiv, Lon and Ruse but it was possible that there were others equally deserving throughout Bulgaria.[34]

Aid

The situation in this field was no more encouraging: given the lack of governmental backing similar to that obtained in Romania, the ICRC realised that it could achieve nothing on a large scale. Everything would depend on the Bulgarian Red Cross which was strictly controlled by the political powers. Therefore no large aid action would be undertaken in spite of the pressing demands from the Joint, since according to the delegate neither the authorities nor the national Red Cross thought it necessary.

In summer 1944 Bulgaria began preparations for its alignment with the Russians. The national antisemitic legislation was repealed. A Jewish consistory was appointed and René Henry himself, of his own admission, dared to depart from the caution with which he had hitherto treated the Jewish question. The Bulgaro-Soviet armistice, the political and social upheavals in the wake of the arrival of the Red Army, made him request his temporary withdrawal shortly afterwards and this was granted by the ICRC without suppression of his post. Moreover, in his opinion the situation of the Jews, or at least those who had stayed in the country, was no different at the time from that of the rest of the population. Thus the Jews did not need special attention.[35]

Italy

Possibilities and means of action

In 1931 the ICRC obtained permission for the president of the Italian Red Cross, but not its own delegates, to visit the 'confinati'. When the fascist regime, as it moved towards antisemitic measures, decided to intern Jews, starting in 1940 with foreign nationals and suspects, it did not place them in the category of political prisoners. In spite of the name, camps 'di concentramento', which it gave to its places of detention, it in fact treated the prisoners as civilian internees who were nationals of enemy countries. The ICRC was thus permitted to enter Jewish camps in Italy, even those which were later to be opened for Italian Jews, whereas in the rest of Europe, dominated or controlled by the Reich, it could only occasionally visit Jews held as civilian internees, that is nationals of enemy countries such as the United States and Great Britain whom the Germans treated with consideration, or people from neutral countries. Until summer 1943 the ICRC delegates Paul Lambert and then his successor Dr Hans Wolf de Salis, who had been assisted since spring 1943 by Dr Bruno Beretta, visited in all about a hundred POW camps and hospitals and thirty-four camps and places of internment for civilians within mainland Italy. Among these there were camps that were entirely or mostly given over to Jewish prisoners like those of Ferramonti-Tarsia (in the province of Cosenza) and Civitella del Tronto (Teramo). Similarly, unlike the situation everywhere else (except in principle in the countries of south-eastern Europe), Italian and foreign Jews could emigrate, provided, of course, they had obtained an entry visa for the receiving country and the necessary authorisations from transit countries, which required a lot of time and money.

The situation began to change from summer 1942 on. The ICRC established contact with the Delasem and from then on was able to begin to fill the role that was its own in aid activities, i.e. to inform the donors of what was needed and to offer its good offices.[36] However, all the internees did not have the same means. The nationals from the warring countries were aided by the intermediary of their Protecting Power. Others were given aid by charitable organisations in their own countries. The German, Austrian and Polish Jews, on the other hand, stateless and without a Protecting Power, with no charitable organisation, looked to the Red Cross as their only hope. Unfortunately the ICRC had got little or nothing to offer them. As Hans Wasmer of the Aid Division explained in a letter to the stateless Jewish prisoners of Ferramonti-Tarsia, the ICRC was merely the collecting and distributing agent and could send aid only to the people indicated by the donor's wishes. Their only hope was the Delasem.[37]

Two states and three wars

On 25 July 1943 Mussolini was overthrown and arrested. On 8 September the armistice was signed between the royal government and the Western Allies. However, the Germans invaded the Peninsula as far south as Rome and just beyond. They reinstated the liberated Mussolini at the head of a satellite government. The war was then made up of three conflicts: firstly that which opposed Kesselring's Wehrmacht to the Allies, then the civil war between the neo-fascist regime and the resistance, and finally the war against the Jews which the SS thenceforth waged in the zone controlled by the Germans.

The ICRC delegation suddenly found itself relieved of an essential part of its mission since the Germans said they wished to evacuate to Germany all the POWs and civilian internees from the camps, leaving only transit camps (Dulags) north of the Po, but at this point it was overwhelmed by numerous requests for aid from a civilian population now drawn into total war. The delegation also had to reorganise to take account of the position of the fronts and the state of communications. The principal delegation under H. W. de Salis, installed in Rome, was joined by assistant delegations in the south, centre and north, the latter including, under the direction of Bruno Beretta, local correspondents in Trieste, Verona, Milan, Florence, Turin and Genoa.

In the part of Italy controlled by the German army which had in its entirety been declared a zone of operations, the Jews were to undergo in a few months all the stages of an ordeal parallel to that of fellow Jews in the rest of Europe under the Germans. At first the several thousand Jews who had found precarious but real shelter in the Italian-occupied zone of France fled to Italy via Nice when the zone was itself occupied by the Wehrmacht.[38] Some of them managed to reach Rome where de Salis tried to welcome them and organise aid with the help of the Delasem. When the Jews were deported from Rome the sense of shock reached even the Vatican and the delegate could only acknowledge his impotence, since the SS justified their action to no-one, not even the German military High Command.[39] A few weeks later, the Italian Jews, now foreigners in their own country following the neo-fascist decree of 7 November, like refugees, foreigners and stateless people, had no option but to reach the Swiss border so as to escape being rounded up and deported. They turned for help to the ICRC but the delegate, assistant delegates and correspondents had very limited means. Indeed, when de Salis suggested searching for missing persons at the time of the deportations from Rome, the ICRC replied that, on the basis of its experiences in Germany, it was useless, even inopportune, to enquire about who had been deported. Any possible action, then, rested on the energy and courage of the men on the ground: discreet passing on of some civilian messages, repeated attempts to get some people liberated, visits to Aryan political prisoners, and meetings here and there with Germans, in particular *Obersturmbannführer* Kappeler after the massacre in the Ardeatine Caves.[40]

Better than a long analysis, this exchange of telegrams and letters describes the situation of the Red Cross delegates in Italy in spring 1944:

a) Leo Kubowitzki (WJC) to the ICRC. Telegram of 6 March, received in Geneva 8 March 1944: 'Our attention called to more than 200 Jewish children incarcerated in Sanvittore Milan please intervene thanks.'

b) Draft reply dated 10 March, reference PK/AP (Paul Kuhne): 'Your cable of 6 March cannot intervene stop committee obliged limit action on behalf Jews to aid distribution when possibility exists.'

c) Handwritten note by Schwarzenberg in the margin of (b) above: 'M. Kuhne. It seems difficult to me to give so negative a reply which could harm our reputation in the USA. On the other hand we can do nothing. That is why it seems preferable to me to file the cable without reacting. Do you think we should notify Beretta for his information? Send to M. Gallopin, please.'

d) Note for Bruno Beretta, assistant delegate for northern Italy, signed by Schwarzenberg on 14 March, confidential: 'We have been asked to intervene on behalf of 200 Jewish children who are thought to be imprisoned in San Vittore in Milan. We know how difficult it is to request even just information in the case of Jews. Therefore we leave you to make a decision about the possibility of raising this question with the Italian people concerned without creating problems for you. It is really only to put you in the picture that we are drawing your attention to this case with the request that you should write us a report if you can find anything out or could obtain an improvement in the treatment of these children.'[41]

e) On 30 March, Beretta, accompanied by Frédéric Zweifel, the ICRC's correspondent for the Verona region, went to the headquarters of the SS forces in northern Italy. He wanted to find out whether Jewish camps had been set up and whether it was possible to obtain lists of the names of those detained. The two envoys from the Red Cross were received by *Sturmbannführer* Fritz Bosshammer in particular, an SS officer, who was apparently responsible for Jewish questions, and who was very reticent but finally admitted that the police were then assembling Jewish detainees in a camp at Fossolo di Carpi (province of Modena) that had been in Italian hands but that there would be no other camp for Jews in northern Italy. This name was not unknown to Beretta who, twice before, had tried to gain entry there. The meeting ended in a fairly heated way since

Bosshammer, getting more and more suspicious, ended up keeping the two men for identity checks for several hours before releasing them. At the end of his report Beretta announced that Zweifel intended to see the officer again in a fortnight since Bosshammer justified his present refusal to let them visit Fossolo di Carpi by the fact that the camp was being done up and the SS leaders did not want to take responsibility for showing it in such a state.[42]

f) Note from Beretta to the ICRC in reply to the note of 14 March (see (d) above) dated 2 May (received in Geneva 19 May): 'Thank you for your note of 14.3.44 concerning the question under reference and we have the advantage of informing you that on 1.5.44, when we visited this House of Punishment, we discreetly questioned *Scharführer* Klimsa. We were given a negative reply, that is: there are now no longer any Jewish children in the prison of San Vittore because they have been transferred to a camp for Jews. We assume that this is the CC Fossolo di Carpi (Modena) and we have taken the steps needed to obtain permission to visit it from the SS Commander.'[43]

g) Note dated 12 May from Schwarzenberg to Beretta, in reply to his report of his visit of 30 March to *Sturmbannführer* Bosshammer (see (e) above): 'We acknowledge receipt of your report H.121/44 of 5 April 1944 which received our full attention. We are grateful for the efforts you made to try to obtain permission to visit the Jewish camps but we feel a need to draw your attention to the fact that these questions must be handled with great restraint. You tell us that Dr Zweifel should renew his approach to M. Bosshammer with a view to obtaining permission to visit the camp at Fossolo di Carpi. It would, of course, be interesting for the ICRC to know what category of detainees is in this type of camp but it would be wise to avoid asking officially to be allowed to visit such camps. Indeed, requests of this sort are outside the remit of the ICRC which could not back them up either with the Geneva Convention or as a practice recognised by the warring parties. We must not forget that under the Conventions it is only the POW and civilian internee camps that can be inspected by the ICRC. Thus it is first and foremost on these two categories of camp that our delegates' attention should be focused and we must avoid compromising our possibilities of action on behalf of POWs and civilian internees by taking steps outside our traditional field of activity.'[44]

h) On 23 May, during a meeting in Milan with Jean-Guy de Rham, secretary of the Foreign Interests Section of the Swiss consulate in the Lombard capital, Beretta learnt that the Protecting Power had been able to visit the Italian part of Fossolo di Carpi which held

1,100 civilian internees, all Aryan, among them about 200 Italian political prisoners, but not the Jewish camp under German control. This information encouraged Beretta to request permission for another visit from the Italians.[45]

i) On 25 May, Schwarzenberg asked the ICRC delegation in Washington to give the Committee's reply to Leo Kubowitzki's telegram of 6 March (see (a) above). It made two points: it was impossible, as the WJC knew, to obtain information about detained or deported Jews; according to details obtained on the ground there were no more Jewish children in San Vittore, because it seemed they had been taken to a camp for Jews.

j) Note from Beretta to the ICRC, dated 12 June, in reply to the note from Schwarzenberg of 12 May (see (g) above): 'Thank you for your note under reference whose content we have studied closely. Following your instructions we have asked our correspondent Dr Zweifel to desist from a second approach to M. Bosshammer. If we have judged it could be useful to approach the commander of the SS troops under whose control the CC Fossolo di Carpi lies, this has occurred after incessant requests from our head of delegation in Italy, Dr de Salis, who urged us to concern ourselves with the plight of the Jews who, according to his information, had been evacuated from the Rome region to camps in northern Italy. We are grateful for your clarification of the situation and we assure you that, unless there is a special order from the Committee, we shall only be concerned in the future with questions affecting POWs and civilian internees as long as these are Aryan.'[46]

k) In a note of 25 September to Albert Lombard, the Committee's vice-president, Schwarzenberg wrote that in his view 'the advanced stage of the war justifies a revision of the classical doctrine of the ICRC', and that he therefore considered it necessary to modify the instructions to the delegates, who up until then had had to concern themselves above all with POWs and civilian internees.[47]

There remained aid. This action took on importance from winter 1943–4 onwards since the Joint declared itself ready to make money available, because the president of the Delasem, Lelio Valobra, was in Switzerland and the ICRC delegate could – with complete discretion – act as intermediary either in giving small sums of money to needy people who might make spontaneous requests or in transferring to the Delasem larger sums of money made available from Switzerland. When in spring 1944 the channels used by the Delasem to introduce money into Italy, especially those of the Catholic church, were interrupted or upset by the repression, then the ICRC delegation intervened, notably to forward the equivalent of a first instalment of 20,000 Swiss francs made by the Joint to the ICRC on behalf of the Jews in Italy. Up until the liberation of the country, other help in the form of money would follow this route and also that of the church, allowing the payment of monthly allocations of up to 2,400 lire per person and also the distribution of clothing and parcels. Furthermore, thanks to a depot created at Ponte San Pietro in buildings belonging to a Swiss industrialist, the sub-delegation in northern Italy would be able to forward significant numbers of parcels, such as the dispatch of half a wagonload that Beretta managed to get into the Italian part of the Fossolo di Carpi camp even though he was unable to enter the buildings himself.

Special mission in northern Italy

In autumn 1944 the violence of the war redoubled in northern Italy which made the task of the sub-delegation all the more difficult since they were cut off from Rome. Besides, the ICRC decided to recall its principal representative, Bruno Beretta, who had become suspect in the eyes of the Germans. Believing his mission to be impossible in the circumstances and urged by his worried family, Beretta sent his report to Geneva and then withdrew. His departure left the correspondent on the ground in a difficult situation.

This situation explained, as did the chaos that reigned in the country, the fragmentary and often contradictory nature of the information reaching Geneva on the plight of civilian internees and of political and racial detainees and on the type of camps where they were likely to be. Two names recurred constantly, the function of which seemed quite clearly defined: Fossolo or Fossolo di Carpi, from which the deportation convoys left for Buchenwald, Auschwitz and Mauthausen. After the closure of this camp there was one at Bolzano/Gries which seemed to be no more than a staging post on the road to deportation. Thus the ICRC did not lack information since it even received (limited) lists of the Jews deported, but it did lack means of action because the traditional intervention through aid would not work here, partly because of the general situation (the depot at Ponte San Pietro had been bombed and its secretary, Jean Obrist, killed) and partly because of the fact that the transit camp at Bolzano was only a staging post for the deported.

The need to pull together again a sub-delegation that had split into several sections and to attempt a special operation on behalf of the deportees, but also the general change in attitude of the ICRC and the balance of the war tipping towards Allied victory, all led finally to the decision, taken seemingly in September or October 1944, to send a special delegate to northern Italy. No trace has, however, been found of a formal decision by the Committee. On the other hand, there is no doubt from reading the correspondence about the title of special delegate and the nature of the mission entrusted to Hans Bon. The new envoy was to get in touch with all the local correspondents, to reorganise the sub-delegation, to carry out a tour of visits to the camps, to renew relations with the authorities in the country and finally to attempt an aid operation for the political and racial detainees and those deported. These were the outlines of his mission if one puts together the written documents with the oral explanations given to the delegates. It was not surprising that the formal decision was never recorded in writing, given the methods of working: it could also be seen as in some way integrated, like a natural consequence, into the efforts made on behalf of the detainees in the concentration camps in Germany.

The idea of special action was born in summer 1944 in the wake of the Red Cross operations in Hungary. It was first presented to the ICRC by an Aid Committee for Italian political and racial deportees which arose in the Italian Free Colony, Lausanne section.[48] At that moment the Royal Government and the ICRC were preoccupied above all with hundreds of thousands of Italians in German hands, especially the military internees for whom they wanted to obtain a treatment similar to that of POWs. They were also concerned by the plight of the POWs whose protection under the Geneva Convention the OKW had taken away. The government in Rome did not, however, neglect other categories of victims. It was seeking at the same time to obtain from the Swiss Federal Council the removal from the Reich of a thousand or so Jews of under sixteen and over fifty years of age. Like Belgium and France it would intercede subsequently with the ICRC on behalf of the detainees in Auschwitz, who, it feared, would be exterminated.

If the ICRC wanted to attempt an approach on behalf of Italian Jews to achieve a suspension of the deportations, visits to the concentration camps, the regrouping of threatened people under its protection and the distribution of aid, should it not have made sure of the agreement of the neo-fascist authorities? Burckhardt had promised the president of the Italian Free Colony in Lausanne, Luigi Zappelli, that he would speak to Count Vinci, who had kept his post in Geneva, still in Mussolini's service.[49] But this appeal, if it was made, was without result. A few weeks later, Mlle Ferrière asked the advice of the Swiss consul in Milan, Franco Brenni, with whom the Red Cross was in correspondence and who was the *de facto* representative of Swiss interests in northern Italy.[50]

Brenni recommended to the ICRC a new intermediary, Valerio Benuzzi, whom he had recently met in Milan. This man, aged fifty-two, was dubious to say the least since the title of inspector of the Italian Red Cross which he had self-flatteringly adopted was visibly usurped and he was in fact trying to withdraw to Switzerland with his wife, hence his contacts with the Swiss consul in Milan. He said he wanted to save the persecuted and could intervene on their behalf with the Germans if they had money. For this reason he was in touch with the Joint and the Delasem, that is with Saly Mayer and Valobra. He had access to the Cardinal Archbishop of Milan, Mgr. Schuster, whose interventions on behalf of Jews and members of the resistance are well known, and to the Cardinal Archbishop of Genoa, Mgr. Boetto, but it seems likely that he was really working for the SS or for those of its leaders of high rank, of whom there were several in northern Italy, who were hoping to end up on the right side.[51] Thanks to the ICRC Benuzzi obtained an entry visa to Switzerland from the Federal Aliens Police who had at first refused his application. Once there he was ready to get down to work to facilitate the ICRC delegation's work in northern Italy.

Hans Bon, a sixty-two-year-old hotel owner in St Moritz, whose brother Rodolphe was also working for the ICRC at the time, was head of the ICRC delegation in Egypt from 1942–3. His experience, his knowledge of the world and of languages were most useful in the mission that was entrusted to him. With regard to the present topic, on the advice of Benuzzi, the ICRC asked him to make contact with General Harster, an SS *Obergruppenführer* who lived in Verona, to obtain:

a) permission to visit the camp at Bolzano and give aid to the detainees;
b) the list of people already deported to Germany;
c) the suspension of deportations;
d) the eventual transfer of the Jews from Bolzano to Switzerland; and
e) the repatriation of the French people from the Alpes-Maritimes who had been taken to Italy by the Germans.[52]

Delayed by illness, Hans Bon only left Geneva during December to settle in Milan from where he began the reorganisation of the sub-delegation in northern Italy, in particular in the field of aid, its storage and distribution. Through the intermediary of Benuzzi, he met, in Milan, not only the leaders of the Italian Red Cross but in particular the highest German military and police authorities, notably General Wolff, *Obergruppenführer* SS, the supreme head of the SS and the police in northern Italy, who took him under his personal protection and designated SS Colonel Rauff as his liaison officer. The ICRC delegate made contact again with the Cardinal Archbishop of Milan, Mgr. Schuster, and with the German ambassador to the fascist regime, Rudolf von Rahn, as well as several dignitaries of the northern Italian Social Republic.

The first results of his conversations were promising. Hans Bon obtained permission to visit the camp at Bolzano but he did not get the right to be given the list of names of those deported. He was promised that the deportations were being suspended while talks about the transfer of the Bolzano Jews to Switzerland and the repatriation of the French to the Alpes-Maritimes were in progress.[53] This was an un-doubted success, comparable to what was happening in a parallel manner in Germany and of course comparable to the many attempts by Wolff to save his skin through direct contacts with the Western Allies. But the ICRC delegate did not let his success go to his head. He knew that there were, in fact, few people left to save. 'It is regrettable', he concluded in his report on his activities dated 15 February, 'that we did not begin this work at the delegation four or five months ago. In the meantime events have brought about great difficulties which are par-ticularly noticeable in the distribution of aid to the POWs and Allied civilian internees and these will take a long time to resolve.'[54]

However, the ICRC had a run of bad luck. In Verona, Zweifel, who also had his contacts with the SS in the person of *Sturmbannführer* Bosshammer, gained permission to go to Bolzano, a journey that would never take place since Biaggi de Blasys, who was to accompany him, was laid up in hospital with sudden appendicitis. At the same time, Bon, who had started to negotiate with the Germans for an exchange on a one-for-one basis of German prisoners and Jewish detainees, was not able to continue his stay in Milan since there had been a new decline in his health. From St Moritz, where he was being treated, he continued the discussion through the intermediary of his assistant, Kurt Tschudi, which was an unfortunate way of conducting so delicate a negotiation. Moreover the ICRC did not always seem to coordinate its efforts. On 6 April, Tschudi informed Mlle Ferrière from Milan that the deportations had stopped, as Hans Bon had announced two months earlier, that the arrested Jews would be interned, at Bolzano for the moment, and that the ICRC now needed to turn to the British and the Americans for an examination of the realisation of the plan for an exchange of German POWs and interned Jews.[55] But it was in vain that Bon telephoned the ICRC to press them to act and that the president of the Delasem, Valobra, expressed his fear of failure if they delayed any longer. The note sent to Tschudi on 19 April 1945, a mere fortnight or so before the war ended, while it announced the Committee's intention, does not appear to bear the stamp of either firmness or urgency:

We will immediately get into contact with the American and British authorities to ask whether they would in theory be ready to proceed to an exchange on the basis suggested by the German authorities and whether they would be prepared in particular to include in this exchange other than Allied Jews.

In any case we must give the Allied authorities as soon as possible details of the people whose exchange could be negotiated.

We beg you to press the German authorities when you next speak to them to provide as soon as possible a list of names or at least the numbers by nationalities of the people they would be prepared to exchange.

On the other hand please include in these negotiations the greatest possible number of detainees and please try to obtain either an exchange proposal or authorisation to transfer to Switzerland not only Italian and Allied Jews but also Aryan detainees.

On 18 April 1945 we had a visit from M. Valobra, the Delasem representative in Switzerland, who told us that according to information that he is sure comes from a completely reliable source, there are at the moment in the camps at Bolzano and Merano at least 200 Jews, not to mention a group of 400 Hungarian Jews who seem to have been brought very recently to Bolzano from Austria.

We would urge you to keep us closely informed of the steps you take and all the information that you can get on Bolzano and Merano. Please do your utmost to visit these camps as soon as possible.

We might finally add that in your talks with the German authorities you should underline the fact that the ICRC is making approaches already to the Allied authorities to find out what compensation they could offer in exchange for the different categories of detainees in the concentration camps in Northern Italy.[56]

No document has been found in the ICRC archives to prove that the announced approach to the Allies was carried out in time. On the other hand, at the end of April, Colonel Bon was informed that following his meeting with Hans Bachmann in Innsbruck, Kaltenbrunner gave the order for the immediate liberation of the thirty-five to fifty Allied Jews in the camp at Bolzano. With regard to the 200 Italian and 400 Hungarian Jews, the ICRC delegation in northern Italy was told to get in touch with General Wolff, but there was no time left.

Colonel Bon's mission largely failed, for accidental reasons certainly, but also because it was quickly overtaken, in the mind of the ICRC members responsible, by the negotiation carried out in Germany itself in March and April 1945. Nonetheless it was highly successful over the question of the deportees. Following repeated French overtures, Hans Bon and Kurt Tschudi obtained agreement from the Germans and Italians on the principle of the repatriation, via Switzerland, of 2,500 French civilians who lived near the Italian frontier and had been taken away during the withdrawal of the Axis forces. On 12 April 1945, the ICRC was thus able to make a public announcement that a first train-load of 1,000 women, children and elderly people had returned to France via Geneva. It was also a small service rendered by the Red

Cross to Switzerland. The federal authorities were indeed trying to
follow up the French request but could not do so since they did not
represent French interests in northern Italy. They were thus able to send
the file discreetly to the ICRC and to obtain a success whose merit,
indeed, was shared equally in the public mind between Switzerland and
the ICRC.[57]

Part III

Another Turn of the Screw

8   The drama of retreat, persecution and action played out in Hungary

Introduction

In a Europe still under Axis control, Hungary remained the only country in the spring of 1944 to have preserved its native Jewish community more or less intact. It is true that as early as 1938 the Horthy regime had drawn up antisemitic legislation, but little use was made of it until April 1941. Moreover there were many Jews among the thousands of civilian and military refugees from Poland, Serbia, Croatia and other places who sought asylum in the country. Everything changed with the coming to power of the Bardossy government in April 1941; not content with persecuting the Jews, it deported to Galicia and the territories conquered by Hungarian troops more than 18,000 internees, most of whom were massacred in the Ukraine. Early in 1942 thousands of Jews and Serbs were murdered, too, in Novi Sad, a Yugoslav town occupied by the Hungarians. The coming to power of Miklos Kallay in March 1942 brought this first wave of terror to an end, but the authorities in Budapest lived henceforth under constant pressure from the Germans, who were keen to see the Final Solution applied in Hungary, to stiffen their antisemitic policies. A precarious balance was maintained between the Nazis' wishes and the Hungarians' determination to safeguard their sovereignty, a situation brought to an abrupt end by the German takeover in March 1944.[1]

First measures and early reactions

After the massacres of August 1941, Jewish organisations drew the persecution to the attention of the Hungarian Red Cross, which sought to repatriate the Jews of Hungarian nationality deported to Galicia, or at least to relieve their suffering. One of its members, Countess Mary Dobrazensky, travelled to Geneva in December 1941, but did not manage to persuade the ICRC to send a delegate to organise assistance on the spot with the help of the German and Hungarian Red Cross (see

p. 58 above). When her request was considered by the Coordinating Committee on 5 December 1941, Max Huber wondered what the ICRC could do, arguing that the issue fell outside the scope, even extended, of the 1929 Convention, that the ICRC had many other tasks requiring its full attention, and that Hungary, as an ally of the Reich, was more likely to get something out of its powerful partner than the ICRC was. The other ICRC members who spoke that day agreed with him.[2]

But this refusal, confirmed in autumn 1942 when the Hungarian Red Cross requested aid for alien or stateless Jewish internees, was only a stage in a longer process. Further information was received during the course of 1942, notably when Werner Rohner was sent on a mission by the Joint Aid Commission (see p. 37 above), on the fate of the thousands of unfortunate émigrés who were living as best they could under the constant threat of deportation eastwards and of death.[3] Since it appeared that certain stateless or refugee Jews holding emigration certificates for Palestine could leave Hungary, the notion of assisting them came up for discussion quite naturally again when the Coordinating Committee decided on 27 January 1943 that the ICRC could not remain indifferent to the Jews and looked into what could be done in certain countries that were allies or satellites of the Reich. During their tour of East European capitals, therefore, Edouard Chapuisat and David de Traz looked into the feasibility of the ICRC sending a delegate to Budapest. This suggestion got such a favourable response from the authorities and the Hungarian Red Cross that the ICRC resolved to do it, in spite of the fact that POWs and interned enemy aliens in the strict sense of the term were few in number on Hungarian soil, and even though emigration matters were more the responsibility of the Protecting Power than of the Red Cross. This mission was entrusted to Jean de Bavier, fifty-one, the brother of the Swiss chargé d'affaires in Athens.[4]

The instructions the delegate was given at the time were drawn up within the confines of a by now familiar tradition: on the one hand, to carry out the tasks which were the ICRC's responsibility under the Conventions and under existing arrangements covering civilian internees, and on the other to keep in close touch with the authorities, and with the Hungarian Red Cross.[5] The oral instructions on the Jewish question referred primarily to an observatory role, though that did not exclude either vigilance or personal contact, as is shown by the discussion that took place in Geneva shortly before de Bavier's departure in October 1943 between him and the Joint's representative, Saly Mayer, which empowered de Bavier to act as intermediary between rich Hungarian Jews and needy Jewish refugees whom the Joint wished to help, promising to reimburse any donors, once the war was over, to the tune initially of $10,000.[6]

So as soon as he arrived in Budapest de Bavier got in touch not only with the Swiss legation, with Red Cross leaders and with the Hungarian authorities, but he also met the chairman of the Jewish community, Samuel Stern, the representative of the Jewish Agency for Palestine, Rudolf Kastner, and several others, including Baroness Weiss. He put together detailed information on what had happened over the past few years to the Jews, visited camps where foreign, Polish and Jewish civilian internees and POWs were being held, and in some cases seems even to have managed to improve difficult conditions and modify regimes that were too harsh. However, the ICRC had no intention for the moment of extending its involvement in Hungary beyond prisoners who could be classified as alien civilian internees. So de Bavier was reminded that he ought not to visit camps where Hungarian internees were held, since as Schwarzenberg had told him at the end of 1943, these people fell within the jurisdiction of their own state,[7] and the ICRC had to confine itself to humanitarian aid, and even then to act with great discretion, so as to avoid at all costs laying itself open to the objection that it was 'interfering in matters that did not concern it'.[8]

De Bavier, who was more *au fait* than headquarters with the threat hanging over the country, contemplated the future with foreboding. He raised his main issues of concern with the ICRC and was told by the CPI that were Hungary to be occupied by the Germans he would probably have to take on responsibility for civilian aliens trapped in Hungary whether they were Jewish or not.[9] Two days later, on 19 March 1944, a pro-Nazi government was imposed on Regent Horthy. This dramatic speeding up of events led the CPI to revive the idea of strengthening the ICRC's presence in Central Europe, chiefly by sending a representative to Bratislava and by increasing the number of delegates in Budapest. While it was happy to respond in this way to requests from Jewish groups the ICRC had no intention of altering the instructions that de Bavier had been given, particularly that nationality should weigh more heavily than race. And in response to American démarches, Schwarzenberg suggested that the War Refugee Board should agree to foodstuffs and clothing being stockpiled in Switzerland as the only way of coming swiftly and massively to the aid of detainees and children.[10]

Change of delegate; change of policy?

De Bavier had guessed right: the Germans' entry into Hungary sealed the fate of the million Jews (of whom 200,000 were refugees, aliens or stateless) who lived there. Draconian antisemitic legislation was imposed as a prelude to first herding people into ghettos and then deporting them, chiefly to Auschwitz, under the direction of a detachment of specialists led by Adolf Eichmann in person. At the beginning of June 1944 the delegate of the Swiss Council for International Aid passed to Max Huber leaked information that 300,000 Jews had already been interned in provincial Hungary, of whom 100,000 had been taken to the 'Auschwitz destruction camp'. Round-ups, deportation and extermination now faced the 300,000 Budapest Jews.[11]

The ICRC, however, no longer seemed satisfied with de Bavier. Being accompanied by his wife and knowing no German he was no longer the right person in the new situation facing Hungary. He had alarmed headquarters, too, by a number of gestures felt to be out of place, such as requesting Max Huber to intervene with the Führer on behalf of the Jews, and although his wire arrived after the decision had been taken to recall him, it served merely to confirm the ICRC in its decision to change its representative in Budapest. It was reluctant to move Julius Schmidlin from Zagreb and opted instead for the appointment – on a temporary basis at first – of Frédéric Born, who until then had been the Swiss Commercial Expansion Bureau's representative in Hungary, and who was in fact due to return to his post in Budapest in spring 1944.

The new acting delegate's brief was essentially the same as his predecessor's, except that its wording allowed more explicitly for the possibility of new humanitarian tasks arising for which the ICRC would give the necessary instructions in good time. Like de Bavier previously, Born met Saly Mayer before his departure, as well as Mihaly Banyai, the head of a new charitable organisation, the Hungarian Jews Support Committee, which, to the Joint's intense displeasure, had just been founded in Zurich by Swiss Jews of Hungarian origin. As the head of the Delegations Commission, Frédéric Siordet, reminded Schwarzenberg in an internal memorandum, Born's discussions in no way implied a change of outlook on the Jewish question in Hungary. Noting that Mayer had complained about what he called the 'negative' attitude of the Red Cross on the Jewish question, Siordet set out the ICRC's position yet again: it made no distinction between Jews and Aryans, the former being on exactly the same footing as war victims of other races. And where others did choose to make a distinction, it was unfortunately not up to the ICRC either to approve or disapprove of the laws enacted against Jews in consequence. The ICRC had to maintain strict political neutrality if it was to remain effective in the humanitarian field. Antisemitic legislation forced the ICRC to act with great discretion;

otherwise its activity might be construed as political rather than humanitarian. So if in certain cases its attitude did appear negative, that was not in any way dictated by principle but solely by the limitations that local circumstances imposed upon it.[12]

Born was on the ground by mid-May 1944 and able to take stock of the situation. He did not take long to realise that in the circumstances the instructions he had received were quite inappropriate, and asked for a new brief that would allow him to persuade the authorities to show less zeal in the application of anti-Jewish legislation. A personal message he sent to Max Huber on 10 June 1944 ended with these words: 'I know the extraordinary difficulties facing the ICRC, but the idea of standing by helplessly, powerless to do anything, is almost impossible to bear.'[13]

So slow were communications that this letter only reached headquarters on 26 June 1944 and thus crossed with a note sent to Born by Schwarzenberg on 14 June which did indeed, as the delegate had requested, give him further instructions, telling him to look discreetly into the possibility of transferring funds (particularly those made available by Saly Mayer in Switzerland), into the chances of emigration (since it appeared that some Jews were able to leave the country and had been assembled for the purpose in special camps), and – just as discreetly – to approach the Hungarian authorities about what possibilities there were for the ICRC to protect the Jews, to distribute aid, and even to visit the ghettos and concentration camps. But a few days later, as we have seen (p. 80 above), in the presence of Albert Lombard, vice-president of the ICRC, Schwarzenberg rejected the démarche of Gerhart Riegner and of the Czechoslovak minister Jaromir Kopecki, who had come to talk about the exterminations at Auschwitz-Birkenau and of the 12,000 Hungarians deported there daily.[14]

This attitude over the Hungarian affair need not surprise us; it confirms what we have seen in other theatres at the same period. In several possible areas where it might have done something, the ICRC contemplated acting only if doing so fell within the confines of its neutrality and its mission as guardian of the Conventions and of agreements made between the belligerents. In this respect Max Huber's reply of 12 May 1944 to démarches by the War Refugee Board – which was touched on when the point at issue was whether Jews should be treated as civilian alien internees – seems entirely in character.

So the ICRC was taken aback, in late June 1944, by the change which had occurred in the attitude of the neutrals and of some of the countries at war with the Reich. The Final Solution was no longer a terrible secret. In the last two years the revelation not merely of massacres, but of a concerted extermination policy, had increasingly gained ground, and people were prepared to think the unthinkable, all the more so since, thanks to the tireless efforts of the Jewish organisations, eye-witness accounts had multiplied. The events in Hungary were not only the last possible chapter in the Final Solution, they were also the first to take place more or less in the open, when the defeat of the Reich was no longer much in doubt.

Sweden, as the Protecting Power of several countries at war with Hungary, was among the first to react. From June 1944 onwards its legation made arrangements to allow emigration to Palestine of a number of the people threatened, and Swedish citizenship was offered to hundreds of Jews able to prove personal or business connections with Sweden. But the Swedish minister hoped for more than this. On 26 June 1944 the ICRC was told by Born that the minister had asked his government to send a high-ranking official of the Swedish Red Cross, probably Folke Bernadotte. This news had a galvanising effect on both the ICRC and the Swiss government.

As Protecting Power to United States nationals, Switzerland stepped into the limelight. Vice-Consul Carl Lutz, head of the Foreign Interests Section of the Swiss legation in Budapest, and his wife Gertrude, were extremely active, issuing emigration certificates for Palestine to thousands of Jews and getting the Hungarian government to agree to the departure of 10,000 children. But as we have seen (p. 111 above), emigration schemes hinged on the Germans authorising transit, and this was always refused since the Reich had no intention either of jeopardising its Arab policy by letting Jews go to their national home or of putting a brake on extermination.[15] Nevertheless, the papers concerned (passports, emigration certificates or simple protection documents) quite often allowed the holders, especially in dealing with minor officials, to live in requisitioned houses and to be relatively shielded from round-ups and immediate deportation.

When in March 1944 President Roosevelt mentioned the Final Solution along with other war crimes for the first time, governments, spurred on by press revelations, began to intervene with the Budapest authorities. First Pope Pius XII, then the American government through the Swiss legation, then Archbishop Francis J. Spellmann of New York, and finally the king of Sweden all asked for the deportations to be suspended. In any case the military situation of the Axis on all fronts was deteriorating, as was shown by the success of the Normandy landings. A failed *coup d'état* attempt by extremist elements in the local fascist party and, it seems, an American air raid on Budapest on 2 July 1944 carried the day, and Regent Horthy, yielding to the more realistic members of his cabinet, ordered the suspension of the deportations.

So some governments, and some moral authorities, at last did what welfare organisations, private citizens and individual Jews had been requesting for months; but they only did so after weighing up the pros and cons of bowing to such private and public pressure on the one hand and of sticking to the national interest on the other. Switzerland and the ICRC, fearing a public appeal – the outcome of which was unpredictable and could well be negative – were no exception. On 3 July 1944, Edouard de Haller, on higher orders, sounded Max Huber out on the ICRC's intentions. Huber replied that the ICRC's primary duty was to concentrate on actions that were effective and not to get sidetracked into making futile gestures. He doubted whether the Hungarian authorities could put the clock back, and as for the Hungarian Red Cross, which had never had much clout, one had to admit that it was powerless to do anything. He added that if the government felt that notwithstanding Swiss neutrality it could intervene, that would do no harm to the ICRC; quite the reverse.[16]

What Huber seems not to have told de Haller is that he had decided to approach Admiral Horthy direct. He did tell Alphonse Koechlin, chairman of the Swiss Federation of Protestant Churches, in a confidential letter dated 3 July 1944, which Schwarzenberg had drafted. As for de Haller, he did not know (or pretended not to know) that a fairly unusual démarche was due to be made on 7 July by minister Maximilian Jaeger on the instructions of the Swiss Political Department, informing the Hungarian Foreign Ministry of the Swiss government's concern over the deportations.

The appeal of the Swiss Protestant Churches to the ICRC did not therefore go unheeded by Max Huber, who was supported by the Bureau: after taking account of the Swiss government's attitude and of the pleas of Jewish organisations and of the War Refugee Board, it resolved that the ICRC should approach the Hungarian authorities at the highest level. A letter would be sent to the government (in fact the Foreign Ministry) approaching the problem from the welfare angle. In addition a special envoy would carry a message to the regent, as Huber had promised Koechlin on 3 July.

Robert Schirmer, the envoy entrusted with this delicate mission, did not get the necessary visas to leave Berlin until 19 July and so could not deliver his message until the 20th or the 21st, by which date the deportations had been suspended for a fortnight. So the ICRC's appeal did not weigh directly with Horthy, even if the documents show that the ICRC took the decision to do something before the Hungarians' volte-face; what it probably did do, however, given the limited room for manoeuvre Horthy enjoyed, was stiffen his resolve. In his very courteous

reply to Max Huber, Horthy was anxious to stress that his government
had taken over the responsibility for the Jewish question.[17]

The ICRC had come to the same conclusion. On 7 July 1944 Max
Huber signed a note to the Foreign Ministry inviting the Hungarian
government to allay people's anxieties by allowing the Red Cross
delegate to visit the camps where the Jews had been assembled and to
distribute food and clothing. The Hungarians were quite happy to agree
to this because in return they hoped the Swiss would help them with
other humanitarian problems. So the reply brought by Imre de Tahy, the
secretary to the Hungarian legation in Berne, on 18 July, was very
largely positive, and the ICRC, contrary to its usual practice, rushed out
a press release about it. The Hungarian government authorised the
ICRC to send aid to all the Jews in ghettos or camps, and agreed to all
Jewish children under ten emigrating to Palestine, together with all
adults in possession of an emigration visa for that destination and
Hungarians under Swedish protection.[18]

This reply was accompanied by action. On 21 July 1944, after
delivering his message to the head of state, Robert Schirmer got in touch
with government officials and was given permission to visit a certain
number of places in Budapest where Jews were under house arrest. On
27 and 28 July he went with Born to the concentration camps of
Kistarcsa and Szarvas not far from Budapest where he was able to
ascertain that the detainees, at least in Kistarcsa, were (given the
circumstances) almost properly treated.

All seemed set therefore for an aid operation on an even larger scale
than the ICRC was attempting in Romania: the Hungarian government
offered its help; an augmented ICRC delegation could act on several
different levels at once, particularly over emigration; and it could
purchase food and medicines locally if the necessary funds were made
available. After taking advice from Saly Mayer, 'a discreet and experienced friend of the firm' as Schwarzenberg put it, the ICRC on 10
August 1944 invited to a joint meeting the main Jewish bodies represented in Switzerland, such as the World Jewish Congress, the Jewish
Agency for Palestine, the Union of Orthodox Rabbis, Agudath Israel,
HIJEFS (Swiss Aid Committee for Jewish Refugees Abroad), the Swiss
Support Committee for Jews in Hungary, and so on, not forgetting of
course the Joint, the Churches' Ecumenical Council, the War Refugee
Board and Rev. Paul Vogt, often nicknamed 'the pastor for refugees'.

It was obviously mainly the Joint that was going to provide the
millions of pengös made available to the ICRC delegation and the
Jewish Senate in Budapest for local purchasing and for the travel
arrangements of people leaving. The War Refugee Board would occa-

sionally lend its help over different ways of raising the finance, which varied, as in Romania, according to what was both legal and feasible: the purchase of pengös in Switzerland, the use via clearing of Swiss assets frozen abroad, or the purchase of pengös in Hungary against Swiss francs deposited by the Joint in Switzerland or against dollar credits realisable after the war.

So money was not the problem; what was soon became apparent when the room for manoeuvre actually enjoyed by the Hungarian authorities turned out to be drastically limited. The Germans were still there, as were their fanatical local henchmen. A few days after Schirmer and Born's visit, and despite Horthy's 7 July ban, thousands of Jews were deported by Eichmann from the camps of Kistarcsa and Szarvas. So the Hungarian government was being ingenuous – or disingenuous – in claiming through Imre de Tahy that the Nazis had agreed to the various emigration measures already mentioned. On the ground, in any case, Schirmer's initiatives were blocked: food parcels could not be sent to people transferred to Germany unless the deportations resumed, and no ICRC delegate could get permission to accompany the deportees on the trains taking them to their destination.[19]

In response to fading hopes and unkept promises, the ICRC's delegation redoubled its efforts to make funds available and send aid. Born and Schirmer were not content with visiting buildings where Jews were confined; they brought aid and assistance to the sick and needy, distributed soup and tonics and, in makeshift homes, looked after many thousands of children awaiting departure (clearance for which had been given in theory but never carried out). On 15 October, with the Soviet vanguard 100 kilometres from Budapest, any hopes of escaping the Nazis' grasp were finally dashed, and Horthy was taken prisoner to Germany. The extremist 'Arrow-Cross' government under Ferenc Szálasi seized power and unleashed a bloody repression on the country. Thousands of enemies of the new regime were imprisoned or executed, and for the Jews the relative calm that had reigned since the suspension of deportations on 7 July came to an abrupt end. A big ghetto was created in the centre of Budapest to shut in the Jews who had not already been arrested. Labour was requisitioned, and 50,000 Jews, including children and old people, were 'lent' to factories in the Reich. Herded together in columns numbering up to a thousand each in the Altofeuer tilery on the outskirts of the city, they were marched without food or blankets towards Germany. This operation of sheer destruction, begun on 9 November 1944, was suspended ten days later, and the haggard faces of the deportees remained forever engraved on Born's mind as a vision of what happens when the purest barbarity and unmitigated hatred that people are capable of are unleashed on their fellow human beings. Of the tens of thousands whipped and shot by the SS on the road towards Vienna, he and his colleagues were able to save only a few hundred.[20]

During those terrible weeks at the end of 1944 the ICRC delegation intervened frequently in this way, trying to supply the inhabitants of the ghetto with clothing, medicines and basic foodstuffs, to provide shelter for orphans and to locate the missing. Since the summer, its staff and organisation had been expanded considerably through the recruitment of some 250 local personnel. After first Luc Thudicum and then Robert Schirmer had left, Frédéric Born (assisted now by a deputy delegate, Hans Weyermann, Ciba's representative in Budapest) worked closely with the Jewish Senate chaired by Samuel Stern and set up inside the delegation a number of special sections: A and B for the Jews and Jewish children, P for Polish internees and Y for the Yugoslavs. On the other hand he did not enjoy very close ties with the neutral legations since they – the Swedes in particular – assisted individuals, whereas Born chose to protect the organisations that aided the population.[21] His report of June 1945 mentions more than 150 clinics, hospitals, homes and various other institutions which the delegation took under its protection in this way in the winter of 1944–5.

Two spheres of activity involving Swiss diplomats deserve special mention: emigration and protection documents. Since an immigration visa constituted in itself a document protecting its holder, particularly against the threat of deportation, the two aspects tend to get confused and it is not easy for the historian to disentangle them. Governments and numerous national and international NGOs were involved and a host of conditions had to be met before the journey could begin: not just an immigration visa issued by the destination country but also an exit visa from the country of origin and a transit visa through the Reich or its occupied territories. All this necessitated lengthy negotiations, some diplomatic and open, others private and secret. In all but a few cases and whatever the category of beneficiary involved, they soon stalled in the face of Nazi intransigence, despite assurances to the contrary from both the German and the Hungarian sides. So, in order for the ICRC's activities to be properly evaluated, the overall picture must briefly be sketched in.

The impossibility of transit to destination countries

As we saw in chapter 4, emigration was dealt with at the level of governments and of the Protecting Power. According to German sources, a few hundred Jews managed to leave Hungary for Palestine every month until March 1944,[22] which explains why the ICRC's interest in the possibilities of emigration from this part of Europe resulted in Jean de Bavier's posting to Budapest and Karl Kolb's to Bucharest. After the Wehrmacht's takeover requests poured in, and the Swiss and Swedish legations undertook to provide the necessary papers: the Swedes' protection documents that they hoped would provide a minimal level of safety in the absence of cast-iron legal protection, and the Swiss emigration certificates for Palestine (about 10,000 visas had been issued by the Palestine government to the Jewish Agency since the autumn of 1943).

In July the Hungarian government's new policy got the ICRC involved in the emigration issue, since the reply brought to Burckhardt by de Tahy on 18 July 1944 dealt extensively with emigration possibilities offered, the note said, as we have seen, with the Reich's agreement. The public announcement of this new development having unleashed a flood of requests and calls for help, Burckhardt went to great lengths at the end of July to be able to send to Budapest 'a special delegate, a man of calibre' to take charge in the first instance of emigration issues in the context of the broader action he outlined to the ICRC on 26 July.[23] Through Fritz Berber (one of Ribbentrop's advisers, then resident in Geneva) he even asked Ribbentrop himself for the necessary visas for Mlle Ferrière, who had long-term responsibilities for emigration, and for Dr Adolf Vischer, the special delegate, and at a meeting of Jewish organisations convened at the beginning of August he renewed his appeal for everyone to act together, whatever their differences.

The route envisaged at the time was via the Black Sea, through Romania and Turkey, which explains why, whilst Gilbert Simond and Karl Kolb pursued their contacts with the War Refugee Board and the Jewish Agency to get visas, the Bureau resolved on 3 August, as we saw in chapter 4, to notify the belligerents of the departure of the ships chartered by the Romanian Red Cross and sailing under its colours. Otherwise the question of settlement in Palestine had not been sorted out. The Swiss legation in Budapest sent Born the names of 8,000 people who had received immigration certificates and wished to leave, and worked closely with Miklos Krausz, the Jewish Agency's representative. But in order to do everything they could, Carl and Gertrude Lutz had also put about 40,000 people on the lists. But the British would never agree to increase the quota of 14,000 immigrants which they had fixed for Hungary, except perhaps for children. Here too the ICRC intervened, to request that more people be allowed into the Mandate.[24]

Considered first by Romania, then by Switzerland and Sweden, transit was to remain impossible because the Germans said no to it, and the 8,000-odd 'Palestinians' (as they came to be known) would not in the end be allowed to leave Budapest, though they at least escaped deportation both before and after the Arrow-Cross's *coup d'état*.[25] The same applied to the 'Swedes' (so called), some 4,000 Jews protected by the Swedish legation because of their special links with Sweden; they could not leave Hungary and lived under constant threat.[26]

The United States intervened in its turn. In mid-July it had refused to accept the families of those Hungarian Jews who had become American citizens, since federal legislation did not allow it to, but at the beginning of August it did agree, at the request of the ICRC amongst others, to take in a certain number of immigrants on the same lines as the Swedes. They then kept extending the practice until in mid-August they finally declared, in concert with Great Britain, that they would grant temporary refuge to any Hungarian emigrant who managed to reach a neutral country. The ICRC was asked to inform the Hungarian government of this development, which could only encourage the neutral countries in their earlier decision to offer temporary residence. In November 1944 the government in Washington assured the Swiss Federal Council of its intention to do everything in its power to move to America any Hungarian Jews granted temporary refuge in Switzerland. But since so few Jews actually managed to reach Swiss territory, these intentions could not be translated into effective action.

All the emigration projects to Palestine or the United States, like the proposals to send children to Mexico or Tangier, involved Switzerland in a pivotal capacity, if only temporarily, because of its geographical position, its neutrality, and its status as Protecting Power for the United States and Great Britain. The ICRC's action, in the Hungarian case more than in most others, was therefore closely geared to what the authorities in Berne felt they could and should undertake.

Their attitude over the Jewish question in Hungary was at first one of great prudence, in sharp contrast to the activity on the ground of Vice-Consul Lutz. But the démarche Maximilian Jaeger was instructed to make with the Hungarian Foreign Ministry on 7 July 1944, coupled with a parallel approach to the Hungarian chargé d'affaires in Switzerland, heralded a change. After the harsh years of 1942 and 1943, when numerous refugees, Jews for the most part, had been pushed back over the Swiss border for having crossed it illegally, the police authorities and the Political Department decided to follow Sweden's example and grant entry visas to three categories of Hungarian Jewish refugees: children under ten, elderly people, and those with business connections or relatives in Switzerland. The instructions issued by the Police Division of the Federal Department of Justice and Police on 12 July no longer stressed the distinction between political refugees (admitted) and people under threat because of their race (who normally could not enter Switzerland).[27] It is true that asylum policy remained rooted in the conviction that Switzerland could serve only as a temporary refuge, and there were few illusions in Berne as to the number of German transit visas that would be granted, especially since, to avoid the disagreeable prospect of a refusal, the Swiss ambassador was told, in all but the most exceptional cases, not to lean on the Hungarian authorities to grant exit visas.[28]

Nevertheless, under the pressure of public opinion and the international situation, a first step had been taken and it was followed a few weeks later by a further liberalisation of asylum. This required the assistance of the ICRC, henceforth given the job of getting exit visas for Switzerland and Sweden out of the Hungarians. Moreover the Federal Council, in the light of the reply brought by de Tahy to Burckhardt on 18 July, revived an offer of hospital beds for children under ten that had been hinted at previously; this time it was made without distinction as to race or nationality even though each trainload contained a certain proportion of young Jews.[29] As early as 19 July the Swiss legation was entrusted with launching negotiations with the Hungarians for a first trainload of 500 children.

In the end none came. Weeks and weeks of negotiations, false hope, even of ingenious ruses, failed to get the Nazis to budge. They were quite happy to see trains leave so long as no German or Jewish children were on them. On Christmas Eve a mere forty-four children finally made it to Switzerland. It was the only success the Swiss authorities obtained on their own.

Paradoxically, behind-the-scenes haggling did lead to a marginally more tangible result. Using what happened in Slovakia in 1942 as a model, a Hungarian Jewish resistance committee had been negotiating since the spring of 1944 with SS leaders to pay the ransom of internees, either in cash or in food and equipment. These negotiations resulted in three developments: the dispatch at the beginning of July 1944 to the special camp at Bergen-Belsen of 1,600 Jews pending exchange or emigration, the creation in Budapest of a small privileged ghetto of 388 people, and at the end of August the removal to Vienna and district of between 15,000 and 18,000 Jews who would, it is true, be held in camps but would thus escape deportation.[30] When a sub-delegation was set up in Vienna at the beginning of December 1944, Luc Thudicum got permission of Karl Ebner, head of the Gestapo in Vienna, to visit the Jews' camps and labour battalions.

In mid-August, as rumours of the imminent arrival of a train from Bergen-Belsen became more insistent, the Swiss authorities clarified and extended their earlier asylum declaration by stressing that they were ready to welcome any Hungarian refugee who turned up. The head of Switzerland's Aliens Police, Heinrich Rothmund, whose name symbolised the policy of closing the frontiers and turning Jews away, displayed in this instance a carefully thought-out wish for openness which did not remain purely verbal and which contrasted with the doubts felt by his superior, the federal councillor Vladimir de Steiger, as it did, too, with Schwarzenberg's reservations about the whole business.

On 22 August it was not 600 refugees as had been announced but 318 who arrived at Basel from Bergen-Belsen. Once over the border they were carefully looked after, but the authorities were puzzled that they came without papers or any indication of ultimate destination. The Swiss wondered whether they had been ransomed or delivered free of charge, and whether a protest should be made to Berlin for what looked like the expulsion on to Swiss soil of people considered undesirable in the Reich. Fortunately, considering the adults interned pending release, they refrained from comment. While, like the ICRC too of course, declining to get involved in dealings that remained a private matter, the Swiss authorities bore them in mind when framing policy, and in October 1944 they even tried to facilitate the process by asking the German Foreign Ministry to assist the transfer to Switzerland of the remaining Bergen-Belsen deportees.[31]

The Arrow-Cross's *coup d'état* and the violent resumption of racial persecution breathed new life into the emigration issue, especially as the Szálasi government decreed that people holding emigration documents were free to leave the country before 15 November. The Germans having apparently given their consent, all eyes turned to Switzerland. The Federal Council confirmed on 31 October that it was ready to receive the 8,000 'Palestinians' even if their stay in Switzerland were to last until the end of the war, and a few days later adopted the same attitude to the 4,000 'Swedes' whom the Hungarian government seemed prepared to let go. The Swiss felt that they could always count on the United States, and the end of the war and the defeat of the Reich was in any case hardly any longer in doubt.

But as some officials in Berne had realised, hopes of saving such a large number were not to be realised. German false promises, the procrastination or cynical lies of the Hungarian fascists, and the passive wait-and-see attitude of the Swiss authorities, all prevented a satisfactory solution. To the 318 escapees from Bergen-Belsen and the forty-four children of Christmas 1944 were finally added only the 1,352 Jews left in Bergen-Belsen who managed in December to cross the Swiss frontier, as a result of undercover negotiations between a Hungarian committee chaired by Rudolf Kastner, the Budapest representative of the Jewish Agency, and *Standartenführer* Kurt Becher, deputy to Dieter Wisliceny, whom we encountered earlier in Greece (see p. 168 above).

Where, it may be asked, did the Red Cross stand in all this? After the collapse of Burckhardt's grand plan and the even more significant failures of Switzerland, Sweden and the USA, the ICRC had to be satisfied with backing through démarches in London and Washington the projects already outlined and the efforts made by others. The same was done in Berne in a well thought-out political manoeuvre, as one of the colleagues of the delegate of the Federal Council for International Welfare Cooperation noted after a visit from Burckhardt when rumours were growing of the imminent arrival of 600 Hungarian Jews from Bergen-Belsen. The colleague noted that Burckhardt seemed not unduly surprised by the news from Budapest and even expressed his delight at it since it was, he felt, a very good thing for Switzerland that something positive could now be done for the Jews. It would, he thought, produce a good impression abroad and could at the same time dispel any anti-Swiss resentment that could arise as a result of the accounts of refugees and interned aliens (intellectuals especially) dissatisfied with their treatment. He thought they should be welcomed straightaway; the official pointed out that the consent of the Swiss authorities should be obtained first.[32]

On the ground the delegation offered to act as intermediary to help get the necessary documents, find missing people and, in general, to support those ready to leave, who having lost or sold everything had nothing to live on when the endless wait began for trains that never left the buffers. So no démarche, no emigration project turned out successfully for the ICRC in Hungary.

Lifesaving papers and signboards

We have described the work of the Swiss and Swedish legations in handing out Palestine immigration certificates and other kinds of protection documents. The ICRC also took part in this kind of activity, after undergoing a significant change of heart.

As the previous chapter has shown, the ICRC confined itself to adopting a principled caution as far as immigration certificates in general were concerned, taking the view that this was a question of relations between sovereign states and fell within the Protecting Power's competence. But during July 1944 the general shift in its position led it, in the wake of decisions taken by governments, to alter its practices over this matter too. At the request of the authorities, notably in Central American republics such as Nicaragua, El Salvador or Mexico, it directly passed on documents known to be phoney – immigration visas or nationality certificates – issued by consulates in Switzerland and handed from then on to their recipients in Hungary by the Red Cross delegation there. However, the ICRC refused right to the end to shoulder the same responsibility vis-à-vis private organisations.

The way it changed is even more impressive where, without proper diplomatic credentials, its own protective action is concerned. From the spring of 1944 onwards, for example, many Jews who were stateless or without Protecting Power – not to mention those who did have citizenship – turned to the ICRC for protection. De Bavier, backed by headquarters, refused to be drawn, and Born was later reminded that he could only issue certificates to delegation employees in the strict sense of the term, which did not include people working for other organisations, even where their welfare work was put in jeopardy by antisemitic legislation, especially the obligation to wear the yellow star.

Since, despite the head of state's order to the contrary, individual deportations continued throughout the summer, the Bureau at its meeting of 28 August 1944 discussed at length the idea of placing the Hungarian Jews under the ICRC's protection, or of putting the houses in which they had already gathered under the same umbrella.[33] Despite the misgivings of Jacques Chenevière and to some extent of other members, it was decided to put up, outside houses or camps occupied by Jews, signboards bearing the Red Cross emblem and a text in French, German and Hungarian to be drafted by Max Huber, Suzanne Ferrière and Jean-Etienne Schwarzenberg. The action was to be as low key as possible so as not to appear deliberately provocative towards the Germans but aimed rather at local mischief-makers.

The ICRC's decision was immediately conveyed to Born who was told to carry it out and at the same time given instructions which profoundly altered his previous brief: from now on he had to visit frequently places where Jews were held and seek to ensure that they were properly housed and not suffering from overcrowding.[34] So Born had signboards made bearing in Hungarian, German and French the following message:

The people held in this camp/house by order of the Hungarian authorities have, with the agreement of the latter, been placed under the protection of the International Committee of the Red Cross and are visited regularly by its delegates. This protection must be respected.
ICRC Delegation [followed by the address]

At first the operation was not a big success, since the leaders of the Jewish community themselves were afraid that the signboards would draw attention to the detainees and that their proliferation would lessen their impact. They were also hesitant in the face of contradictions and uncertainties on the part of the authorities themselves. This gave rise to a certain number of criticisms to which, in a striking turn-up for the books, the ICRC decided this time to reply publicly. Schwarzenberg drafted a note for Burckhardt suggesting the publication in Swiss newspapers of a press release on the following lines:

We have ascertained from sources close to the ICRC that several weeks ago the Red Cross responded to numerous requests for protection from Hungarian Jews by asking the Hungarian government to allow its delegation to take all Jews held in Hungary under its protection and to post on all the houses and camps where Jews were to be found signboards indicating everyone inside was protected by the Red Cross.[35]

The Szálasi *coup d'état* forced the ICRC to broaden its activities. If headquarters, after reminding the minister of foreign affairs that the outgoing government had ordered the suspension of deportation, was basically content to cover its delegation, Born and Schirmer[36] – the latter soon to be relieved by Hans Weyermann – undertook endless démarches with the authorities in difficult conditions, as Robert Schirmer related (see Appendix, document VIII). From September 1944 onwards they handed out letters of protection to their (increasingly numerous) Jewish aides, and after 15 October 1944 they stepped up the policy, issuing these so-called passports to any Jew claiming a connection, however tenuous, with the delegation, so that within a few weeks 15,000 people were in possession of such documents. After putting their signboards up on Jewish hospitals, clinics, hostels and soup kitchens, the delegates began responding to requests from the Hungarian authorities and civic leaders to take under their protection a growing number of public buildings in the capital. With the onset of a very hard winter, and on the eve of a merciless pitched battle between the Wehrmacht and the Red Army, the delegation turned its attention to the entire civilian population. This enormous undertaking caused the ICRC some concern; it had, after all, to worry about the prestige of the institution being dragged into an impossible mission, and about the legal aspects of this kind of blanket cover jeopardising the protection guaranteed by the Red Cross emblem to installations and staff that met the strict criteria of the 1929 Geneva Convention. Nevertheless, in return for certain precautions being taken over the use of the emblem, the ICRC covered its delegation from that point onwards.

The delegation shared the fate of Budapest's inhabitants until the end of the battle. On 18 January 1945 the Russians conquered Pest, and on 13 February fighting ended in the streets of Buda. Born (unlike Kolb, who was allowed to remain in Bucharest) had to leave on the orders of the Soviet command. Still, after making contact with the new government in Debrecen, Weyermann stayed in Hungary, and carried on aid work in difficult circumstances which help explain why questions were raised later about his handling of affairs during this period. The American Jewish Joint Distribution Committee, the chief backer responsible for putting millions of Swiss francs at the delegates' disposal, and the ICRC even lodged a complaint; the matter was subsequently settled out of court.

Unlike Raoul Wallenberg, but like Carl Lutz, Frédéric Born (d. 1963) was quickly forgotten, only to be rehabilitated quite recently. On 5 June 1987 he was awarded posthumously the medal of 'Just Among the Nations' and a tree was planted in his honour in the Avenue of the Just at the memorial to the victims of Nazism in Jerusalem. Whereas the activities of people like Marti, Kolb and Dunand still remain largely unrecognised, Born's work in Hungary has taken its rightful place in Holocaust history.

9   Aid and protection on the eve of liberation

Introduction

The success of the Allied landings in Normandy and the failure of the German counter-offensive in July 1944, followed by the liberation of Paris on 25 August – an event as symbolic as the city's fall on 14 June 1940 had been – not only altered the military balance of power but had profound repercussions in the diplomatic sphere as well. The resumption of hostilities in the West brought its own crop of civilian victims, but in ever greater numbers than before, and for Switzerland and the ICRC, caught between combatants and battlefields, it marked a return to the situation at the beginning of the World War: humanitarian aid was needed on its doorstep once again. By the end of July 1944 the French Committee of National Liberation's representative had, with the Swiss government in Berne and with the ICRC in Geneva, begun looking into the possibility in due course of repatriating through Swiss territory the three million or so French POWs, civilian workers and deportees held in the Reich.

A fresh démarche in Berlin

On his return to Berlin in August 1944, Roland Marti, a practised connoisseur of things German, was able to grasp the full extent of these changes. The defeats suffered by the Wehrmacht, the stepping up of air raids and above all the SS takeover of the apparatus of army and state following the failed coup of 20 July, were a direct threat to the well-being and particularly the food supply of POWs and civilian internees. There was a serious risk that total war could end up making the Geneva Conventions null and void. Indeed, irregular combatants like partisans, on whose behalf the ICRC had never ceased to intervene, were already paying the price for this tougher line; they found themselves henceforth at the mercy of the political police, whereas until then certain groups had been considered *de facto* POWs by the Wehrmacht. There was likely to be a similar worsening of conditions for millions of foreign civilian workers in the Reich. As for administrative detainees, whose number the retreating German army continually added to by seizing thousands of partisans and innocent hostages that crossed its path, Marti feared the worst, and with good reason: SS officers at Natzweiler, Dachau and Buchenwald had let it be known that in the event of Germany losing the war, most if not all concentration camp prisoners would be exterminated, in order to prevent 'communist elements reappearing on the public stage'.[1]

Similar fears were entertained in Belgium and France. During the first fortnight of September the ICRC received several appeals from the Liberation authorities, such as the new head of the French Red Cross, or the Archbishop of Paris, requesting that a démarche be attempted to assist civilians arrested and deported to the Reich. The French government and Red Cross were even ready for the ICRC to allocate to the Concentration Camp Parcels Scheme part of the stockpile of food and clothing which could not for the time being be sent to POW camps because of military operations.[2] Also, when the DRK representative Walter Hartmann arrived in Geneva in mid-September 1944 for another round of discussions, he was asked several questions concerning *inter alia* the resumption of correspondence between deportees and their families, suspended after the Allied offensive began, and the fate of civilian internees as a result of various events during the preceding weeks such as the evacuation of prisoners from Fresnes prison near Paris to Buchenwald, questions which Hartmann felt he could not pass on to the German authorities for the present because of the military situation.[3]

Schwarzenberg realised acutely that such an approach was inadequate. The Liberation had restored France to its position as belligerent, so the time had perhaps come (he wrote on 14 September 1944 to Chenevière) for the ICRC to call for Jews and other French deportees to be accorded the status of civilian internees. But for such a strategy to have any chance of success Schwarzenberg and Marti were agreed that the usual methods were ineffective. Himmler had to be approached direct by sending a leading figure, such as a member of the ICRC, to Berlin, or failing that by inviting to Geneva the president of the DRK, the Duke of Saxe-Coburg-Gotha, or a high-ranking SS officer.[4]

The die was cast on 20 September 1944: the Bureau resolved to bow to French demands and make a démarche in Berlin 'to explore the possibilities of humanitarian aid in favour of political deportees'. Max Huber noted that 'the ICRC can seek to guarantee them the minimum treatment of civilian internees, since they too are enemy aliens on the territory of a belligerent'.[5] So, through the French and Belgian Red

Cross societies, the ICRC asked the two governments to assist its démarche in Berlin in favour of their deported citizens, promising for German civilians in their hands treatment similar to that requested of the Reich.[6] On 2 October 1944, Huber signed the letter addressed to Ribbentrop and sent via the German consulate in Geneva, which enclosed the important note of the same date (translated in the Appendix, document IX).

This letter is of major importance, pointing out as it did that in the case of such categories as the French *Schutzhäflinge* (people held in preventive detention) the ICRC was the only body able to offer any moral or material support, and that it was even-handed, as its work on behalf of German nationals held in Brazil and in the United Kingdom demonstrated. With the exception of the note of 24 September 1942 the ICRC undertook no official or general démarches directly concerning detainees in German concentration camps. The difference was that whereas the 1942 note was signed by the secretary, Roger Gallopin, for Roland Marti to use in his discussions with the German Foreign Ministry, the covering letter of 2 October 1944 was addressed by Max Huber to the foreign minister in person.

The two texts obviously have a lot in common. In both cases, the démarche is concerned with generalities. In 1942 the reference to even-handedness made up a significant part of the introduction, whereas in 1944 it features only in the covering letter, probably through having failed up till then to be of much use. The two notes refer to the Tokyo proposal to base the treatment of civilian internees on the POWs' code; both deal with enemy civilians taken to the Reich (deportees, in other words) and not political prisoners in general, since the démarche's purpose was to draw a parallel with enemy civilians interned on a belligerent's territory; and in both the concrete demands made on behalf on these prisoners were more or less identical.

Although the victims concerned were not precisely the same – in 1942, French Jews primarily, in 1944, Belgian and French deportees, including Jews if any remained – the ICRC stuck to the same legal basis as it had always done. Besides, on the same day, 2 October 1944, as he was addressing the German government in this official manner, Max Huber sent Gerhart Riegner and Paul Guggenheim the memorandum in which he explained why he could not, in law, entertain the World Jewish Congress's proposal to obtain for the Jews the status of civilian internees, or their *de facto* assimilation to such a statute: the Jews were not a state, so they had no place in existing international humanitarian law.

Even so, humanitarian action on their behalf continued to gather momentum. We have noted its impact in Hungary and Slovakia, for example, Romania and Bulgaria having left the war by then and ceased to be Axis partners. With the ICRC's permanent encouragement Marti tried to enter Bergen-Belsen, where it was certain that Jews were being held. The note from Schwarzenberg dated 25 September 1944, to which reference has frequently been made already, shows how far thinking had progressed in only a few weeks, since it envisaged shifting the focus of the instructions given to delegates even if the Jews were still not referred to as a specific category. Remarking that deportees in Germany now represented a substantial proportion of all detainees, POWs included, and yet enjoyed the least legal protection and were most vulnerable to food shortages, Schwarzenberg felt that at this late stage in the war a revision of the ICRC's classic stance was justified and that it was now indispensable to make regular visits to concentration camp commandants: 'we have promised such visits to aid-donor governments and we must keep our word', he concluded.[7]

Waiting impatiently

The provisional government of the French Republic responded favourably to the ICRC's request for reciprocity, stressing that this would mainly involve passing on the names of detainees, Red Cross visits to internment camps, and the immediate repatriation of women, the elderly, and the sick[8] – proposals, except for repatriation, all contained in the ICRC's submission to the German authorities of 2 October 1944. For its démarche the ICRC could therefore also envisage seeking the support and understanding of the British, the Americans, the Norwegians and the Dutch.[9] The British were, however, only interested in the fate of POWs, as was shown by their laconic reply of 14 February 1945, and chose, as did the Americans, to operate mainly through the Protecting Power.

October and November 1944 were spent waiting for a reply from the Germans. An official acknowledgement was not sent until 13 December; and, even though it was in possession of the French overtures, the German Foreign Ministry stuck to a silence which even the goodwill of the DRK, personal and confidential contacts in Berlin, and the visit to Geneva of the head of the Ministry's legal department, legation councillor Eric Albrecht, were powerless to overcome.[10] This lack of response was worrying and embarrassing for the ICRC, compelled to keep this exchange of letters absolutely secret, since information about the concentration and extermination camps and about the terrible things going on there was becoming ever more precise and detailed. The press in Allied and neutral countries was devoting more and more attention to it and public opinion was showing ever greater intensity of feeling about it, as we have seen in the summer of 1944 in connection with the Jewish question in Hungary.

At the same time, too, ICRC delegates were increasingly encountering difficulties in fulfilling their missions in the Reich. Parcels were no longer reaching several camps, particularly at Auschwitz-Monowitz; contacts with commandants were becoming less and less frequent, not only because of the military situation, but also because of manifest ill will on the Nazis' part, and without such dialogue the parcels operation and the possibilities of locating 'layers' of detainees, to use the term common at the time, were threatened. The visit to Bergen-Belsen, which had several times been promised, still had not taken place. The German Foreign Ministry admitted its powerlessness, and suggested that the police be approached over the démarche in mid-November on behalf of the thousands of Poles deported to Auschwitz and Birkenau. Marti himself began to fear that his credit would soon be exhausted in empty gestures of this kind. On the other hand, the success obtained by Thudicum and Schirmer over the setting up of a new sub-delegation in Vienna at the beginning of December seemed to confirm that it could still be advantageous to approach the SS. As was noted above in the previous chapter, the two delegates on the ground secured from the head of the Gestapo in Vienna, Karl Ebner, from the prefect of police Hans Delbrügge, a high-ranking SS officer, and from *Obersturmbann-führer* Hermann Krumay, the head of the special commando, the most extensive facilities for their work under the Conventions and for their activities on behalf of the more than 15,000 displaced Hungarian Jews who had been moved to that part of Austria. Thanks to the support of these Nazis, to the help of Dr Josef Löwenherz, the head of the Viennese Jewish community, and to the clothing, foodstuffs, staff and premises put at their disposal, the ICRC's representatives were able to accomplish a fairly unusual welfare operation.

Otherwise, the appeals and requests for intervention emanating from Jewish organisations, especially after the Arrow-Cross's *coup d'état* in Hungary, only served – diplomatic démarches even more so – to under-line how cruel the German delay in replying was becoming. At the beginning of November 1944, at the prompting of the Polish govern-ment in exile in London, the Holy See, followed by Portugal and even the Swiss Confederation, protested to the Foreign Ministry in Berlin about the Polish deportations to Auschwitz that have already been mentioned. The Swiss minister took the opportunity to suggest to his German opposite number, in vain of course, that the ICRC should visit the camp.[11]

A few weeks later Burckhardt sent a similar request to the German government over the camp at Ravensbrück, about which news of the most alarming kind was beginning to circulate. In handing this note to Werner von Holleben, the German consul in Geneva, Burckhardt again asked for a reply to the 2 October letter. But on 4 December the consulate passed Burckhardt a note couched in very different terms. Using as an excuse the executions, arrests and ill treatment inflicted on former French collaborators, German civilians, and Alsatians and Lorrainers who had entered the Reich's service, the Berlin government promised to take revenge on the Gaullists it held and placed all responsibility for it fairly and squarely in advance on the shoulders of the French authorities.[12]

Freed from the dilemma which it would have faced over passing such a letter of threats to an adversary government by the fact that the Foreign Ministry made it public, the ICRC was able to establish a connection – that of reciprocity – between German civilians in French hands and French civilians in German hands, and in this way link the Reich's note of 4 December with its own of 2 October.[13] This interpretation was borne out by Fritz Berber (Ribbentrop's adviser, then resident in Geneva), so on 9 December Max Huber signed a letter from the ICRC to Ribbentrop proposing that France and Germany open negotiations under Red Cross auspices, as was done in 1914–18, to resolve the question of the civilians held on both sides.[14]

There was to be no direct follow-up to this note. However, on 1 February 1945, the German consulate-general in Geneva finally conveyed Ribbentrop's reply to the note of 2 October 1944. In it, the Reich accepted that French and Belgian detainees, using Red Cross forms, could correspond with their families and tell them how they were; that they could receive parcels of food, clothing, medicines and books, either individually or in groups; that people arrested would be informed of the offences with which, under German law, they were being charged; and that the authorities would respond to enquiries about individuals. But for reasons of national defence, visits to camps and labour battalions remained impossible, and as for the question of repatriation raised in the 9 December letter, this was still under discussion.[15]

Despite its lateness the German reply was significant; at least, that was what the ICRC seems to have considered it to be, since they mentioned it in a press release. But, at this late stage in the war, would not a different approach have produced more in the way of tangible results? Throughout the long months of impatient waiting that had led finally to this outcome, some people had thought so, as we shall now see.

In the summer of 1942, bombarded with questions and demands about deportees, both Jewish and non-Jewish, Marti had pointed out to headquarters that in the circumstances only one channel seemed open, that leading to the Gestapo and its supremo Heinrich Himmler, or failing him the Ministry of Justice and its head Georg Thierack. He was not listened to, since the note of 24 September 1942 told him to speak to his usual contacts in the legal section of the Foreign Ministry. But Marti – who was, after all, the chief delegate in Germany – stuck to his guns and every so often, in the next few years, returned to the attack. In September 1944 the head of the Special Aid Division, Jean-Etienne Schwarzenberg, rallied to his side; being convinced of the humanitarian and political necessity of attempting what he called 'one last effort' on behalf of the French and Belgian deportees, Schwarzenberg proposed energetically, as we have seen, that a leading figure such as Burckhardt should go and see Himmler.[16] Towards the end of October 1944, in spite of the note of the 2nd, or perhaps because of it, Mme Frick-Cramer took up the cudgels with Burckhardt in her turn and even suggested that an approach be made to Hitler himself, putting forward for the purpose somewhat naïvely the name of Pastor Adolphe Keller, a leading light in Swiss Protestantism and in the ecumenical movement.[17]

Three days later, on 26 October 1944, Mme Frick wrote by hand to Max Huber and urged him, even more insistently, to go to Berlin himself, in spite of his still shaky health. Her plan was that Marti be given instructions to try by all means at his disposal to obtain for Max Huber a private audience with the Führer, and she suggested that the ICRC's request be drafted along the following lines:

Professor Max Huber considers it a matter of the utmost importance that he be received by the Führer and Reich Chancellor in person to discuss the situation of certain categories of war victim who, whatever nationality they belong to, are not covered by the International Conventions. The president of the ICRC is convinced that urgent measures are now needed and must be put to all the belligerents. Professor Huber is ready to go at once (the sooner the better) to anywhere that the Führer cares to suggest as the place of their meeting.

Mme Frick believed, she went on, that this request stood more hope of being granted if it was made by Huber personally rather than being sent through diplomatic channels. Even if it were refused, she believed it to be of the utmost importance that the démarche be attempted, because the ICRC could not in her opinion morally fail to do its utmost to try to prevent the development of certain methods of war. She thought that the situation was so serious that the ICRC, knowing what it now knew, could not be content with a written démarche that was very likely to be ignored. The president's personal intervention was in her view the only way of mitigating the evils increasingly afflicting unfortunate civilian populations, and she felt sure, she concluded, that he shared her sense that not to attempt it would incur a heavy responsibility.[18]

In November 1944 Mme Frick and Marti returned to the issue of the need to seek direct contact, and for its part the Swiss Political Department, concerned at its failure to accredit a new Swiss minister to General de Gaulle's administration, left Burckhardt in no doubt that it would be very useful for the ICRC, as well as for Switzerland, if the Committee were to meet with some success over the question of the French political prisoners.[19]

The paths leading to the grand master of the black order

From the beginning of 1945 onwards, things became more and more difficult for delegates on the spot, what with the damage to roads and railways, the disruption of telephone and telegraphic communications, and the dispersal of the German authorities. Organisation was breaking down at the same time as the withdrawal of prison camps from front-line areas was being speeded up. What was now being put in jeopardy was the whole of the ICRC's work in arranging visits to and the feeding of POWs and internees, not just the parcels operation. Decentralisation measures, such as the creation of sub-delegations at Uffing (where Marti was posted) and Vienna, and the setting up of depots at Wagenitz (north-west of Berlin, where the delegation under Otto Lehner remained), Lübeck and Moosburg, no longer sufficed to guarantee the supply of aid. In mid-February, the ICRC had to appeal to Allied governments to help in ensuring that food supplies arrived from Switzerland and Gothenburg. Even then there was the need to get aid through to the camps themselves, since the ICRC would only accept responsibility for transports that it could ensure reached their destination. At the beginning of March, a Swiss trainload of fifty wagons was sent to Stalag VIIA (Moosburg) where evacuated POWs had been assembled. Twenty-five lorries put at the ICRC's disposal by the American and the Canadian Red Cross left Switzerland, six of which went via Berlin to Lübeck, and from there to the main POW and civilian camps. It was thus only in the last few weeks of the war that the ICRC (and indeed the WRB and the national Red Cross societies) began to overcome the obstacles encountered for months past by the Concentration Camp Parcels Service.

All this upheaval impelled headquarters and delegations staff to exhausting efforts of energy and improvisation. It gave rise to the most contradictory fears and rumours. At one moment the main risk seemed to be isolated acts of butchery, at another that the regime would stage a

Götterdämmerung-style apotheosis of horror. The concentration camps in the East, which were being evacuated in appalling conditions, gave these gruesome suggestions a particular resonance. But, overwhelmed by work, Burckhardt still awaited a reply which he apparently hoped to hasten through secret diplomatic channels.[20]

Anxiety was at its height in Jewish circles. More insistently than ever they called for victims of racial persecution to be given the status of civilian internees and for measures to be taken to prevent an impending massacre of Jewish POWs. But Leo Kubowitzki, one of the people in charge of the World Jewish Congress's aid service, was virtually ignored when he went to London in January 1945 on a mission to win over the Allies. In Geneva, Gerhart Riegner had hoped to bolster these efforts with the help of his pressure group, but the meeting he arranged between Burckhardt and Kubowitzki on 20 February turned into a dialogue of the deaf, since the ICRC's new president kept repeating that the World Jewish Congress's public demand for Jews to be given the status of civilian internees could only hinder the traditional operations of the Red Cross. He then revealed that he had decided to see Himmler, however unpleasant the meeting might be, since he shared his visitors' point of view that the Reich's political leaders were now divided over what to do with POWs and civilian prisoners. A few days later, once more at Riegner's instigation, the delegates of the national Red Cross societies in Czechoslovakia, Poland, Yugoslavia, the Netherlands, Belgium, Norway, Italy, Romania and Greece, backed by the French Ministry for Prisoners, Deportees and Refugees, asked Burckhardt in writing for the ICRC to make every effort on behalf of the civilian detainees in the Reich by sending to Germany a delegation with power to negotiate. The Churches' Ecumenical Council made a similar request from their particular angle.[21] So Burckhardt did not fail to notify the World Jewish Congress at the beginning of March about the contacts he had just made with what he called 'the competent top people in Germany'; he subsequently informed both the World Jewish Congress and the representatives of the national Red Cross societies of his negotiations with Ernst Kaltenbrunner.

From the second fortnight in January onwards the governments of the occupied or liberated countries also made it patently clear to the ICRC the importance they attached to the fate of the deportees, France in particular, since all Switzerland's efforts to secure the representation of French interests in Berlin came up against the Reich's repeated refusal to recognise the provisional government of the French Republic, which now could play only the ICRC card. On 16 January 1945 it authorised the ICRC's delegates to visit all the German prison camps and declared itself ready to repatriate certain categories of civilian internees without waiting for reciprocity, and at the end of January it asked the ICRC to start negotiations with the German authorities on a range of matters including an exchange of French deportees and German civilian internees. Meanwhile the State Department and the WRB, in the wake of the World Jewish Congress, called upon the ICRC to intervene using every means at its disposal, because of the increasingly sinister rumours circulating about the massacres perpetrated or planned in the camps. These rumours were also conveyed to the neutral countries. The Swedish government suggested to Switzerland and the Vatican that a discreet but firm démarche be made to the German Foreign Ministry; on 12 February 1945 the Swiss minister informed the German secretary of state that his country was ready to admit other Jews under threat with the help, if necessary, of Swiss transport, and backed up the ICRC's request to be allowed to look after Jews, particularly at Bergen-Belsen, where conditions were terrible.[22]

The visit which the Swedish consul in Paris, Rolf Nordling, paid Burckhardt on 31 January certainly played a role too in the decision to attempt direct contact with the SS. Nordling was an enterprising individual who maintained that he had links with Himmler himself; and when Burckhardt, having just learned that the ICRC's delegation in Berlin was in constant touch with the police authorities, told Nordling so, the latter replied that it was not enough. Last-minute catastrophes could be unleashed both from the top and the bottom. The only solution was therefore to install a medical team in each camp to dispense health care and keep an eye on the situation. This idea had already been put to Burckhardt in December 1944 by Herbert Siegfried, the Reich's consul in Geneva. When Nordling had left, Burckhardt noted that the delegation in Berlin would be informed of his discussions with the Swede, in a speedy and secure manner, to prevent the ICRC being outstripped by another organisation if it turned out that Nordling's proposal was a practicable one.[23]

On the eve of this meeting, in fact, a report of the utmost importance had been received at headquarters. It had been sent from Berlin on 20 January 1945 by Robert Schirmer. This was not of course the first time that the delegates had got in touch with Nazi authorities other than their usual contacts in the Foreign Ministry and the OKW. Marti and his colleagues had, after all, held meetings from autumn 1943 onwards with several concentration camp commandants and SS cadres, but this time Otto Lehner and Robert Schirmer had managed to establish relations not only with the General Directorate of concentration camps, based at Oranienburg (*Hauptquartier der SS für die Verwaltung aller KZ*), but with the representatives of the Reich Central Security Bureau (RSHA). These contacts seemed to be bearing fruit: according to the delegation, an agreement had been reached which would benefit French, Belgian, Dutch and Scandinavian detainees by allowing the receipt of parcels on a generous scale, the setting-up of a central depot at Dachau, the appointment of persons of trust as in POW camps, and the official return of all receipts. As for visits properly speaking, Schirmer announced that the request had been passed to Himmler and was being looked into.[24]

In this way the parcels operation received a kind of official blessing, which is why Schwarzenberg described Schirmer's report as 'the first light glimpsed at the end of the tunnel in our negotiations with the SS'. But the news also represented a breakthrough in its reference to Himmler. In the circumstances it is therefore understandable that the reply to the letter of 2 October 1944, which arrived in Geneva on 1 February 1945, lost some of its impact. For one thing the Foreign Ministry's note concerned only the deportees from France and Belgium; it did, it is true, offer concessions over detainees' correspondence and to some degree put an end to arbitrary police involvement in legal proceedings. On the other hand, it firmly turned down the ICRC's request for visits, and the parcels authorisation did not go as far as the detailed plan for the delivery of foodstuffs worked out in Berlin between the ICRC's delegates and the SS.

The immediate outcome of the Swedish competition and of the Berlin delegation's appeals to, pressure on and contacts with the SS was to encourage the ICRC to reply to the Germans now in a more active way than could have been imagined, given the stance it took up as recently as December 1944. Indeed, not content with expressing satisfaction at the results achieved thus far, the ICRC asked the Reich authorities on 15 February 1945 to provide lists of names of detainees for the purpose of making a proper card-index, to undertake technical measures for easing food supplies, to accord detainees the minimum judicial guarantees granted to POWs, to allow visits by delegates after all, and lastly to organise the repatriation of several categories of French and Belgian internees (the sick, the wounded, women, children and people not under criminal investigation or who benefited from prescription), and it repeated its invitation for a prominent figure to be delegated to pursue negotiations face to face in Geneva.[25]

The second result of shifts in the balance of power was obviously the refloating of the idea of dialogue at the highest level, and in this respect things moved swiftly. Independently of Nordling, who was popping up all over the place in Switzerland, Burckhardt learned from the delegate in Stockholm, Georg Hoffmann, that the Swedes too were poised to act in Germany. Referring at the Bureau meeting on 7 February 1945 to the presence of Swedish representatives in the camps, Burckhardt concluded that the time seemed to have come to send an ICRC delegation to talk to the Germans.[26] The arrival at the Swiss border the next day of 1,200 Jews from Theresienstadt accompanied by the former president of Switzerland Jean-Marie Musy, whose intervention aroused public interest (see p. 192 above), does not appear to have influenced the ICRC's decisions, because what Burckhardt seems not yet to have told the Bureau is that on 2 February he had already had a letter from Himmler, inviting him to a meeting.

Before accepting, Burckhardt took a fortnight to think it over. On 19 February he told the Swiss Political Department that he had said yes, following, he said, requests by Allied governments (the envoy extraordinary of the United States in Geneva, Laughlin Currie, was also put in the picture about the projects envisaged during his visit to the ICRC on 26 February). On 19 February too, Himmler met at Hohenlychen another neutral representative, the vice-president of the Swedish Red Cross, Folke Bernadotte.

Himmler's intentions were obvious: he was trying to extricate Germany from the war. But at this date the ICRC was conducting various other negotiations with the Nazis, whether through the delegation in Berlin, through Hans Bon's mission in Italy, or through the Foreign Ministry via Fritz Berber in Geneva, a channel that was not without its usefulness since it was through him that the Foreign Ministry indicated on 2 March its agreement to an exchange between France and the Reich of interned old men, women and children. So even though belated and fraught with difficulty (because there were far more Allied civilians interned in Germany than German civilians in Allied hands), this major operation seemed feasible as long as adequate material resources, particularly lorries, were made available by the Allies. So Burckhardt replied in the following terms to the Americans who were urging him to intensify the ICRC's efforts in all fields and throughout the Reich:

Only large-scale measures and rapid decisions can guarantee results. We are often expected to produce miracles. That is obviously impossible, but by lending all our efforts and focusing all our attention on a problem we can achieve something, provided we are given the tools to do the job.[27]

A meeting on the Arlberg road

Prevented by his military responsibilities on the Eastern Front, Himmler could not in the end find the time for a meeting, and suggested instead that Burckhardt meet in southern Germany a leading figure who would represent him. On Monday 12 March 1945 at midday the president of the ICRC, accompanied by his faithful aide Hans Bachmann, crossed the Swiss border close to Feldkirch. The two men were driven straight-away to a discreet rendezvous at an inn on the road between Feldkirch and Bludenz, where their host was waiting. He was Dr Ernst Kalten-brunner, *Obergruppenführer-SS*, Waffen-SS and Police General, head of the Sipo and the SD, and the person in charge of the Reich Central Security Bureau and of all the Nazi concentration camps.

There are several sources of information about this meeting, which lasted all afternoon. All are Red Cross sources. They consist principally of an account written by Burckhardt for Fritz Berber on 14 March, another drafted in French by Burckhardt on 17 March for the head of the Swiss Political Department, Max Petitpierre, and a document in the form of minutes drawn up by Hans Bachmann on 19 March. The dates are significant because on 13 and 15 March discussions continued in Kreuzlingen, just inside the Swiss border, with the representative of the Foreign Ministry, Adolf Windecker, who since the end of January had been conducting unofficial negotiations in Konstanz to make the town once again a centre for exchanges and hospitalisation as it had been during World War I. But when Burckhardt met Fritz Berber in Zurich on 16 March, it was clear that the two Foreign Ministry spokesmen were at loggerheads both with each other and with Kaltenbrunner, the one invoking powers given him by the head of the Legal Section, the other those given him by Ribbentrop himself. Finally, for good measure, the replies sent on 29 March by Kaltenbrunner to Burckhardt following their meeting still left many questions unanswered. In spite of this imbroglio, it is worth trying to understand what the SS general and the ICRC president said to each other on 12 March, the real scope and significance of Burckhardt's proposals, and the precise value of these famous negotiations, made public at once, but in garbled form, due to a slip-up in the Swiss Political Department.

Apart from Burckhardt's request that various leading figures be freed, two major problems were tackled that afternoon, if Burckhardt is to be believed; both concerned as a top priority the French detainees. The discussions then turned to concentration camp internees, and finally, at Burckhardt's insistence, to the Jews.

The first problem was that of the evacuation and hospitalisation of several categories of POWs and detainees on Swiss soil. Appointed Swiss ambassador in Paris on 20 February in order to cement relations between the Confederation and the French provisional government, Burckhardt was here on solid ground. He therefore proposed, after raising the question of the wives and children of members of Bor-Komorowski's Polish army, that the exchange of civilians between France and the Reich, which the German note of 2 March had accepted in principle, be carried out. Kaltenbrunner said that he was unaware of this note, but that he had no objection to the proposal, or for including Belgians in it, but that it would have to be done via Switzerland, since the Baltic was mined, and the ICRC would have to provide the necessary transport, which did not seem impossible.

During the next few days solid prospects for exchanges remained at the heart of the Kreuzlingen discussions, though little actual progress was made, and in his letter of 29 March Kaltenbrunner harked back to the assurances sought by the Reich from the French over the Alsatians, Lorrainers and the collaborators. So démarches and preparations continued until the first exchange took place. Against 454 German civilian internees some 300 French women from Ravensbrück, mainly Jewish, arrived in Switzerland on 11 April in such a state that several of them could not continue on their journey to France straightaway. This first trainload would be followed on 24–26 April by another, consisting of about a thousand people, mostly French, Belgians and Dutch, chiefly from Mauthausen. Registered, fed, their medical needs attended to, the deportees, several of whom died en route, were kept apart from the population and moved as quickly as possible to the Franco-Swiss border; indeed since the French government was urging the ICRC to hasten the repatriation programme, the Federal Council decided on 27 April to intervene as well and, despite the reservations of General Henri Guisan and the Swiss postal authorities, to make available two columns of yellow mail vans, providing 1,600 seats on each journey. On their side Marti, head of the ICRC delegation now installed at Uffing, and the Swiss minister in Germany, Hans Frölicher, who had been withdrawn to Bernried near Tutzing, prevailed upon the Federal Council to accept in principle the hospitalisation of 3,000 sick and wounded people and the transit of 1,500 liberated prisoners daily. But their plan to use food lorries returning empty from the camps they had supplied met with a number of difficulties, not least the general chaos, the exhausted state of many deportees and internees, and the reservations of the Swiss military, police and health authorities, who were willing to accept after the briefest of checks all categories of prisoner freed from the camps, provided that these people did not try to stay in Switzerland but were content just to pass through on their way to the Franco-Swiss border. But then neither were the French, notwithstanding a generally sympathetic attitude, prepared to admit all those to whom the term 'displaced persons' was already being applied, particularly when the people in question were from Eastern Europe and spoke no French.

Burckhardt also raised with Kaltenbrunner the question of the Jews, and here too he had something to offer. He was able to submit to Kaltenbrunner a WRB memorandum which in proposing a vast programme of aid to civilian detainees not classifiable as POWs and their transfer to Switzerland, promised the ICRC all necessary funds, diplomatic support, and means of transport. Kaltenbrunner, pointing out that the Musy and Saly Meyer–Becher operations showed a certain flexibility on the part of the German side, promised to look into the matter with the competent authorities.

The re-grouping of Jewish survivors and their transfer to Switzerland did not in the end take place even though Kaltenbrunner still held out the hope on 29 March of a certain opening in this direction in return for some form of *quid pro quo*. Later meetings at Kreuzlingen and at Innsbruck on 24 April did not enable any progress to be made on this point, which was increasingly becoming academic given the chaos spreading through the Reich and the small number of Jews who had managed to survive.

At the meeting between Burckhardt and Kaltenbrunner on 12 March the protection of detainees and internees was the second basic problem to be addressed, involving as it did the question of POWs such as the Free French forces and Germans in French hands. But the main issue was obviously the fate of concentration camp detainees and the German reply of 1 February 1945. Kaltenbrunner straightaway accepted the principle of extending to other nationalities the concessions that the ICRC had obtained for the French and the Belgians. On the other hand, it did not appear possible, given the large number of camps and nationalities involved, to gather together prisoners by country and then repatriate them, as Bernadotte had done for the Scandinavians, and Kaltenbrunner also ruled out visits by delegates, since too many camps were supplying labour for the defence industries. There remained the same possibility as had been envisaged for POWs, namely, to install delegates, accompanied by medical teams, in the camps, which they would only leave at the end of the war. Kaltenbrunner promised a written reply on this point, but it never came. As will be seen, the delegates carried on for over a month longer continuing their visits on the usual basis, that is, being content with meeting the *Kommandanten* and handing over parcels. Only the approach of Allied troops or the liberation of the camps would sometimes give them access to the inside of the installations. There was the same lack of progress on the question of aid, since at the 12 March meeting no advance was made on the proposal, which had first been aired two months earlier, to set up a central parcels distribution point in Dachau, from which the SS, with transport provided by the ICRC this time, would supply the camps. On the other hand, the SS chief acceded to Burckhardt's request that Jews be treated henceforth in the same way as other detainees, that is granted similar benefits in their camps in respect of concessions obtained for correspondence, access to food supplies, and so on.

Any verdict on the Arlberg meeting, even one made in the light of subsequent discussions, must finally remain a matter of doubt. Kaltenbrunner did not agree to very much, except to pass on Burckhardt's desiderata to Himmler, and to intervene with the Foreign Ministry, on whom chiefly depended the issue which, in his capacity as Swiss minister-designate in Paris, Burckhardt was particularly keen to see resolved, namely the exchange or repatriation of Allied detainees, especially French ones. A face-to-face encounter had taken place, something which since the war started had seemed unimaginable to the ICRC. Due partly of course to the circumstances, the results would not be commensurate with the goodwill displayed, but it is tempting to speculate whether things would have turned out any differently if the meeting had taken place in 1942 or even in 1944.

In any event Burckhardt, back from his discussions with Fritz Berber in Zurich, lost no time in urging the ICRC to make the most of the meeting with Kaltenbrunner. On 14 March he established a permanent bureau in Kreuzlingen in order to maintain contact with the Germans through their envoy Adolf Windecker; a technical commission was set up in Geneva; the Swiss authorities were kept fully in the picture; through Jean Jardin at the French embassy in Berne the Masson–Schellenberg link was made to help out, and new life was breathed into the channel provided by Fritz Berber. At the end of March, a new delegate, Dr Hans E. Meyer, arrived in Berlin at the head of a column of ten lorries, loaded with supplies for POWs at Torgau and bearing a letter in which in the spirit of the Arlberg discussions Burckhardt proposed to Kaltenbrunner that henceforward, rather than return empty, the trucks supplying POW camps bring back political prisoners to Switzerland.[28]

In the ruins of the Third Reich

Not only was the ICRC delegation in Berlin not kept informed of the outcome of the Arlberg discussions, but headquarters had every intention of keeping it in ignorance, since it forbade its special envoy Hans Meyer to tell his colleagues what the real aims of his mission were; he did not, however, keep to those instructions. This excessive compartmentalisation in the conduct of negotiations, which we have already encountered several times, was in this instance particularly unfortunate in that Otto Lehner and his colleagues had pursued their contacts with the SS and had managed to reach some high-ranking people. Their discussions in mid-March with the head of the SS's espionage section, Amt VI, Walter Schellenberg, proved that the leaders not only of the Reich but of the SS itself were more and more split into two camps, the fanatics and the moderates (or realists). Schellenberg was one of the latter, and he managed to pull his chestnuts from the fire. Using him as intermediary, Marti met on 23 March 1945 the head of the Reich Central Security Bureau, Heinrich Müller, known as Müller-Gestapo. The latter was privy to what his chief had discussed with Burckhardt; Marti was not, but what he asked for obviously tallied with what was talked about in the Arlberg discussions: sending parcels to the concentration camps, extending to all deportees the right to receive letters, and visiting the camps (particularly Theresienstadt and Bergen-Belsen). Hans Meyer tried for his part to secure the repatriation of a first batch of French women prisoners from Ravensbrück. And since he failed to get anyone to listen to him in Berlin he went straight to ask Himmler in Hohenlychen. The place, an SS medical establishment, where a commando from Ravensbrück was also active, was one he knew well from having worked there between 1943 and August 1944 as assistant to Professor Karl Gebhardt, chief SS surgeon, close friend of Heinrich Himmler, Grawitz's successor (albeit briefly) at the head of the German Red Cross, and hanged at Nuremberg for his involvement in pseudo-medical experiments. People have wondered if Meyer was at all aware of the experiments carried out on concentration camp inmates. A little belatedly, the ICRC would express surprise at the past of a delegate who had travelled extensively in the East in 1943–4, forgetting that in support of his candidature at Geneva the doctor had concealed nothing about his placements with Gebhardt and his SS colleagues. Whatever the case, Meyer soon pulled off a success when he left Ravensbrück for Switzerland with a convoy of 299 French women and one Polish woman; subsequently he went to Dachau and Mauthausen as well.

Frédéric Siordet, head of the Delegations Committee, and Paul Dunant went on a tour of inspection that took them to Theresienstadt at the end of March and then on to southern Germany, Berlin, Prague and Vienna, but they were allowed neither into the ghetto-camp, nor into what was called the little fortress where thousands of prisoners rotted completely cut off from the world. Paul Dunant took up quarters in Prague, hoping through his negotiations with the *Reichsprotektor* Karl-Hermann Franck to secure at last permission to visit it (something granted in principle at the end of March to the Swiss legation in Berlin). Heinrich Müller gave permission to Otto Lehner in Berlin, and on 6 April he and Dunant, accompanied by Eberhardt von Thadden of the Foreign Ministry, entered the ghetto, but not the little fortress. Then during an evening at the Hradschin (Hradkany Castle) they discussed Theresienstadt and the Jewish problem in general with Erwin Weinemann, head of security in the Protectorate, and with Adolf Eichmann who, despite his modest rank, was correctly identified by Lehner as having played a central role at Lublin, Auschwitz and in Hungary, and who in any case introduced himself as Himmler's direct plenipotentiary for the entire Jewish question (see Appendix, document X).

After two unsuccesful attempts at the end of April to gain access to the ghetto, Paul Dunant finally moved in on 2 May, when with the agreement of the Germans and the Council of Elders, he took it under ICRC protection. It was in that capacity that on 8 May he was to hand over the survivors, including nearly 5,000 prisoners at last freed from the little fortress, to the new Czech authorities. So here the ICRC was to play an important role in the delivery of aid to the population, in the protection it afforded them at the moment of the transfer of power, and last but not least, in the repatriation of deportees.

In his reply of 29 March to the questions raised by Burckhardt at their meeting on the 12th, Kaltenbrunner proposed that the ICRC's Berlin delegation get in touch at once with the Foreign Ministry to follow up proposals for exchanging French and Belgian POWs, improving food distribution in their stalags, grouping the Poles in Bor-Komorowski's army, and transferring Jews to Switzerland. As for the exchange of French and Belgian civilians, including deportees, one of the chief themes, it will be recalled, of the ICRC's démarche, Kaltenbrunner designated two colleagues who had remained at Konstanz and the Foreign Ministry representative, the envoy Adolf Windecker, to study the proposal. But there was no longer any question of visiting the camps, even less of installing delegates in them until the end of the war. It was obvious that the idea had either been dropped by Kaltenbrunner himself or had been vetoed by Himmler. The delegates on the ground realised it as soon as they presented themselves at the gates of the camps, despite the letters they bore from Burckhardt referring to his negotiations with the SS. On 4 April Otto Lehner and Gustave Moynier talked at Oranienburg to the former commandant of Auschwitz, Rudolf Hoess, now attached to the Central Directorate of the camps, and they even met the men holding positions of trust, but without of course being able to question them closely, and sending Moynier to Buchenwald turned out to be impossible. In any case a few days later a new piece of information temporarily diverted the Berlin delegation's attention to another danger: the Gestapo had carried out the destruction of the papers and documents of political prisoners in Berlin, perhaps indicating thereby that the latter were going to be made to disappear. Lehner, accompanied by Emil Boesch, hurried to the Foreign Ministry and the Ministry of Justice and Police, and got assurances from Heinrich Müller and a representative of the Ministry of Justice which he lost no time in confirming in writing. There was, no doubt, little more he could do.[29]

On 15 April 1945 the British liberated Bergen-Belsen, and the photographs and films of corpses in piles, of human skeletons staggering towards their liberators and of the wooden shelving on which the dead and dying were crammed together, were flashed around the world. It was the first camp to fall intact, so to speak, into Allied hands, since the camps in the East, like Auschwitz, had been evacuated before the Russians arrived and the extermination facilities (or, in the case of Treblinka and Sobibor, the camps themselves) had been destroyed. By mid-April the only major installations remaining under German control were Dachau and Mauthausen-Gusen (with their many commandos and annexes, such as Landsberg) in the south, Buchenwald in the centre, and Neuengamme, Ravensbrück and Oranienburg-Sachsenhausen in the north. In an attempt to get the SS to fulfil the promises it had made both on the Arlberg road and in Berlin, the ICRC now concentrated all its efforts on these camps.

At first these efforts were confined to organising the food supply, no easy matter in the current situation, with everybody working more or less, given the circumstances, on their own initiative. Jean Briquet arrived on 18 April at Dachau, but had to be content with leaving parcels there. On 20 April, being unable to contact Schellenberg or Himmler, Lehner met Müller at Wannsee to discuss the fate of Ravensbrück and Oranienburg. In spite of the Russian artillery bombardment which made him distinctly jittery, the SS boss maintained that he could not allow the delegates to enter the camps, but he did agree to refer the matter to Himmler. Meanwhile the delegates took concrete action on the ground and went to 78 Schulstrasse, the Berlin Jews' assembly camp (for a few were still left in the capital), and to the infirmary of the Reichsvereinigung der Juden in Deutschland at 2 Iranische Strasse, which they took under their protection. Subsequently Emil Boesch and Albert de Cocatrix managed to secure the release of numerous political prisoners.

Having heard nothing from Himmler, Lehner sent Willy Pfister to Oranienburg to see Hoess, but Pfister came back empty-handed. This confirmed that the SS had no intention of opening the camps up to the

Red Cross. On the other hand they wanted to prevent the Allies seizing camps which were still inhabited, as had happened at Bergen-Belsen, the liberation of which had provided Allied propaganda with a terrible weapon. While headquarters tried to organise a base at Lübeck for food supplies and even for repatriation, via Gothenburg, of civilian prisoners in north Germany, the political police got directly in touch with delegates on the ground. During the night of 21 April, Hoess called Lehner from Oranienburg to tell him that many tens of thousands of deportees were about to leave for Wittstock, a journey of 100 km on foot. Sent back there post-haste, Pfister, who had at his disposal a little aid dispatched from the depot at Wagenitz while supplies were being organised at Lübeck, was to witness the horrifying march and to try unsuccessfully to prevent summary executions. He would accompany the deportees as far as Schwerin, where they were met by the Americans, before he withdrew, struck down by illness. At Ravensbrück too Albert de Cocatrix tried in vain to dissuade the commandant Fritz Suhren from evacuating the detainees. He was to witness the same horrors and, like his colleague, was to follow the columns in order to bring a little material and moral comfort.[30] So Lehner had good reason to write in his final report that thousands of wretched prisoners owed their lives to the presence of the Red Cross, who made a real impression on the SS guards who were fearful, now that the war was nearly over, about how their actions would be judged.

In the south things were somewhat different. On 22 April Jean-Maurice Rübli and Dr Claude Mayor presented themselves at the gates of Mauthausen with lorries loaded with food supplies. The commandant Frantz Ziereis took the parcels but forbade access, but when the delegates left this time they took with them 817 French, Belgian and Dutch deportees, and the next day Charles Steffen repeated the exploit, this time with 183 French prisoners. So it seems that Kaltenbrunner was telling the truth, at least partially, when in Innsbruck on 24 April he assured Hans Bachmann and Hans Meyer, who pressed him to fulfil the undertakings given and the promises made to save such of the camp populations as could still be snatched from death, that he had given the necessary orders for evacuation (or exchanges) to be carried out, starting with women, children, the sick and the elderly. He also assured them that he had arranged for delegates to be allowed into the camps.[31] But what is not clear is how much real power he possessed. However well disposed his contacts found him, they had no way of knowing whether he was covered by his boss or able to command the loyalty of his subordinates. He was later to tell the Allied Military Tribunal in Nuremberg (where he was condemned to death for war crimes) that he had been given full powers by Himmler on 19 April to negotiate with the ICRC, something he does not appear to have revealed to Bachmann and Meyer on 24 April.

On the same day, 24 April, the Russians completed the encirclement of Berlin, and two days later the forward troops of the Allied armies linked up on the Elbe at Torgau, cutting the Reich, or what was left of it, in two. On the same day, 26 April, Robert Hort and Raymond Moynier entered the Jewish camp at Türckheim, although almost all the 15,000 inhabitants had been taken to Dachau. Their intervention did, however, make it possible to remove to safety some 500 survivors before the final pitched battle between the camp guards and the liberators took place. At Dachau, Victor Maurer's presence helped in the negotiations over surrender, which took place on 28 April. Lastly, at Mauthausen Louis Haefliger, arriving at the head of a column of nineteen lorries, was met at first by Frantz Ziereis's refusal to let him in, because in spite of rumours spreading among the prisoners that the Red Cross was about to arrive, the gassings continued almost to the end of April. On 29 April the SS did away with the gas chamber's technical apparatus, and on the same day Haefliger, who on 27 April had finally badgered his way into being allowed to take up quarters in the camp, tried to get the commandant to agree to improve food and accommodation in a camp that was seriously overcrowded and above all to refrain from blowing up Gusen I and II, the huge aircraft factory and the slave labourers employed there. Finally, on 5 May, having probably helped forestall the worst in this respect, he went in person to meet the advance detachments of the American armoured corps which was stationed nearby at Linz. Having ushered them into the compound he witnessed scenes of relief and joy, but also the disarming and beating up of the SS guards by their former captives. By noon Mauthausen was liberated, and he proceeded to open up the annexes at Gusen. Whatever the immediate problems raised by what he called 'the encounter between freedom and hunger', he had succeeded in what he had set out to do: 60,000 human beings had been freed and the camps had not been destroyed.[32]

Thus in the Third Reich's last days the ICRC's delegates not only managed to enter some of the camps, but worked hard to repatriate their prisoners, especially citizens of Western European countries. All in all, according to André Durand, they succeeded before and after the German surrender in securing the return of 10,750 detainees in round figures, about half of them after the Allies had taken charge of the camps.[33] But in the weeks following the opening up of the concentration camps the ICRC's attempts to persuade the Swiss government to let in deportees fell on deaf ears because the army and police authorities were afraid that their poor state of health would give rise to epidemics and preferred allocating scarce beds in hotels, sanatoria and hospitals to sick and wounded soldiers belonging to the victorious Western powers, expecting in general that once the war was over refugees would go on their way.[34] The ICRC carried on its activities for several years more, for instance in the search for displaced persons, chiefly concentration camp detainees and families scattered by the war. The International Search Service at Arolsen, successor to institutions set up by the Allies for the purpose, continues to this day to carry out the task under the auspices of the ICRC. But that is another matter, which falls outside the scope of this book.[35]

10   Conclusion

It is not easy to conclude, since it involves, on the one hand, measuring the distance which separates the historian from the subject studied: if the attempt to explain does not always lead to sympathy, it usually results at least in a certain understanding of what had seemed simply inadmissible. On the other hand it also means emphasising everything that separates the time of the historical events from the narrator's own time. In the present case this period is particularly long, not in respect of the number of years but of what is sometimes called the evolution of mentalities – the extent to which attitudes change over time – so that we today sometimes find it difficult to understand, to interpret correctly and in the end to accept the ways of thinking of a past epoch.

Throughout the Nazi period, and especially during the war, the ICRC looked upon the concentration camp internees, political prisoners and people persecuted on grounds of race as groups of victims worthy of interest and therefore of compassion and support, but at no point as a distinct category, even at the end of the war, when, under pressure from the French and Belgian governments, the ICRC finally came to a decision and made a concerted effort to help them. Attempts at intervention rooted in humanitarian law tended to leave them on the sidelines whereas, of all war victims, their fate was the most tragic. As a result the ICRC has often been asked to explain its apparent lack of interest and to analyse why it was powerless to act. Based on a close scrutiny of the documents the present study has confirmed what was already well enough known (chiefly that the Nazis always said no, and that the Conventions had their limits), but it has been able to nuance and complement the picture in three ways in particular.

The philosophy and traditions of the ICRC

Firstly, the ICRC's philosophy and traditions need to be taken into account. It was a private body, born out of the compassion felt by the Genevan Henri Dunant at the battle of Solferino (1859), and in the

273

1930s and 1940s the ICRC and the Conventions of the Red Cross remained close to their nineteenth-century roots, aiming at attenuating the evils of international war in a society which had a number of values in common and acknowledged no higher reality – in judicial terms – than that of the nation-state. The ICRC derived its strength as a humanitarian organisation from its recognition of this fact and from its observance of strict neutrality towards states at war with each other. It also drew strength from the moral authority it exerted over national Red Cross societies, bodies under the control of their respective countries, especially in time of war, and subject to the principles of national sovereignty. So in the last analysis the ICRC had only one weapon in its armoury when it came to protecting the victims, and that was its credibility in the eyes of all concerned. That credibility in turn depended entirely on its neutrality and on the discretion it observed where nations in conflict were concerned.

But every time hostilities broke out they edged closer to total war, and the ICRC made efforts to adapt. After the wounded or sick combatant, after the POW, there loomed in the 1930s, in the so-called Tokyo project, the civilian alien interned on a belligerent's soil or captured by belligerents in territory occupied by them, and worse, the spectre of civilian populations threatened by gas attack, aerial bombardment and, just around the corner, atomic weapons. The Red Cross went even further, since, without challenging the nation state's sovereignty over its citizens and territory, it embarked in the early 1920s on an internal debate on conflicts which broke out within a country's borders. In the wake of these discussions the ICRC reacted spontaneously to the first complaints about Germans being locked up in concentration camps by the government of the Reich. Even though the term 'civil war' – despite the excesses of the 'brown revolution' – did not strictly speaking apply in this case, it decided that the *Schutzhäftlinge*, or people in preventive detention, fell squarely within its competence, and asked the national Red Cross society, the DRK, to make sure that these men and women were held in decent conditions, that they were properly treated, and that clearly established administrative procedures applied to them. The question, however, was what could be done if a national society failed to cooperate. As early as 1935 the ICRC appeared to have few illusions about this extension of its competence in humanitarian matters, since it concluded that in a case like that, as with opposition coming from a nation-state, it would have to publish the relevant documents, that is bring before the bar of world opinion the defaulting state or national society. Such an appeal to an authority higher than the state heralded a change in Red Cross thinking, but the International Committee was not yet ready to draw all the conclusions that flowed from it, since at no time before 1945 was it to have recourse to this form of action, even after it became crystal clear that the DRK was departing fundamentally from the Red Cross ideal.

The ICRC did not, however, turn a deaf ear to accusations about the concentration camps; it managed in 1935 and 1938 to send one of its members to Germany, but it is open to question who gained most from these missions. The prisoners did not in truth see their lot improve at all. But since Burckhardt and Favre could not but conclude that so far as hygiene, food and housing were concerned, conditions were satisfactory in the camps, the Nazis alone benefited from these visits. This was because the ICRC, while realising that the DRK was becoming increasingly aligned with the regime, was not willing, indeed could not imagine being able, to indict the German Reich or its Red Cross society, fearing both to compromise its neutrality and worsen the detainees' lot. Having given in to the Bolsheviks in the 1920s and to Mussolini in 1931, it bowed to Nazi Germany's conditions, even when they amounted to a denial of the Red Cross's universality, as when Jews were thrown out of the DRK, for example. Like national governments at the time, it was loath to express an opinion about the Third Reich's antisemitism, as that would amount to passing judgement on the regime itself, and giving up on the belief that action on behalf of victims was the movement's sole guiding principle. But since it did not wish to wash its hands of the Jews either and since it refused to accept any limits set by others to what might properly be said to fall within its purview, it was to attend to the Jewish question after 1938 from the point of view of emigration, which was above all the business of governments. So its plans, like those of the League, were to remain as vague and ineffective as those outlined by the Intergovernmental Committee for Refugees, born in 1938 of the otherwise fruitless Evian Conference.

Once war broke out in Europe it is not easy, given such doctrinal and intellectual tendencies, to see how things could have turned out differently. Ever since the warning of Munich, world war had been on the agenda, and war was the Red Cross's real challenge, its true mission, which repositioned it firmly in its tradition and rooted its activities in international Conventions signed and ratified with few exceptions by all belligerents. Two new developments, however, combined to alter fundamentally the angle from which the ICRC had previously viewed its work: on the one hand the lightning victory of the Axis in Europe and the extension of hostilities first to the East, then to the Pacific; on the other, the recourse on a scale never before seen to the taking of hostages and above all to the deportation and imprisonment in the concentration camps of the Reich of enemy civilians guilty or suspected of threatening the security of the occupant's armed forces. So the ICRC was in demand in new theatres of operations; it felt it had to be present there; and it watched the list of non-military victims being extended indefinitely. It feared not only that the task might prove too much for it, but also that its credibility might be undermined, therefore its moral authority over the Red Cross movement, and thus the Red Cross's universality.[1] So worries about its effectiveness were bound up with preoccupations about what was to become of the Red Cross as an idea and an institution wrong-footed by modern warfare and sapped by totalitarianism.

It was in the context of such doubts and anxieties, coming on top of the issue of deportees, that the Jewish question was posed with particular acuteness. The ICRC, as we have shown, enjoyed through its delegates the benefit of several indirect pieces of information and even of eyewitness accounts of the round-ups, the deportations, and the massacres in the East. That it did not at the end of 1941 immediately realise that these terrible events were part of a systematic programme of physical elimination is not in any way surprising or extraordinary. And that the idea of the Final Solution then met with a degree of resistance on its part had, at the institutional level at least, nothing to do with antisemitism: those in charge, and particularly the delegates who were in daily contact with death, showed a remarkable degree of sensitivity to the massacres, especially if one compares it, for example, to the discreet antisemitism of many senior British civil servants. And even if they lacked the imagination to encompass the unimaginable, they did not turn their backs on that reality. The question was, what could they do and where? The internal discussions of 1942 prove that they had abandoned all hope of a legal solution, in any case impossible in time of war, except to raise the issue of the deportation of enemy civilians from occupied territory to the Reich and to bring up again, in the note of 24 September 1942, the Tokyo project and the reciprocity principle. It did not amount to much, since the Jews were not explicitly mentioned and in any case stateless people, or people deprived of their nationality, would have slipped through the net, even if something could have been attempted along these lines. It was, however, a worthwhile gesture, even though there was never any question of giving deportees and victims of racial persecution priority over POWs and civilian internees. So as not to take any risks that might endanger the latter or compromise efforts to help POWs on the Eastern Front, all the démarches on behalf of the former – such as the note of 24 September 1942 or that of 2 October 1944 – were addressed to bodies like the Foreign Ministry or the OKW which ICRC chiefs knew lacked all competence where the camps were concerned. Today it is still not easy to disentangle how far, in arriving at this decision, they were motivated by a fear of spoiling everything by provoking an outright refusal, and how far they were anxious to act effectively by getting material concessions while keeping a low political profile. Unfortunately the ICRC was at fault in never making an in-depth study of the people they were dealing with or the best ways of going about things.

There remained the solution of publishing the relevant documents. It was first considered in 1935 by the Boissier commission and later examined by the ICRC under the watered-down form of an appeal denouncing violations of human rights. With regard to what was going on, that too did not amount to much. But it could have become so, and straightaway too, since Allied propaganda could be relied upon to latch on to the ICRC's gesture, and public opinion would soon have realised that the Reich alone was the focus of this public act of indictment, so in a certain sense it was a solution of last resort, as Gerhart Riegner himself recognised.[2] Thus what stood between him and Burckhardt in the autumn of 1942 was less their assessment of the Final Solution than their analysis of the timing. Notwithstanding the decision of the Plenary Assembly, the highest organ of the ICRC, those in charge rejected the very idea of an appeal for two reasons: the existence of the Conventions, which the Dieppe Raid handcuffs crisis appeared to put in jeopardy, and fears expressed in Berne about the implications for Swiss policy. The first reason is well known: the Vatican too allowed other considerations to temper its denunciation of racial persecution. The other reason is worth pausing over, since its profile has been raised as our research has progressed. So we should look at the diplomatic and political context in which the ICRC found itself, since this is the second factor which, when taken into account, nuances and complements the overall picture.

Toeing the Swiss line

The ICRC sought within this context to influence governments, but it was also influenced by that context and reacted variously to the pressures exerted upon it. For example, Max Huber set great store by the Protestant churches, and among the Jewish organisations Schwarzen-berg did not conceal his preference for the American Jewish Joint Distribution Committee, which provided funds and kept quiet, whereas he felt that the World Jewish Congress sought to act politically. But above all the ICRC looked to national Red Cross societies, and although any illusions it may still have had about the DRK as an institution were rapidly dispelled by the war, the position and the resources of the Swedish Red Cross (which enjoyed governmental support) increased to such an extent that Max Huber felt it was laying claim to equal status with the ICRC.[3] As a neutral country, Sweden, like Switzerland, needed to make its good offices available to the belligerents, even if its neutrality was not of the same kind as Switzerland's, and since it had far fewer Protecting Power mandates than Switzerland, it made the activities of its national Red Cross society one of the key instruments of its humanitarian policy.[4] This can be seen in the case of the aid mission to Greece, in the rescue of the Danish Jews (albeit few in number), and in Bernadotte's intervention in 1945 on behalf of the Scandinavian prisoners in the concentration camps. So, while paying close attention to Swedish initiatives, the ICRC could not ignore Switzerland's attitude; throughout the Second World War relations between Switzerland and the ICRC were at once close (because of the geopolitical situation) and not infrequently difficult. The ICRC's *de jure* and *de facto* independence did not prevent Switzerland intervening directly, if discreetly, either to encourage major initiatives in the national interest, as in the summer of 1940 and 1944, or to urge the ICRC to be careful, as in October 1942 when the public appeal was being discussed. Burckhardt did not question this community of interest – quite the reverse; in 1946 he was after all still writing to federal councillor Max Petitpierre that the ICRC was an institution of crucial importance to Switzerland because at certain moments it had made it possible for their small country to act like a great power. This did not stop him calling for complete freedom of action for the ICRC, which he seemed to believe was enshrined in the existing Conventions. For example, in December 1942 he found it most regrettable that in carrying out its traditional tasks the Red Cross was being made to toe the Swiss line:

In fact the ICRC has a task on which its very existence depends: everything else, practical issues, are purely accessory. This task is to fight for respect of the Conventions. But the Protecting Power is increasingly taking this task away from us. Whereas during the last war, under Mr Ador's courageous chairmanship, the ICRC's tasks and privileges were tirelessly defended, we have always in the present conflict given in to the authorities; Haller's Bureau has turned a blind eye to the ICRC's regrettable and increasing dependence on Berne, something which unfortunately has not escaped the notice of any of the belligerents. The ICRC has suffered an irreparable loss of prestige through being kept out of activities like the exchange of badly wounded POWs, and again in the present instance. Other *ad hoc* institutions are just as capable as we are of communicating lists of POWs or of transporting food supplies. Once lost, moral authority, which the ICRC still possessed at the 1918 Peace Conference, cannot be restored. In my view a policy of always seeking to put the Protecting Power first is pure short-termism, even in the country's own interests, since there will be other conflicts but Switzerland will not always be a Protecting Power. But whatever happens the ICRC ought to continue in being and therefore emerge from the current war strengthened rather than weakened.[5]

Since the Nazis did not reply to the note of 24 September 1942, the ICRC, without calling into question the general instructions given to its delegates, embarked from 1943 onwards on a twin-track aid operation, the first concern being to send food parcels to concentration camps, and the second to target aid more precisely at Jews in countries allied to or satellites of the Reich. In both instances the results were to remain limited, even where the policy of some governments gave grounds for hoping that there would be support at local level for curbing racial persecution. It was only the setting up of the WRB early in 1944 that opened up new possibilities, but the British accorded a higher priority to their Palestine policy than to emigration schemes, and right to the end turned a deaf ear to requests for relaxation of the blockade regulations. The Concentration Camp Food Parcels Scheme only got the full benefit of American generosity in the closing months of the war, at a time when transportation difficulties and the Allied advance into Germany disrupted food shipments from both Gothenburg and Switzerland. The question may therefore be asked why between, on the one hand, the aid operation, derisory from the point of view of the victims of racial persecution in particular, and on the other the public appeal, a weapon of last resort perhaps which the ICRC, under pressure from the Swiss authorities, felt it could not use, no diplomatic initiative was launched that was both worthy of the drama being enacted before everyone's eyes and based on a precise calculation of risks, such as a protest letter to Hitler or Himmler, or better still a mission by Huber or Burckhardt to Berlin or Berchtesgaden. The answer perhaps is that the memory of similar missions by Kurt von Schuschnigg and Emil Hacha caused their nerve to fail. Perhaps, too, the Concentration Camp Food Parcels Scheme subtly put the damper on the search for other kinds of activity by harnessing the energies of those who wished to do something, by imposing specific criteria for success and above all by observing the Red Cross's golden rule that priority should be given everywhere to concrete gestures affording the victim immediate relief rather than to the formulation of general principles or comprehensive demands. Perhaps in choosing between feasible aid and seemingly unrealisable rescue operations the ICRC succumbed not to cowardice or fear but to an excessive respect for its own principles, without asking what they signified in practice, or what new forms its humanitarian policy should take in the particular case of the concentration camps. Finally, it is quite clear today that if it could not do much against Nazi fanaticism in the Reich and the occupied territories, the ICRC could, in the satellite countries or those allied to Hitler, have relied more on well-disposed local people of various kinds in the civil service and the government and taken action earlier and on a wider scale, on the lines for instance of what was achieved in Hungary.

The Allies drag their feet

But if it did not of its own accord do so, or if its will to innovate remained trapped in the manner described in traditional habits of thought, this was perhaps also because in the face of Nazi intransigence it felt that the Allies and the Swiss government gave it little incentive to do much else. This aspect leads on to the third strand of a possible explanation for the failure of the Red Cross to do much to assist Jews suffering persecution at German hands. If this study has not concerned itself directly with the reasons for Allied reticence (to use a euphemism) about the Jewish question, it has shown that this reticence weighed heavily with the ICRC.

As early as 1943 André de Pilar, a Joint Committee delegate and personal friend of Burckhardt's, told Gerhart Riegner that knowing the Red Cross as he did he was sure that so long as the Allies did not officially call upon the ICRC as a neutral institution to concern itself with the Jews in the occupied territories little would be done and the whole issue would get smothered in bureaucracy and paperwork, and stressed that it was absolutely necessary for the Americans, the British and in due course other Allied governments to entrust the international Red Cross with a mission along these lines. He did not know whether the Red Cross could accept such a mission, since the Conventions did not apply to Jews in the occupied territories, but he was certain that without such an Allied démarche the Red Cross 'machine' would never be set in motion at governmental level. Nothing had so far happened: although the British Red Cross and other institutions had raised the matter with the ICRC, they lacked the authority that governments themselves possessed, so he urged Riegner once again to put pressure on them.[6] The origins of the note of 2 October 1944 and the arrangements made for the meeting between Burckhardt and Kaltenbrunner do indeed confirm that the ICRC's restraint was largely dictated by the attitude of Switzerland and of the coalition ranged against Hitler.

The role of the delegates

Now a word about the role played by the delegates: some of them were not only the first to be able to grasp on the ground the significance of what was going on, or at least its immediate consequences, but also, insofar as their resources allowed, to act outside the limits of their instructions and take risks. We have seen how in Berlin, Bucharest, Budapest, Croatia, Italy and Slovakia the more active delegates and those least burdened by duties under the Conventions sought to make use of such room for manoeuvre as already existed at the risk of being officially disavowed by headquarters, but however much we may admire people of this temper we cannot overlook the fact that the sum of individual acts does not constitute a policy. Even before the end of the war the ICRC was aware of this. Jean-Etienne Schwarzenberg, conscious of all that had been attempted, undertaken and achieved, wrote in February 1945 that the ICRC's policy with regard to the Jewish problem had been subtle and therefore difficult to sustain; during the early years of the war it did not consider itself competent to deal with it, and, fearing that too overt a stand might compromise its traditional activities and in particular hamper the work it was doing on behalf of POWs in Germany, instructed its delegates to exercise the greatest prudence and discretion in getting involved with the Jews. As a result some delegates refrained from giving any help at all to Jews within their jurisdiction. This, Schwarzenberg went on, led to people behaving like Born who, during the first part of his stay in Budapest, did as he was told and had nothing to do with the Jews; then, inundated by messages and cables from Geneva and yielding to pressure from Jews on the ground, he went almost too far in the other direction and overreached his powers. Meanwhile Jews abroad were paying close attention to the way the ICRC's attitude was developing, and had gained the impression that, not wishing to campaign actively for their cause, it was playing for time; although it did all in its power to keep its delegations in London and Washington informed of its actions, they were not in a position to give a full explanation of its attitude and in particular of the difficulties it faced. Too many details escaped them; Jewish leaders were keen to discuss these problems with people who, having been closer to Germany and the Axis countries, were fully acquainted with every aspect of the question. These leaders, Schwarzenberg concluded, expected the ICRC to raise its profile in Germany and, since they had considerable clout in Britain and America and were in a position to influence public opinion and that of their national Red Cross societies, they could well get the ICRC into trouble if it did not manage to persuade them that it really was doing all it could.[7]

The moral authority question

So this brings us back to the problem of the moral authority on which, as much as on the Conventions, the ICRC based its activities and in the name of which it felt it necessary to extend its interest to concentration camp prisoners, deportees and victims of racial persecution. But even the material aid it was able to deliver has not succeeded in convincing the world that it had given sufficient proof in this instance of its effectiveness, all the more so because it did not take the supreme risk of throwing the full weight of its moral authority into the scales on behalf of these particular victims. In spite of all the explanations offered, in spite of its satisfaction at having been able to provide some help at least, we have no choice but to recognise that it really should have spoken out. The reasons for this error of judgement appear clearer to us now than they did at the outset. In its way of working, in its methods of analysis, in its political perspective, the ICRC was by then out of phase with the ideological struggle that was what World War II was really about. The institution and the ideal were thwarted and the limitations inherent in the ability of their instruments to cope were exposed.

The importance the ICRC attached to its credibility took it paradoxically down a road that led to a loss of credibility and therefore of authority within the Red Cross movement and in the wider world. The political instruments needed to carry out the mission were seen to fall short both of the attachment to principles and of the will to act. The ICRC was an apolitical institution facing a totalitarian state, a situation new to it despite the Soviet and Italian precedents, and it was no more adept than anyone else at the time in grasping the fundamental changes brought about by the Third Reich in international relations, including humanitarian affairs, and in the role of law in national and international society. It tried to counter the challenge to its liberal values by intensifying its own neutrality, but it was not entirely immune from Swiss chauvinism in time of war, nor from the way people tended in moments of crisis to fall back on the most conservative features of the Red Cross tradition. And finally, in the practice of international humanitarian law, faced with appeals from victims who were juridically innominate, the ICRC habitually sought not ways of getting things done but instead reasons for doing nothing, so as not to undermine the missions carried out under the auspices of the Conventions upon which, in its eyes, its very existence depended.

Biographical notes: who was who in the ICRC

1. Max Huber (1874–1960)

Born into a Protestant patrician family in Zurich, Huber was for many years chairman of two large companies, Maschinenfabrik Oerlikon and Alusuisse. He held the Chair of International Public Law at the University of Zurich for some twenty years, and wrote several landmark works of scholarship. As legal adviser to the Swiss government's Political Department he drafted a number of key opinions on, for example, neutrality and on the entry of the Confederation into the League of Nations. In that capacity he was asked to undertake diplomatic missions of some delicacy. In 1922 he was elected to the International Court of Justice in the Hague and presided over it from 1924 to 1927. He joined the ICRC in 1923 and became its chairman in 1928, remaining in that post until the end of 1944 despite increasing ill health. A few weeks after his retirement from that office he was recalled to deputise for Burckhardt (see below) when the latter was appointed Swiss ambassador in Paris. Huber was widely respected, both as a legal authority of international reputation and as chairman of the ICRC, for his moral integrity and his intellect, as evidenced by the award of ten honorary doctorates, including one in theology from Zurich. He was a man of deep religious faith, from which he drew the strength to cope with sickness, disappointments, anxiety caused by his wife's prolonged depressive illness, and worries about the spread of violence, totalitarianism and materialism in the world.

In politics he was a member of the Liberal-Democratic party and sat on the Grand Council of his canton during the 1914–18 war. In the 1930s his conservatism, deep patriotism, and belief in a strong and righteous community led him to incline towards the then fashionable ideas of national renewal, to the point where he sometimes speculated publicly whether an authoritarian state, on the lines at least of the aristocratic tradition of the old Confederation, was not to some extent, from the point of view of Gospel teaching, the sole legitimate one. He therefore embraced the ideology of national spiritual defence, based on three tenets: the safeguarding of neutrality, the defence of institutions, and the exercise of Christian charity. Although keen to see these embodied in concrete action, he was modest about the importance of his own role in achieving this. Modesty sprang, too, from great caution: Huber was a person given to reflection, even to meditation, rather than a man of action, preferring decisions arrived at after the most careful thought and the weighing of all the pros and cons. Recklessness was never his defining characteristic. He was, someone close to him said, a man who hoped always to unravel Gordian knots rather than be forced to cut through them.

2. Carl J. Burckhardt (1891–1974)

Born in Basel, the last male of an old and famous line, Burckhardt could be said to have lived several lives, usually concurrently. He began his career in Vienna, where he served from 1918 to 1922, and occupied a series of important and even dangerous posts. For instance, he served as League of Nations high commissioner in Danzig on the approach of war, and in 1945 was entrusted with the task of re-establishing traditional friendly relations between the Swiss Confederation and the French Republic. He was also a writer and historian who enjoyed (especially through his biography of Richelieu) a reputation which extended well beyond the university institutions he taught at (first Zurich and then Geneva).

His work in the Red Cross made full use of his diplomatic experience and personal skills. In 1923 he was sent by the Red Cross as an observer when war broke out between Greece and Turkey, and joined the ICRC itself ten years later. His role on it during the Second World War was preeminent: he was in fact its president in all but name, and was the natural successor to Max Huber when the latter finally stood down; only his appointment as ambassador to Paris prevented his taking up the post.

His was a complex, even contradictory personality: he displayed both intellectual arrogance and tireless curiosity; he was both reserved, intimidating even, and keen on (and good at) dealing with people face to face; and he could swing from doubt and hesitation to brazen assurance. By nature an intellectual and writer, a worrier, prey to world-weariness, even depression, he was propelled by circumstance into activity on a number of fronts, first in Danzig, and then during the war in Geneva, where he had to deal with people and with a vision of the world that represented the antithesis of all he believed in and stood for.

Contemporaries had nothing but praise for his lucidity, perspicacity and far-sightedness. But he was at bottom a pessimist with a 'catastrophist' view of history; in theory a liberal, he was in practice a conservative, hostile to progress and mechanisation, so that despite his Basel origins and his cosmopolitanism he shared the social and political apprehensions of the Geneva bourgeoisie who made up the ICRC. Moreover, his culture was Germanic and French – he had studied at Basel, Munich, Göttingen and Paris, and his years in Vienna exerted a particularly powerful influence on him – but he had never studied in England and had only a superficial understanding of the British. The antipathy was reciprocated: he had few friends at the Foreign Office, where his stock stood fairly low throughout the war, largely because his essentially Eurocentric view of the world led him for a long time to overestimate the chances of a German victory, a misconception he shared, it is true, with the majority of the Swiss establishment, the Federal Council, army chiefs, senior diplomats and top civil servants. But if the ICRC's thinking, like that of Switzerland itself, sometimes suffered a timelag with regard to events and especially in its tendency to judge the Second World War in terms of the First, Burckhardt read signs of change before many others did, although he never saw them as changes for the better.

Burckhardt was easy-going, charming, and by no means indifferent to the honours associated with the posts he held. As League of Nations high commissioner in Danzig, for instance, he was invited by the Germans as guest of honour at the 1937 Nazi Party Congress, but was unable to attend. The same supple person was made an honorary member of the Weizmann Institute after the war, as a reward for his efforts as head of the ICRC – the citation said – 'to bring succour to populations in distress, especially the Jewish people'.

3. Edouard de Haller (1897–1982)

Edouard de Haller was born at Cologny (Geneva) of a patrician Protestant family which had been part of the Berne bourgeoisie since the sixteenth century and had produced many remarkable people, most notably the famous scientist Albert de Haller; Edouard's father, a Geneva engineer, had been among other things delegate-chairman of Conrad Zschokke SA and chairman of the Société Générale pour l'Industrie Electrique, while his mother, née Mallet, belonged to a family that had been part of the Genevan bourgeoisie since 1566 and had fanned out over France, Britain and the United States. Edouard's wife, née Bonna, came from a mainly banking family that had been part of the Genevan bourgeoisie since the seventeenth century, and during the war his brother-in-law Pierre Bonna was, as head of the Foreign

Affairs Division of the Political Department, Switzerland's top diplomat. After studying law at the universities of Geneva and Zurich, Edouard was first appointed secretary of the presidency of the Council of the Port and Waterways of the Free City of Danzig, then general-secretary of the joint Greco-Turkish commission for the exchange of populations. In 1926 he became a League of Nations civil servant and worked in the Mandates Section, which he headed from 1938 to 1940. In 1941 he became a member of the ICRC and shortly afterwards honorary member as a result of his appointment in January 1942 as delegate of the Conseil fédéral aux œuvres d'entraide internationale in Berne. In 1948, the same year as he represented Switzerland at the seventeenth International Red Cross Conference, he took charge of the Swiss legation in Oslo, moving on to become Swiss minister in the USSR in 1953 and ambassador to the Netherlands in 1957. He was a first lieutenant in the army and member of several traditional clubs for good Genevan families such as the Société de lecture and the Cercle de la Terrasse.

4. (Renée-)Marguerite Frick-Cramer (1887–1963)

A member of the ICRC from 1918 to 1946, then honorary member, Mme Frick came from a family that had been part of the Genevan bourgeoisie since 1668; in fact, she was related to seven other members of the ICRC. After studies in Geneva and Paris leading to a law degree, she did a Ph.D. in history and was for a time assistant lecturer at the University of Geneva; in her publications she concentrated particularly on the principle of nationalities. She headed the Agreement Services section of the POW Agency from 1914 to 1918, and was the ICRC's representative at (among others) the 1929 diplomatic conference.

5. Jacques Chenevière (1886–1979)

A member of the ICRC from 1919 to 1959, vice-president from 1950 to 1952, and honorary vice-president from 1959 onwards, Chenevière came from a mainly banking family that had been part of the Genevan bourgeoisie since 1631. Born in Paris, he did a literature degree at the Sorbonne and became a writer, gaining a number of prizes for his fiction and poetry. During the First World War he worked in the Central POW Agency and headed it from 1939 to 1945.

6. Suzanne Ferrière (1886–1970)

A member of the ICRC (in succession to her uncle Frédéric Ferrière) from 1924 to 1951, and honorary member thereafter, Mlle Ferrière came from a predominately clerical family that had been part of the Genevan bourgeoisie since 1788, and devoted her life to social work; she was particularly active in the Union internationale de secours aux enfants, and also held until 1945 the post of secretary-general of the International Migration Service, and for ten years thereafter served as deputy director of its successor body, the Service social international.

7. Edouard Chapuisat (1874–1955)

A member of the ICRC from 1938 to 1955 (when he was succeeded by his nephew Guillaume Bordier) and vice-president from 1946 to 1947, Chapuisat belonged to an old Vaudois family. He studied law in Geneva, Paris and Berlin, qualified as a barrister, and became chief executive of Geneva city council. He then turned to contemporary history and a career in journalism. He was editor-in-chief of the *Journal de Genève* from 1918 to 1933 before becoming a lecturer and writer of books on history. He was a colonel and chief auditor of the First Division. He sat on the Genevan Grand Council as a member of the National Democratic party (liberal right) from 1913 to 1952 and in 1932 became president of the parliament of the canton of Geneva.

8. Johannes E. von Schwarzenberg, aka Jean-Etienne Schwarzenberg (1903–1978)

A wartime volunteer in the service of the ICRC. Sometimes called 'the Prince' on account of his delicate features and thin moustache, Schwarzenberg was born into a noble Austro-Swiss family which counted among its members Franz Joseph I's chancellor. While still young he gained a doctorate in law and embarked on a long career in the Austrian diplomatic service, serving in Vienna, Rome and Berlin before the war and Rome, London and the Vatican afterwards. He carried out a number of humanitarian missions on behalf of the Food and Agriculture Organisation and the Order of Malta in the 1960s before retiring in 1969. He had just taken up a new post in Brussels in 1938 when news of the Anschluss reached him, and he at once left government service; on being repatriated to Switzerland two years later he put himself at the ICRC's disposal, working first as head of the translation service, then taking responsibility for civilian internees before, at the end of 1942, being put in charge of the Jewish question under Suzanne Ferrière's direction. While he never forgot the war years and his work for humanitarian causes, he experienced periods of discouragement, threatening in February 1944 to resign, feeling demoralised both by an awareness of his own limitations and by the impossibility of overcoming the obstacles in the path of his mission. There were, however, compensations, such as the moving moment when the first chits signed by concentration camp detainees reached Geneva, acknowledging receipt of the parcels they had been sent.

9. Other members of the ICRC (as of spring 1942; dates in parentheses indicate year of election to the Committee)

(i) Full members

Frédéric Barbey-Ador, former Swiss minister in Belgium (1915)

Paul des Gouttes, doctor of law, barrister (1918)

Paul Logoz, doctor of law, professor of criminal law at the University of Geneva, general staff colonel (1921)

Rodolphe de Haller, banker (1924), treasurer

Dr G. E. Audeoud, colonel, former Swiss army divisional medical officer (1925)

Dr Georges Patry, colonel, former Swiss army divisional medical officer (1929)

Mlle Lucie Odier, former head of the Service des infirmières-visiteuses de la Croix-Rouge genevoise (1930)

Franz de Planta, colonel (1930)

Guillaume Favre, divisional colonel (1932)

Heinrich Zangger, doctor of medicine, honorary professor at the University of Zurich (1932)

Jacques-Barthélemy Micheli, engineer (1935)

Georges Wagnière, doctor of law, former Swiss minister in Rome (1936)

Paul-E. Martin, doctor of letters, professor of history at the University of Geneva (1937)

Mlle Renée Bordier, former head nurse at 'Bon Secours' (1938)

Dr Alec Cramer, colonel (1938)

Martin Bodmer (1940)

Philippe Etter, federal councillor, president of the Swiss Confederation (1940)

Albert Lombard, banker (1942)

(ii) Honorary members

Edmond Boissier, colonel (1914)

Lucien Cramer, doctor of law (1921)

Appendix

Document I

Anonymous, undated (though from internal evidence c. October–November 1939; see note 12 to chapter 2 above).

The resettlement of the Jews

The evacuation of the Jews from the Reich began on 17 October this year. It was ordered by Heinrich Himmler, *Reichsführer-SS* and Chief of the German Police. The evacuation is proceeding in the following three stages:
1) evacuation from the Protectorate of Bohemia and Moravia,
2) evacuation from the East March (Austria),
3) evacuation from the Old Reich.

The Jewish communities of the various districts have been forced to take over the task of *actively* carrying out this evacuation, that is, they are having to organise and finance it themselves. To this end they have sent out circulars to the members of the communities, with the prior agreement of the Gestapo head-quarters in Mährisch-Ostrau, which is headed by Detective Superintendent Eichmann of the Gestapo. Mährisch-Ostrau is the central point from which deportations from all four districts of the German Reich to Poland are organised.

The following groups of persons are involved: approximately 150,000 Jews from the Protectorate, approx. 65,000 from Vienna, approx. 30,000 from Poznań and West Prussia and about 20,000 from the Old Reich.

In general it has been decreed that every deportee may take a maximum of 300 Reichsmarks, should he be in possession of this much. Any remaining assets must be left behind and will be automatically liquidated. This applies equally to personal belongings and furniture, business equipment and stock, and also to houses and land.

Deportees are to be told officially that they are being taken to retraining or resettlement camps. In actual fact, the first transportations (they have not yet begun in the Old Reich) went to Nisko-on-the-San in Eastern Poland, to the south-east of Lublin. There some of the deportees have been interned in villages which were partially destroyed in the war and some in camps surrounded by barbed wire. In both instances the deportees have to build or restore their quarters themselves. Because the San forms the border between German and Soviet interests, the area along the banks is also sealed off by barbed-wire fences in order to prevent flight to Russia.

Polish, German and Ukrainian inhabitants of all villages and towns in this area will be evacuated within the next months so that before long there will be a vast reservation, about 80–100 square kilometres in size, occupied solely by Jews. It will be completely surrounded by barbed wire and be under the permanent control of SS groups. After the new, reduced state of Poland has been founded, in the form of a protectorate, the area is to be overseen by official bodies of the new state of Poland.

At the same time as the Jews are being deported from the German Reich, there will be forced resettlement of the $1\frac{1}{2}$ million Polish-born Jews now living in Poland to the same reservation. *The whole resettlement programme is to be completed by 1 April 1940.* Deportations have already taken place from both new Reichsgaus, above all from Gdynia, Grudziadz, Toruń, Poznań and Katowice. From Vienna at least 2,000 men, women and children are to be deported every week, but the second transport at the end of October this year only contained about 1,400 persons, because many Jews escaped deportation by means of flight or suicide. Between 20 October and 2 November 1939, eight-two Jews in Vienna alone committed suicide, among them thirty-six women.

The enclosed documents give more details and information about the method of deportation.

Document II

Memo from the American consul, Paul C. Squire, about his interview with Carl J. Burckhardt, 7 November 1942

STRICTLY CONFIDENTIAL

MEMORANDUM

Interview with Dr. Carl J. Burckhardt
11:30 a.m. November 7, 1942
re *Jewish Persecutions*

Following my receipt of more than one report that Hitler had issued a written order for the extermination of the Jews when, at the suggestion of the Honorable Leland Harrison, I asked Dr. Carl Burckhardt, distinguished member of the International Committee of the Red Cross, whether he was in a position to confirm the existence of such an order, he replied that while he had not actually seen the order he could confirm to me *privately and not for publication* as follows: that Hitler at the beginning of 1941 signed an Order that before the end of 1942 Germany *must be free of all Jews*. He emphasised that his information came independently from two 'very well informed Germans' in whom he allowed me to understand that he placed unlimited confidence. (Note: there is an intimation that the two sources are (1) an official of the German Ministry of Foreign Affairs and (2) an official of the German Ministry of War, at Berlin.)

I then asked him whether the word *extermination*, or its equivalent, was employed, to which he replied that the words *must be Juden-frei* (free of Jews) were utilised. He then made it clear that since there is no place to send these Jews and since the territory must be cleared of this race, it is obvious what the net result would be.

Dr. Burckhardt attempted to obtain information from the German Red Cross representative who visited Geneva about three weeks ago by requesting 'verbally but officially' news regarding the situation of the Jews. To which question the response came that nobody in Germany knows the real situation, but it is in any case greatly exaggerated. Dr. Burckhardt commented that this was the only sort of reply that the representative could afford to make.

Dr. Burckhardt, who deals with External Affairs in the International Committee of the Red Cross, informed me that it was his plan to direct a public appeal throughout the world on the question of the Jews and hostages and that

293

the matter was discussed at a full meeting (about 24 present) of the International Committee on October 14, 1942. It was decided, however, that such an appeal (1) would serve no purpose, rendering the situation even more difficult and (2) would jeopardise all the work undertaken for the prisoners of war and civil internees – the real task of the Red Cross.

I then inquired whether any sort of intervention by the Red Cross had been made, to which Dr. Burckhardt referred to the Committee's pronouncement on September 22, 1942 to the effect that (translated from French) 'we are unable to envisage an intervention in the various countries at war with Germany if we are not able to act precisely in the same manner in Germany and in the territories controlled by her for the benefit of the *political* prisoners or evacuees.'

On October 30, 1942, the Red Cross, added Dr. Burckhardt, made an intervention in the following sense (translated from French): 'When the German Red Cross, the OKW (German Army High Command), and the German Ministry of Foreign Affairs requested that the Red Cross intervene to go visit the German internees retained not as *civil* internees but as *political* internees in the countries of South America, the Committee replied yes . . . but only when we can occupy ourselves in Germany and in the occupied countries with persons arrested or deported for political reasons.' The reference to 'arrested or deported for political reasons' obviously embraces the Jews.

Paul C. Squire
American Consul

American Consulate,
Geneva, Switzerland

November 9, 1942

Document III

Annex to an ICRC note drafted by Jean-Etienne Schwarzenberg and signed by Roger Gallopin; dated 23 September 1942, it was intended for Roland Marti to use as a basis for a verbal démarche at the German Ministry of Foreign Affairs (see p. 65 above).

Notice

The authorities of the Reich have on numerous occasions drawn the attention of the International Committee of the Red Cross to the situation of German citizens who have been arrested for reasons of security in countries at war with Germany and who are being detained by judicial or police authority. Every time the Germans have expressed such worries we have instructed our delegates in the enemy country in question to intervene and try to improve the position of the detainees. These prisoners are not covered by the statute governing the treatment of civil internees. In both the United States and Great Britain we have been allowed to visit police internees and inspect their place of internment. We hope to be able to follow a similar procedure in Latin American countries such as Brazil and Venezuela which have recently entered the war.

The International Committee of the Red Cross has every intention of continuing and extending this practice, especially as it conforms well with traditional practices of the Red Cross and the mandate given it by the conferences of the International Red Cross. It would be happy to be of assistance to the Reich authorities if its services are ever required again in similar cases.

Our actions in this matter are based on our aim of working together with the imprisoning country in order to achieve the same advantages for this group of persons as were achieved for civil internees by the extension of the 1929 agreement on the treatment of prisoners of war to cover them. These advantages were also provided for by the Tokyo Plan, which was agreed to by all the delegates from the governments and Red Cross Organisations taking part in the conference. In the course of the present conflict the Foreign Office has said it is prepared to abide by the rules of the plan, as long as this is done by both sides.

We are receiving requests from areas under German occupation which relate to foreigners who have been taken prisoner by the Germans and which are exactly analogous to those cases mentioned above which have been put to us by the German Reich. The government of the Reich will certainly understand that our present world-wide policy is largely made possible by observing the principle of mutuality. By making our services available to all parties in a war in the same way and to the same extent, we have managed to gain trust, and this has allowed us access to all victims of war without prejudice. And it is for this reason that we feel we can and must approach the Foreign Office on behalf of all those foreigners arrested in occupied territory who have either been interned there or transported to Germany without, in the majority of cases, any information being given as to their whereabouts or their situation.

We should like to make the following requests in this connection to the Foreign Office:

1. We should be most grateful to receive individual details about the present whereabouts of interned and imprisoned persons and those who have been deported from their home country, so that their relatives, and in some cases members of the general public who are concerned for their safety, could be given information.

2. Would it be possible to allow these persons to contact their families? If correspondence in the normal way is not considered possible, perhaps the possibility of their receiving forms to fill in, similar to the cards approved for prisoners of war, might be considered.

3. Could the relatives of these persons as well as the national Red Cross societies be allowed to send packages to them?

4. Could the delegates of the ICRC be given the opportunity to visit these persons from time to time? This is particularly recommended for the reason given above (visits to Germans interned in enemy countries).

It seems to us that this assistance is of particular importance in view of the fact that the German Red Cross has just informed us it is no longer in a position to conduct individual inquiries about these persons, though we receive large numbers of requests from relatives in the various countries to carry out just such inquiries.

The ICRC has felt able to state its position in this matter because it has great faith in the help and understanding which the Reich authorities have always shown towards it. Furthermore, its absolute neutrality means it has a duty to apply the same rules and guidelines in all countries and under all circumstances, and always to ask for the same assistance in its work.

Document IV

Written from the section 'Interior II' of the German Ministry of Foreign Affairs and addressed to Heinrich Müller, head of the Gestapo (see p. 111 above).

Berlin W 35
Rauchstrasse 11
13 July 1943

Dear *Gruppenführer*,

The British government has approached the government of the Reich through Switzerland to ask whether permission could be granted for 5,000 Jewish children to leave the Reich's administrative area and the occupied Eastern territory and emigrate to Palestine. The British government has also asked to be informed of the Reich's position on whether Jewish children might be permitted to leave occupied territory to the West.

This matter has been discussed between the Foreign Minister and the *Reichsführer-SS* and I have been instructed to prepare the following answer:

In principle, the government of the Reich is willing to negotiate. Exit permits will be granted, possibly in exchange for internees, but emigration to Palestine will not be allowed. The basic condition is that the children must be taken to England and that this agreement must be sanctioned by the English House of Commons.

Discussion of this matter in the Foreign Office is nearly complete, so the draft answer to Switzerland can be got ready within the next few days.

I shall be in contact with you very soon to tell you how the matter is progressing. But it seemed desirable to give you this information now. The proposed answer is intended to put Great Britain in the uncomfortable position of having to take in 5,000 Jewish children, with all the unpleasant consequences of this situation, or else to meet with reprobation because the intended emigration has failed owing to British opposition. In addition, the answer will serve to confirm the Arabs in their view that the Axis powers are pursuing an honest and friendly policy towards them. And even if it seems extremely unlikely that England will accept our condition, it is nevertheless not impossible that there might one day be an exchange of Jewish children for German internees. Such an exchange would certainly need to be prepared for in good time by the Reich's Security Office.

Heil Hitler!

Document V

Report from Dr Max von Wyss to the Joint Aid Commission (CMS), 14 April 1943 (see p. 143 above).

Jews: Reliable information about number and place of residence not available. Ghettos apparently still exist in Warsaw and Cracow (Weihrauch). The latter is being 'reorganised', i.e. the inhabitants are being taken from their present locations to a camp. Most of them are being used for the weapons industry and other jobs. Because of the 'reorganisation' it was not possible to give them their 16 per cent share of the earlier delivery of supplies. Driving in the vicinity of Cracow recently we met a column of Jews, both men and women, perhaps 400–500 of them, who were being taken back from their work to the camp by policemen.

Locals give the approximate number of Jews as: Kielce, earlier 15,000–20,000, now about 1,000; Radom, earlier 30,000, now about 3,000.

Herr Hartmann asks that parcels of supplies for Jews or portions of other larger consignments intended for them should in future be kept in Geneva. He says that their safe delivery by the DRK [German Red Cross] cannot be guaranteed because of the 'reorganisation'. I have the impression that the whole Jewish question – a definite 'noli me tangere' – is causing serious concern to the authorities and the DRK.

Document VI

Letter from Ernst Grawitz, acting head of the German Red Cross to Carl J. Burckhardt, 7 July 1942 (see p. 163 above).

Your letter of 1 June has given me a great deal to think about. You know how important I consider the work of the International Committee of the Red Cross and how this makes me sympathise with any worries you have concerning your role as intermediary and provider of aid, especially in connection with the events you mention in the Netherlands. I can fully understand your concern. And indeed it would be completely justified even if you were not afraid that there might be serious consequences for our German compatriots.

I am afraid that my present knowledge of this particular question is not sufficient to enable me to give you an answer at the moment which would satisfy all parties. Nevertheless, like you, I very much hope that any deterioration in the position or outlook of my compatriots can be avoided, because measures of this sort always tend to provoke retaliations, especially as there is clearly a difference between the duties of the German officials in an occupied territory such as the Netherlands and the treatment of civil internees, for whom an exact system of treatment has been agreed upon.

We are most grateful to the International Committee of the Red Cross for the improvements in the prisoners' lot which it has managed to bring about on any number of occasions, thanks to its inexhaustible efforts. So I am sure you will believe how sorry I am, in view of this, not to be able to offer effective intervention by the German Red Cross in connection with the events you describe in your letter. I ask you to accept that it was only because of unavoidable military necessity that those responsible took the measures they did and that, in the face of such necessity, even aspects of particular importance to us have to take second place.

Document VII

Mgr. Tiso to Max Huber, 10 January 1945 (see p. 195 above).

The President of the Slovak Republic

Bratislava, 10 January 1945

Professor Max Huber
President of the International Committee of the Red Cross

Dear Professor Huber,

On 2 January 1945 Mr Georges Dunand, the delegate of the International Committee of the Red Cross, handed me your letter, in which you ask me to state my position on the Jewish question in Slovakia. I am happy to respond to your request; there are quite a number of points I should like to make.

The solution of the Jewish question in Slovakia, which manifested itself in the removal of economic and social rights from the Jewish element, was a correction of the disproportionately large influence which the Jews had in this respect as an advantaged element under both the Hungarian and Czech governments, to the disadvantage of the native Slovak population. Their influence seems to have arisen from the imbalance between the prosperity of the Jews and that of the Slovaks. Because a Jewish minority of 80,000 had 38 per cent of the national income, the 2.5 million Slovaks, together with people of other nationalities, were forced to make do with the remainder. Thus the Jews in Slovakia were a privileged social class and when the Slovakian people took over the government of their country, they saw no reason to protect the rights and positions the Jews had acquired. In this context it is important not to forget the political role played by the Jews in Slovakia as supporters of government policy – until 1918 that of the Magyars, and then after 1918 and until 1939 that of the Czechs – which was directed against the Slovakian people. In general it would be true to say that until then the Jews were more ready to identify themselves with the Hungarians, or the Czechs and the Germans, than the Slovaks, both in census and vote. Thus they indicated that it was their choice to remain a foreign element among the Slovak people. This fact puts the Jewish question in Slovakia in a particular local and political perspective.

After 1939 the Slovak state, for obvious reasons, put a stop to the stream of Slovakian émigrés, which has amounted to 70 per cent of all Czechoslovakian emigration during the existence of the Czechoslovak Republic, and guaranteed every one of its people the essential conditions of their existence, even if this had to happen at the expense of the Jewish element.

The exclusion of the Jewish element from Slovak life manifested itself in numerous ways. Above all, the Slovak government allowed some Jews to leave Slovakia of their own free will. Others were made expatriates and were evacuated. The government regarded these measures as justified because many of the Jews had entered Slovakia only a few years before from a number of different European countries – from Poland during the First World War and from Hungary after the defeat of the Communist Revolution of Béla Kun by Horthy in 1920. There was a further large influx of Jews into Slovakia in the years 1933–39 from Germany.

Of those Jews who remained Slovakian citizens, many were allowed to stay in their normal jobs, while others were legally restricted as to the occupations they could carry out. These latter were concentrated according to the relevant laws and they were given the opportunity to do non-professional jobs in factories they ran themselves.

I gave concessions to many Jews, some with the effect that they would not be regarded by the law as Jews and others which allowed them to stay in their posts and professions, some of them even as civil servants and in other public offices.

There was a big change in the Jewish question in Slovakia as a result of the partisan uprising in the months of August, September and October 1944. The majority of free Jews left their workplaces and those who were in concentration camps left their camps and joined the partisans. Thus they joined the enemies of the Slovak state.

And thus during the battles against the partisans there were several interventions by the German army, who for security reasons did not want any enemies – whether actual or potential – to remain and for this reason deported not only a large number of Jews from Slovakia but also Slovaks, both military and civilian persons. The Slovak government protested but until now has not been able to obtain the return of all these people from Germany.

In view of the fact that Slovakia has become a zone of operations, the deciding factor in whether such regrettable attacks occur in the future is simply the question of whether a particular sector holds the position of ally or enemy.

Finally, it must be admitted that the solution of the Jewish question in Slovakia did in certain cases cause tangible invasions of individual liberty. It was the honest intention of the Slovak government to prevent or to alleviate the effects of such occurrences. But it must be understood that they resulted from the war, which always gives rise to much harsher social, political and economic problems both between and within nations than would arise in a time of peace.

But the plain truth of the matter is that we tried to be as humane as circumstances permitted in the solution to the Jewish question.

I would ask you to regard the contents of this letter as confidential. My very best wishes to the International Committee of the Red Cross for its work and to you yourself as its president.

Document VIII

Note by Gerhart Riegner about his debriefing on 9 November 1944 of the ICRC's delegate in Hungary, Robert Schirmer (see p. 249 above).

On 18 October after the new foreign minister had given his famous speech, Dr Schirmer and Herr Born managed to obtain an interview with him. They were apparently the first people to be allowed to meet him. Dr Schirmer has given a very colourful description of their meeting with the foreign minister, who was dressed in a green uniform shirt and wore a revolver in a holster; Schirmer had thought he was the doorman. He continually addressed them as 'Comrade Schirmer' and 'Comrade Born'. They spoke out very forcefully during this meeting. Knowing that the only way to deal with gangsters was to use the methods of gangsters, they simply bluffed. They told the new foreign minister about the CICR and the Geneva Convention and described what was stated in the Convention. They made all sorts of demands which legally were quite without basis. Because the foreign minister had no idea what the Geneva Convention was, he fell for all this and believed everything they told him about it. They told him the treatment of Jews was an absolute 'disgrace' and that the rules of the Convention must be kept and that they would on no account tolerate that persons and buildings under their protection should be in any way subjected to harassment. They threatened that there would otherwise be serious international complications. The foreign minister then promised to comply and said there would be no more persecution of the Jews.

And in fact instructions were immediately issued to the effect that the status of buildings under the CICR's protection was to be respected as were documents of safe-conduct issued by the CICR or foreign missions in Budapest. On 19 October they saw the minister of the interior again and also put their views to him most emphatically. At this meeting they managed to extract promises of protection for the Jewish Senate, saying they needed it for their work. They simply maintained that the work of the Jewish Senate was allowed in all other countries.

Document IX

Note drafted by Jean-Etienne Schwarzenberg and enclosed with Max Huber's letter to Joachim von Ribbentrop, 2 October 1944 (see p. 253 above).

Geneva, 2 October 1944
Metropole Hotel

To: The Foreign Ministry
Wilhelmstrasse 74/76
Berlin

Because there was no protection officially recognised under international law for civilians living during a war in enemy states, the Tokyo plan* was formulated in the period of time between the World Wars. The plan represents a substantial step forward in the treatment of this particular category of citizen of an enemy country. Unfortunately this plan, which the German government[†] said at the start of the war formed the basis for an agreement, could not be put into practice. Though the powers at war have not agreed to give residents who are citizens of the enemy country all the advantages the Tokyo plan had envisaged, they have, during this present conflict, at least consented from the start to give them treatment analogous to that of prisoners of war in the sense of the 1929 Convention.

However, treatment based on the Convention's rulings for prisoners of war was not accorded to the category known as political detainees (*Shutzhäftlinge*); these are civilians whose internment is not merely the result of their belonging to an enemy state. The International Committee of the Red Cross, however, has never stopped trying to obtain for civilians in this category a form of treatment analogous to that given to the type of civil internees mentioned above.

It is usually in occupied territory that the internment of such persons or their transfer to the country of the occupying power takes place. Whatever the reasons for this, the following minimum guarantees of safety and acceptable treatment of foreign political detainees, regardless of nationality or place of internment, should be regarded as absolutely essential:

---

* 'Projet de Convention internationale concernant la condition et la protection des civils de nationalité ennemie que se trouvent sur le territoire d'un belligérant ou sur un territoire occupé par lui.'
[†] Foreign Office, R29347 of 30 November 1939.

a) Release of detainees' names, place of internment, state of health; communication of news between detainees and their relatives.
b) Permission for them to receive gifts in the form of food, clothing, medicines and books.
c) Permission for a neutral organisation such as the International Committee of the Red Cross to visit the detainees in order to make sure their circumstances are acceptable as regards accommodation, food, hygiene and general treatment.
d) The right, if legal measures are to be taken against detainees, to know the charge and to have their case dealt with as rapidly as possible

In the present circumstances the growing numbers of civilians who are imprisoned and separated from home and country deserve the particular care and support of the International Committee of the Red Cross. Thus the International Committee believes it must leave no stone unturned in obtaining permission to perform the same tasks for these detainees as it does in countries at war for prisoners of war and civil internees.

Thus the International Committee requests that the appropriate authorities of the Reich be kind enough to grant at least the following points as soon as possible:

1. The delegates of the International Committee of the Red Cross shall be allowed to visit concentration camps and other places of detention both within the German Reich and in occupied areas where non-German political detainees are held.
2. The International Committee of the Red Cross shall be allowed, on the basis of needs thus established by its delegates, to distribute food, clothing and medicines to these detainees.
3. Lists shall be supplied to the International Committee of the Red Cross containing the names and addresses of these detainees.

The International Committee of the Red Cross wishes to emphasise once more that these suggestions, urgent though they are, only represent a minimum of those concessions granted to civil internees in countries at war. It trusts, therefore, that the authorities of the German Reich will agree to them and requests that an answer be given as soon as possible.

Document X

Note dated 22 April 1945 by Otto Lehner about his meeting in Prague on 6 April with Erwin Weinemann, head of the SS in the Protectorate of Bohemia-Moravia, and Adolf Eichmann, Himmler's plenipotentiary in all matters concerning the Jews (see p. 268 above).

At a reception held in Hradschin I had the opportunity to talk to these two men until late at night and to discuss the various problems. What the International Committee of the Red Cross particularly wanted information about was not really the living conditions and amenities of the Theresienstadt ghetto so much as whether the ghetto was simply a transit camp for the Jews and to what extent deportation to the East (Auschwitz) had taken place. As I discovered while in the Theresienstadt ghetto, the camp's representative, Dr Eppstein, an elder of the Jews, had himself, along with many others, been deported to Auschwitz. So I asked Dr Weinemann directly when the deportations had occurred and what their extent was. Dr Weinemann replied that the last deportations to Auschwitz had taken place 6 months before. They involved 10,000 Jews. They were employed to work on further extensions to the Auschwitz camp, he said, and were mainly working in the camp administration. Some were being used as trench-diggers in the East. I asked whether there was any remaining communication between these people and Theresienstadt, to which he replied that there was not. He also said he knew nothing further about their fate, adding that they had probably been taken by the Russians who had advanced into the region. Their transfer had not been at his command, he maintained; he received his orders from higher up.

In the course of the evening, Eichmann developed his theories about the Jewish question. According to him, the Jews in Theresienstadt were in a much better position as regards food and medical care than many ethnic Germans. He maintained that Theresienstadt was the creation of *Reichsführer-SS* Himmler, who wanted to give the Jews in the ghetto there the opportunity to create a community, under Jewish leadership, with almost complete autonomy. He said that in this way the Jews were to be given a sense of national community. The Jews of Therensienstadt were to be transported later to some area where they would live separately from the German people.

As regards the overall problem of the Jews, Eichmann maintained that Himmler was in favour of humane methods. He himself was not completely in agreement with these methods, but as a good soldier he of course followed the commands of the *Reichsführer* with total obedience. At this meeting I made an agreement with Dr Weinemann that a delegation would be set up in Prague. The delegates would be able to visit the camp in Theresienstadt at any time. I also mentioned the concentration camp at Theresienstadt, which was next to the ghetto, and extracted a half-promise that this too could be visited. I should of course have preferred it if the delegate could have actually lived in Theresienstadt. Dr Weinemann contacted *Obergruppenführer* Kaltenbrunner about this by telegraph but had received no answer by the time I had to leave.

Notes

INTRODUCTION

1 See chapter 7, n. 29.
2 See under Laqueur in the 'Studies' section of the Bibliography.
3 For the full text of the Tokyo project, see pp. 381–5 of the original edition (J.-C. Favez, *Une mission impossible?*, Editions Payot, Lausanne, 1988).
4 For full details see the box on p. 139 of the original edition.
5 See also Cornelio Sommaruga, 'Croix-Rouge: des errements passés, des dangers actuels' (*Le Monde*, 26 September 1996, p. 13); Nicolas Weill, 'La responsabilité des démocraties dans la "solution finale"' (*ibid.*, 27 September 1996, p. 16); and Jean-Dominique Merchet, 'Déportation nazie: le CICR joue la transparence' (*Libération*, 28 March 1997, p. 13).

1 THE RED CROSS, POLITICAL PRISONERS AND RACIAL PERSECUTION BEFORE 1939

1 Max Domarus, *Hitler: Reden und Proklamationen, 1932–1945*, vol. II, p. 1058.
2 AG, G 59/2, note of 28 February 1945, and *L'activité du CICR en faveur des civils détenus dans les camps de concentration en Allemagne (1939–1945)*, 3rd edn, Geneva, April 1947.
3 Jean Pictet, *Les principes de la Croix-Rouge*, Geneva, 1955, p. 45.
4 Diego Fiscalini, 'Des élites au service d'une cause humanitaire: le Comité international de la Croix-Rouge', licentiate thesis, Geneva, 1985.
5 'It is free to take (. . .) any humanitarian initiative within the scope of its traditional role' (Statutes, Article 5, as they stood in 1939).
6 Articles 79 and 88.
7 'Projet de convention internationale concernant la condition et la protection des civils de nationalité ennemie qui se trouvent sur le territoire d'un belligérant ou sur un territoire occupé par lui', *RICR*, August 1934, pp. 657–62.
8 Jacques Moreillon, *Le CICR et la protection des détenus politiques*, Lausanne, 1973.
9 AG, CR 110/I–II. The text was adopted on 1 May 1935.
10 Resolution XIV, Sixteenth International Conference of the Red Cross, London, 1938. Report, p. 104.

11 PVCICR, meeting of 18 May 1933.
12 AG, CR 110/I–II. Letter from Prince Charles of Sweden, president of the Swedish Red Cross, to Max Huber, 18 September 1933.
13 In the early 1930s the DRK was a large organisation with more than 1.5 million members. It was first brought to heel in November 1933 under a new chairman, Duke Charles Edward of Saxe-Coburg-Gotha, then it was bound even more closely to the regime by the appointment in 1938 of the chief SS doctor, *Brigadeführer-SS* Dr Ernst Grawitz, as *Stellvertretender Präsident* or serving chairman. (Grawitz, one of the leading people involved in pseudo-medical experiments in the concentration camps, committed suicide in Berlin in April 1945.) Very little remains, it seems, of the DRK archives; such fragments as have survived do not enable us to assess how much room for manoeuvre was enjoyed by people faithful to the Red Cross ideal such as the vice-chairman Paul Draudt or the man who succeeded him as the head of the external relations bureau, Walter Georg Hartmann, who in 1943 moved his office far from headquarters in Berlin to Ettal in Upper Bavaria.
14 AG, Box. Max Huber archives. Personal letter to Paul Draudt, 3 November 1933.
15 *Ibid.*, telegram from Draudt, 30 July 1934.
16 *Ibid.*, Missions Committee, meeting of 27 February 1935, Suzanne Ferrière's contribution.
17 Carl J. Burckhardt, *Ma mission à Dantzig*, Paris, 1961, pp. 60–9 and UB, Burckhardt papers, B II 34, for the report and the written text of his briefing to the ICRC. The report of Burckhardt's 1935 visit to Lichtenburg, Esterwegen and Dachau is reproduced in full on pp. 385–6 of the original edition.
18 AG, CR 110/I–II. Letter from Carl J. Burckhardt to the DRK chairman, 21 November 1935.
19 *Ibid.*, letter of 13 February 1936.
20 IfZ, Akten der Parteikanzlei der NSDAP, CJB, no. 11489; AG, PVCICR, meeting of 25 June 1936; and UB, Burckhardt papers, B II 46b, letter from Heydrich, 18 June 1936.
21 AG, CR 110/4 and CR 110/I–II, letter from Favre to Himmler, 31 August 1938. For the full text of Favre's report on his 1938 visit to Dachau, see pp. 387–90 of the original edition.
22 *Ibid.*, CR 110/I–II, telephoned note of 14 June 1938.
23 *Ibid.*, personal note for Col. Favre, n.d.
24 Daniel Bourgeois, 'La porte se ferme: la Suisse et le problème de l'immigration juive en 1938', *Relations Internationales*, 54 (1988), 181–204.
25 AG, CR 123, letter from the secretary-general of the League, Bernard de Rougé, 24 November 1938, and minutes of the League's Executive Committee meeting, same date.
26 *Ibid.*, letter from Georges Bonnet, 19 November 1938; see also *Documents diplomatiques français relatifs aux origines de la Seconde Guerre Mondiale*, 2nd series, vol. XII, pp. 680f, note from the Sous-direction des Affaires administratives et des Unions internationales, 21 November 1938.
27 AG, CR 123, letter of 5 December 1938.
28 *Ibid.*, letter of 30 December 1938.

29 *Ibid.*, CR 110/I–II, letter to Huber of 9 January 1939 and CR 123, letter to Huber of 24 March 1939.
30 *Ibid.*, PVB, meeting of 13 January 1939.
31 Max Huber, 'L'idée de la Croix-Rouge au temps présent', *RICR*, December 1934.

2 SECRECY, RUMOUR, INFORMATION

1 W. A. Visser't Hooft, *Le temps du rassemblement*, Paris, 1975, p. 212.
2 Christopher Browning, *The Final Solution and the German Foreign Office*, London, 1978.
3 Walter Laqueur, *Le terrifiant secret*, Paris, 1981.
4 FA, E 4800 (A) 1, Notiz über meine Besprechungen in Berlin, end of January 1943.
5 Jean-Claude Favez and Ladislas Mysyrowicz, 'Que savait-on en Suisse en 1942 des crimes commis par les Nazis?', *Journal de Genève*, 21 April 1979, and *La politique pratiquée par la Suisse à l'égard des réfugiés au cours des années 1933 à 1955*, report prepared for the [Swiss] legislative councils and submitted to the [Swiss] Federal Council by Professor Carl Ludwig (henceforth Ludwig report).
6 AG, PVPIC, meeting of 10 November 1942.
7 *Ibid.*, G 59/8, letter of 19 November 1941.
8 *Ibid.*, G 3/24b, extract from a report of 2 November 1943.
9 *Ibid.*, G 3/Jun/1b, Ferrière note of 27 October 1939.
10 *Ibid.*, PVCC, meeting of 27 December 1939.
11 Marcel Junod, *Le troisième combattant*, Lausanne, 1947, pp. 129–30.
12 AG, G 59/8. On the document (reproduced in French translation on pp. 88–9 of the original edition; translated from the German for this edition and reproduced in the Appendix as document I) there is this manuscript note: 'Rapporté par le Dr Junod auquel il a été remis par la Légation de Suisse. Confidentiel. Novembre 1939.' Two appendices, not reproduced in the original edition, deal with the organisation of the Jewish reservation and a public notice from Mährisch-Ostrau.
13 *Ibid.*, G 10, note from Huber of 16 December 1939.
14 *Ibid.*, G 59/8.
15 *Ibid.*, telegrams of 3 March and 8 March 1940.
16 *Ibid.*, Box, Jacques Chenevière, private correspondence, strictly confidential report of 6 September 1940.
17 *Ibid.*, G 3/14b, confidential report of 14 August 1940.
18 *Ibid.*, G 59/8, 'Confidentiel. Ne pas copier', undated but marked with the date of receipt, 26 November 1941.
19 *Ibid.*, letter signed W. A. Visser't Hooft of 29 October 1941.
20 *Ibid.*, letter to Miss Warner.
21 *Ibid.*, G 17/Fr., note of a discussion with Sir Herbert Emerson and G. G. Kullmann of 17 December 1941.
22 *Ibid.*, G 59/8, letter to Miss Warner.
23 *Ibid.*, G 48/1, letter of 5 December 1941.
24 *Ibid.*, G 3/26e, note of 16 February 1942.

25 *Ibid.*, G 59/8, note of 11 September 1942.
26 *Ibid.*, document received by W. Rohner on 4 April 1942.
27 *Ibid.*, G 3/26f, note of 27 August 1942.
28 *Ibid.*, file with no shelfmark, 'France. Camps'.
29 *Ibid.*, G 3/36e, note of 16 February 1942.
30 *Ibid.*, G 59/8, reports handed on 10 April 1942 to Rohner and note of 22 April 1942.
31 *Ibid.*, G 3/26f, note of 25 August 1942.
32 Laqueur, *Le terrifiant secret*, pp. 97–100.
33 Meir Dworzecki, 'The International Red Cross and its Policy vis-à-vis the Jews in the Ghettos and Concentration Camps in Nazi-Occupied Europe', in *Rescue Attempts during the Holocaust*, Jerusalem, 1974, p. 85. See too Dworzecki's interview with Riegner on 13 July 1972 and my conversations with Riegner in January 1987.
34 AG, G 59/8. Lieber's report of 6 October 1942 has been found in the ICRC archives, but not Zivian's of 1 October.
35 *Ibid.*, note of 13 October 1942. On 22 October Riegner sent the US minister in Berne a memorandum accompanied by detailed documents such as the Lieber and Zivian reports. A few days later Paul C. Squire, US consul in Geneva, passed to his minister the same information which he had just received from a leading figure in international circles in Geneva, none other than Carl J. Burckhardt (AWJC, Riegner memorandum of 22 October and note of 29 October 1942 from Paul C. Squire).
36 AG, PVCC, meeting of 21 October 1942.
37 AWJC, Squire memorandum of 7 November and letter from Squire to Leland Harrison, 9 November 1942.
38 *Ibid.*, note of 17 November 1942.
39 AG, G 59/8, letter of 2 November 1942.
40 *Ibid.*, G 3/26f, note of 14 November 1942.
41 *Ibid.*, G 59/8, Schwarzenberg note, 4 December 1942.
42 *Ibid.*, G 44/00, letter of 8 March 1943.
43 *Ibid.*, G 59/8, note of 15 April 1943.
44 *Ibid.*, note of 30 April 1943.
45 *Ibid.*, G 59/2, Pro Memoria dated 12 September 1944.
46 *Ibid.*, G 59/7.
47 *Ibid.*, G 44/13, note of 8 December 1944.
48 *Ibid.*, G 3/26f, reproduced in the original edition, p. 101.
49 *Ibid.*, note to the Secretariat dated 22 December 1944 about a visit to Flossenburg on 9 December (for further details see the document reproduced in the original edition, pp. 100–2).
50 *Ibid.*, confidential note of 29 September 1944; see original edition, p. 103.
51 *Ibid.*, confidential note of 14 October 1944; see original edition, pp. 103–4.
52 *Ibid.*, G 3/26f, note of 12 June 1944.
53 *Ibid.*, G 59/8, private letter of 29 November 1944.
54 André Durand, *Histoire du Comité international de la Croix-Rouge*, vol. II, Geneva, 1978, p. 529.
55 See also p. 269 above. For Rossel's wry account of his visit to the RVJD, see the box on p. 105 of the original edition.

56 AG, various minutes, 9 February 1944.
57 *Ibid.*, G 59/12, Theresienstadt ghetto, visited on 23 June 1944.
58 *Ibid.*, G 59/12, note of 19 July 1944.
59 *Ibid.*, G 59/8, note of a discussion on 23 June 1944.
60 FA, E 2001 (D) 1968/74/14, Pilet-Golaz letter to the Swiss minister in Budapest, 7 July 1944.
61 AG, G 59/3, letter from Zurich of 4 July 1944.
62 *Ibid.*, G 17/51, note for Schwarzenberg, 2 June 1944.
63 *Rapport du Comité international de la Croix-Rouge sur son activité pendant la Seconde Guerre Mondiale (1 septembre 1939 – 30 juin 1947)*, Geneva, 1948, 3 vols. (henceforth *Rapport général*), vol. I, p. 44.
64 *Ibid.*, p. 58.
65 See the box on pp. 108–9 of the original edition for an illustration of this: the complaints made in summer 1942 by Roland Marti of the Berlin delegation.
66 AG, PVCC, meeting of 28 December 1942.
67 *Rapport général*, vol. II, pp. 322–3.
68 AG, Box, Max Huber archives, letter of 12 August 1942.
69 *Ibid.*, letter of 11 April 1944.
70 *Ibid.*, Box B, CICR 1b, letter from Mlle Odier, 21 March 1944.
71 *Ibid.*, Box, Max Huber archives, letter of 12 August 1942.

3 THE DOOR THAT STAYED SHUT

1 Durand, *Histoire du Comité international de la Croix Rouge*, vol. II, p. 502.
2 AG, PVCC, meeting of 27 December 1939.
3 *Ibid.*, G 23, visit by Mr Hartmann to Mr Huber, 5 March 1940; PVCC, meeting of 9 April 1940; and CG 2, Junod, note from the ACPG, 10 April 1940.
4 *Ibid.*, G 17/All., letter of 20 August 1941.
5 *Ibid.*, PVSvCi, meeting of 2 September 1941.
6 *Ibid.*, PVCC, meeting of 16 September 1941; for the text of the minute, see pp. 124–6 of the original edition.
7 *Ibid.*, G 23, notes of 24 and 26 September and meeting with Mr Hartmann on 1 September 1941.
8 *Ibid.*, PVCC, meeting of 9 December 1941.
9 *Ibid.*, PVCC, meeting of 7 January 1942 and CMS, Burckhardt report on his London visit, 20 March 1942.
10 *Ibid.*, G 44/13, letter of 16 March 1942.
11 *Ibid.*, letter of 29 April 1942.
12 *Ibid.*, letter of 1 May 1942.
13 *Ibid.*, letter of 20 August 1942.
14 *Ibid.*, G 59, note for the technical directorate of the Agency, signed Schwarzenberg, 21 September 1942.
15 *Ibid.*, Informations services civils, 7 December 1943.
16 Friedrich Forrer, *Sieger ohne Waffen*, Hanover, 1962, pp. 134–8.
17 AG, PVCC, meeting of 6 January 1942.
18 *Ibid.*, meeting of 28 April 1942.

19 *Ibid.*, G 59/1, note of 27 April 1942.
20 *Ibid.*, G 3/26e, confidential letter of 30 March 1942.
21 *Ibid.*, G 8/M/I, note for Marti from Roger Gallopin, 16 April 1942.
22 *Ibid.*, PVCC, meeting of 15 May 1942.
23 *Ibid.*, G 3/26e, letter from Marti, 20 May 1942.
24 *Ibid.*, G 85, visit by Burckhardt to Metternich, 4 August 1942, and PVPIC, meeting of 1 September 1942.
25 *Ibid.*, G 48/France, note of 10 June 1942; for the text, see pp. 132–3 of the original edition.
26 *Ibid.*, 3/26f, note of 17 September 1942.
27 *Ibid.*, G 59/8, letter signed J. Chenevière of 3 September 1942.
28 *Ibid.*, note for Marti of 24 September 1942; see pp. 134–8 and p. 393 n. 28 of the original edition for further details about the notice or *Aufzeichnung* (dated 23 September 1942) sent via Marti to the German Foreign Ministry.
29 UB, Burckhardt papers, B II 46b, letter from Major Suchanek, written on Himmler's orders and dated 27 October 1942. On 19 June 1987 Hans Bachmann confirmed to the author that it most probably concerned an intervention on behalf of an individual, and not a general démarche, judged impossible by Burckhardt at the time. All attempts to find a copy of Burckhardt's letter to Himmler of 21 September, including a search through the section of the Burckhardt bequest still closed to public access, have been unsuccessful. Countess Lanskoranska's case is dealt with by Kaltenbrunner in his letter to Burckhardt of 2 April 1945 (AG, G 44/13).
30 AG, G 3/26f, letter from Marti of 7 November 1942, PVPIC, meeting of 24 November 1942, and H. G. Adler, *Die verheimlichte Wahrheit*, Tübingen, 1958, pp. 293–4.
31 AG, PVCC, meeting of 30 December 1942.
32 *Ibid.*, G 44/00, memorandum for the attention of Carl J. Burckhardt on the problem of the Polish civilians by R. de Graffenried-Villard, 15 January 1943.
33 *Ibid.*, G 3/26f, note from Marti of 10 September 1942.
34 *Ibid.*, PVPIC, meeting of 28 October 1942.
35 *Ibid.*, G 3/26f, note of 18 January and letter from Huber of 30 January 1943.
36 IfZ, Fa 506/12.102, Himmler's decision of 29 October 1942 authorising the dispatch of foodstuffs to detainees by their relatives, and AG, Div. Secours, corr. AA, letter from the AA on the aid sent to the French at Hagenau, 17 October 1942.
37 AG, G 85, letter from Sethe, 15 February 1943, and G 3/26f, note to Marti of 6 May 1943 drafted by Schwarzenberg and signed by Chenevière.
38 *Ibid.*, G 44/00, note of 11 August 1943.
39 *Ibid.*, PVCC, meeting of 27 January 1943.
40 *Ibid.*, G 3/48c, minutes of the extraordinary meeting of 2 July 1942.
41 *Ibid.*, G 59/8, note for Mr Duchosal, 31 March 1943.
42 *Ibid.*, G 3/26f, Marti note of 26 July 1942; BA, R 58/89, unsigned Aktennotiz, n.d.; Secretariat of State of His Holiness, *Actes et documents du Saint-Siège relatifs à la Seconde Guerre Mondiale*, Vatican City, vol. IX, p. 470.
43 On Rossel's instructions see the notes of the CMS and CI (AG, G 3/26f, 1 June 1943).

44 AG, G 59/12, Rossel's report, and BA, R 58/89, Besichtigung der Judensied-
   lung Theresienstadt, 23 June 1944.
45 FA, E 2001 (D) 1968/74/114, confidential report of 7 July 1944; for more
   detailed discussion of the extent to which Rossel may or may not have been
   taken in (the author concludes that on balance he was not) see p. 394 n. 45
   of the original edition.
46 AG, G 59/12, letter from Hartmann to Burckhardt, 5 June 1943, and IfZ,
   Eich 1418, note from the AA (Abt II) to Eichmann, 12 August 1943.
47 AG, G 59/12, note to the Berlin delegation, 15 November 1944.
48 *Ibid.*, G 44/13, note of 31 May 1943.
49 *Ibid.*, G 23, note by Hartmann for Bachmann, 19 November 1943, and
   Informations services civils, minutes of the meeting of 8 February
   1944.
50 *Ibid.*, G 17/53, note for Jean d'Amman, 1 February 1943, quoted on
   pp. 150–1 of the original edition.
51 *Ibid.*, G 3/48e, note for Mr Lombard, 25 September 1944.
52 *Ibid.*, G 59/1, proposed text (dated 1 February 1943) of the talk given on 12
   February to a group of organisations concerned with Jews convened by the
   ICRC, 12 February 1943.
53 *Ibid.*, G 59, letter from A. L. Eastermann, 6 January 1943, and F. Barbey's
   reply, 10 March 1943.
54 *Ibid.*, G 59/7, letter of 16 June 1943 and letter from Schwarzenberg to Peter,
   30 August 1943.
55 *Ibid.*, G 59/7, note from the ICRC delegation in London of 12 August 1943;
   G 59/4, Max Huber's note of 26 August 1943 about this appeal; and GG
   59/7, the ICRC's reply to the WJC, 30 August 1943.
56 See especially *ibid.*, G 59/2, note to Peter of 2 March 1943 telling the WRB
   not to pass on to the WJC Kolb's report on his visit to the Transnistrian
   ghettos; G 59/4, letter from Schwarzenberg to the delegation in London, 13
   June 1944; and G 59/2, Kuhne note on a Schwarzenberg–Riegner conversation, 27 June 1944.
57 *Ibid.*, G 59/8, Paul Kuhne note on the conversation, 30 June 1944.
58 FA, E 2200 Washington, Archive no. 16/2, letter from Burckhardt to Karl
   Bruggmann, Swiss minister in Washington, 20 June 1944.
59 AG, Box, Huber–Burckhardt correspondence, letter from Burckhardt to
   Huber about a conversation with Pilet-Golaz on 20 July 1944.

4 WAYS AND MEANS

1 ICRC statutes, 1939, Art. 4d and 4e.
2 Durand, *Histoire du Comité international de la Croix Rouge*, vol. II, pp. 251f.
3 *RICR*, April 1940, pp. 321f.; for further details and the text of the so-called
   'Whitsun appeal', see pp. 157–8 of the original edition.
4 AG, G 44/00, letter from the army adjutancy, 'Armée et Foyer' section, 18
   June 1942, and draft by Jean Pictet of a projected reply from Max Huber, 25
   June 1942.
5 *Ibid.*, PVCC, meeting of 19 June 1942.
6 *Ibid.*, meetings of 5 and 12 August 1942.

7 FA, E 2803 1969/302/1, handwritten letter from P. Bonna to Edouard de Haller, 2 September 1942, and letter from de Haller to Max Huber, 4 September 1942.

8 AG, PVCC, meetings of 22 and 30 September 1942; FA, E 2803/302/1, note from Edouard de Haller to federal councillors Etter and Pilet-Golaz, 30 September 1942, and handwritten note by de Haller, 5 October 1942.

9 AG, CR 73, document dated 14 October 1942. In a personal letter to Hans Bachmann on 4 September, kindly shown to the author by Mr Bachmann, Burckhardt reaffirms his conviction that the ICRC can do nothing: 'Vor dieser Tatsache kann das Komittee nur vernehmlich vor der Welt protestieren und dann demissionieren.'

10 FA, E2803 1969/302/1, note from Edouard de Haller to Pilet-Golaz, 30 September 1942, and handwritten note by de Haller, 9 October 1942.

11 AG, CR 73; the fourth draft is dated 16 September 1942 and the summary of members' opinions 6 October 1942.

12 FA, E 2803 1969/302/1, note for Mr Pilet-Golaz dictated by Edouard de Haller over the telephone, 14 October 1942.

13 AG, PVCICR, meeting of 14 October 1942; for the full text, see pp. 161–4 of the original edition.

14 PRO, FO 371, 30925, 19363, conversation between F. K. Roberts and Mr Brotman of the Board of Deputies of British Jews, 18 December 1942; for the text of the Allied appeal, see pp. 162–3 of the original edition.

15 AG, CR 201, excerpt from PVB, meeting of 16 June 1943, and project of P. Ruegger, 22 June 1943.

16 Ibid., PVB, meeting of 30 June 1943, and CR 73, Ruegger project, 6 July 1943.

17 Ibid., Box, Max Huber archives, correspondence with Philippe Etter, conversation of 13 July 1943.

18 RICR, August 1943, p. 607.

19 AG, PVB, meetings of 13 and 27 October 1943.

20 Ibid., CR 225, message of 30 December 1943, and PVB, meeting of 17 November 1943.

21 RICR, August 1943, pp. 1–2.

22 Jacques Chenevière, 'Le Comité international de la Croix-Rouge, 1.9.39–30.6.46', in Géographie de la solidarité. L'œuvre du Don Suisse pour les victimes de la guerre, by Guido Caligari, Jacques Chenevière, Fritz Ernst, Camille Gorgé, Albert Malche and Maurice Zermatten, cyclostyled, n.d.

23 Rapport du Comité international de la Croix-Rouge sur son activité pendant la Seconde Guerre Mondiale (1 septembre 1939 – 30 juin 1947), vol. III, Actions de secours, Geneva, June 1948.

24 Rapport de la Commission mixte de secours de la Croix-Rouge internationale, 1941–1946, Geneva, 1948.

25 AG, G 3/26f, Marti note of 18 November 1943.

26 Ibid., DAS, Schwarzenberg memoir of 30 June 1944.

27 Ibid., PVDAS, meeting of 8 May 1944.

28 Ibid., G 44/13, Marti note of 26 January 1944; for Marti's report on his visit to Ravensbrück, see pp. 172–3 of the original edition.

29 Ibid., 3/26f, Schwarzenberg note of 19 May 1944.

30 *Ibid.*, G 59/7, letter from L. Kubowitzki to the WRB, 9 August 1944; G 59/
    2, Tartakower letter of 9 April 1945.

31 *Ibid.*, PVDAS, meeting of 21 September 1944.

32 *Ibid.*, meeting of 16 November 1944. For the contents of a standard food
    parcel, see the box on p. 175 of the original edition, and for graph and
    statistics relating to the Concentration Camp Parcels Scheme, see the box
    on p. 176 of the original edition.

33 AG, CG 16, note of 12 February 1942.

34 *Ibid.*, G 59/1, proposed text (dated 1 February 1943) for the talk on 12
    February 1943 to a group of organisations concerned with Jews convened by
    the ICRC.

35 *Ibid.*, G 59/12, Ferrière letter to Riegner, 7 December 1942; G 59/7,
    Riegner telegram to the WJC of 17 December 1942; WJC reply of 18
    December 1942.

36 *Ibid.*, G 59/1, note by Gallopin for Dr Junod drafted by Schwarzenberg, 23
    December 1942.

37 *Ibid.*, G 59/2, note signed Duchosal drafted by Schwarzenberg, 10 February
    1943.

38 *Ibid.*, G 59/2, letter from Hartmann to Burckhardt, 5 June 1943; note for a
    Burckhardt–Hartmann conversation, 11 May 1943; AWJC, Aktennotiz from
    Riegner of 18 May 1943; and BA, R 58/89, letter to the CMS, 26 June 1943.

39 AG, dossier CMS, Germany, de Pilar's strictly confidential report, 7 July
    1943. De Pilar, in regular contact with Riegner, gave him the same informa-
    tion (IfZ, Eich. 1058, Aktennotiz, 7 July 1943). See also AWJC, Riegner's
    Aktennotiz on a conversation with de Pilar, 24 June 1943, and BA, R 58/89,
    letters to the RSHA of 4 January and 7 August 1944.

40 AG, G 59, meeting of 10 August 1944, talk to the associations convened by
    the ICRC, and CMS, *Déportés, réfugiés et internés israélites dans les divers pays
    d'Europe*, Geneva, July 1944.

41 AG, G 59/7, note on a meeting with Saly Mayer, 7 August 1944.

42 *Ibid.*, G 59/5, Schwarzenberg note of 29 March 1944, note for de Haller for
    the attention of Simond of 29 March 1944, note for the ICRC delegation in
    Washington of 11 May 1944, with report of 16 April 1944 on the ICRC's
    activity in relation to Jewish emigration from Romania, Hungary and
    Bulgaria, and chronological summary of 24 April 1944 on the same subject.

43 *Ibid.*, PVCC, meeting of 29 September 1942, and G 59/5, project of M. Jean
    Faure, *inspecteur général* of civilian internment camps in France, passed to
    Dr Cramer, 5 February 1942.

44 *Ibid.*, G 59, prefatory note (confidential) to the study of the evacuation of
    the European Jews to the Americas, 1 October 1942.

45 *Ibid.*, G 59/5, letter from S. Ferrière to G. G. Kullmann, 16 February 1943.

46 See on this problem Bernard Wasserstein, *Britain and the Jews of Europe,
    1939–1945*, Oxford, 1979.

47 AG, G 59/5, letter from R. de Weck to the ICRC, 4 April 1943.

48 *Ibid.*, G 59, report from Mlle Ferrière, 25 March 1943; PVCC, meeting of
    10 February 1943.

49 *Ibid.*, G 59/5; for the full text of the note, see pp. 185–6 of the original
    edition.

50 *Ibid.*, note of 9 June 1943, E. Berthoud's note of 18 August 1943 for Schwarzenberg and Ferrazino and Berthoud's handwritten comment in the margin.

51 *Ibid.*, note to de Haller, 23 September 1943; for the full text of the note, see pp. 187–8 of the original edition.

52 *Ibid.*, Schwarzenberg note to Duchosal and Burckhardt, 8 June 1943.

53 *Ibid.*, Aufzeichnung f. die HH. Bachmann u. Füllemann, 20 January 1944.

54 *Ibid.*, G 59/3, note for Marti, 22 March 1944; for the full text of the note, see pp. 189–91 of the original edition.

55 *Ibid.*, G 59/5, Simond letter, 14 March 1944.

56 *Ibid.*, note from Füllemann to Kolb, 31 March 1944 (for the full text of the note, see pp. 191–2 of the original edition); see also PVB, meeting of 22 March 1944.

57 *Ibid.*, Kolb letter, 7 July 1944.

58 *Ibid.*, PVB, meeting of 3 August 1944.

59 *Ibid.*, IMPA Archives (henceforth IMPA), box 29, prefatory note for Mlle Ferrière, 14 February 1945.

60 *Ibid.*, G 59/4, letter from Kahany to the ICRC, 31 May 1943, and PVPIC, meeting of 4 June 1943.

61 *Ibid.*, G 59/5, letter to Simond, 23 August 1943.

62 *Ibid.*, IMPA, box 29, questionnaire of 21 January 1946 and activities report, 1 December 1946.

63 FA, E 2001 (D) 11/9, de Haller note, 7 February 1944.

64 *Ibid.*, E 2001 (D) 3/484, de Haller note, 29 September 1943.

65 AG, G 59, notes for Carl J. Burckhardt, 28 and 30 December 1943.

66 *Ibid.*, Aufzeichnung f. Herr Hartmann, from H. Bachmann, drafted by Schwarzenberg, 17 February 1944, and Hartmann–Bachmann discussion.

67 FA, E 2001 (D) 3/484, memorandum of 10 April 1944; personal and confidential letter from Pilet-Golaz to Frölicher, 8 May 1944.

68 AG, G 59/4, *streng vertraulich* letter from Born, 23 October 1944.

69 FA, E 2001 (D) 11/59, letter from the head of the DIE to the Swiss legation in Budapest, 21 July 1944. At the same moment Schwarzenberg went to enquire of de Haller how civilian internee exchanges were going, about which Switzerland had to maintain discretion even towards the ICRC (FA, E 2001 (D) 1968/74/17, de Haller note, 21 July 1944).

70 AG, G 59/5, Schwarzenberg note, 4 August 1944.

71 FA, E 2001 (D) 11/8, letter from J. Chenevière to de Pury, head of the DIE, 20 October 1942.

72 *Rapport général*, vol. I, p. 202.

73 AG, PVCC, meeting of 28 April 1942.

74 *Ibid.*, G 25/34, Marti note of 17 September 1942.

75 *Ibid.*, G 59/7, letter from the WJC to the ICRC, 14 April 1943, and reply of 5 May 1943 signed J. Duchosal and drafted by Schwarzenberg.

76 PRO, FO 916/567/79115, telegram from the Foreign Office to the British legation in Berne, 9 March 1943, and Swiss reply of 22 April 1943.

77 *German Regulations pertaining to Prisoners of War*, Befehlsammlung 1, Nr. 7, Befehlsammlung 6, Nr. 11, Befehlsammlung 11, Nr. 5, etc.

78 *Ibid.*, Befehlsammlung 48, Nr. 876.

79 AG, G 25/34, minutes of meeting with Marti of 16 October 1944.
80 *Ibid.*, Riegner letter of 13 March 1945; AWJC, Riegner–Chenevière discussion, 13 March 1945.
81 Ibid. Letter to Riegner of 23 March 1945.
82 *Ibid.*, letter of 29 March 1945.
83 *Ibid.*, letter of 5 April 1945; for full text, see pp. 204–5 of the original edition.
84 Monty Penkover, 'The World Jewish Congress Confronts the International Red Cross during the Holocaust', *Jewish Social Studies*, 41, 3–4/1979; AWJC, conversation of 11 April 1945, proposed letter, etc.
85 AG, G 25/34, letter of 27 April 1945.
86 *Ibid.*, letter signed by David de Traz, and Riegner reply, 10 June 1945. The ICRC after the war, in response to several questions, carried out small sporadic searches in its archives. See the letter of M. René J. Wilhelm to M. M. Alberti, 3 November 1959, and the note by Mme G. Durouvenoz, 25 January 1974.
87 *Ibid.*, G 59, Riegner letter to Burckhardt, 19 November 1942; G 59/7, Peter letter to the ICRC, 16 March 1943 and copy of Tartakower letter to Peter, 4 March 1943, and Stephan Wise and Nahum Goldmann letter to the Board of Economic Warfare, 25 February 1943.
88 *Ibid.*, G 59/7, Duchosal letter to Peter, 5 May 1943; for full text, see pp. 206–7 of the original edition.
89 *Ibid.*, letter from Peter, 25 May 1943, and copy of letter from Arieh Tartakower, 12 May 1943.
90 *Ibid.*, G 44/13, visit from Guggenheim and Riegner, Bachmann note, 6 July 1943 (compare Riegner's account of the same day in AWJC, and G 59/1, Bachmann letter to Guggenheim, 6 August 1943); FA, E 2308 1969/302/2, notes on the discussions of 9 and 12 July 1943.
91 IfZ, ED 201/4, letter from Tartakower and Kubowitzki to Peter, 10 December 1943.
92 AG, G 59/8, letter from Eastermann to Huber, 11 July 1944.
93 *Ibid.*, G 59/7, letter from Riegner, 22 August 1944, and Stephan Wise and Nahum Goldmann telegram, 19 December 1944.
94 *Ibid.*, letter from Harrison, 2 May 1944, and reply from Huber, 12 May 1944; FA, E 2001 (D) 1968/74/13, de Haller notes of 20 and 26 May 1944; for the text of a summary of the ICRC's reasons for refusing, see the box on p. 208 of the original edition.
95 IfZ, ED 201/4, Riegner to Huber, 23 October 1944; see too letter from Tartakower and Kubowitzki to Peter, 10 December 1942, and AG, G 59/2, Tartakower to Marc Jarblum, G. Riegner and Adolf Silberschein, 12 January 1944.
96 AG, G 59/7, letter from Peter H. Bergson, 28 February 1945.
97 *Ibid.*, G 59/9, note of 29 September 1944.
98 IfZ, ED 201/4, letter from Huber to Guggenheim and Riegner, 2 October 1944, and memorandum on the notion of civilian internee.
99 *Ibid.*, letter from Riegner to Goldmann and Kubowitzki, 25 October 1944 (for the full text, see p. 211 of the original edition), and AG, G 59/4, letter from Guggenheim and Riegner to Huber, 23 October 1944.

5 THE OCCUPIED COUNTRIES

1 The history of this negotiation remains to be written, since the chapter devoted to it in the *Rapport général* (vol. I, pp. 419–53) is short on detail.

2 AG, CR 00/47, summary of the relations between the ICRC and the Polish Red Cross, 16 October 1945.

3 *Ibid.*, G 23, Frick–Hartmann conversation, 7 May 1940.

4 *Ibid.*, PVPIC, meeting of 24 October 1942, and Serv. Pol., Marti note of 26 February 1942.

5 *Ibid.*, G 3/26f, notes for M. Huber, 30 June 1942 and 1 July 1942.

6 *Ibid.*, G 85, note of 26 January 1942.

7 *Rapport général*, vol. II, p. 128.

8 AG, G 48, letter of 1 May 1940.

9 *Ibid.*, G 23, Bodmer note on his conversation with Hartmann, 5 May 1940.

10 *Ibid.*, G 48, letter of 30 May 1940. According to one deportee, Professor Henryk Batowski, small food parcels bearing the international Red Cross stamp did, however, arrive in the second half of 1940, at the rate of one parcel per person per month.

11 *Ibid.*, letter of 9 May 1940.

12 *Ibid.*, G 40, letter from Hartmann, 13 November 1939.

13 *Ibid.*, SG 3/5, letters to Max Huber of 4 September 1939 and to J. Chenevière of 14 September 1939.

14 *Ibid.*, letter to Max Huber of 27 September 1939.

15 *Ibid.*, unsigned note of 9 November 1939.

16 *Ibid.*, letter of 12 December 1939. See too Adam Czerniakow's note in his ghetto diary: Adama Czerniakowa, *Dziennik getta warzowskiego*, ed. Marian Fuks, Vacs, 1983, p. 62.

17 AG, G 40, note handed to Hartmann on 29 November 1939.

18 *Ibid.*, G 10, note by M. Huber about a conversation with Hartmann, 16 December 1939.

19 *Ibid.*, PVCC, meeting of 27 December 1939.

20 *Ibid.*, G 23, Hartmann's visit to Huber, 29 February 1940.

21 *Ibid.*, G 3/10, diplomatic mission to Berlin, note by Mme Frick, 24 February 1940. Mme Frick asked Burckhardt again on 19 and 21 February 1940 to get permission for the ICRC to set up a permanent delegation in Cracow (UB, Burckhardt papers, B II 46d).

22 'The sending of a delegate to those places which are the theatre of the terrible events reported to you by your correspondent seems to us out of the question, since in the end the authorities concerned have every interest in preventing any intervention which could interfere with the orders given. Any attempt on our part to get information about the situation under some pretext or other, and so to create the possibility of later action, would be at odds with our basic attitude, leaving aside the fact that the attempt would be doomed to fail. Extremely painful as it is for us to do nothing in many instances where our help is expected, we must nonetheless resist the temptation to intervene when we consider that the intervention would be hopeless. We must not abuse the goodwill of the authorities and the national Red Cross societies who are indispensable for the pursuit of our traditional and

generally recognised activities, for that could directly compromise certain proceedings. It is all the more difficult for us to ask permission to send a delegate or to do anything at all when the mission envisaged departs from that of a neutral intermediary holding the ring between the warring factions with the aim of helping the actual victims of the conflict and looks like involvement in matters seen by governments as being of purely internal political concern. It is precisely because people often ask the impossible of us that we avoid doing the same with the authorities whose support we rely on to carry out our main tasks. Nevertheless our constant preoccupation is with the fate of the unfortunates who can least be helped, and we never pass up an opportunity to do something or to seek openings which might offer some chance, however remote.' AG, G 59/7, letter to W. A. Visser't Hooft, 17 December 1942.

23 *Rapport de la commission mixte*, pp. 216–19.
24 AG, G 3/48, report of Dr von Wyss, 13 October 1942.
25 *Ibid.*, PVPIC, meeting of 19 June 1942.
26 *Ibid.*, G 3/48, letter from Dr von Wyss of 16 September 1942.
27 *Ibid.*, CMS, report of Dr von Wyss of 14 April 1943.
28 'To finish the discussion of Poland, Mr Hartmann tells me that aid, even medicines, can no longer be sent to the JUS in Cracow. On this point I wish to clarify whether this is a precautionary measure on the part of the German Red Cross which perhaps feels that it can no longer shoulder responsibility for the distribution of aid, or whether it is a final decision taken by the authorities. Mr Hartmann, who is not at ease when discussing these matters, says that in any event the German Red Cross could no longer accept any responsibility and that the local authorities had decided to cease distribution. I asked if he did not think it possible for the Joint Commission's aid to be distributed at the donors' risk, without even the knowledge of the DRK and outside its responsibility, and he replied that he was of the opinion that a Red Cross organisation should steer clear of any involvement in the distribution of these supplies and that it was up to private organisations to carry on this work at their own risk, while hinting that the aid might not reach its destination. I pointed out to Mr Hartmann the very unfortunate impression that this decision would create abroad seeing that over the last few weeks the parcels had been got ready and that some were even already on their way. He answered that he could perhaps raise this question again if he could be given arguments proving that the resumption of these supplies might offer the German authorities some advantage and facilitate German activity in enemy territory. I told him that I would try to find a form of words to this effect but that I considered the situation clear enough not to need other arguments. We then went on to examine possible ways of ensuring the dispatch of aid to the JUS in Cracow via Theresienstadt, a formula that had been mentioned by the German authorities and passed on to the Joint Commission by the DRK. Mr Hartmann declared himself ready to support the plan of conducting a trial by sending a consignment to the Landstelle des Deutschen Roten Kreuzes in Prague for Theresienstadt. The DRK should be notified at the same time that it was a supplementary consignment which could be sent on to Cracow for distribution in the

camps of Jewish workers in the district. In this way the DRK would be able to undertake the necessary démarches with the authorities following the precedent of a previous permit. I tell him that I am ready to discuss this formula with the organisations involved, but I stress once again the serious consequences of the General-Government authorities' change of attitude and the painful impression it would create in British and American circles.' *Ibid.*, de Pilar note about a visit from Hartmann, 23 September 1943.

29 *Ibid.*, G 3/26f, report on the von Wyss journey, 30 November 1944.
30 *Ibid.*, CMS, report by Mr Burckhardt on his visit to London, 20 March 1942.
31 *Ibid.*, PVCC, meeting of 29 July 1942.
32 *Ibid.*, G 3/26f, letter from Burckhardt to Marti, 9 September 1942.
33 'As was indicated in our note 1652 [note to the Service internés civils] of 12 September 1942, this activity falls right outside the domain of the OKW and is the responsibility of the AA. This is our frank opinion: the German government will not accept your aid for Poles interned in prisons or camps. As was indicated in my note no. 1645 of 11 September 1942 to the Service secours individuels, food aid is flatly refused. Clothing is only distributed when prisoners are released since inside they wear convict uniforms, and their money is also held for them until they leave prison. Furthermore ICRC delegates will never be let inside prisons or concentration camps, and even if by some chance they were allowed into a prison or a camp, they would not be able to carry out a proper inspection. Several of the ICRC's services have asked me recently whether aid is allowed for prisoners in these kinds of prison or camp. For once and for all I will try and make things clear. Here we can do nothing. The ICRC must deal, as I have already said, with the *Reichsminister der Justiz*, Berlin W 8, Wilhelmstrasse 65, who alone is in a position to give you information. But do not expect too much. I have already raised these issues with the German Red Cross, the OKW and the AA, but they all claim that they are not competent to deal with them, repeating constantly "It is the Gestapo's business". We are already overwhelmed with work for the POWs and the "official" civilian internees, and we are anxious to avoid damaging our prestige by continually making vain demands in relation to the prisoners mentioned in your note, so we insist that the ICRC itself tries its luck with the competent Minister.' *Ibid.*, note of 17 September 1942.
34 *Ibid.*, report of December 1940.
35 *Ibid.*, letter of J. Chenevière, 13 January 1941.
36 *Ibid.*, G 59, meeting of 10 August 1944, Burckhardt's account.
37 *Ibid.*, G 17/Fr., note of a conversation with Sir Herbert Emerson and G. G. Kullmann, 17 December 1941.
38 *Ibid.*, minutes of the meeting of 28 July 1941. The report was published in the October 1941 number of the *RICR*, pp. 813–15.
39 *Ibid.*, confidential note by Mme Frick, 4 November 1941.
40 *Ibid.*, G M/8/I, report by de Morsier, 22 December 1941.
41 *Ibid.*, PVCC, meeting of 30 December 1941.
42 On 7 August 1942 the ICRC received a detailed report on the big July round-up: 'During the night of 15–16 July the French police carried out a vast programme of arrests among non-French and recently naturalised Jews.

Some 28,000 people were arrested, all of whose names had appeared on a list drawn up several months before. Many people had been warned in advance either by strangers or by the police themselves, some of whom were dismissed for doing it. Six thousand Jews were also able to hide in the eighteenth *arrondissement*, so that the number of arrests was only between 12,000 and 14,000 and the operation is therefore continuing at a slower pace. Both men and women were arrested and their money was confiscated before they were taken separately to either the Vélodrome d'hiver or the Parc des Princes. No exception was made for the sick, even when they had undergone operations only the day before. Thus the surgical unit at the Rothschild Hospital which dealt solely with patients from the camp at Drancy was emptied in one go and all the patients were returned to the camp however ill they were and even if they had only just been operated on. Children of three and over were taken from their mothers. Some policemen showed pity and entrusted the children to neighbours, but for the most part they shut up the flats and turned the little ones out on to the street or loaded them into lorries already full to bursting with hundreds of such youngsters. Their cries, their sobbing, and their desperate appeals for "maman" could be heard the length of the dark, deserted streets. In all about 5,000 children were herded into three schools. The social services and the UGIF were told to look after some of them. Measles and scarlet fever spread quickly and four children died within twelve hours of their arrest. Because of their poor state of health many of the adults needed treatment, so ten doctors were allowed by the occupation authorities to look after them, but the French Bureau for Jewish Affairs cut the number to three. The men and women have been taken to camps for the time being. The government dispatched the National Aid Organisation, but the German authorities banned it. The Quakers, the Salvation Army and the UGIF are trying to feed this starving multitude whose situation is even worse than in the Parc des Princes since they lack proper billets and sanitary installations, surgical dressings and cooking facilities. A large number of children do not know their names and for the moment it is impossible to find out who they are. Since the arrests there has been a virtual news blackout over the detainees. There have been an estimated 300 to 400 suicides; women have thrown their children (six in one case) out of the window and jumped out after them. In many cases the women had been thought to be safe from such measures, so the men had fled to avoid arrest, leaving their wives, mothers and children all their money and jewellery which have been seized and the women arrested. Children – boys and girls – have been arrested from fourteen to fifteen years of age. In Paris most of those arrested were not French nationals, but in the provinces French Jews, foreign Jews, men and women were taken into custody by the German police. Surrounded by soldiers with fixed bayonets, men and women were loaded separately into lorries and then provisionally interned, thousands of them in the camp at Pithiviers. Youngsters were thrown on the street, the flats were boarded up and the neighbours warned not to look after the children. Even the remotest village with only one Jewish inhabitant had a visit from the police coming to arrest him. Thanks to the active solidarity of many non-Jewish French people many Jews were able to escape and their children were hidden or removed to the unoccupied zone in spite of the danger to those adopting this attitude. At the same time anti-Jewish measures have been strengthened against those who stayed in Paris. They had their telephones cut off, even the UGIF, and were only allowed an hour for shopping for essential supplies when the stores were closed. In Paris and the provinces, especially in the no-go zone, there is widespread panic. Very many Jews are trying to escape to the unoccupied zone: a continuous stream of men, women, children and sick people cross the demarcation line in various places after covering anything up to 75 kilometres on foot. A real smuggling racket in people has grown up and prices have leapt from around 400 to 500 francs to between 5,000 and 10,000 francs. The administration is on the whole tolerant and understanding towards foreign Jews who cross the demarcation line and thus find themselves without the requisite permits. Nevertheless in the unoccupied zone 10,000 foreign Jews must be handed over to the German authorities. A census of internees in the camps in the south of France has been carried out and at the moment all the places of internment are out of bounds and completely cut off from the outside world. Three thousand men and women are due to be deported on 6, 8 and 10 August. The remaining 7,000 must be taken from those foreign city-dwellers in a "floating" situation, that is those who are not in possession of a receipt for an application for an identity card. Thus the foreigners who have fled from the occupied zone are likely to be picked up first. There have been round-ups in Lyons, Marseilles and Toulouse and other towns on the 4, 5 and 6 August, and they are still going on.' (AG, G 58/8, report submitted by Dr Weil.)

43 *Ibid.*, G 59/8, letter from Col. Garteiser, head of external relations in the French Red Cross, 28 April 1942.

44 *Ibid.*, G 17/Fr., note written by Col. Garteiser and submitted during his visit to Geneva, 7 July 1942.

45 *Ibid.*, PVCC, meeting of 28 April 1942.

46 *Ibid.*, G 44, note of 10 June 1942.

47 FA, E 2308 1969/302/2, MS notes, meeting of 24 August 1942.

48 AG, G 59/2, letter of 30 March 1942.

49 *Ibid.*, G 8/M/I.

50 *Ibid.*, G 8/26e, Marti notes of 13 and 24 April 1942.

51 *Ibid.*, G 3/36f, Schirmer note of 20 July 1942.

52 *Ibid.*, note of 20 May 1942.

53 *Ibid.*, G 44, letter of 20 May 1942.

54 *Ibid.*, G 59/8, notes of 20 August and 7 September 1942.

55 *Ibid.*, PVCC, meeting of 29 July 1942.

56 *Ibid.*, G 59, letter to the Foreign Ministry's Administrative Affairs and International Relations subdivision, signed by Jacques Chenevière, 3 September 1942; for the full text, see p. 234 of the original edition.

57 *Ibid.*, PVPIC, meeting of 3 November 1942.

58 *Ibid.*, PVCC, meeting of 29 September 1942; for the full text, see p. 235 of the original edition.

59 *Ibid.*, G 59/5, minutes of the meeting of Agency services heads, 24 September 1942; for the full text, see p. 235 of the original edition.

60 *Ibid.*, G 59/5, letter from G. G. Kullmann to Mlle Ferrière, 9 October 1942, and PVPIC, 28 October 1942.
61 *Ibid.*, letter from G. G. Kullmann to Mlle Ferrière, 23 October 1942, and PVPIC, 24 November 1942.
62 'French Service – Civilians Section – Detainees and Deportees. Numbers: To date the number of people that the Service has been asked to investigate totals 1,288 (men, women and children). Women and children: These make up 33 per cent of total arrests. Jews: These make up 62 per cent of arrests. They represented an average of 65 per cent of monthly new arrests but this figure fell in April to 34 per cent. Enquiries: 649 requests for information were made to the DRK with the following results: positive replies 12 per cent; negative replies 28 per cent. The Service has received several interesting replies from the DRK to do with illness and deaths, medical bulletins, releases, places of work; one civilian unheard of since his detention at Compiègne in 1941 and subsequent deportation in June 1942 was reported by the DRK to be working at the Messerschmitt factory in Augsburg. Information: Amongst the 1,288 cases investigated nine deaths and fifteen releases were reported. Remarks: During April ninety-nine enquiries were made about French Aryans. Enquirers had often not been given any reason for the arrest; in several cases the families mention false denunciations for Gaullist sympathies or weapons caches, even the seizure of a foreign radio receiver. Attention is drawn to the fact that many civilians held at Compiègne for some time (eighteen months or more) have left the Camp for an unknown destination. The families were informed (in German) by the Camp Authorities that the detainee was leaving to work and that he would write in due course. Several months have passed and the families have still heard nothing. In two cases there had been an official announcement of the release of the detainees. Some sources suggest that departure for a work camp must be considered as a reprisal for several escapes from the Compiègne Camp.' AG, G 44, 30 April 1943.
63 *Ibid.*, G 44/13, sent by Garteiser, 6 September 1943, and conversation with the Marquis de Mun, 10 November 1943.
64 *Ibid.*, PVPIC, meeting of 19 November 1943.
65 *Ibid.*, G 44/13, note from the OKW to the German delegation at Rethondes, 25 June 1943, produced at Nuremberg (RF-326).
66 *Ibid.*, G 44, confidential letter signed by J. G. Lossier, 6 March 1944; for the full text see pp. 237–8 of the original edition.
67 *Ibid.*, G 54/3, note for Schwarzenberg, 2 June 1944.
68 AG, G 3/26, Gallopin note to Marti of 23 September 1942 and Marti note of 1 October 1942.
69 *Ibid.*, Marti notes of 16 April and 13 May 1943.
70 *Ibid.* On the slip accompanying the Marti note of 13 May 1943 are the words *ad acta*.
71 *Ibid.*, G 44/13, letter from Schmid-Koechlin, 16 September 1944.
72 *Ibid.*, G 44, letter of 21 September 1944.
73 *Ibid.*, G 59/12, letter from the Belgian legation in Berne to Max Huber, 28 June 1944, and letter from A. Leo Kubowitzki to Marc Peter, 15 August 1944.

324 Notes to pages 157–170

74 *Ibid.*, letter from Schwarzenberg to the Belgian chargé d'affaires in Berne, 11 July 1944; for the full text see p. 240 of the original edition.
75 *Ibid.*, letter of 17 October 1944; for the full text see p. 240 of the original edition.
76 *Ibid.*, Marc Peter letter of 6 March 1945.
77 *Ibid.*, G 17/Be., Schmid-Koechlin report of 31 December 1943.
78 *Ibid.*, G 3/14b, strictly confidential report.
79 *Ibid.*, Descoeudres report of 4 June 1941 and PVCC, meeting of 24 June 1941.
80 *Ibid.*, G 17/All., letter signed G. Favre, 8 August 1941.
81 *Ibid.*, G 3/26d, Marti note of 25 November 1941 about the Haaren camp.
82 *Ibid.*, G 44, letter of 1 June 1942; for the full text see pp. 245–6 of the original edition.
83 *Ibid.*, letter of 7 July 1942. For the full text see Appendix, document VI.
84 AG, G 3/26f, note by Bubb on his visit to Stanislau and the General-Government, 21 September 1943.
85 *Ibid.*, Mayer report, n.d.
86 *Activités du CICR en faveur des ressortissants hollandais de 1940 à 1947*, report by Georges Hoffmann, January 1952, p. 22. For the full text of Marti's note, see the box on p. 248 of the original edition.
87 AG, G 3/26e, Marti note of 28 January 1942.
88 *Ibid.*, undated report on the visit of 13 to 15 December 1942.
89 *Ibid.*, CMS report, July 1944, pp. 40–1 and 44.
90 *Ravitaillement de la Grèce pendant l'occupation 1941–44 et pendant les cinq premiers mois après la libération*, final report of the Commission de Gestion pour les Secours en Grèce under ICRC auspices, and *Rapport général*, vol. III, pp. 487–519.
91 AG, G 3/27c, Jean d'Amman report of 10 November 1942; Dr René Burkhardt report, 1942–3, n.d.
92 *Ibid.*, G 17/Gr., note drafted by Schwarzenberg, signed Duchosal, 1 February 1943.
93 *Ibid.*, G 44/Sec, d'Amman note for the Swedish head of the Commission de Gestion, 3 May 1943.
94 *Ibid.*, G 44, letter from Jean Munier to Carl J. Burckhardt, 24 July 1943; for the full text, see pp. 252–3 of the original edition.
95 *Ibid.*, G 3/26f, Marti note to the AA, n.d., and IfZ, NG 3329.
96 AG, G 3/27c, report by Dr Burkhardt, winter 1942–3, n.d.; for the full text, see p. 253 of the original edition.
97 FA, E 2001 (D) 1968/74/6, letter from the Swiss chargé d'affaires in Athens to the DPF, 24 March 1943.
98 AG, G 59/8, letter from F. Jenny to the ICRC, 18 March 1943.
99 FA, E 2001 (D) 1968/74/6, letter from the Swiss chargé d'affaires in Athens to the DPF, 24 March 1943; for the full text, see p. 254 of the original edition.
100 AG, G 59/8, note for Duchosal, 31 March 1943; for the full text, see p. 254 of the original edition.
101 *Ibid.*, note for the Division PG/IC, attention of Roger Gallopin, 28 April 1943; for the full text, see p. 255 of the original edition.

102 *Ibid.*, G G3/27c, note for the delegation in Athens, drafted by Schwarzenberg and signed Gallopin; for the full text see pp. 255–6 of the original edition.

103 FA, E 2001 (D) 11, file 9, letter from the acting head of the DIE to the DPF, 20 October 1943.

104 AG, G 59/2, Schwarzenberg letter to F. Jenny, 27 September 1943; for the full text, see p. 256 of the original edition.

105 *Ibid.*, letter from Jean d'Amman, 5 June 1943; for the full text, see the box on p. 255 of the original edition.

106 *Ibid.*, PVCC, meeting of 7 July 1942.

107 *Ibid.*, G 44, note of 16 November 1942.

108 *Ibid.*, G 3/26f, oral report by Marti, meeting of 5 October 1943.

109 *Ibid.*, G 44, report B (written) by Marti on his mission, 6 October 1943.

110 *Ibid.*, Box B, Norway, report 55, Stockholm, 10 November 1944.

111 *Ibid.*, G 44, letter to Schwarzenberg of 30 October 1943; for the full text see pp. 257–8 of the original edition.

112 *Ibid.*, G 44/13, note of 25 May 1944.

113 Edgar Bonjour, *Histoire de la neutralité suisse*, vol. VI, Neuchâtel, 1970, pp. 139–40.

114 AG, Box B, Norway, manuscript note by Huber on Hoffmann's report 55, 27 November 1944.

115 *Ibid.*, CR 00/54, report by the vice-president of the Swedish Red Cross, Count Folke Bernadotte, on his visit to Berlin and Geneva, 1 December 1943, passed on to the ICRC by Hoffmann.

6 THE SATELLITES

1 AG, G 48, letter from Col. Favre to the Italian Red Cross, 24 October 1941.

2 *Ibid.*, Div. Secours PG/IC, discussion with Valobra, Luzzato and Riegner, 29 July 1942.

3 FA, E 2001 (D) 1968/74/16, letter from the Swiss consul of 26 September 1942.

4 AG, G 17/Cro., letter from the president of the Croatian Red Cross to Schirmer, 21 December 1942.

5 See p. 261 of the original edition for Schwarzenberg's reference to Schirmer's report on the Croatian Red Cross.

6 AG, G 17/Cro., note of 8 February 1943; for the full text, see pp. 260–1 of the original edition.

7 *Ibid.*, Schmidlin's first report, Geneva, 15 March 1943; for the full text see pp. 261–2 of the original edition.

8 *Ibid.*, minutes of the conference of 25 March 1943; for the full text see pp. 262–3 of the original edition.

9 *Ibid.*, G 59/2, letters from Schmidlin of 27 April 1943, 12 May 1943, etc.

10 *Ibid.*, *streng vertraulich!* letter from Schmidlin of 10 May 1943.

11 *Ibid.*, letter from Schmidlin of 5 July 1943 and letter from Gallopin of 14 July 1943.

12 *Ibid.*, G 3/48c, minutes of the meeting of 2 July 1943.

13 *Ibid.*, G 59, meeting of 10 August 1944, account by Carl J. Burckhardt.

14 *Ibid.*, G 59/2, Schmidlin note of 25 April 1944.

15 *Ibid.*, letter from F. Barbey, 17 March 1944.

16 *Ibid.*, G 17/Cro., minutes of the working meetings with Schmidlin of 17 and 23 March 1944.

17 *Ibid.*, G 59/2, Schmidlin note of 7 April 1944, and G 17/Cro., Schmidlin notes of 23 May, 12 June and 23 June 1944.

18 *Ibid.*, G 92, *streng vertraulich!* report of 31 October 1946.

19 *Ibid.*, G 17/Cro., report of 2 August 1944.

20 *Ibid.*, letter of 4 July 1944, and see the box on p. 267 of the original edition.

21 *Ibid.*, and see the letter, signed Chapuisat, of 24 November 1944, not sent if the MS note on the first page is to be believed.

22 *Ibid.*, G 85, letters of 18 September 1944 and 21 March 1945.

23 *Ibid.*, G 59/7, confidential note by Schmidlin, 7 November 1944.

24 *Ibid.*, G 92, report of 31 October 1946, and G 59/3, confidential note of 23 March 1945; FA, E 2001 (D) 1968/74/16, note for minister Stucki of 2 March 1945.

25 AG, G 59/8, Rohner report, document handed to Budapest on 10 April 1942.

26 *Ibid.*, letter from the Slovak Red Cross, 9 June 1942.

27 *Ibid.*, PVPIC, meeting of 20 July 1942, and PVCC, meetings of 22 July, 26 August and 2 September 1942.

28 *Ibid.*, G 59/1, letter to the Slovak Red Cross, signed J. Chenevière, 3 September 1942.

29 *Ibid.*, G 59/2, letter from D. de Traz of 13 May 1943.

30 *Ibid.*, G 59/3, letter from the Slovak Red Cross, 15 September 1944.

31 *Ibid.*, G 59/2, note by Leclerc on a discussion of 12 October 1944. The credit was later raised to 1 million, including 200,000 francs to the end of 1944 (G 59/2, letter from Saly Mayer of 27 October 1944).

32 *Ibid.*, Box B, Czechoslovakia, letter from Dunand of 8 November 1944.

33 *Ibid.*, letter signed A. Lombard of 28 November 1944.

34 *Ibid.*, G 59/3, letters from Dunand of 24 November, 4 and 18 December 1944.

35 *Ibid.*, G 59/4, letter from Dunand of 2 January 1945.

36 *Ibid.*, G 59/4, letter from Dunand to the head of the Political Affairs division of the Foreign Ministry, and G 59/2, letter from Dunand of 24 January 1945.

37 *Ibid.*, G 59/8, letters from Dunand of 6, 14 and 16 November and 4 December 1944.

38 *Ibid.*, G 3/63, Ferrière note of 21 December 1944.

39 *Ibid.*, letter from Lossier of 10 January 1945.

40 *Ibid.*, letter of 18 November 1944.

41 *Ibid.*, G 59/2, letter of 18 December 1944.

42 *Ibid.*, letter of 7 January 1945.

43 *Ibid.*, Box B, Czechoslovakia, letter of 1 November 1944.

44 *Ibid.*, G 85/Slovakia, letter of 21 November 1944.

45 *Ibid.*, G 59/8, letter of 15 December 1944, drafted by Schwarzenberg.

46 *Ibid.*, G 85; see document VII in the Appendix.

47 *Ibid.*, G 59/4, Schwarzenberg note for Bachmann, 9 February 1945.

48 *Ibid.*, G 59/2, letter of 4 December 1944.
49 FA, E 2308 1969/302/2, minutes of the meeting of 7 November 1944.
50 AG, G 59/2, letter from Dunand of 18 December 1944.

7 THE AXIS ALLIES

1 AG, Box B, Romania 1, confidential letter of 29 November 1941 to Jacques Chenevière.
2 *Ibid.*, letter from Jacques Chenevière of 6 January 1942.
3 *Ibid.*, G 3/48, telegram from the Romanian foreign minister of 23 March 1942.
4 *Ibid.*, G 3/36, CID note to de Steiger of 6 October 1942.
5 CMS Germany, report on the situation of the Jews in Romania, handed to Dr A. Cramer, 14 August 1942, and AG, G 59/3, letter from G. Riegner to Schwarzenberg, 28 January 1943.
6 AG, G 59/2, note to de Steiger, signed by J. Duchosal, drafted by Schwarzenberg, 10 February 1943.
7 *Ibid.*, confidential note from Pilar to Burckhardt, 7 April 1943.
8 *Ibid.*, PVB, meeting of 22 March 1943.
9 *Ibid.*, G 3/48, de Haller telephone call, 25 March 1943.
10 *Ibid.*, note signed J. R. Wilhelm, 7 June 1943.
11 *Ibid.*, G 59/2, note from David de Traz, 27 May 1943, and G 3/48, minutes of the special meeting devoted to the Chapuisat–de Traz report, 2 July 1943.
12 *Ibid.*, G 59/5, note of 28 June 1943; for the full text, see pp. 285–7 of the original edition.
13 *Ibid.*, PVB, meeting of 7 July 1943.
14 *Ibid.*, G 3/48b, Burckhardt, Bachmann, de Steiger discussion, 16 July 1943.
15 *Ibid.*, note on the discussion between Ruegger, Siordet and Kolb, 29 October 1943.
16 *Ibid.*, G 59/5, de Steiger letter, 28 September 1943.
17 *Ibid.*, G 3/48, note from Schwarzenberg to de Steiger of 30 September 1943; for the full text, see p. 288 of the original edition.
18 *Ibid.*, G 59/2, report dated 14 January 1944.
19 *Ibid.*, letter from Kolb of 9 February 1944; see also the box on pp. 290–1 of the original edition for Kolb's letter to Antonescu of 13 January 1944 (written on his return from Transnistria).
20 *Ibid.*, letter sent via the Swiss legation to Kolb, 9 February 1944; for the full text, see pp. 290–1 of the original edition.
21 *Ibid.*, letter from Kolb of 20 March 1944.
22 *Ibid.*, 59/4, letter from Kolb of 29 June 1944; for the full text, see p. 292 of the original edition.
23 So as not to be accused of 'trading with the enemy', Schwarzenberg refused to let the WRB know how the ICRC managed to change at the free market rate the money deposited at the Société de Banque Suisse (AG, G 59/2 note from Schwarzenberg to Roswell MacLelland, 25 May 1944), but he assured them that the Swiss francs had stayed in Switzerland and that the money had been used exclusively for the purpose for which it had been given.

24 AG, G 59/2, letter from Albert Lombard to Kolb, 24 May 1944; for the full text, see p. 293 of the original edition.
25 *Ibid.*, G 59/5, letter of 15 May 1944; for Kolb's controversial certificates, see the box on p. 295 of the original edition.
26 *Ibid.*, letter from F. Siordet to Kolb, 29 June 1944; for the full text, see pp. 295–6 of the original edition.
27 *Ibid.*, letter of 25 July 1944.
28 *Ibid.*, letter of 9 June 1944.
29 *Ibid.*, G 59, letter from Schwarzenberg of 14 August 1944; for the full text, see pp. 298–9 of the original edition.
30 *Ibid.*, G 59/2, Kolb's report, 5 April 1946, and personal file, particularly the letter of 29 February 1968.
31 *Ibid.*, G 59/7, letters of 7 May and 8 June 1948.
32 *Ibid.*, G 59/2, note from Sofia by David de Traz of 7 June 1943.
33 *Ibid.*, G 59/5, letter of 10 August 1943.
34 *Ibid.*, G 59/2, confidential note for the delegation in Sofia, 2 May 1944; for the full text, see pp. 302–4 of the original edition.
35 *Ibid.*, G 59/2, Leclerc note of 8 January 1945 and Leopold note of 22 March 1945.
36 *Ibid.*, Div. sec. PG/IC, note of a discussion with Mlles Odier and Bordier and Messrs Schwarzenberg, Wasmer, Valobra and Riegner. For the aid sent by the CMS, see *Rapport*, pp. 372–9.
37 *Ibid.*, G 59/2, letter from H. Wasmer of 27 August 1943 to the stateless Jews interned at Ferramonti-Tarsia.
38 FA, E 2001 (D), cl. 9, letter from the Swiss legation at Vichy, 17 September 1943.
39 AG, G 3/24b, letters from de Salis, 2 October and 2 November 1943.
40 *Ibid.*, G 3/24b, letter from de Salis of 6 April 1944.
41 *Ibid.*, G 59/2 (in English in the original).
42 *Ibid.*, report by B. Beretta of 5 April 1944 (received in Geneva on 24 April 1944).
43 *Ibid.*, G 59/2.
44 *Ibid.*, G 3/24b.
45 *Ibid.*, letter from B. Beretta of 25 May 1944.
46 *Ibid.*, G 59/2.
47 *Ibid.*, G 3/48c.
48 *Ibid.*, G 59/4, letter from Luigi Zappelli of 28 July 1944. On this recently created committee, see Michele Sarfatti's article listed under section VI, 'Studies', in the Bibliography.
49 AG, G 59/2, Carl J. Burckhardt–L. Zappelli discussion of 28 July 1944.
50 *Ibid.*, G 23/74, letter of 1 September 1944 and reply of 19 October 1944.
51 I would like to thank Mr Klaus Voigt for his information on this matter.
52 AG, G 59/2, letter from Albert Lombard of 21 December 1944.
53 *Ibid.*, G 3/24b, H. Bon's report of 15 February 1945 on his activities, and a note from him to Lombard of 6 February 1945.
54 *Ibid.*, activities report of 15 February 1945.
55 *Ibid.*, G 3/24b, letter of 6 April 1945.
56 *Ibid.*, G 59/3, note of 19 April 1945 drafted by P. Kuhne.

57 FA, E 2001 (D) 3/474, Walther note of 23 February 1945 and ICRC communiqué no. 274 of 12 April 1945.

8 THE DRAMA OF RETREAT, PERSECUTION AND ACTION PLAYED OUT IN HUNGARY

1 On the events in Hungary, see Randolph L. Braham, *The Politics of Genocide: the Holocaust in Hungary*, New York, 1981; on the attitude and activities of the ICRC, see Arieh Ben-Tov, *Facing the Holocaust in Budapest*, Geneva, 1988.
2 AG, PVCC, meeting of 5 December 1941.
3 *Ibid.*, G 59/8, document received on 10 April 1942 in Budapest.
4 *Ibid.*, PVPIC, meeting of 27 May 1943, and PVB, meeting of 7 July 1943.
5 *Ibid.*, G 3/48e, instructions signed J. Chenevière of 20 October 1943.
6 *Ibid.*, confidential note signed Schwarzenberg of 18 October 1943; for full text, see p. 317 of the original edition.
7 *Ibid.*, G 59/5, note from Schwarzenberg to de Bavier, 30 December 1943.
8 *Ibid.*, PVPIC, meeting of 27 January 1944.
9 *Ibid.*, G 59/2, de Bavier letter of 18 February 1944, and PVPIC, meeting of 17 March 1944.
10 *Ibid.*, PVPIC, meeting of 24 March 1944, and G 85, letter from Schwarzenberg to Daniel J. Reagan, commercial attaché at the United States legation in Berne, 27 March 1944.
11 *Ibid.*, Hungary box, 6 June 1944.
12 *Ibid.*, G 59/5, note of 4 May 1944; for full text, see p. 319 of the original edition.
13 *Ibid.*, G 59/4, note to Huber of 10 June 1944, note from Schwarzenberg to Born, 14 June 1944, and G 59/2, Born's final report to the ICRC, June 1945, pp. 26–7.
14 *Ibid.*, G 59/8, note from Paul Kuhne, 30 June 1944.
15 AA, Inland IIg/209, note for Ribbentrop's attention, 6 July 1944.
16 FA, E 2001 (D) 1968/74/14, note of 4 July 1944, and AG, discussions with M. de Haller, vol. I, no. 40 (3 July 1944).
17 AG, G 59/1, letter of 12 August 1944. The author wishes to thank Dr Robert Rozett for drawing his attention to the fact that Max Huber's letter to the Foreign Ministry, the carbon copy of which cannot be traced at the ICRC, is reproduced in the documents assembled by Professor Elek Karsai (*Vadira a Nacizmus Ellen*, vol. III, Budapest, A magyar Izraelitak orzsagos kepviselete kiadasa, 1987, pp. 100–1).
18 AG, G 59/3, note by C. J. Burckhardt of 18 July 1944.
19 IfZ, Eich. 970, telegram from Veesenmayer, the Reich's representative in Hungary, 2 August 1944.
20 AG, G 59/2, Born's report, June 1945, p. 6.
21 *Ibid.*, G 59/5, letter from Born of 11 December 1944, and Gilbert Joseph, *Mission sans retour*, Paris, 1982.
22 AA, Inland IIg/209, secret note for Ribbentrop, 27 October 1944.
23 See box on pp. 328–9 of the original edition for the text of the minute.
24 FA, E 2001 (D) 1968/74/14, note of 17 August 1944 about a conference

held the day before between representatives of the Political Department and of the Justice and Police Department, Dr Rothmund, Mlle Ferrière, Mr Bachmann and Mr Schwarzenberg.

25 *Ibid.*, de Haller note about his telephone call to Mr Tyler of UNRRA, 29 December 1944.

26 IfZ, NG 4287, telegram from Veesenmayer of 18 November 1944.

27 FA, E 2001 (D) 1968/74/14, letter from Pilet-Golaz to Jaeger, 7 July 1944, and Ludwig report, pp. 287f.

28 *Ibid.*, letter from P. Bonna to Jaeger, 15 July 1944.

29 AG, G 59, Schwarzenberg note of 4 August 1944.

30 IfZ, Eich. 29, Wisliceny's evidence at Nuremberg, 3 January 1946.

31 FA, E 2001 (D) 1968/74/14, letter to Frölicher in Berlin, 20 October 1944.

32 *Ibid.*, note by Revilliod, 14 August 1944.

33 AG, PVB, meeting of 28 August 1944; for the full debate, see pp. 333–4 of the original edition.

34 FA, E 2001 (D) 1968/74/6, telegram from Schwarzenberg to Born, 29 August 1944.

35 AG, G 59/4, note from Schwarzenberg to Burckhardt, 17 October 1944; for the full text, see p. 335 of the original edition.

36 *Ibid.*, G 85, telegram from Schwarzenberg of 26 October 1944.

9 AID AND PROTECTION ON THE EVE OF LIBERATION

1 AG, G 3/26f, confidential letter, 13 August 1944.

2 *Ibid.*, G 44/sec, PV, meeting of 19 September 1944 with the Comte de Gramont of the French Red Cross, de Leusse, representative of the Commissariat aux prisonniers et déportés, etc. See also the de Leusse discussions in summer 1944, both in Berne and in Geneva, in AF, E 2001 (E) 1/134.

3 AG, G 59/2, Bachmann note, 14 September 1944.

4 *Ibid.*, G 44/00, note from Schwarzenberg to J. Chenevière, 14 September 1944.

5 *Ibid.*, PVB, meeting of 20 September 1944.

6 *Ibid.*, G 44/00, Huber letter to J. de Bourbon-Busset, 21 September 1944.

7 *Ibid.*, G 59/2, note for A. Lombard, 25 September 1944; for full text, see pp. 342–3 of the original edition.

8 *Ibid.*, G 44, letter from Henry Frenay to Max Huber, 9 October 1944.

9 *Ibid.*, G 85, letters to the British and American governments, signed J. Chenevière, of 16 October, and to the national Red Cross societies of Norway and Holland, of 3 November 1944. The Americans supported the ICRC, but the British replied that German civilian internees in the UK already benefited from Red Cross guarantees and that there was no similarity between them and the civilians deported to the Reich (G 85, letters of 18 January and 14 February 1945, and PRO, FO 916/938).

10 AG, G 3/26f, strictly confidential note from Lehner, 16 October 1944, and G 85, protocol of the meetings of 30 October 1944.

11 FA, E 2001 (D) 3/475, letter from Frölicher, 16 November, and telegram to same, 20 November 1944.

12 AG, G 85. Simultaneously the DRK and AA suggested to the SS that they negotiate through the ICRC improvements in the conditions under which

German POWs were held in France (IfZ, MA 288/8522, letter from Grüneisen to the head of the Heeresverwaltungsamt, 8 December 1944).
13 AG, G 44/00, Mme Frick's reflections, note by R. Gallopin, discussion between Mme Frick and M. Berber, 8 December 1944.
14 *Ibid.*, G 85, note for the German consulate and letter to von Ribbentrop from Huber, 9 December 1944.
15 *Ibid.*, G 85.
16 *Ibid.*, G 44/00, note from Schwarzenberg to J. Chenevière, 14 September 1944.
17 *Ibid.*, Box, Max Huber archives, correspondence with Mme Frick, 23 October 1944; for full text, see pp. 347–8 of the original edition.
18 *Ibid.*, 26 October 1944 letter.
19 *Ibid.*, note from Louis H. Micheli, 3 December 1944.
20 *Ibid.*, PVB, meeting of 13 December 1944.
21 AWJC, *inter alia* note from Riegner, 20 February; note from Kubowitzki about his conversation with Burckhardt, 3 March; letter from Burckhardt to Riegner, 5 March 1945; and minutes of the meetings held on 5 December 1944 and 26 March 1945; AG, G 59/1, de Traz note, 22 February 1945.
22 FA, E 2001 (D) 1968/74/14, note of 5 February and telegram of 13 February 1945.
23 AG, G 44, note of 31 January 1945. See too the reports of the ICRC delegate in Stockholm, G. Hoffmann, 15 February, 18 February, and summary of 4 July 1945 (G 44).
24 *Ibid.*, Schirmer note, 20 January 1945.
25 *Ibid.*, G 44/13, letter signed Burckhardt.
26 *Ibid.*, PVB, meeting of 7 February 1945.
27 *Ibid.*, G 44/13, letter to Leland Harrison, 19 February 1945, and UB, Burckhardt papers, B II 46h, letters to Heinrich Himmler and Walter Stucki, 19 February 1945. For details about attempts made by Musy and Bernadotte to 'buy' Jews, see the box on p. 352 of the original edition.
28 AG, G 44/13, Besprechung mit *Obergruppenführer* Dr Kaltenbrunner, vom 12. März 1945 (drafted by Hans Bachmann and dated 19 March) and letter from Burckhardt to Berber, 14 March; FA, E 2803 1969/302/112, letter from Burckhardt to Petitpierre of 17 March; also AG, G 44/13, PVB, meeting of 19 March, and letter from Burckhardt to Kaltenbrunner, 23 March. Burckhardt was informed of the place and date of the rendezvous with Kaltenbrunner by an Austro-German businessman, Johann Heinrich Franck (Inga foods, Franck chicory, etc.) who lived in Zuoz (Engadine). From the 1930s onwards it seems that J. H. Franck (together with the lawyer Fritz Bon, one of the signatories of the Petition of the Two Thousand and brother of Hans Bon, who as has already been mentioned was the chief ICRC delegate in northern Italy in 1944–5) supported the Nazis and Frontism in Switzerland financially. Franck was certainly well known to Burckhardt even if they were apparently not close friends, and he used Burckhardt as a reference when he tried in summer 1945 to change his image by joining the Frei-österreichische Bewegung in der Schweiz (UB, Burckhardt papers, B II 46h). After the war an Inga-controlled Zurich investment and securities bank was strongly suspected by the Swiss authorities of money-laundering to finance German espionage operations.

29 For everything concerning the Berlin events see the Lehner 23 November 1945 and Boesch reports (AG, G 59/1, G 44/13).

30 *L'activité du CICR en faveur des civils détenus dans les camps de concentration*, pp. 111f.

31 AG, G 44/13, conversations with Kaltenbrunner, note of 14 May 1945.

32 *Ibid.*, G 44/13, report by Louis Haefliger on his activities from 27 April to 8 May 1945; P.-S. Choumoff, 'Des chambres à gaz à Mauthausen', *Le Monde juif*, Paris, 123, 1986; Albert Haas, *Un médecin en enfer*, Paris, 1986, pp. 315f. Louis Haefliger (whose account is given in full on pp. 363–4 of the original edition) undoubtedly kept a level head and showed much personal courage during the liberation of Mauthausen, but he was summarily dismissed in June 1945 after barely three months in office; although the author considers the ICRC's action deplorable, he refrains from further comment on its reasons other than quoting the ICRC's public justification for its actions: 'Mr Haefliger was no longer fulfilling his mission with all the discretion required and was abusing his position as delegate of the International Committee of the Red Cross for purely personal ends.'

33 Durand, *Histoire du CICR*, vol. II, p. 530. In order to set this figure in context it should be compared with that given for the WRB by David S. Wyman in *L'abandon des Juifs. Les Américains et la solution finale*, Paris, 1987, p. 368; according to Wyman the WRB, between the time it was set up in January 1944 and the German surrender on 8 May 1945, evacuated 35,000 Jews and Aryans from the occupied territories. No attempt has been made in the present work to calculate the figures relating to people who were saved wherever they happened to be, like the internees who survived thanks to the Concentration Camps Parcels Scheme, the deportees repatriated from Transnistria, or the 120,000 Budapest Jews; the ICRC kept no statistics and Wyman's and the WRB's figures can only be rough estimates.

34 FA, E 2001 (D) 1968/74/19, minutes kept by the ICRC's P. Kuhne of the meeting in Berne on 16 May 1945.

35 Early in 1946 the office of the delegate of the Conseil fédéral aux œuvres d'entraide internationale, a Swiss government body, drew up the first official balance-sheet of the ICRC's work on behalf of deportees and of racial and political detainees in the concentration camps. Drawing on the ICRC's figures, later confirmed in the ICRC's general report to the seventeenth International Red Cross Conference in Stockholm in 1948, the Conseil fédéral document concluded that in conjunction with the Protecting Powers the ICRC took care of seven million POWs and 175,000 civilian internees, to whom its 173 delegates made more than 5,000 visits. (For other detailed statistics relating to POWs and civilian internees given in the document, see p. 366 of the original edition.)

10 CONCLUSION

1 AG, PVCICR, meeting of 20 November 1941, declaration by Max Huber.

2 AWJC, note by Riegner, 17 November 1942.

3 AG, PVB, meeting of 27 October 1943.

4 Interview with Georg Hoffmann, ICRC delegate in Stockholm, 13 March 1984.

5 AG, Box B, 'Politique du CICR', letter to Albert Oeri of 11 December 1942, and UB, Burckhardt papers, B/Ic, letter of 1 January 1946.

6 AWJC, Aktennotiz, 3 February 1943.

7 AG, G/2, note by Schwarzenberg for F. Siordet, 28 February 1945.

Bibliography

MANUSCRIPT SOURCES

Archives of the International Committee of the Red Cross, Geneva.
Archives of the Red Cross League, Geneva.
Archives of the World Jewish Congress, Geneva Bureau.
Bundesarchiv, Koblenz.
Centre for Contemporary Jewish Documentation, Paris.
Deutsches Zentralarchiv, Potsdam.
Document Centre, Berlin.
Institut für Zeitgeschichte, Munich.
Politisches Archiv des Auswärtigen Amtes, Bonn.
Public Record Office, Kew (London).
Swiss Federal Archives, Berne.
University Library, Basel (Burckhardt papers).

PRINTED SOURCES

CICR, *L'activité du Comité international de la Croix-Rouge en faveur des civils détenus dans les camps de concentration en Allemagne (1939–1945)*, 3rd edition, Geneva, April 1947.
  Commentaire, ed. Jean S Pictet. *I. La Convention de Genève pour l'amélioration du sort des blessés et des malades dans les forces armées en campagne*, Geneva, 1952.
CICR, LSCR, *Manuel de la Croix-Rouge internationale. Conventions, statuts et règlements, résolutions des conférences internationales et des assemblées de la Ligue*, 8th edition, Geneva, 1942.
Rapport du Comité international de la Croix-Rouge sur son activité pendant la Seconde Guerre mondiale (1 septembre 1939 – 30 juin 1947), Geneva, 1948, 3 vols.
Revue internationale de la Croix-Rouge, Geneva, 1933–1945.
Dix-huitième conférence internationale de la Croix-Rouge, Toronto, juillet-août 1952, proceedings, Toronto, 1953.
Quinzième conférence internationale de la Croix-Rouge à Tokyo, du 20 au 29 octobre 1934, proceedings, Tokyo, 1934.
Seizième conférence internationale de la Croix-Rouge tenue à Londres du 20 au 24 juin 1938, proceedings, London, 1938.

COLLECTIONS OF DOCUMENTS

Adler, H. G., *Die verheimlichte Wahrheit. Theresienstädter Dokumente*, Tübingen, J. C. B. Mohr, 1958.

Akten zur deutschen auswärtigen Politik, 1918–1945, in the Archiv des deutschen Auswärtigen Amts, Series D: 1937–41, Göttingen, Vanderhoek und Ruprecht, 1950–91, 17 vols.

Akten zur deutschen auswärtigen Politik, 1918–1945, in the Archiv des deutschen Auswärtigen Amts, Series E: 1941–5, Göttingen, Vanderhoek und Ruprecht, 1969–79, 8 vols.

Documents diplomatiques français, 1932–1939, Ministère des Affaires étrangères, Commission de publication des documents relatifs aux origines de la guerre 1939–1945, Paris, Imprimerie nationale, 1963–86, 32 vols. in two series.

Domarus, Max, *Hitler. Reden und Proklamationen, 1932–1945*, Wiesbaden, 1965, 4 vols.

Foreign Relations of the United States, Diplomatic Papers, 1939–, Washington, United States Government Printing Office, 1956–, several vols.

German Regulations Pertaining to Prisoners of War: Translations of Collections of Orders Issued by the Supreme Command of the Wehrmacht from 16 June 1941 to 15 January 1945, prepared in the Office of the Provost Marshal General, n.p., 29 December 1945.

Mitscherlich, Alexander, Mielke, Fred, *Medizin ohne Menschlichkeit. Dokumente des Nürnberger Ärzteprozesses*, 7th edition, Frankfurt a. M., Fischer Taschenbuch Verlag GmbH, 1983.

Nationalsozialistische Massentötungen durch Giftgas. Eine Dokumentation, ed. Eugen Kogon, Herrmann Langbein and Adalbert Rückerl, Frankfurt a. M., S. Fischer Verlag GmbH, 1983.

Secretariat of State of His Holiness, *Actes et documents du Saint-Siège relatifs à la Seconde Guerre Mondiale . . .* ed. Pierre Blet and Angelo Martini, Vatican City, Libreria editrice vaticana, 1965–82, 12 vols.

Das Sonderrecht für die Juden im NS-Staat. Eine Sammlung der gesetzlichen Massnahmen und Richtlinien – Inhalt und Bedeutung, ed. Joseph Walk, Heidelberg/Karlsruhe, C. F. Müller Juristischer Verlag, 1981.

Die Weizsäcker-Papiere 1933–1950, published by Leonidas E. Hill, Frankfurt a. M., Propyläen Verlag, 1974.

RECOLLECTIONS, MEMOIRS AND DOCUMENTS

Batowski, Henry K., 'L'Allemagne hitlérienne et l'Université jagellonne ("Sonderaktion Krakow")', *La Pologne et les affaires occidentales*, Poznan, 1979.

Berber, Friedrich, *Zwischen Macht und Gewissen, Lebenserinnerungen*, Munich, C. H. Beck'sche Verlagsbuchhandlung, 1986.

Burckhardt, Carl J., *Briefe 1908–1974*, published by the Kuratorium Carl J. Burckhardt, ed. Ingrid Metzger-Buddenberg, Frankfurt a. M., S. Fischer Verlag GmbH, 1986.

Ma mission à Dantzig, Paris, Arthème Fayard, 1961, translation of *Meine Danziger Mission*.

Chenevière, Jacques, *Retours et images*, Lausanne, Rencontre, 1966.

Dunand, Georges, *Ne perdez pas leur trace!* Neuchâtel, Baconnière, 1950.

Haas, Albert, *Un médecin en enfer*, Paris, Presses de la Renaissance, 1986.

Huber, Max, *Vermischte Schriften*, Zürich, Atlantis Verlag, 1947–1948, 3 vols.

'Interview du Dr Gerhart Riegner par Meir Dworzecki', Geneva, 13 July 1972, cyclostyled.

Junod, Marcel, *Le troisième combattant. De l'ypérite en Abyssinie à la bombe atomique d'Hiroshima*, Lausanne, Payot, 1947.

Levi, Primo, *Se questo è un uomo*, Turin, Einaudi, 1976.

Nowak, Jan, *Courrier de Varsovie*, Paris, Gallimard, 1983, translated from the Polish.

Safran, Alexandre, *Resisting the Storm. Rumania 1940–1947, Memoirs*, Jerusalem, Yad Vashem, 1988.

Schwarzenberg, Johannes E., *Gedanken und Erinnerungen*, private publication, n.d.

Visser't Hooft, Willem Adolf, *Le temps du rassemblement: mémoires*, Paris, Seuil, 1975, translated from the English.

Vrba, Rudolf, *Escape from Auschwitz (I Cannot Forgive)*, New York, Grove Press, 1986.

Waibel, Max, *1945, Die Kapitulation in Norditalien. Originalbericht des Vermittlers.* Basel and Frankfurt, Helbing und Lichtenhan, 1981.

REFERENCE WORKS

Dictionnaire de la Seconde Guerre Mondiale, published under the direction of Philippe Masson, with the assistance of the Services historiques de l'Armée de terre, de la Marine et de l'Armée de l'air, and with the assistance of Alain Melchior-Bonnet, Paris, Larousse, 1979–1980, 2 vols.

Encyclopaedia Judaica, Jerusalem, Keter Publishing House Ltd., 1971–1972, 16 vols.

Gilbert, Martin, *Endlösung. Die Vertreibung und Vernichtung der Juden, ein Atlas*, Reinbek bei Hamburg, Rowohlt Taschenbuch Verlag, 1982, translated from the English original, *Atlas of the Holocaust*, 1982.

International Tracing Service, *Catalogue of Camps and Prisons in Germany and German-Occupied Territories, September 1939 – May 1945*, prepared by Records Branch Documents Intelligence Section, Arolsen, 1949–1951, 2 vols. and 1 supplement.

Verzeichnis der Haftstätten unter dem Reichsführer SS, 1937–1945, Arolsen, 1977.

Note concernant la distribution des colis CICR pendant la Seconde Guerre Mondiale, Arolsen, 19 August 1987.

STUDIES

Adam, Uwe-Dietrich, *Judenpolitik im Dritten Reich*, Düsseldorf, Droste Verlag, 1972.

Adler, Jacques, *Face à la persécution. Les organisations juives à Paris de 1940 à 1944*, Paris, Calmann-Lévy, 1985.

L'Allemagne nazie et le génocide juif, Colloquium of the Ecole des Hautes Etudes en sciences sociales, Paris, Gallimard/Le Seuil, 1985.

Amicale d'Oranienburg-Sachsenhausen, *Sachso. Au cœur du système concentrationnaire nazi,* Paris, Librairie Plon, 1982.

Arndt, Ino, Scheffler, Wolfgang, 'Organisierter Massenmord der Juden in national-sozialistischen Vernichtungslagern', *Vierteljahreshefte für Zeitgeschichte,* 24, 1967.

Arsenijevic, Drago, *Otages volontaires des SS,* 2nd edition, Paris, France-Empire, 1984.

Assouline, Pierre, *Jean Jardin, 1904–1976. Une éminence grise.* Paris, Balland, 1986.

In Auschwitz vergast, bis heute verfolgt. Zur Situation der Roma (Zigeuner) in Deutschland und Europa, ed. Tilman Zülch, for the Gesellschaft für bedrohte Völker, Reinbek bei Hamburg, Rowohlt Taschenbuch Verlag, 1979.

Ben Elissar, Eliahu, *La Diplomatie du IIIe Reich et les Juifs, 1933–1939,* Paris, Julliard, 1969.

Ben-Tov, Arieh, *Facing the Holocaust in Budapest,* Geneva, Henry Dunant Institute, 1988.

Billig, Joseph, *Les camps de concentration dans l'économie du Reich hitlérien,* Paris, PUF, 1978.

L'Hitlérisme et le système concentrationnaire, Paris, PUF, 1967.

Boissier, Pierre, *De Solférino à Tsoushima. Histoire du Comité international de la Croix-Rouge,* vol. I, 2nd edition, Geneva, Henry Dunant Institute, 1978.

Bonjour, Edgar, *Histoire de la neutralité suisse,* vols. IV to VI, Neuchâtel, La Baconnière, 1970.

Bourgeois, Daniel, 'La porte se ferme: la Suisse et le problème de l'immigration juive en 1938', *Relations Internationales,* 54, summer 1988.

Braham, Randolph L., *The Politics of Genocide: the Holocaust in Hungary,* New York, Columbia University Press, 1981, 2 vols.

Browning, Christopher R., *The Final Solution and the German Foreign Office,* New York/London, Holmes and Meier, 1978.

Buchheim, Hans, Broszat, Martin, Jacobsen, Hans-Adolf, Krausnick, Helmut, *Anatomie des SS-Staates,* Gutachten des Instituts für Zeitgeschichte, 2nd edition, Munich, Deutscher Taschenbuch Verlag GmbH & Co. KG, 1967, 2 vols.

Burleigh, Michael, Wippermann, Wolfgang, *The Racial State. Germany 1933–1945,* Cambridge, Cambridge University Press, 1991.

Calic, Edouard, *Himmler et son empire.* Paris, Stock, 1966.

Reinhard Heydrich, Schlüsselfigur des Dritten Reiches, Düsseldorf, Droste Verlag, 1982.

Choumoff, P.-S., 'Des chambres à gaz à Mauthausen', *Le Monde juif,* 123, 1986.

Dauer im Wandel, Festschrift zum 70. Geburtstag von Carl J. Burckhardt, ed. Hermann Rinn and Max Rychner, Munich, Verlag Georg D. W. Callwey, 1961.

Durand, André, *De Sarajevo à Hiroshima. Histoire du Comité international de la Croix-Rouge,* vol. II, Geneva, Henry Dunant Institute, 1978.

Durand, Yves, *La captivité. Histoire des prisonniers de guerre français 1939–1945,* Paris, [1982].

Dworzecki, Meir, 'The International Red Cross and its Policy vis-à-vis the Jews in Ghettos and Concentration Camps in Nazi- Occupied Europe', *Rescue Attempts during the Holocaust*, in Proceedings of the Second Yad Vashem International Historical Conference, Jerusalem, 1974.

Ebrei in Italia: deportazione, resistenza, edited by the Centro di Documentazione Ebreica Contemporanea di Milano, Florence, Tipografia Giuntina, 1974.

Eichmann par Eichmann, ed. Pierre Joffroy and Karin Königseder, Paris, Grasset, 1970.

Les etats neutres européens et la Seconde Guerre Mondiale, ed. Louis-Edouard Roulet, Neuchâtel, La Baconnière, 1985.

Evrard, Jacques, *La déportation des travailleurs français dans le IIIe Reich*, Paris, Fayard, 1972.

Favez, Jean-Claude, 'Le prochain et le lointain. L'accueil et l'asile en Suisse au printemps 1945', *Revue suisse d'histoire*, 4, 1988.

Favez, Jean-Claude, Mysyrowicz, Ladislas, 'La Suisse et la "Solution finale"', *Journal de Genève*, 21 April, 28 April, 5 and 12 May 1979.

Feingold, Henry L., *The Politics of Rescue, the Roosevelt Administration and the Holocaust, 1938–1945*, New Brunswick, NJ, Rutgers University Press, 1970.

Festgabe für Max Huber zum sechzigsten Geburtstag, 28. Dezember 1934, Zürich, Berichthaus, 1934.

Festschrift zum 50jährigen Bestehen. Schweizerischer Israelitischer Gemeindebund, Fédération suisse des communautés israélites, 1904–1954, n.p., n.d.

Fiscalini, Diego, 'Des élites au service d'une cause humanitaire: le Comité international de la Croix-Rouge', licentiate thesis, Geneva, April 1985.

Forrer, Friedrich, *Sieger ohne Waffen: das Deutsche Rote Kreuz im zweiten Weltkrieg*, Hanover, Adolf Sponholtz Verlag, 1962.

La France et la question juive, 1940–1944, proceedings of the conference of the Centre de documentation juive contemporaine, 10–12 March 1979, published under the direction of Georges Wellers, André Kaspi and Serge Klarsfeld and with the assistance of the Memorial Foundation for Jewish Culture, Paris, Sylvie Messinger, 1981.

Friedlaender, Saul, 'L'extermination des Juifs d'Europe: pour une étude historique globale', *Revue des études juives*, 135, 1–3/1976.

Gascar, Pierre, *Histoire de la captivité des Français en Allemagne (1939–1945)*, Paris, Gallimard, 1967.

Genschel, Helmut, *Die Verdrängung der Juden von der Wirtschaft im Dritten Reich*, Göttingen, Zürich, etc., Musterschmidt Verlag, 1966.

Gilbert, Joseph, *Mission sans retour, l'Affaire Wallenberg*, Paris, Albin Michel, 1982.

Gilbert, Martin, *Atlas of the Holocaust*, London, Michael Joseph, 1982.

The Holocaust, The Jewish Tragedy, London, Collins, 1988.

Grossmann, Alexander, *Nur das Gewissen, Carl Lutz und seine Budapester Aktion, Geschichte und Porträt*, Zürich, Verlag im Waldgut, 1986.

Grossmann, Kurt R., *Emigration. Geschichte der Hitler-Flüchtlinge 1933–1945*, Frankfurt a. M., Europa Verlagsanstalt, 1969.

Hilberg, Raul, *La destruction des Juifs d'Europe*, Paris, Fayard, 1988.

Hutchinson, John F., *Champions of Charity. War and the Rise of the Red Cross*, Boulder/Oxford, Westview, 1996.

Kaspi, André, *Les Juifs pendant l'Occupation*, Paris, Seuil, 1991.

Katz, Schlomo Z., 'L'opinion publique en Europe occidentale face à la conférence internationale pour les réfugiés d'Evian en juillet 1938', Geneva, Institut universitaire des Hautes études internationales, diplôme, 1971.

Kielar, Wieslaw, *Anus Mundi, Fünf Jahre Auschwitz*, 3rd edition, Frankfurt a. M., S. Fischer Taschenbuch Verlag, 1984, translated from the Polish, *Anus Mundi*, 1972.

Klarsfeld, Serge, *Vichy–Auschwitz. Le rôle de Vichy dans la solution finale de la question juive en France, 1942–1944*, Paris, Fayard, 1983–5, 2 vols.

Kolb, Bernhard, *Bergen-Belsen, 1943 bis 1945*, Göttingen, Vandenhoek und Ruprecht, 1984.

Langer, Lawrence L., *The Holocaust and the Literary Imagination*, London, Yale University Press, 1975.

Laqueur, Walter, *Le terrifiant secret. La 'solution finale' et l'information étouffée*, Paris, Gallimard, 1981, translation of *The Terrible Secret. An Investigation into the Suppression of Information about Hitler's 'Final Solution'*, London, Weidenfeld and Nicolson, 1980.

Laqueur, Walter, Breitman, Richard, *Breaking the Silence*, New York, Simon and Schuster, 1986.

Lasserre, André, *La Suisse des années sombres. Courants d'opinion pendant la Deuxième Guerre Mondiale, 1939–1945*, Lausanne, Payot, 1989.

Lévêque, Gérard, *La Suisse et la France gaulliste, 1943–1945, Problèmes économiques et diplomatiques*, Geneva, privately printed, 1979.

Lichtenstein, Heiner, *Angepasst und treu ergeben. Das Rote Kreuz im 'Dritten Reich'*, Cologne, Bund-Verlag, 1988.

Marrus, Michael, *The Holocaust in History*, Toronto, Leister and Orpen Dennys, 1987.

Marrus, Michael, Paxton, Robert O., *Vichy et les Juifs*, Paris, Calmann-Lévy, 1981, translated from the English.

Michaelis, Meir, *Mussolini and the Jews, German–Italian Relations and the Jewish Question in Italy, 1922–1945*, Oxford, Clarendon Press, 1978.

Moore, Bob, Federowich, Kent, eds., *Prisoners of War and their Captors in World War II*, Oxford/Washington DC, Berg, 1996.

Moreillon, Jacques, *Le Comité international de la Croix-Rouge et la protection des détenus politiques. Les activités du CICR en faveur des personnes incarcérées dans leur propre pays à l'occasion de troubles ou de tensions internes*, Lausanne, L'Age d'Homme, 1973.

Morley, John F., *Vatican Diplomacy and the Jews during the Holocaust, 1939–1943*, New York, Ktav Publishing House, 1980.

Morse, Arthur D., *While Six Million Died. A Chronicle of American Apathy*, New York, Random House, 1967.

Mysyrowicz, L., Favez, J.-C., Schaerer, M., Meurant, J., 'Refuge et représentation d'intérêts étrangers', *Revue d'histoire de la Deuxième Guerre Mondiale*, 121, January 1981.

Neumann, Franz, *Behemoth. Struktur und Praxis des Nationalsozialismus, 1933–1944*, Frankfurt a. M., S. Fischer Taschenbuch Verlag GmbH, 1984; original American edition 1942, expanded 1944 under the title *Behemoth*, first German edition, 1977.

Penkover, Monty Noam, 'The World Jewish Congress Confronts the International Red Cross during the Holocaust', *Jewish Social Studies*, 41, 3–4/
1979.
Pictet, Jean, *Les principes fondamentaux de la Croix-Rouge*, Geneva, 1979.
Poliakov, Léon, *Bréviaire de la haine*, Paris, Calmann-Lévy, 1951, reissued Livre
de poche, 1979.
*La politique pratiquée par la Suisse à l'égard des réfugiés au cours des années 1933 à
1945*, report prepared for the [Swiss] Legislative Councils and submitted to
the [Swiss] Federal Council by Professor Carl Ludwig, n.p., n.d. (Ludwig
report).
Pollak, Michael, 'Des mots qui tuent', *Actes de la recherche en sciences sociales*, 41,
1982.
'Reflexions on the Holocaust', *The Annals of the American Academy of Political
and Social Science*, 450, July 1980.
Riegner, Gerhart M., *A Warning to the World. The Efforts of the World Jewish
Congress to Mobilize the Christian Churches Against the Final Solution*, The
Inaugural Stephen S. Wise Lecture, Cincinnati, OH, Hebrew Union
College – Jewish Institute of Religion, 1983.
'Switzerland and the Leadership of the Jewish Community during the Second
World War', in *Jewish Leadership During the Nazi Era, Patterns of Behavior in
the Free World*, ed. Randolf L. Braham.
'Zur Klarestellung', *Israelitisches Wochenblatt*, 22, 1984.
Sarfati, Michele, 'Il "comitato di soccorso per i deportati italiani politici e
razziali" di Losanna (1944–1945)', *Ricerche storiche*, 2–3/1979.
Schleunes, Karl S., *The Twisted Road to Auschwitz, Nazi Policy towards German
Jews*, Chicago/London/Urbana, University of Illinois Press, 1970.
Silvain, Gérard, *La question juive en Europe 1933–1945*, Paris, Jean-Claude
Lattès, 1985.
Stauffer, Paul, *Zwischen Hofmannsthal und Hitler. Carl J. Burckhardt. Facetten
einer aussergewöhnlichen Existenz*, Zurich, NZZ Verlag, 1991.
Streit, Christian, *Keine Kameraden. Die Wehrmacht und die sowjetischen Kriegsge-
fangenen, 1941–1945*, Stuttgart, Deutsche Verlagsanstalt, 1978.
Studien zur Geschichte der Konzentrationslager, Stuttgart, Deutsche Verlagsanstalt,
1970.
'Le système concentrationnaire allemand (1940–1944)', *Revue d'histoire de la
Deuxième Guerre Mondiale*, 15–16/1954.
Ternon, Yves, Helman, Socrate, *Histoire de la médecine SS. Ou le mythe du
racisme biologique*, Tournai, Casterman, 1969.
Vichniac, Isabelle, *Croix-Rouge. Les stratèges de la bonne conscience*, Paris, Alain
Moreau, 1988.
Vogelsanger, Peter, *Max Huber, Recht, Politik, Humanität aus Glauben*, Frauen-
feld, Huber, 1967.
Voigt, Klaus, 'Gli emigrati in Italia dai paesi sotto la dominazione nazista:
tollerati e perseguitati (1933–1940)', *Storia contemporanea*, 16, 1/1985.
'Notizie statistiche sugli immigrati e profughi ebrei in Italia (1938–1945)', in
Israël, Un decennio, 1974–1984, Roma, Carucci, 1984.
Wasserstein, Bernard, *Britain and the Jews of Europe, 1939–1945*, Oxford,
Clarendon Press, 1979.

Weingarten, Ralph, *Die Hilfleistung der westlichen Welt bei der Endlösung der deutschen Judenfrage. Das 'Intergovernmental Committee on Political Refugees' (IGC). 1938–1939*, Berne/Frankfurt a. M., Peter Lang, 1981.

Wyman, David S., *L'abandon des Juifs. Les Américains et la solution finale*, Paris, Flammarion, 1987, translated from *The Abandonment of the Jews. America and the Holocaust, 1941–1945*, New York, Pantheon Books, 1984.

INTERVIEWS

Hans Bachmann, 8 May 1985 and January 1987.
Georges Dunand, 14 January 1984.
Charles-Albert Egger, 13 May 1985.
Georg Hoffmann, 13 March 1984.
Gerhart Riegner, 24 January 1983 and 8 January 1987.
Alexandre Safran, 19 September 1987.
René-Jean Wilhelm, 19 February 1987.

Oral History ICRC, interviews by M. P. Reynard with
Otto Lehner, 16 December 1986.
Albert de Cocatrix, 23 February 1987.

Index